BEYOND THE LIMITS

A Planet in Crisis

by

TOM JAGTENBERG

CILENTO
PUBLISHING

This book is dedicated to all those who have devoted their efforts to defending the sustainability of our increasingly fragile habitat.

Contents

PART 1

ECOLOGICAL CRISIS

INTRODUCTION

In the twenty first century there is no shortage of information. Mobile phones and the Internet allow individuals to be immersed in communication and information. In my imagination the faint sounds of a violin are discernable in this vast symbolic churn. Could we be fiddling while our planetary habitat is dying?

There are good reasons to be overwhelmed by a sense of imminent doom. The effects of a globalised consumer culture are becoming ever more apparent in the form of climate change, pollution, resource decline, habitat destruction, over-population and slowly declining rates of global economic growth. Global decline seems inevitable, but hope does 'spring eternal'. This book has been motivated by the impotence and futility generated by a destructive juggernaut called *humanity* – and the hope that closer analysis of the situation will yield something constructive. *Beyond the Limits* seeks to examine the key factors at play in the destabilisation of our planetary ecosystem and what cultural forces drive and sustain our inability to change.

It seems obvious that some kind of mass denial characterises our daily life and the more institutionalised cultures of professional experts. In a world so full of information this might appear a puzzling phenomenon.

Closer inspection of media and professional cultures provide some understanding of how this denial is perpetuated as a mass phenomenon. The first chapter looks at a popularised 'apocalypse culture' which normalises violence, death and destruction. At the same time the 'business as usual' imperative that dominates markets, media and government is in itself a global process of denial that the 'natural' world is in decline.

Subsequent chapters reveal that despite mounting scientific evidence that is so persuasive, governments and political parties in liberal democracies appear incapable of taking the big decisions that might guarantee a habitable world for future generations. For reasons discussed, professional cultures seem incurably optimistic. In consequence of that (but only partially) individuals and liberal democracies continue to prioritise economy over ecology and return governments that can best manage a continually growing economy. Yet growth economies would seem to be reaching a 'use by' date – endlessly growing populations will eat the Earth.

Meanwhile the media – old and new – create 'popular' cultures (in film, television, music, literature and electronic media) that contribute to a culture of excess – excessive violence, sex, drama and consumption in the endless portrayal of human suffering and desperate aspirations. The combination of apocalyptic themes and a general cultural excess (of emotions, consumption, violence, sex, and even love) constitute what one might call a post-modern opium for an era participating in planetary decline.

In an increasingly frantic world there is no shortage of books and television that describe this apparent madness, that prescribe solutions, and that even describe post-apocalyptic worlds that we might eventually inhabit – fiction and non fiction. Most of this work requires a great leap of faith given the 'dysfunctionality' of political systems locked onto the *status quo* and an apparent mass ecological apathy – despite abundant evidence that should be cause for great alarm. Constructive next steps are obviously very hard to contemplate, and even harder to make. An author such as Paul Gilding, for example, tells us in *The Great Upheaval* that he has 'moved on' – telling a story about what must happen. Persuasive as his story may seem, in the absence of a mass appetite for change, it is hard to take recommendations that corporate leaders should 'think positively' and 'act ecologically' too seriously – necessary as such steps are. The lure of continuing economic growth still motivates every large corporation. Much more integrated systems analysis, and determined political change, needs to occur first if we are to prevent a future coping with the consequences of a global ecological collapse. Last century's spin is becoming less convincing: 'moving on', or 'going forward', or 'progressing matters' is much favoured corporate talk, but it's not so easy to be relaxed about the future when we are surrounded by an exploding media scape and an imploding ecology. The idea of progress and the optimism traditionally inspired by science, technology, professionalism, economic growth, and political ideals is running out of steam. Re-negotiation of the meaning of 'progress' is a continuing theme in the chapters that follow.

Scientific knowledge allows evidence based political decision-making and can provide confident judgements about the declining condition of environments and ecologies. Science is the least ideological knowledge available. So can science and technology save the day? There are many enthusiasts who believe so, but most 'high-tech' schemes are still unproven and risk further ecological damage. Whatever technologies are maintained or innovated there is an imperative that they be ecologically sustainable.

The most challenging chapter – looking at the need for urgent attention to global ecology and ecological decline – is a chapter titled 'the big three': climate change, economic growth and over-population. The conjunction of these three globally affective processes appears to pose an insuperable ecological problem. Most fundamentally, the argument and discussions contained in this book circle around the imminent catastrophe 'the big three' threaten.

The greatest obstacle to building industries and economies that are ecologically sustainable, for the long term, is the assumption that economies must grow. Current economic orthodoxy, 'neoclassical' economic theory, is the subject of a chapter concerned to debunk this assumption with the intention of providing an analytic basis for the competing ideas of 'sustainable economics'. The anti-ecological nature of prevailing economic theory and practice is at the base of so many of our ecological problems – including over-population, a much-neglected cause of environmental and ecological decline. Analysis of over-population raises serious dilemmas – for reasons to be explored. Most fundamentally, economic growth and continuing population growth are inextricably related as part of economic orthodoxy.

The first six chapters of *Beyond the Limits* provide a critique of growth oriented social and economic practices. They have been separated as Part One of the book. This section constitutes an analysis that is interdisciplinary but still, in a deep sense, sociological insofar as social relations and cultural analysis provide a starting point for consideration of other disciplinary concerns. Nonetheless, the analyses of climate change, ecological limits, and economics in Part One are meant to be substantive. Interdisciplinarity requires a starting point but is no substitute for the detailed findings of specialists. The phenomenon of climate change denial is an eloquent testimony to the idiocy of ignoring experts.

There should be no doubt that all humans on the planet face a very uncertain future that has already been pre-determined by the fact that, collectively, humanity has gone beyond the limits of many ecological systems – climates, rates of pollution, growing populations, and growth oriented economics all provide evidence that 'we' have, in many cases deliberately and determinedly, gone 'beyond the limits'.

Part Two provides a more focused analysis of green politics and social movements. It has been separated from material that is more scientifically focused – including economics, even though that is a discipline that cannot claim the certainties of natural sciences. Climate science, in this book, definitely trumps economics as a guide to ecological problems and knowledge of natural limits. Economics that ignores ecological limits is a recipe for disaster. Part Two is more programmatic than Part One and will probably be considered more partisan. For that reason the book has been divided in two. Those uncomfortable with a focus on green politics, philosophy and history may choose to remain more focused on the issues raised in Part One.

CHAPTER
1

WHY BOTHER?

We'll all be 'rooned' said Hanrahan,
In accents most forlorn
Outside the church ere mass began
One frosty Sunday morn.

John O'Brian
Burra Record (South Australia),
1 December, 1920.

It's hard to look the other way. The evidence is clear that the world is disaster bound. The planet is warming, the climate less predictable, sea levels are rising, human populations are increasing at exponential rates, the pollution of air, sea, and land, continues unabated with alarming consequences. The rates of extinction of animal and plant species are higher than ever, and whole ecosystems are threatened. Onto this list of ecological disaster we need to add the chaos of human systems: *global* terrorism, warfare, financial crises, nuclear meltdowns, poverty, floods of refugees, remorseless urban expansion . . . Expert panels agree - mass media agree – but all appear powerless.

Governments, corporations, international organisations, trade unions, social movements and philanthropic individuals all seem dwarfed by the sheer scale of these problems. Even more dispiriting is the appearance that these peak bodies and custodians of public welfare are unable to do much that might unsettle the status quo.

The fate of future generations is looking grim. It is hard to be complacent about even the next ten years of planet Earth's future. This is a realistically bleak outlook. Given the overwhelming nature of the problems that surround us all, and the great difficulty of a change of direction, surely one has to ask why bother engaging with processes seeking a solution to future impacts of human behaviour? When the optimism or pessimism of experts seems pointless, why bother?

These are not just rhetorical questions. This book is an attempt to understand why it is that around the issue of climate change large numbers of people appear determined to sleep walk into the future. If the scientific facts are known, and technological solutions are available, why doesn't humanity simply change direction and respond rationally to events that increasingly threaten the very survival of future generations?

Answers to these questions are not straightforward. Human behaviour is not fully rational; social institutions are usually slow to respond to crises; human culture has a momentum that carries reason and emotion along pathways that are often dark and threatening, and often apparently self-defeating; 'human nature' can be selfish and cruel – and compassionate and creative.

This first chapter is an exploration of the psychological and cultural terrain that appears to pre-dispose what appears to be very strange behaviour indeed. If there ever was a time when 'sociological reasoning' was required this is it: many of the reasons for collective behaviour to be so apparently strange and impotent, and organisations to behave so badly, are just that – collective, or social. Often we do not have adequate ways of describing, or even identifying, what is going 'wrong' – reducing explanations to bad behaviour, or criminal negligence, or personality, or other individualised explanations are simply not adequate, as will become evident. Nor are the formulaic responses that come from many established disciplinary traditions adequate – in the final analysis, being totally human-centred is no longer useful in an era of ecological decline.

Some of the terrain of this chapter, and other material in later chapters, is therefore unavoidably philosophical or 'theoretical'. I hope to explain why that is a necessary step by virtue of the light such excursions can cast on what seems to be an intractable set of problems.

The questions already raised have implications that reveal 'sociological' reasoning. For instance, why bother worrying about things that seem beyond individual control? This question divides populations between those who see their individual spheres of influence as limited to self and family, and those with a more expanded sense of their ability to affect change in the world around them. Yet all people are part of ecologies, societies and the structures and processes that will determine outcomes to all efforts to address the effects of climate change and ecological decline. This book seeks to accommodate differences in personal orientation, by exploring issues that are deeper than personal behaviour and what might be termed 'common sense'.

Why bother about things that are not immediately self-evident? If global warming seems to be at odds with cooler or wetter climates, can we really believe the scientists and other self- appointed experts? And if these people can't agree, how reliable is science anyhow? So if things are going well now, why should we turn everything upside down at the whim of experts that claim to know better? These issues call basic evidence into question and cast doubt on our ability to be confident about judgements made on the basis of evidence – particularly if judgements are made by others, 'on our behalf', or 'in our best interests'.

It is highly likely that our ecological predicament is far worse than commonly known. We should be alarmed because the sky really might be about to 'fall down' – that is, heat up mightily. This book has also arisen out of desperation shared by all those with one eye (and ear) on the scientists, and another eye on a long history of human excess. Responses to those bigger issues have required more than sociological reasoning. Only multi-disciplinary research and an effort to provide an over-view could possibly begin to integrate science with the perspectives of other disciplines.

There are two different, but connected, reasons why there is not enough 'bothering': one is 'rational', the other 'emotional'. Firstly, rational discussion and argument about climate change and ecological crisis has been, and still is, limited – particularly in Australia. There are many considerations, or facets, to this observation. Media coverage, for instance, is piecemeal, occasional, largely reported by non-experts, 'balanced' by editors, and submerged in a flow of competing 'news' and information. Media are the most important source of mass, 'popular' knowledge, but if we turn to more specialised cultures we find other biases and constraints that also limit the communication of vital information. By addressing both popular and professional cultures, this book attempts an over-view that is more revealing of the ecological crisis we are in, and shows why action now is so vital to our common future.

Secondly, there is an unhelpful 'emotional' terrain that is constructed in popular culture, professional cultures, governments, and political cultures that dispose optimism as an anaesthetic balm. This subject will be addressed through an analysis of 'professional optimism', 'denial', and outmoded political ideologies.

The resolution of the many related issues that arise is suggested to be a 'pragmatic eco-centrism'. This 'new' perspective is similar to pioneering green philosophical works in arguing that an ecologically, and economically, sustainable philosophical and political position requires, among other things, a much less human-centred perspective.

THE BIGGER PICTURE

Bothering, or not, requires the will to act - which unavoidably raises political and philosophical issues. Later chapters investigate reasons *why* we need to act politically to bring about ecological change and *how* Green politics has emerged as a 'progressive' force. That investigation is the culmination of a longer exploration of the relationship between human society and global ecology. Before that discussion can sensibly proceed, some digression into 'common sense' is necessary. Why anyone might 'act', or take a position on any issue will always depend upon prior 'emotional' attitudes - whether considered as individual attributes or social products. The subject has emerged in renewed popular discourse about optimism versus pessimism, but in this book the discussion has been given much sharper focus: how useful are these attitudes in allowing us to deal with the likelihood of a future collapse, and can they be counter-productive in achieving positive ecological outcomes?

Human emotion is fundamentally important in any analysis of the future. Everyone may need good reason 'to bother', but we all need to *feel like* bothering, and that is partly an emotional matter bearing on how we are motivated, and what projects we might take up. There are many ways individual emotion can be analysed as a cause of action; in this book an 'institutional' approach has been chosen. It seems more relevant to wonder how particular emotions and feelings can be manufactured than to marvel at the emotions themselves. Optimism, in particular, has been subject to closer examination.

Also basic to any discussion of bothering, or not bothering, is the fact that we are social individuals, and we are ecologically connected; these are *natural* and in our natures as human beings. We are born with our individual differences and different perspectives; we are socialised and immersed in families, groups, institutions, political processes and cultures such that our power to choose is always limited. And we are all individually connected to the world in ways that go well beyond the scope of conscious awareness and conscious choice. This connectivity extends to the non-human world. We are organically part of natural ecologies and human systems. Most of this huge and tangled web of connection we normally take for granted, and are not aware of its subliminal powers. This complex situation has, of course, unavoidable consequences for what we might expect of human behaviour, and for the likelihood of effective social change.

Most critically, many people do not accept individual responsibility for the welfare of other species and their ecological support systems, or indeed for most of the worlds beyond one's immediate interests. There are good reasons for this, founded in successful survival mechanisms. Normally the complex social and ecological systems that sustain us function smoothly enough to be left alone. Local councils, government bureaucracies, small and large businesses, and all the other structures and organisations of human society articulate with natural systems to provide food, goods and services, and safety on the streets. Rarely does everything go totally pear shaped, or grind to a halt. Accidents, disasters and wars are common enough, but most societies have mechanisms at the ready for crisis management. Global catastrophes, and the threat of them, are much less frequent but certainly known to the historical record. The ancient history of global fire, flood, pestilence, or starvation may be too far removed to provide an immediate understanding of how humanity will respond to any future ecological cataclysms, but recent history is certainly relevant.

The twentieth century was distinguished by two world wars, the threat of a nuclear exchange between the Soviet Union and the United States, and the beginnings of a noticeable global ecological decline. Most of the survivors of world wars were able to start again, or somehow continue their shattered lives. There is an established pattern of survival here – we are the survivors of cycles of violence and hardship that go back into the mists of time.

The threat of nuclear war, and now of global ecological decline, present problems of a different order of complexity. The degradation and decline of natural systems caused by these potential events threaten the 'commons' that are the most basic support structure for all human societies. Dealing with these problems requires much deeper thought, and new and different strategies to be developed.

Can we look to new technologies to redress these problems? Without doubt new technologies will shape, and reshape, the future. Any future ecological crisis will benefit from technological innovations in all fields. The main issue concerns the adequacy of technological assessment processes and the incorporation of ecological considerations into new, and existing, technological designs. It may also be that new technologies have already transformed the future into something beyond redemption. Possibly new communication technologies are already absorbing the future into a world of instantaneous connection capable of transfixing whole generations. Perhaps machines running on artificial intelligence will make humans totally redundant.

Whatever outcomes future technologies deliver will need to be increasingly underpinned by ecological considerations – and the goal of ecological sustainability. For instance, every technological device and process has a 'carbon footprint': from nano-technology to rocket ships, everything that requires power is in some way connected to a carbon cycle. Humanity is a technological species, but this does not mean we can escape the basic 'laws' of physics, or limits imposed by ecological systems. All technologies are essentially *machines*, 'intelligent' or not, and this has major implications ecologically and economically, as will be discussed at greater length in Chapter 6.

It is particularly disturbing that our current ecological crisis appears to be largely a consequence of human activity. This chapter explores the idea that it is not simply the machine processes of technologies that are blameworthy - all human culture is deeply implicated. Indeed, all efforts to mitigate human-produced global warming and ecological decline will fail if the cultures that produce such anti-ecological consequences are not addressed at the same time as we change technologies.

Certainly, as human products, technologies are cultural; their machines and systems are designed in meaningful human processes and impact natural worlds to achieve human ends. However, as this chapter shows, we are deeply enmeshed in many cultural processes that produce meaning and purpose in human lives. Technologies are only part of the problem.

Technologies can indeed be relatively easy to change – for instance, alternative technologies to generate power are available; deeply engrained social practices can be much harder to change, or even identify as problematic. Media cultures and many professional cultures – including economics and politics - can be far more subversive ecological villains, as I go on to discuss.

This first chapter observes ecological concerns submerged in a deluge of popular media that actively seeks to incorporate ecological concerns into 'apocalypse culture'. Such efforts may be in the interests of mass emotional control (of anxiety, panic and anger, one would suppose), but we should wonder whether streams of 'popular' information are over-controlled by wider political agendas - and commercial interests.

In daily life the demands of work and family life are absorbing enough in worlds that are becoming increasingly regulated. Media-scapes that are seductive and catastrophic only increase the distance between daily life and the larger systems that govern our lives. Indeed, large numbers of people in many societies are disinterested, sceptical and even cynical about governments and the intentions of politicians and their corporate patrons to safeguard public welfare. To cap it all, the possibility that the climate is becoming 'weird' and that economies are ecologically unsustainable are overwhelming and catastrophic ideas.

However, before surrendering to the inevitability of imminent doom, we should review some of the reasons why passive fatalism is not the most effective response. Some evidence-backed opinion suggests things are not, as yet, hopeless. In this book a range of expert opinion will be reviewed, and two related questions addressed: what traps us into an apparently impossible situation, and how might we avoid the worst outcomes? The fact that it is our very way of life, as modern humans, that is the cause of so many ecological problems raises questions that are quite 'existential', and therefore very confronting.

For instance, because the mere suggestion that life on earth faces imminent decline raises the prospect of death - of individuals and species, human and non-human – the question of how we cope with crises such as death and dying becomes more relevant to the meaning of life now. The sense of urgency that comes with having to confront our mortality raises related 'big' personal questions. Two other issues raised in later chapters concern sex and technology: is sexual reproduction the primary purpose of life? And, why do we become addicted to new technologies?

The analytical approach taken in dealing with these inquiries is inter-disciplinary in scope – but underpinned by a sociological orientation; in the sense that all these deeply personal concerns, and other perennial concerns, are formed in particular social and cultural circumstances, and it is these circumstances that can help make particularly useful sense of them. This also implies that responses to many existential questions are variable – for example, the production of large families is not favoured in all societies; non-human life is not universally a high value; even human life is not universally valued. However, one assumption made in this book is that all these differences are relativised by the recognition of ecological values and their transcendent importance.

Our current circumstances are unique, but not everything is new; history, society, culture, and our individual responses have been created in long, slow processes involving patterns of social behaviour ('institutions') and emotions that are very old. Some human responses have never changed. We can take for granted that when confronting such unpleasant realities as death, whether individual or ecological, everyone will run through a gamut of emotional responses – such as anger, denial, grief, despair, resignation, and so on.

Confronting the end of our comfortable worlds raises similar issues - except for the scale of the deaths involved and what kind of life is dying. Of course, human death tends to be taken far more seriously than the death of other species, or the termination of other worlds, such as ecologies and environments. Perhaps this is the inevitable consequence of the survival instincts of our species. Such a perspective will be referred to, in this book, as *human-centredness*. As an existential condition it may prove fatal.

Discussion of ends and beginnings is everywhere. From archetypes to zeitgeist, human culture is an ongoing discourse about beginnings, endings and the enduring of time in between. But things have become a little more pressing. Whereas priests once urged populations to prepare for death tomorrow, and presumably were discredited somewhat on the morrow, today scientists are much more measured as prophets of doom. Their pronouncements are in terms of probabilities rather than absolute certainties – which is one of the reasons they are so much more persuasive. But not to all.

The great mystery that challenges some minds today is: if the evidence of impending disaster due to global warming and climate change is so compelling why do governments, corporations and great masses of people continue to effectively ignore the bad news? Why, if vigilance comes so easily, and perhaps is even hard wired into our psyches, is denial so easy? Do all religions that defer human fulfilment and the completion of life's meaning to some other time and place interfere with our ability to take ecological decline as seriously as necessary? Does a belief in God encourage ecological fatalism? Is there a deep and disabling layer of fear, anxiety and guilt that somehow perpetuates cultures of denial and over-consumption? Is over-absorption in families and reproduction some kind of existential solution?

These are questions that need to be asked - with the risk of finding no easy answers. It might be assumed that some recourse to theology or the mass psychology of catastrophe and crisis could be useful, or even necessary. This book takes a very different path because of the ecological vacuum in most religious, philosophical, and psychological efforts to diagnose the general problems of economics and modern life. It has been assumed (not unreasonably, I contend) that over-engagement with established religious or psychological models will result in a journey away from ecological imperatives.

The possibility that religions have played a role in encouraging desire for an apocalyptic end is clear, but the apocalyptic nature of contemporary media is at least as compelling today. Globally, citizens have to deal with a constant onslaught of crisis, disaster, misery and violence that comes as 'the news' and 'popular' culture. Not only are the images we receive disturbing, most things are endlessly deferred. Political crises unfold slowly through investigations, committees, courts, and the rehashing of journalists. Even science is deferred as journalists present 'balanced' and conflicting views as a means of developing a narrative that can be endless – about everything from diet to the methods used by terrorists, and to climate change. This immersion in endless possibilities might be reasonable as a simulation of scientific method, but it leaves audiences moving from day to day, from fad to fad, and hopefully (in the minds of advertisers and programmers), from product to product. Perhaps immersion in contemporary culture that is so apocalyptic and uncertain makes us more ecologically complacent, and more susceptible to bad decisions forced upon us by powerful elites in business and politics.[1]

APOCALYPTIC CULTURES

Fears about the end of the world, and our sense of connection to others in the world, are everywhere today produced and affected by media culture (including advertising) that influence our social and political responses. Most contemporary culture (including new technologies) deflect awareness of a natural world in crisis into 'more urgent' human concerns. A world in ecological crisis is not good for business and markets, and interferes with established narratives that depend on nature and the environment to be beautiful, bountiful and an appropriate setting

for human dramas. Such economic and cultural deflection is not altogether simple, or just a deliberate manipulation by evil capitalists and
media barons: it is also deeply rooted in cultural traditions, and particularly in religious teachings. Religious teachings contain well-developed
attitudes to nature and what is 'natural', and well developed ideologies
to deal with fears about the end of the world (including the end of the
natural world).

Worrying about the end of the world is not a new concern. Indeed,
humanity has always had a fascination with the end of things. The
world-views of most major religions have disposed whole populations
towards the idea of an afterlife in either heaven or some other realm.
Christianity gave hell and purgatory as particularly clear-cut options, but
all major religions agree that heaven is not an inevitable destination for
the immortal part of human beings.

One of the distinguishing features of Christianity, Islam and Judaism,
however, is that God can end things, or create apocalyptic conditions, at
any time of his choosing. Because of this doctrine, European Christians,
and their descendants around the planet, have had the end of the world
in mind for ages. In that religiously inspired angst the end of millennia
have been particularly troublesome - but for some fundamentalists there
is no time like the present. Suicide pacts and plots to bring on an early
end are now well known, much feared, and not restricted to funda-
mentalist Christians. It cannot be surprising that there are 'survivalists'
making bunkers, storing food and rehearsing strategies for worse case
scenarios.

We might wonder whether these religious doctrines have inhibit-
ed humanity from seeking deep fulfilment here on Earth. Waiting for
heaven to come, waiting for the end of the world, waiting for signs
– waiting, always waiting. Even in secularised views, hope for a better
society must wait – whether we are waiting for a revolution or waiting
for common sense to prevail. We are still waiting.

Fear of the unknown has fortunately been tempered by systematic observation and science. Scientific reason has liberated us from the
disempowerment that superstition brings. Behind this, the simple observation and experience of cause and effect has enabled the great successes

of human technological arts and sciences - including engineering and architecture, which continually transform our material worlds. Yet still, superstition abounds. Fear of the unknown, and fear of future disaster, spawns all manner of responses – rational and irrational. Fear continues to motivate future scientific and technological responses to impending disasters. Fear is an emotion exploited by media - 'disaster watch' and 'disaster alert' continue on a daily basis in all media. In modern times where over-consumption and excess in all things are the norm, the constant deployment of fear should make us wonder whether we are all just waiting for a catastrophe of some kind. The problem is that we may be waiting for the wrong catastrophe.

The response of all developed societies to mass existential threats appears the same: institutionalisation, or the creation of specialists whose job it is to deal with direct threats (such as hostile neighbours), or more intangible threats such the displeasure of the gods. Traditionally shamans and priests were apocalyptic specialists; today scientists are more at the leading edge of 'disaster watch'. Today, however, there is no simple division of labour that can control the dissemination of 'news' about 'the end'. In a highly connected world, large numbers can access the prophetic visions of any sect, cult or individual that can post a tweet, open a facebook page, or make a website. New media have enabled ancient mythologies to become part of a very eclectic modern popular culture. Thus, the correlation of heavenly events with earthly disasters is an ancient practice whose busy timetable now extends into modern times. In the space of just a few recent years we have been warned about the arrival of Comet Kahoutek, planetary alignments, the turn of the century, the year 2K computer bug, the end of the Mayan calendar, and now ecological collapse. This last threat is substantively different, but still open to mythologisation – ancient mythology and modern cosmology have significant parallels.

In many cultures it has been considered that the relationship between Heaven and Earth determines the fate of humans. This is still true today, even in secular worlds. Although it may be easy to shrug off the astrology of disaster as a kind of pre-scientific activity that has so far failed to deliver, the heavens are still the major partner in all modern cosmology.

However, the advent of highly sophisticated telescopes and space technology have resulted in the heavens becoming far more than a symbolic vista. As our scientific knowledge of the universe has grown, the heavens have become a real landscape in the sense that they can be observed, described and predicted using theory and methods that can be more reliably tested than ever before. Science and scientists have also become cemented in popular culture – today every creation story has to contend with 'the big bang'.

Death and disaster have always been part of the human condition; so while 'disaster watch' and apocalyptic fears have been transformed into mythology in all cultures, it is certainly worth reassessing mythology as a record of the human experience of catastrophe. Further, there are probably other important practical considerations implicit in the process of mythologisation - that may bear on what we are, and how we might react to the threat of a global ecological disaster. The urge to explain 'the big picture', from the beginning of time to the end of everything, is universally human – cosmology is an ancient obsession. The impacts of modern science on ancient mythologies are critical in the creation of new narratives that can cope with the realities of ecological change. The frameworks of the production of cosmologies are less obvious – there are institutional considerations that are highly relevant in understanding how it is that new narratives are framed and transmitted. Apart from the social organisation of specialists, such as shamans, priests, and more recently scientists, economists, and others who generate narratives and provide advice, the 'paradigms', or cognitive frameworks that specialists produce tend to incorporate the concerns and values of their funders and supporters.

What is directly portrayed in narratives that deal with unpleasant or forgettable events is the most obvious part of institutionalised coping mechanisms. Absences and omissions are also part of these processes. What specialists say is always interesting, but what they don't say can also be highly revealing. What is not said can be read in many ways – sometimes as tacit support for a controversial position, but also as a polite form of denial. In general, 'denial' is a response that resonates with the conservatism of many institutions and professions, and will be pursued as a major theme relevant to understanding the slow acceptance of climate change. It is hardly controversial to assume that denial is a very traditional (and natural) way of coping with our deepest fears – of death and other horrors.

For instance, the recurring occurrence of denial of genocide is a baffling phenomenon – in a highly mediated era, there are publicly available records; investigative journalists and other professionals 'expose the facts'; individuals and groups who survive provide testimony. One wonders whether climate change denial can reveal something more about the deeper sources of denial in the human psyche. Perhaps the imminent threat of climate change arouses very ancient responses that are 'hard wired' – global climate change is, after all, just a slowly emerging natural disaster.

To whatever extent our cultural records can be regarded as fact or fiction, it is certain that our distant ancestors have witnessed ice ages, dark ages, floods and fires on an epic scale. Perhaps there are historical records other than texts and the debris of disaster. It may be that this history of trauma is encoded in our genes, and even in the dark spaces of 'junk genes'.

Genetic research has, indeed, become much more relevant to our understanding of ancient history and the evolution of humanity. Professor Lars Olov Bygren of the Karolinska Institute demonstrated, in a ground breaking Swedish study published in 2000, an apparent relationship between the experience of 'feast and famine' by parents and the acquisition of acquired genetic characteristics in some of their children. If the descendants of survivors of famines can pass on some acquired 'epigenetic' changes – due to parts of genes being caused to switch 'on' or 'off' - then the possibility that all survivors may carry some acquired characteristics is clear.[2]

ECONOMIC FORCES

Work, business, trade, finance and markets are fundamentally determining of society, culture and any individual's 'life chances'. The effects of economic processes, and economic reasoning, are essential component in any explanation of human history and the impacts of human activities on environments and ecologies. Even climate change denial can be sourced in economic behaviour.

The imperative of 'business as usual' is one of the more obvious causes of most kinds of mass denial. The need for work, business and trade is such a powerful collective force that it can overcome all vague fears and most personal scruples. Politicians know this better than most since their election campaigns are extensively funded by the private purse, which depends on 'business as usual'. In that process, political systems become captives of business interests, and politicians seek to control the outcome of elections through appeal to voters' 'hip-pocket nerve'. Manipulation of 'the system' by external vested interests has undoubtedly been with us since the beginnings of organised trade, and indeed is so 'normal' that it now has its own legitimate industry – 'political lobbying'. In this tradition of economic behaviour ecological needs have to be economically rational or they will be ignored. Environmental degradation and pollution can be so expensive to remedy that it is often far easier for companies and workers to simply ignore environmental accidents and routine pollution.

Economic forces work in both war and peace. The thought that profit can be had from war and disaster is unpalatable to most, but undoubtedly true. Joseph Heller's novel *Catch 22* expressed this brilliantly by exposing how war is profitable for smart entrepreneurs. Despite the apparent contradiction, it can be profitable to bomb yourself. Heller's main protagonist, Yossarian, may have been a crazy comic hero, but the popularity of the book (and film) indicates that mass audiences understand that the twisted economic stimulus war provides to some is economically rational in the end. [3]

As Naomi Klein put it, 'Now wars and disaster responses are so fully privatised that they are themselves the new market; there is no need to wait until after the war for the boom – the medium is the message.'[4]

Similarly, today's global warming challenges are easily understood as economic opportunities for some, despite being a tax burden for most. Even more disturbing is the prospect that energy producers may cry poor about the cost of pollution abatement and conversion to sustainability, but they know that costs will pass along to the consumer. In the

longer term large corporations have the ability to control the economy
with or without government intervention.

Even if governments, businesses and markets will work to make sustainable energy an available choice in the market place, it is clear that
coal is still the immediately cheaper option for powering the global grid.
Economic rationality is an overwhelmingly powerful force. There are,
however, some signs that coal is becoming less popular as a source of
electricity because of its role as a green house gas producer (particularly
CO_2) and because of international efforts to promote sustainable energy
sources. There have even been dramatic declarations by some more morally driven organisations – the Uniting Church in Australia has recently
introduced a policy of disinvestment from the coal industry, and other
large organisations, including universities and the Catholic Church, have
followed. These are positive steps, but as will be explained at greater
length in Chapter 6, 'Changing Economics', until economic reasoning
incorporates ecological costs there can be little hope that fossil fuel usage
will decline quickly enough to prevent serious global warming.

Further, many of the most economically attractive alternatives to coal
are, unfortunately, unsustainable. For instance, if natural gas is substituted
for coal the likelihood that atmospheric methane concentrations will
skyrocket appears high. Because 'methane is roughly 30 times more
potent as a heat trapping agent' it would accelerate catastrophic global
warming.[5]

Already evidence is mounting that 'fugitive' methane gas emissions
are much higher than the gas industry admits (at most stages of the gas
cycle – extraction, distribution, storage and possibly even combustion).[6]

In addition to methane emissions directly caused by our high levels
of demand for power, there are other natural sources of atmospheric
methane: cattle, rotting vegetation, and 'vents' from various methane
sinks, including those under melting permafrost on land and under the
Arctic ocean. If global warming accelerates, as widely predicted by scientists, the increasing scale of future methane emissions may force a much
higher rate of warming than already predicted.

The worst fear of most environmentalists is, however, that nuclear power will make a comeback as a 'clean' and economically rational
source of energy. A well known history of environmental disasters from

power station failures, failure to solve the problem of waste storage, the connection with the production of nuclear weapons (including the use of depleted uranium in conventional ordinance), the known health risks of radiation, and an unconvincing economic return on investment in new power plants does, however, make the possibility of future nuclear energy production being ecologically or economically rational unlikely. That may not deter governments from making desperate decisions at a later stage when green house gas concentrations become a much more serious political issue.[7]

Alarm bells should be ringing loudly *now* as we are on an imminent collision course for 450ppm of atmospheric CO_2, the tipping point for an inevitable 2° C global temperature rise.[8]

By 2013 we passed 400ppm CO_2, and chances of slowing increasing atmospheric concentrations of either CO_2, or methane appear slim. It is hard to fathom why governments, business and the mainstream media should continue to pursue such obvious programs of mass impression management about increasing concentrations of greenhouse gases – except by assuming that there is still good money to be made using old, dirty technology. Even the more outspoken journalists in Australia, such as the economist Ross Gittens, and environmental writers Tom Arup and Ben Cubby (all employed by the *Sydney Morning Herald*), find their commentary published well away from pages one, two or three. Cricket, Rugby, Horseracing, Sailing, Celebrities, and now soccer, are more likely to find page one. Audiences want to be entertained. In Australia, depressing stories without the possibility of clear and progressive narrative lines are not likely to sell even the most highbrow newspapers, or attract advertisers.

Market forces are unavoidably important in determining the success or failure of ecological programs. In a global capitalist economy we need to proceed with a clear view of market forces and the ability of economies to price in the costs of habitat regeneration, wilderness preservation and the reduction of carbon pollution. Capitalism is not intrinsically opposed to idealism, but any idealism needs to be grounded in the realities of how people behave when left free to lead lives in market-based economies. Ecological idealism needs to be considered in the light of market forces. This discussion will be pursued in later chapters, but the point is well made by the wide international consensus of economists that, in a market economy, a carbon trading scheme is the best way forward in dealing with carbon pollution. Consumers and business will pay for the costs of all kinds of pollution, but 'certainty', or stability in markets is also required. This means that governments need the courage to levy taxes, and businesses the courage to raise prices as necessary. So far, these carbon costs and taxes do not appear likely to cripple economies, or ruin budgets. A strong international consensus about the need for carbon trading schemes is a very encouraging sign of change being possible. However, in Australia it is clear that efforts to make CO_2 production part of a market economy are likely to stall into the near future. At the time of writing, the latest party of government, the Liberal Party, have only recently overcome outright and strident climate change denial. The government is determined to disengage from an existing policy of taxing carbon production, and the option of engaging with international carbon markets. Current government policy in Australia has a long way to go in dealing with a changed and increasingly unpredictable global habitat.

RISK SOCIETY

It is puzzling that many industrial processes, particularly since the nineteenth century, have been so polluting and dangerous that they could be tolerated to the point of impending ecological collapse. Economic imperatives and new narratives about modernisation and progress explain much, but without some new ideas about the normalisation of risk in modern life, the real and present dangers associated with economic success could never provide a fully adequate explanation for increasingly dangerous situations.

The causes of global pollution are obvious enough. Smoke-belching, dirty industrial complexes have been part of city landscapes since the mid nineteenth century. The sights, sounds and smells were immediate and obvious; the mysterious deaths, blights, and slow wasting of the land, people, and animals, less obvious. The destructive impacts of large-scale industry on environments and natural systems were never fully celebrated, but grudgingly accepted as part of the price to be paid for industrially based lifestyles – and the main choice available for workforces then was work, or starve. Of course, industry has moved on. Many industries have changed over the last two hundred years and efforts to control emissions and other harmful effects on people and environments have been made. Governments have legislated about pollution abatement; the idea that 'the polluter pays' is virtually common sense. Harm minimisation may have become best practice, but the increasing global scale of industry generates myriad unanticipated consequences; environmental, social and ecological impacts have only become more profound - and more disturbing.

The massive urban expansion that has devoured grassy plains, forests and ecosystems is also a cause of global pollution. Urban development has been less noted as a major cause of pollution because of its association with 'progress' and human welfare. However, the combination of environmental and ecological destruction, population growth and the industrial infrastructure required to sustain urban expansion everywhere are now obvious as sources of pollution and loss of habitat; urban development is well understood to be inevitable as a correlate of population growth and human welfare, whatever risks that process may present.

The escalating risks 'modernisation' and 'development' pose to human health and safety, as well as to the health and safety of animals and plant ecosystems, are now better known. To various extents they are factored in, and widely accepted as part of the costs of better lifestyles. Yet workers in hazardous jobs often still have the same limited choice of work, or poverty. The threat of catastrophic climate change alters none of that. Ecological damage does already raise the bar for all risk assessment and planning processes, and the costing of new development – including insurance and reinsurance. But now with climate change and ecological decline much more imminent, life 'suddenly' does seem a lot riskier.

Climate change is particularly challenging in the way it forms a new boundary for a globalised industrial society. This product of human activity had been anticipated in previous decades, but now looms as such a threat to life as normal to have generated high levels of deferral

and denial. Certainly, governments and local councils have been alerted
to the consequences of climate change, and are in many cases beginning to make plans. But risk is a very grey area for public officials – and
would seem to be for the general public too. If it's not a current or very
recent disaster, deferral and denial are more likely immediate strategies
of coping – *Yes, Minister,* indeed. The dangers of climate change – such
as the likelihood of significant sea level rises soon, or the likelihood of
severe weather events in the near future - are not yet easily calculable.
Governments are very reluctant to scare the voters; markets rely on the
growth of consumption. The calculation of future probabilities that go
beyond election cycles remains a very dark art – any results are usually
buried with little ceremony.

For all their concern with the risky nature of capitalism, the sociologists Ulrich Beck and Anthony Giddens did not anticipate catastrophic
climate change. Nonetheless, they have become famous for the way they
focussed academic attention on the phenomenon of risk as an organising
principle in contemporary industrial capitalist societies. The idea that
risk (and danger) is now a way of life was novel in 1986 when Beck published *Risk Society: Toward a New Modernity.* The idea was novel insofar as
it was a sensible and hugely plausible intellectual response to an otherwise crazy scenario – in large and complex societies increased security
and prosperity comes at the cost of ever-greater risk-taking. Risk has
been normalised – and it would seem, often hidden from common and
expert view alike. The global financial crisis of 2009 – 2011 demonstrated this so well.

People of my parent's generation were generally not the economic risk takers that their children have become. They were reluctant to
borrow large amounts of money to buy the family home – and banks
then were also much less likely to lend money to working people. In
one short generation that has all changed, leaving many older people
still scratching their heads over the levels of debt their children accept as
absolutely normal. In growing economies it may be sensible to extend
the opportunities of increased debt levels to all – however not all economies do grow, as we see with such tragic effects in the case of Greece in

2015. Not all people alive today have actually experienced an economic depression of the depth of the Great Depression of last century – it is not surprising that people of my parent's generation were reluctant to take major economic risks.

There are benefits in at least recognising the centrality of risk in modern life. In particular, if risk is increasingly part of the rationale of all development, then the inevitability of unanticipated ecological consequences should be more easily contemplated. Indeed, 'risk assessment' has become part of many planning processes, and was traditionally part of many legal and commercial ideas (as insurance, re-insurance, trading in markets, gambling and contingency planning) but the idea that increasing levels of risk are essentially 'normal' was, and still is, challenging. What if the risks become a real and present danger of an overwhelming kind? How can we change everything? Do insurance companies have a way of realistically factoring in future global disasters? Probably not. It seems we are all playing an increasingly high-risk game with no insurance.

ANYONE FOR A REVOLUTION?

Some on 'the left' in politics still harbour the hope that revolutionary consciousness will soon erupt from the discontent of the working class. In the context of the big changes to society and culture that saving the planet's ecological viability apparently require, the idea of a social revolution might seem appropriate – however, in Australia there is little sign of serious class based discontent. Increasing numbers of working people are more 'aspirational' than ever before. The 'good life' is available in Australia to increasingly large numbers.

The class structure of Australia and other wealthy countries has changed significantly in recent times. The growth of the services sector and the proportional decline of manufacturing industries (both as employers and contributors to economic wealth production) correspond with falling rates of membership of trade unions and increasing 'aspirationalism'. Despite the distribution of wealth remaining massively skewed toward the rich, people in wealthy countries increasingly identify with being 'middle class', and are 'upwardly mobile' in terms of economic and lifestyle aspirations.[9]

With the rise of middle class security, 'class consciousness' has radically declined as a revolutionary force.

Mark Latham, an ex-leader of the Australian Labor Party, explains the situation colourfully:

> Unionisation in Australia has fallen to 18 per cent econo-my wide, with private sector coverage at just 13 per cent. Whether the traditionalists like it or not, minority union membership is here to stay . . . For all the commentary about 'Howard's battlers' and Rudd's 'working families under financial pressure' the statistical evidence suggests a different dynamic. . . This is what Laborism is supposed to achieve: to lift up the bottom, to break down class barriers and to make social mobility possible. Not surprisingly this has ignited further aspiration, even greater ambition for the economic success of the next generation. What was the old working class supposed to do, having enjoyed more money in its kick? Go back to low-paid factory work and rented fibro cottages?'[10]

Employment patterns in Australia have also changed dramatically over the last fifty years. Between 1960 and 2012 employment in the services sector has grown from 50% to over 75% (or over 85% if 'construction' and 'utilities' are included). Meanwhile the proportions in manufacturing and agriculture have declined steadily from 28% to 8% and 11% to 3%, respectively. Employment levels in mining and construction industries have remained roughly steady at 1% and 9%, respectively. The growth of employment in service industries and the decline of manufactur-ing is common to all wealthy countries. For example, in 2005 levels of employment in service industries in Australia, Canada, France, the Netherlands, the UK, and the US only varied between 74% and 79% – excluding construction and utilities.[11]

The days of national strikes appear over; workers have gained sufficient rights, and rates of pay, to permit the lowest rates of union membership since the early days of Federation. The most disadvantaged sections of the population (indigenous people, disabled people, and refugees) are not able to organise and strike in ways that would engender mass support. Common wisdom is that Australians are generally too well off to be seriously bothered about changing the system. Education levels have risen and good health care is widespread. Australia scores consistently high on the OECD wellbeing index (and all other wellbeing indexes) - despite countervailing survey evidence that prosperity and happiness are not directly correlated.[12]

In 2013, the OECD found that Australia was the world's most prosperous and happy country.[13]

Elections in Australia continue to be dominated by public concerns about the economy, health, and education. Concern for the environment seems to have fallen away as a priority, roughly in concert with the level of media attention to ecological and environmental problems. This observation is widely shared by media watchers, but statistics are not readily available – determination of environmental attitudes by media is an under researched subject. There is a broader trend of public disengagement with media reportage of political campaigns that may also bear on a relatively low level of concern with environmental issues and climate change.[14]

In campaigning before the last Federal election in 2013, the Liberal Party branded the Labor–Green–Independent backed government initiative for a carbon tax as 'a great big new tax'. This worked well and seems to have been more polarising than the threat of global warming itself. In that year Australians overwhelmingly endorsed a new government that promised to minimise the costs to industry and taxpayers of carbon pollution abatement – these measures have rolled out to include removal of the carbon tax and de-funding Climate Change Commission. The government has initiated measures to remove and downsize all research and development premised on the need for it to change policy directions in response to current scientific evidence about the threats posed by climate change; it has also reduced levels of government assistance to wind and solar power initiatives in the renewable energy sector. It has slashed the budget and staffing of the CSIRO, the nation's peak research organisation, and threatens the funding of environmental groups across the country. We have a Prime Minister, and a Minister for the Environment, and indeed governments, who regularly either ignore climate science, or argue illogically on the basis of the science, or other information at their disposal.[15]

The refusal of scientific evidence and informed reason by our political leaders in their judgements about climate science, do not appear to be of concern to anywhere near half the population. When economic growth and quality of life are used as bargaining chips, sloganeering can easily substitute for reasoned debate. Economic rationalism, or the perception of economic rationalism and economic growth, still win elections - even when the reason is hard to find in the economics. Despite dissatisfaction with politicians because of widespread perceptions of corruption[16]- Australia is not currently a candidate for radical social change.

The idea of a class-based revolution happening in Australia is simply not on the agendas of either of the two largest parties, or the voting public. In Australia there are far more 'white collar' workers than 'blue collar' workers. Voters are 'aspirational'. By any measures 'working class consciousness' is in decline in Australia – a likely source of frustration for many remaining socialists.

Clearly, financial prosperity, good health, good education, and plenty of sport, do not stimulate class based 'revolutionary consciousness' in Australia. If we accept that 'class warfare' is not going to erupt in Australia, or in most wealthy countries, and yet hold out hope for changes to lifestyles and industry that might save declining ecologies, we should wonder how those kinds of changes can occur. This book addresses the question by reassessing the possibilities for change without assuming that there is only one way that radical change can occur – by class warfare. More modest changes that involve beliefs and values, and gradual changes to industry and governments, might be called *cultural change*. This includes changing the ways we generate and consume energy and changing the way we think about nature. Such 'modest' changes are our best hope for enduring change in countries like Australia.

Cultural change should not be off the agenda of political radicals. The best recent Australian historical examples of cultural change concern attitudes to women, sexuality, and a far greater tolerance of multicultural and racial diversity - but these cultural changes have been slower to translate into changes in workplaces, salaries and boardrooms. Indigenous Australians still suffer poor health and lower access to education, but there are many more opportunities for indigenous Australians now compared to fifty years ago. Similar remarks could be made about other cultural minorities in Australia – such as gay, lesbian and transgendered people, and those with disabilities.

Attitudes about the importance of nature and the environment have certainly changed over the last fifty years, but not enough to prevent a level of despair arising among environmentally focused individuals. Do we have another fifty years to wait for changed attitudes to transform economic and political life? The responses of governments and industry to scientific evidence about climate change and ecological decline have been, so far, very restrained.

PSYCHOLOGICAL CONSIDERATIONS

Perhaps there are unconsidered psychological factors in these preliminary investigations of apathy, angst and anti-ecological resistance. We might wonder whether another round of worry about 'the end of the world' could be sufficiently plausible to add more weight to shoulders already bearing the weight of mortality. At what point does the threat of ecologically sourced destruction begin to exceed the normal psychological balance routinely achieved in the face of personal decline and mortality? Does the threat of an impending ecological meltdown make community mental health an issue? Does living with risk and uncertainty cause mass neurosis, mass denial, and an unconscious brinkmanship?

These important questions will be, however, only partially pursued in the analysis that follows. The focus here is placed on systemic causes and effects, the normalisation of such increased psychological pressures, and the importance of political action to deal with crises we can easily anticipate. It is assumed that individuals adjust to inconvenient truths about life and death. Some kind of 'denial' is a routine part of daily individual and collective behaviour. Anyone who has witnessed extreme poverty, or extensive suffering, death, and dying, will have experienced the speed of adjustment processes – 'life must go on'. Nonetheless, the experience of trauma, whatever the causes, has negative effects. In developed countries western psychiatry and psychology do report increasing rates of mental illness. In Australia the rate of suicide of young men is high, and depression is an increasingly common illness among women and men.[17]

Before any conclusions about the causes of social statistics - such as rates of suicide or mood disorders - might be attempted, it is noteworthy that the interpretation of mass statistics is never straightforward. Aggregation of data may result in the loss of regional and individual issues, making the attribution of 'causes' very difficult. Further, the range of possible causes in most cases of public interest is usually wide. Disentangling factors such as unemployment, drug use, isolation, and over exposure to violence, from vague fears (such as that of impending disaster or loss of ecological and environmental quality) makes it difficult to be confident about particular causes of apparently high rates of mental illness and suicide.

Another issue of relevance to the generation of medical and psychological statistics is the apparent willingness of many psychiatrists and psychologists to pathologise and medicalise 'unusual' individual behaviours and states. Some conditions - such as 'hyper-activity', 'attention' disorders and some kinds of depression - can certainly be linked to an over-enthusiastic and globalised pharmaceutical industry that has a profit-oriented interest in new disorders.[18]

So, although it is possible to appreciate why a psychoanalyst as eminent as Julia Kristeva might say '[t]he despoliation of nature, lives and property is accompanied by an upsurge, or simply a more obvious display, of disorders whose diagnosis are being refined by psychiatry – psychosis, depression, mania, depressive states, borderline states, false selves, etc.'[19] , in the absence of a better researched 'ecopsychology', it is sensible to leave such intuitive professional judgements with psychoanalysts, psychologists and psychiatrists.

Theodore Roszack observes that 'few psychologists have any interest in relationships that reach beyond couples, families, and maybe the workplace . . . the environmental crisis remains of little interest to practising psychologists'. This is despite a substantial amount of research that does find that the experience of nature and wilderness is almost always therapeutic. Roszack concludes that the modern relationship of humanity to nature is 'crazy'. His book *The Voice of the Earth* is typically brilliant and persuasive, but not quantitative. Fortunately, the hard facts about ecological decline are becoming more persuasive than post-Freudian analyses of Gaia.[20]

WHY BOTHER?

The future looks very unpleasant in the estimations of leading ecological scientists, climate scientists, and many social scientists. To bother now can still save us from a lot more bother in the future. The alternative is far worse – governments locked into a continual mode of crisis management. To 'not bother' puts us all at greater risk of enduring an increasingly fragmenting global society where conflict over basic resources, such as water and food, becomes normal. Not bothering will contribute to the destabilising effects of global warming on social structures – it is easy to predict increasingly large numbers of refugees arising from large-scale destruction of habitat and rising sea levels. A more dislocated and conflicted world means increases in crime and violence domestically, and a greater rate of warfare between nation-states. It is easy to imagine a spiralling vortex of chaotic dysfunction directly caused by climate change alone. When climate change is added to the list of other known global threats – war, terrorism and organised crime, particularly – it should be obvious that under-estimating the level of threat presented by climate change is just silly.

We have to face up to the most obvious consequences of humanity's dominant presence on Earth. Presently, the leading ecological challenge is climate change, which seems unavoidable:

> So it seems that even with the most optimistic set of assumptions – the ending of deforestation, a halving of emissions associated with food production, global emissions peaking in 2020 and then falling by 3 per cent a year for a few decades – we have no chance of preventing emissions rising well above

a number of critical tipping points that will spark uncontrollable climate change. The Earth's climate would enter a
chaotic era lasting thousands of years before natural processes eventually established some sort of equilibrium. Whether
human beings would still be a force on the planet or even
survive, is a moot point. One thing seems certain: there will
be far fewer of us.[21]

2

THE BIG THREE

I've never seen a problem that wouldn't be easier to solve with fewer people, or harder, if not impossible, with more.

Sir David Attenborough
(quoted in Dick Smith, *Population Crisis*. Sydney: Allen and Unwin, 2011, p.5.)

Why bother, indeed! When the situation is far worse than most can admit, why bother?

Climate change, economic growth and the growth of global population, create problems that may be nearly impossible to 'fix'. Could it be that humankind is slowly adjusting to an awful fate? In Chapter 1 it was suggested that we are already immersed in cultures that are sufficiently apocalyptic to create mass indifference to visions of doom. Disturbing as exposure to human chaos and suffering is, they become culturally normalised with prolonged exposure.

In this chapter evidence will be presented to support the claim that there is a 'wicked' set of global problems that may be impossible to fix.

Climate change, economic growth and over-population are complex and inter-related problems whose enormity will challenge all conventional strategies, particularly insofar as they do not acknowledge that there are, indeed, limits to growth. Later chapters will look more closely at the rhetoric, logic, and history, of 'going forward' optimistically, and the possibility of changing direction economically and politically. I would emphasise that this line of analysis is not just 'doom and gloom'. Without mass acceptance of a serious existential dilemma there can be little reason for hope at all. The skies are dark, but not yet impenetrable to the light of reason.

TALKING ABOUT THE WEATHER

Apocalyptic cultures are part of an exciting and newsworthy foreground – even if they slowly acclimatise audiences to horror and disaster in the process. In contrast, the long slow cycles of the climate, and even occasional natural disasters, have not been particularly captivating as media events. Normally, the weather has not been as exciting, or threatening, as wars, accidents, crimes of violence, or even sport. Essential as weather reports are, they have traditionally been placed after the 'real' news, or towards the back of the newspaper. Similarly, human agriculture and industry have been generally placed in the 'comfortably slow and unexciting' category. The encroachment of humanity on forests and wilderness, and the hardly noticeable decline and extinction of other species have also inched along sporadically in the media, effectively out of the public gaze.

That was before extreme weather events and the threat of climate change were able to inject a new frisson into television news and on-line reportage. Extreme weather events and climate change not only provide new challenges to everyone's normalising abilities, they also threaten the order of traditional media worlds. Unlike wars, violence, epidemics and sport, climate change and extreme weather threaten to be uncontrollable.

This presents an exciting problem to all media because much as the new and the wild are exciting and attention grabbing, order and the appreciation of order are two of the intended effects of all mass media.

The rule of law and all the institutions of state and society may be threatened in media, but this only serves to strengthen our attachment to order. Through cultural rituals like the news and the normal routines of work, leisure and family life, social life is stabilised and made comfortably predictable. The construction of order is also part of the agenda for all that is exciting or disturbing on 'the news' and current affairs programs. Wars, for example, are often protracted affairs – but eventually, peace breaks out; epidemics are either controlled or 'die down'; crime can be managed by police and the courts. Further, life is resilient. These are the sources of security that have made it easy for populations to become complacent about 'apocalyptic' news cycles and chaos that occurs 'out there', somewhere else. However, media reportage of wild and unpredictable weather will demand new sources of order and comfort – particularly if 'denial' is to be cultivated, as normal.

Accepting wild weather as to some extent human made will be part of this new adjustment – in the media and in common perception. Indeed, the advent of a new era of global climate disasters should alter the status of natural disasters forever. Bushfires, droughts, floods, cyclones, tornadoes, rising sea levels, storm surges, and coastal erosion are now more than the unpredictability of an awesomely powerful nature. Now these disturbances can be seen to have human influence – signifying anything from the mark of Cain, to the natural decline of all civilization. Green house gas emissions from the burning of fossil fuels cause global warming which de-stabilises climates and causes extreme weather events. That is a chain of cause and effect that has taken decades for most politicians to accept – and still some Australian politicians lag well behind an international political consensus about climate change.[1]

Science may not as yet be able to prove beyond all doubt that the increasing frequency and intensity of Australia's bushfires, or draughts, are the product of global warming, but the evidence is mounting rapidly. Events that might once have merely raised more doubts about the wisdom of farming 'marginal' land, or living in bushland, now have the full attention of climate scientists and ecologists. This is unwelcome news for all those who believed in 'acts of god' as a way of excusing human agency. Human caused climate change and extreme climatic events are here already, and being studied; the statistics confirming global warming (and the role of humanity as a cause) are firming with each passing year.[2]

The problem is bigger and scarier than many wish to recognise. The evidence is in that we are rapidly approaching many tipping points for ecological instability. Even if atmospheric concentrations of CO_2 were to decrease by technological innovation to 350 ppm, there are other reasons to worry about the possibility of ever re-achieving ecological sustainability. Changing atmospheres and oceans have a 'forward momentum' – such that the effects of 400-450 ppm CO_2, now, guarantees many more years of global warming, particularly if rates of emissions do not actually decline. Just as the forward momentum of an ocean liner makes turning around a protracted event, so too the 'forward momentum' of the various effects increasing levels of CO_2 will take time to slow, or even reverse. Global warming has a 'snowballing' effect on the environment creating many chains, or cascades, of cause and effect – for example melting glaciers change ocean temperatures, sea currents, ocean habitats, and so on. As particular species become extinct in the process they are lost forever – a cooling planet will not simply reverse biological changes that have already occurred. Human populations that are forced to move because of rising sea levels and other effects of global warming (such as increasing desertification) will have enormous social and political effects – just as refugees fleeing war and poverty today are already changing societies and economies, and will continue to do so.

The combined effect of increasing greenhouse gas emissions is alarming, but they are only the 'tip of an iceberg' – the production of greenhouse gases is inextricably linked to the increasing size of populations and the growth of economies. It could also be said that the apparently irresistible rise of atmospheric greenhouse gas concentrations is a clear sign of economic excess – and that has a great deal of forward momentum. As this chapter shows, the continuing growth of economies and populations are scary problems of an unprecedented scale – this is the root cause of the chaos that threatens to become normal. Failure to appreciate that is symptomatic of very deeply rooted denial.

ECONOMIC EXCESS

As long ago as 1972, the first Club of Rome Report began to detail the way increasing populations will cause resource depletion and increasing pollution.[3]

Global warming was not yet an imminent threat, yet the catastrophic effects of human population growth alone were clear. The general relationship between ecological decline and economic activity was also becoming of great concern to a gathering environmental movement. Now, more than forty years later, the unfolding effects that humanity's population explosion is having on the resources of a finite planet should be obvious to all. The economic impacts of climate change are guaranteed to be huge – the impacts of increased refugee numbers alone are likely to be considerable – world wide. Unfortunately, the myriad effects climate change will have are only now being digested by economists and business leaders.

In Australia, where climate change denial is still a part of popular politics, it is a remarkable event when an economic journalist has a climatic epiphany. The Sydney Morning Herald's economic columnist Ross Gittens, a well-respected commentator and writer of books about wellbeing, recently had such an experience:

> Did I ever doubt that climate change represented by far the greatest threat to Australia's future economic prosperity? Never. Should I have said this more often, rather than chasing a thousand will-o'-the wisps? Yes. Dear grand children, I can only say sorry.

We might hope that among economists Ross Gittens is not alone in realising that

> eventually the environment would hit back and do great damage to the economy ... we rationalised our selfishness – our willingness to avoid a tiny drop in our standard of living at the expense of a big drop in our offspring's – by telling

ourselves half truths and untruths about the global nature of climate change.

We've told ourselves there was nothing Australia could do by itself to effect climate change (true), that at the Copenhagen conference in 2009, countries had failed to reach a binding agreement on action to reduce enormous emissions (true) and that the world's two biggest polluters, China and the US, were doing nothing much to reduce their emissions. We had no excuse for not knowing this was untrue because successive government reports told us the contrary. [4]

As great as damage to the economy may prove to be – and even including costs of transitioning to renewable sources of energy production and other more ecologically sustainable activities – the economic crisis we face is more systemic than the blow out of future costs. Economies cannot grow indefinitely on a finite planet. That's a fundamental problem. There is something seriously wrong with current economic logic. Every school child can understand the basic idea of a *limit*. This is not a hard idea – however, the ramifications of such a situation on the foundations of our economy and culture are presently just unacceptable to those committed to the proposition of sustainable endless growth. That fantasy is deeply embedded in the 'common sense' of big business and the professional economists that guide business practice, the necessity of increasing consumption, linked in turn to the necessity of population growth. At present the economic consensus is that growth is the only way to maintain prosperity and wellbeing. Every national Treasurer says so. Further, because economic theory is thoroughly institutionalised as a profession and a tertiary discipline, it is likely that economists will lag behind business leaders in being able to respond quickly to rapidly changing circumstances.

As welcome as Ross Gittens' comments are, the development of alternative economic models factoring in environmental costs, a flat economy, and the needs of future generations, appears to be more difficult than most economists can contemplate. Changes in economic thinking of that kind would amount to a 'paradigm change' – which in the case of economics would also require radical changes to business practices and consumption patterns. Such a 'paradigm change' would cost real money, threaten economist's jobs (and many other jobs and careers), and change society and culture.

There are smaller steps available. It is likely that Ross Gittens, and other progressive economists, will soon promote 'low growth' scenarios. The move to 'sustainable' models, even zero growth models, will take longer to surface in the mainstream, if ever. Without growth, modern economics falls apart. As Herman Daly put it:

> The fundamental axiom of growth [. . .] is that 'when something grows it gets bigger!' When the economy grows it too gets bigger. So dear economist, when the economy grows, (a) exactly what is it that is getting bigger? (b) How big is it now? (c) How big could it possibly get? (d) How big should it be? Given that economic growth is the top priority for all nations, one would expect that all these questions would get major attention in all economic textbooks. In fact (b), (c) and (d) are not raised at all, and (a) is answered unsatisfactorily.[5]

Daly is right to point out that growth is an assumption rarely challenged by economists. Economies are widely held to be so vast and complex that no one can individually understand, or predict, them. This does not stop market analysts from trying – the rewards for any successful predictions (or 'gambles') are large, and well worth the effort. Doubtless such financial incentives help sustain fantasies of endless economic growth.

The basic dilemma for the 'sustainability' of growing economies is how a viable resource base and ecology can be retained while human demands (and their effects) continue to rise. If populations continue to grow, can their demands for quality life styles and economic wealth be sustained if the supply of necessary resources shrinks?

Economies require strong connections between 'capital' and material resources. Both are valued, and exchanged, through negotiation in social processes, but they are fundamentally different: 'you can't eat money'. The fact that modern economies undergo cyclic 'corrections' indicates there is a tendency for these negotiated values to get so out of step that markets, businesses and individual investors 'fail' in large numbers. Governments may intervene in times of crisis by injecting financial capital into markets (by 'printing more money'), or use tariffs and taxes, but this only works if markets and investors remain confident that material assets (like houses, oil, or gold) will retain a certain value. The big question for market economies is what will happen when there are global shortages in basic commodities (such as food, clean water or energy supplies). Presumably the value of scarce resources will skyrocket, and major political unrest will result.

PRICING 'THE COMMONS'

The growth of human systems is a conundrum that orbits the generation of wealth. Economic growth requires increasing numbers of consumers, more production, more profit, and more waste products in a materially finite world. The necessary correlates of economic growth are depletion (of fossil fuel resources, other mineral ores, top soils, and other 'non-renewables'), pollution (of the atmosphere, oceans, rivers and the land), and increasingly large populations (to sustain growing production and consumption).

Endless growth leads to endless problems; at some stage natural resources and space will become exhausted. As the first report of 'The Club of Rome' demonstrated, at that point (however hard it is to predict quite when that might be) ecological systems on Earth will seriously decline, and collapse.

> We can thus say with some confidence that, under the assumption of no major change in the present system, population and industrial growth will certainly stop within the next century [now this century], at the latest.[6]

In economic terms, one very basic ecological issue concerns the 'real' value of natural resources. Markets only value some resources; others are ignored. The value of natural resources that are 'commons', or shared by all, is not a factor in current calculations of economic profit and loss. For instance, the quality of the atmosphere, water and 'land' does not enter the economic calculations of governments or industry – despite the fact that future generations will pay for remediation programs through government taxation and rising prices of commodities caused by scarcity of natural resources. The biological decline of big ecosystems which support all the little projects of human entrepreneurs, are called by economists 'externalities', or what we might otherwise call 'collateral damage', in the creation and advancement of human civilization. So far, present generations have determined that the costs of creating new eco-logical balances will be borne by future generations, some time in the future. Such anticipated costs do not ever appear to enter into present economic calculations because a competitor can always provide a cheap-er product by not factoring in costs that have not yet arisen, and that will eventually be shared by all.

A more basic consideration is that the value present in all econo-mies comes from something and somewhere (as opposed to the printing of money, or 'quantitative easing'). This 'something' is not just human labour but the combination of labour and 'natural capital' – that is, raw materials that come from the Earth (or 'nature') and which may not be in endless supply. The most radical shift that standard economics (the neoclassical model), and more radical political economy (Marxist economics), have still to make concerns the *economic valuing* of natural resources and ecological systems, which include 'the commons' of air, land and water, and the costs to future generations of remediation of all these 'externalities'. These factors need to become part of all economic modelling – as further discussed in Chapter 6. However important it is to appropriately value natural resources, ecosystems and externalities, we can easily assume that any valuing of natural assets, and charging of costs beyond the taxes and licensing agreements already imposed, will be vigorously opposed.

As well as an emerging ecological critique of conventional eco-nomic assumptions, there are a number of criticisms of capitalism that have emerged over many centuries. Political economy (since the time of Marx) is the best known and best developed critique of capitalism – but the left have not been the only source of criticism. Religions (such as Christianity and Islam) have condemned money lending over the centuries, and the excessive accumulation of wealth has always been identified with greed and other personal moral failings. The critique of capitalism from the left is simply the most systematic, and persuasive, of all basically non-ecological approaches. Chapter 6 looks more closely at the ecological shortfalls of conventional economic theory. This chapter is more concerned to demonstrate that the material conditions for sustained economic growth (that is, *endless* economic growth) are simply not available.

DEALING WITH COMPLEXITY

In the twenty-first century it has become essential to model Earth's population, rates of resource consumption, pollution production, and other aspects of ecological systems, using 'global' computer programs. Science, industry and commerce, for instance, routinely require the modelling of global flows of energy, materials and money. The enormous quantities of data involved, and the complexity of interacting systems, necessitate professional computer modelling for even short-term management and record keeping. Although computer modelling cannot deliver absolute certainty about the behaviour of any complex system, it has become a routine and highly effective tool in many professional fields. The main challenge for global modelling today is overcoming the disciplinary divide between economics and ecology. Without a sustainable economy and the ability to use computer modelling as a management tool, the possibility of reigning in the destructive excesses of global expansion are very limited, if not impossible.

The prediction of trends, however, does become quite political, as the Limits to Growth project proved. The conclusions the MIT group were able to make about rates of pollution, the declining availability of stocks of natural resources, and likely rates of growth in economies and populations sent alarm signals to markets and voting publics. The assumptions made in the generation of the various graphical scenarios were highly contentious – how confident can anyone be, for instance, in extrapolating from figures provided by governments and industry about resource availability, rates of pollution, or any other statistics describing growth and depletion of resources and commodities that effect the behaviour of markets? It is not surprising that the original report was controversial, and followed by a much more optimistic second report – but still predicting disaster unless major change could occur.[7]

The possibility of international agreement to pursue an ecologically rational 'equilibrium strategy' are still remote – the economic and political changes required are enormous, as all Reports to The Club of Rome recognise. The actual predictions about likely outcomes, including various scenarios of 'system collapse', need to be highlighted, nonetheless; we need to know! The economics and politics of future processes can, therefore, only be regarded as 'works-in-progress'.

The 'collapse' of global systems modelled by computer programs is a *theoretical* collapse. This means that the solutions to systems of equations modelling 'sustainable' practices 'run out', and the only way forward is if 'new' (simpler) systems and strategies are allowed to emerge out of a tangle of declining curves on graphs – for example, a world with fewer people and different (lower) patterns of resource usage. Given that computer modelling is instrumental in much of the technological wizardry that we now take for granted – such as landing a 'rover' on Mars, or money being available in the bank – then one has to take the disaster scenarios of ecological modelling seriously, even though they are 'theoretical'. Computer modelling is capable of matching the behaviour of many, many systems with great accuracy; contemporary scientists and engineers rely on computer modelling to 'solve' problems that involve multiple complex simultaneous equations. Systems analysts and computer programmers may never get the details exactly right but, consistently, most programs modelling global ecology, or large ecological systems, run up against limits to growth and eventual system collapse – unless major social and technological changes occur.

However, not all modelling of global ecologies leads to inevitable collapse. One of the earliest and simplest models to stimulate popular interest in the idea of Earth as a *self-regulating* natural global system was 'Daisyworld', developed by James Lovelock – and criticised by John Dawkins and many biologists as a 'new age fantasy'.[8]

Daisyworld was an interesting innovation to computer systems that were too limited in their abilities to self-adjust – such as the modelling in *Limits to Growth* – and, further, as Lovelock claims, Daisyworld stimulated new research in mathematics and physiology. Today, self-adjustment defines 'artificial intelligence' and the field of robotics. The difficulty of testing the hypothesis that Earth is a self-regulating system will be discussed in Chapter 5.

For all the sophistication of computer modelling, even in 1970, it is worth repeating how very qualified that first report to the Club of Rome was:

> Is the future of the world system bound to be growth and then collapse into a dismal, depleted existence? Only if we make the initial assumption that our present way of doing things will not change. We have ample evidence of mankind's ingenuity and social flexibility.[9]

In 1970 there may have been more grounds for optimism about the powers of human ingenuity. As Meadows and his colleagues could confidently say, the Green Revolution was raising agricultural yields in non-industrialised countries, and knowledge of modern methods of birth control was spreading rapidly. Climate change and global terrorism were only distant threats in most expert considerations. Nonetheless, the MIT team were hedging their bets – they were aware that because computer models cannot accurately predict human behaviour and innovation, the quality of future human existence is to some extent indeterminable. Indeed, the whole team was *hoping* that their report would quickly stimulate productive change, thus averting global disaster.[10]

Forty-five years later, it is harder to be optimistic, despite technological innovations that were barely imagined, even then. Today, human systems appear less flexible and responsive than necessary to avoid exponential growth of population and capital followed by 'collapse'. It is still not at all clear whether it is possible to prevent a major human decline led by global population growth and climate change, and consolidated by economic practices focused on growth and the generation of wealth. It is clear that the main drivers making 'no growth' an urgent ecological problem can be reduced to these three interdependent problems: climate change, population growth, and growth economics. These pressures are global in scope. If there is 'a solution' to an impending planetary crisis, these three will have to be dealt with, together, as a priority, by all nations. Even if we could avert disastrous climate consequences, by the end of the century demographers estimate that there will be 9-10 billion people on Earth. What that means in terms of economic growth, consumption, and social conflict, is difficult to contemplate.

The way we measure growth is fundamental. Unless economic calculation can factor in the circulation of things other than 'financial capital', 'investment', human labour, and other basic parameters of the dominant 'neoclassical' model, we seem doomed to hit an ecological wall. An economic model that doesn't allow for limits – both ecological and social – can only hasten ecological decline. But the situation is even more complex because just as an economic model that doesn't factor in the interacting complexity of all these related systems seems likely to fail, conversely an ecological model that doesn't allow for the economically caused production and distribution of energy and materials will also struggle to be predictive. Some now speak of 'wicked problems'.

WICKED PROBLEMS

Economist and policy analyst Eric Knight says that 'climate change has quickly become the quintessential wicked problem of politics today'. He believes simplification of climate change to issues of the weather, or conflict between sceptics and believers, or the moral problem of excessive consumption, makes the problem harder to solve because 'it does not sufficiently balance the probabilities latent elsewhere' – in other words, climate change is a complex problem that cannot be reduced to single issues. That the complexity of social issues should be able to contribute to study of the global effects of climate change is noteworthy – it seems likely that the complexity of societies and ecologies are strongly related.

The term 'wicked problem' has been attributed to two Californian urban planners, Horst Rittel and Melvin Webber, as away of describing social problems that could not be simplified.[11]

At that time, in 1976, there was an increasing appreciation that social problems are complex by nature and need to be approached holisticly. This intellectual response appears to be a direct consequence of changing social and cultural conditions – the decade of the 1970s was a time of great social upheaval. The civil rights movement in the USA, the women's movement, the environmental movement, and the peace movement had all rebelled against societies that were unequal, discriminatory and destructive in a variety of ways. Societies and cultures were shown to be stratified, gendered, ethnically stereotyped, anti-ecological, and violent. The 'new social movements' that exposed this complexity were also complex, often involving mass mobilisations of people from all walks of life operating 'informally' – well outside the structures of conventional organised politics and trade unions.

Partly because of the immediate consequences of social upheavals on public order and 'business as normal', many governments and businesses slowly became more focused on social inequalities due to race and gender; economists also became much more aware that inequalities in the distribution of wealth relate to inequalities other than differences in social class. However, economists were not the first to realise that complex social problems had implications for their discipline. The strongest reminder came from non-economists – from social activists and a few radicalising academic disciplines – sociology in particular – and from radicalised students. The closest most academic economists came to the fray was in increasingly vitriolic wars between 'old school' economists and the break-away discipline of 'political economy', and through the subsequent infiltration of tertiary trained political economists (Marxists) into other academic disciplines, political parties and trade unions.

This recent history is relevant not only to the emergence of new ideas about complexity, to which we will return, but also situates Eric Knight in the context of decades of slow response to the radicalisation of Western societies in the decades of the 1960s and 70s. In his short but incisive book on climate change Eric Knight presents an analysis that would resonate with views to the left of the Australian and British Labor

Parties. His is a relatively restrained post-sixties 'left Labor' optimism – proper investment strategies, confidence in new technologies, and a 'bottom up' approach to community empowerment, are at the core of his analysis. He approvingly refers to the work of Elinor Ostrum, winner of the 2009 Nobel Prize for economics:

> Ostrum's thinking challenges us to set realistic expectations for what 'solving climate change' looks like. It will be fragmented and competitive, rather than singular and globally agreed. There will not be panacea technologies, but rather a patchwork of technologies and interventions. More importantly, success does not require everyone to agree at every point in time. There is no finishing line. Instead, progress is a process of continuous incremental improvements.[12]

The over-riding issue with Knight's analysis, like that with the work of other professional optimists, is a commitment to there being a positive 'solution' to ecological problems. Counter-indications, such as population pressure, are often brushed aside as if they were just irritating negativity. Knight simply dismisses such concerns as environmentalist hysteria, based on the thoughts of the eighteenth century economist Thomas Malthus – who famously warned that Britain was on the brink of economic and ecological collapse because the current growth of population would outstrip the carrying capacity of the land: 'what they never tell you is that Malthus turned out to be spectacularly wrong [. .] Malthus's error was that he had missed an immense technological change occurring: the Industrial Revolution.'[13]

Currently the relative effects of new technology on societies and economies do not remotely match those of the Industrial Revolution in the nineteenth century; further, as will be argued in the next chapter, commitment to economic growth based on new technology is an optimistic fantasy that simply does not respect ecological limits. The environmental impacts of a global population of 9 or 10 billion people by the end of the century will be highly significant. Knight's 'new approach' of generating 'a clear roadmap for technologically re-tooling the economy over the long term', separating local from global, such that Australia's particular contribution might not be conflated with some kind of global average, and respecting the freedom of all 'to live the life we have reason to value'[14], is a positive contribution but suffers from the 'professional optimism' of most contemporary futurologists. Well known commentators (including Al Gore and Niall Ferguson, whose work will be discussed in the next chapter) do not seem willing to tackle the profound complexity that cultural commitment to growing economies and making babies adds to the problem of climate change. The last thing anyone wants to hear, it seems, is that there is decreasing cause for optimism.

Despite the simplifying allure technological change has for professional policy makers, the complexity of social and ecological problems requires urgent analytic attention. The worst outcome from an assessment that 'things are going pear-shaped' is to ignore possible solutions that seem too difficult, or cynically defer action until 'certainty' can be achieved in analysis. These tactics were employed to market advantage by tobacco companies, chemical companies, oil companies, and the asbestos industry to avoid compensation claims and loss of revenue through more restrictive legislation. 'Everybody knows' now that this was unconscionable, ruthless behaviour, driven by the dollar, and careless of human health.

Complex issues require decisions about best outcomes under circumstances that may seem difficult or impossible. This terrain will be familiar to all those working with social problems and other complex systems – such as engineers and technologists, and indeed everyone who needs to do practical things in limited time frames. This is the world where precise calculations and exact science may give way to assumptions, simplifications and some inspired guesswork. In the worlds of organised human affairs, the negotiation of complexity can be where 'the arts' of politics are required. However, in the twenty-first century, politics increasingly involves environmental and ecological problems such that the complexity of all issues has a considerable ecological dimension. It has also become abundantly clear that human activity is the cause of serious environmental and ecological damage – and so, in later chapters it will be argued that there is an increasing need for an ecologically based political philosophy to help steer political processes.

The main proposition here is that climate change, population growth and economic growth are the three interrelated human phenomena leading to an all-encompassing ecological conundrum. They have become defining social, cultural and material problems of this present time. It will be the social and cultural responses to these interlinked causes that will define any new way forward.

There is very limited wriggle-room for any of these problems. There may be many different and important strategies to achieve some measure of sustainable growth, and mitigation of adverse effects of human activity on Earth's ecology, but there is no getting round the inevitable consequences arising from this catastrophic conjunction. Arguably, this is our 'mother' of all wicked problems.

Focus on just three 'big' phenomena forming a complex knot, or 'wicked problem', has the virtue of avoiding analytical distraction by other problems that are important, but which do not define an imminent 'end game' scenario – or so completely dominate all other outcomes. This focused approach is also intended to avoid the kind of blatant ideology contained in religion, Marxism, and most narratives of 'left' and 'right'. Today these are all outmoded visions of the future.

It seems likely that future historians will reflect on the current era as a time of ecological crisis. However, if there are any future historians looking back, they will more likely celebrate pragmatism than ideology. More than ever before there is widespread cultural awareness that something is wrong with our ecological home – it's just so difficult to pin it down, and even more difficult to get governments and industry to discuss ecological issues in the public arena.

IPAT

In the recent history of ecological thought, the famous IPAT equation could be described as pragmatic. The equation, developed in the 1970's by Paul Ehrlich and John Holdren, is a simple and convenient way of characterising the relationship between highly complex variables.[15]

The IPAT equation asserts: I(ecological impact) = P(population) x A(affluence) x T(technology) – defining a simple proportional relationship between the thee variables on the right hand side of the equation and the 'independent' variable on the left hand side. There are ways in which this relationship can be made to function as a 'real' equation – for instance, the economist Tim Jackson uses the equation to calculate the impact of CO_2 emissions in terms of dollars. This is a kind of sleight of hand, but does actually work – provided, among other simplifications, that the definition of impact is a tangible dollar cost, and 'technology' is the cost of production of CO_2.[16]

The 'equation' is better described as an arithmetic metaphor that simplifies a profoundly complex situation, and facilitates the making of comparisons. A number of assumptions are necessary to make this equation work.

First, we must agree that, in general, more affluent societies have bigger ecological impacts (per head of population, and assuming the presence of industrial technology) than less affluent ones. It is hard to deny this, and indeed one of the major obstacles to the reaching of agreements over internationally binding targets for CO_2 production by individual nation states is that countries like the USA and Australia produce far more CO_2 emission per head of population. It has been successfully argued in international forums (such as the climate control summit meetings in Kyoto, Bali and Copenhagen) that it is unfair to handicap the growth of developing economies by lumping them together with wealthy countries. Why should poorer countries with much lower emission rates (per head) bear the burden of emissions targets when wealthy countries have already had the economic benefits of being heavy polluters? It is undoubtedly true that societies with high affluence consume more of everything, per head, compared with poor countries. Yet, the situation is more complex if we focus on transnational ecologies and the future costs to the whole planet of, for example, the deforestation of developing countries like Brazil, Indonesia, India, and various African nations, such as the Democratic Republic of the Congo. It is true, however, that deforestation, loss of habitat, species decline and extinction are occurring at very high rates in developing countries. Of course, these countries all have different ecological histories. Arguably India, like England, had been largely deforested hundreds of years ago; Brazil and Indonesia are still deforesting at a rapid rate. Perhaps different considerations should apply according to past histories – fair enough, particularly when the beneficiaries of ecological devastation have been old colonial powers. Nonetheless, the global ecological impacts of 'economic development' are not simply in proportion to average levels of affluence, or even individual levels of affluence. In the case of Brazil one could make the case that the future costs to 'the lungs of the world', are totally out of proportion to the increasing affluence of Brazilians.

There is no moral judgement intended here – the point is to question the supposed linearity of relationship between average levels of national affluence and ecological impacts. Just how the international community can deal with the sovereignty of individual nation states – for the sake of collective benefit – remains a defining problem for bodies such as the UN. More aid, and more internationally funded conservation programs are obvious answers – but countries like Australia still need to be persuaded of the economic benefits to all that can flow from such increased levels of targeted assistance.

The second assumption is that 'technology' lines up with 'population' and 'affluence' as a cause of 'environmental impacts'. In absolute terms this is obviously meaningless, since the impacts of individual pieces of technology are so varied in their environmental impacts. A brown coal burning power station is very different to a water wheel. If individual technologies can be so different in their ecological effects (by orders of magnitude) how can they be placed in a simple linear relationship in the IPAT equation? Only if one reduces the meaning of impacts and technology to dollar costs, as Jackson and others, as economists, do. Any ecologist will tell you, however, that 'the lungs of the earth', are beyond price.

The third assumption is that it can make sense to think of 'dependent' and 'independent' variables in the context of an already complex social-ecological interaction. Why a simple linear relationship at all? Many functions that model complex situations in science or engineering give weightings to different factors – variables may be raised to higher or lower 'powers', involve logarithms, or multiplied by 'fudge factors' that may themselves be complex relationships.[17]

For instance, environmental impacts might already be an intrinsic component of all the variables on the right hand side of the equation, giving a much more complex final equation. Thus, a population in any given region might be expressed as a relationship between available space, past environmental impacts (such as presence or absence of toxic wastes), present and projected levels of affluence, and various local and regional technologies (such as skills in high-rise building construction). And, further, it seems essential to factor in considerations such as the availability of food, availability of paid work, etc. The list of relevant variables could go on and on, and become more and more complex as the mixing of material and social considerations are explored.

The IPAT equation makes better sense, however, when used as a basis for comparison. Given the environmental impacts of *increases* in population, affluence and technological intensity are of major concern for future planning, it makes perfect sense to say, for example, that without improvements in technology, or changes in affluence, the ecological impacts of a population doubling will be greater by a factor of (at least) two. Or conversely, to maintain ecological impacts at current levels, the levels of pollution of a particular type of power station will have to be halved if a doubling of population doubles the demands for electricity. IPAT, so used, is a great heuristic device. It forces obvious answers out of complex situations. IPAT is also a forerunner of the bigger and slightly different combination of climate change, population growth, and economic growth, which are gathered together in this chapter. The similarities between the 'variables' are clear enough, but all forward projections now involve ecological 'tipping points'. As the first report to The Club of Rome demonstrated, irreversible declines occur once certain limits are exceeded: for instance once certain levels of population are reached levels of consumption and resource extraction will rapidly decline; average living standards will decline – initially because of the effects of scarcities on prices, and the lack of availability of some goods and services, but also because of the likely social 'chaos' such a situation will produce. In today's world, once particular limits of green house gases are exceeded (at various 'tipping points') the heating of Earth will cause profound climate effects – extreme weather, diminished crop growth, rapid melting of land ice, rising sea levels, and so on. Any of these events are capable of producing social chaos.

In all these calculations, economic growth (caused by population growth) is the hidden engine of tipping points. Most fundamentally, population growth is the remorseless force that allows profitability to come from endlessly increased consumption and production, which in turn encourages (and requires) growing economies, and creates higher levels of pollution and decreasing stocks of resources. This combination of forces and effects, while still normal and 'business as usual', will obviously lead to systems collapse.

COLLAPSE

If processes with high ecological impacts continue without major change, it is inevitable that climate change and unsustainable demands on natural resources will lead to collapse of eco-systems, big and small. Human population increase alone will eventually cause shortages of food, water, energy, and other basic requirements, in whole countries, and the poorest parts of wealthy societies. Exacerbated by climate change, these shortages will just show up sooner. If the only way 'forward' requires increasing levels of demand on human systems and ecologies that are already being driven to breaking points, collapse will come even sooner, and even more surely. This kind of bleak view was established with the publication of the first report of the Club of Rome – which hadn't even factored in the full effects of climate change. The circuit breaker for the dire predictions made in that report (of total collapse by about 2050) was technological innovation, which has led to improvements in productivity and efficiencies in most industries, agriculture, resource extraction, and communication. Not surprisingly, the optimism of most futurologists is based on a stirring belief in technological silver bullets. They are confident that some combination of nanotechnology, fusion power, new generations of information processors, the internet, genetically modified crops and humans, other biotechnology, and technological manipulation of Earth's climate can transform everything and give us a brand new day. So far, only the Internet can be said to have been fully transformative – but not of ecologies. Therefore, without denying future possibilities, it has to be said that there are very limited grounds to defer ecological pro-activity in favour of undeveloped future possibilities. Further, the ecological impacts of past transformations of any society's productive processes do not provide much in the way of pro-ecological precedents.

In 2005, the anthropologist Jarred Diamond published a now famous book titled *Collapse: How Societies Choose to Fail or Survive*. In the process of studying historical examples of societies that had undergone environmental collapse, Diamond devised a five-point framework. By separating out broad categories he hoped to with deal with a great complexity of data, and to facilitate comparisons. The first four categories – environmental damage, climate change, hostile neighbours, and friendly trade partners – 'may or may not prove significant for a particular society'. The fifth set of factors – society's responses to its environmental problems – 'always proves significant.'[18]

This also gave him a schematic approach for examining cases of potential environmental collapse, for any particular society. Although this approach rather restricts itself to particular societies, as opposed to more global critiques, it does show that, historically, ecological collapse has not been just a random series of events, dictated by an infinitely complex set of possibilities. There have been recurring factors, such as population growth and exhaustion of natural resources.

On the other hand, Diamond's approach is 'scientistic' insofar as a global picture does not emerge from his historical case-by-case approach. Diamond's application of 'scientific method' enables him to effectively bypass the most important and politically contentious factors that require consideration: the global nature of modern capitalism, the anti-ecological cultural blindness built into consumer capitalism, the ecological impossibility of a model based on endless growth, the cultural causes of excessive human reproduction, the increasing irreversibility of climate change, and the global need for a 'non-sectarian' green political vision. Diamond does raise many of these considerations, but only briefly, preferring a narrower focus on specific causes – and the professional optimism critiqued in Chapter 2. Yet, Diamond's review of ecological collapses, ancient and modern – on Easter Island, on the Pitcairn and the Henderson Islands, on Greenland, and the collapse of bigger societies such as the ancient Mayans and modern Rwanda, Haiti and the Dominican Republic – is the first such account that has become a best-seller. This is a great achievement for the raising of environmental awareness, and establishes obvious baselines for ecological research.

As Diamond points out, unintended ecological suicide (or 'ecocide') has been extensively confirmed to fall into eight categories of environmental damage: deforestation and habitat destruction, soil problems, water management problems, overhunting, overfishing, effects of introduced species on native species, human population growth, and increased per capita impact of people.[19]

The way these different types of environmental damage manifest, and their particular local causes arise, will vary as a function of the other set of four categories listed earlier. As Diamond says, it is the way that any of these particular crises are handled ('social responses') that is universally critical. By the second decade of the twenty first century we can assume that environmental damage is a global problem, and an increasing consideration for every society. This has been a defining concern for the environmental movement over many decades. Despite many positive outcomes as a result of activist's campaigns, government initiatives, and various activities in the private sector, it is the intractability of environmental damage – the increasing rates of species decline and extinction, the increasing rates of habitat destruction – that is the central concern of this chapter. This, like the related problem of climate change, has huge future consequences.

THE END OF THE WORLD AS WE KNOW IT

The idea that societies can 'choose to fail', as Jared Diamond puts it, is too comforting. Choice may have become harder to exercise. At roughly the same time Diamond was publishing his book, a Canadian political scientist, Thomas Homer-Dixon, produced a sobering analysis of the way modern societies might fail. In his view there are five 'tectonic stresses' that run through all societies: population stress, energy stress, environmental stress, climate stress and economic stress. With the exception of the singling out of energy, these stresses are roughly similar to Diamond's schema, except Homer-Dixon has focused on a bigger picture. As soon as the focus is broadened, the availability of 'choices' becomes a more complex issue. For instance, the idea that the West has chosen the terrorism of radical Islam (a proposition advanced by radical leftists) is as simplistic as supposing that people choose to be unemployed, or that societies 'choose to fail'. Choice is a right and freedom that must be protected, but the choices we can make are defined in the context of available possibilities. We cannot simply choose to have fusion power, or to reverse the atmospheric concentrations of CO_2, for example.

Nonetheless, Homer–Dixon is reassuringly optimistic in thinking that current challenges can be turned to our advantage:

> We need to be comfortable with constant change, radical surprise, and even breakdown, because these are now inevitable features of our world, and we must constantly anticipate a wide variety of futures [...] In other words, we'll be better able to achieve what I call catagenesis – the creative renewal of our technologies, institutions, and societies in the aftermath of breakdown.[20]

Homer Dixon's view evolves as his book progresses. His narrative structure is interesting in the way it illustrates this point about the creative renewal of the world after 'breakdown'. The author's personal and professional development is unfolded as a series of revelations, beginning with his study of the decline of ancient Rome, the bedrock of the book. We proceed through an encounter with the energy industry stimulated by reminiscing about being a worker on an oil rig, we drive in California, home to tectonic stresses, we go back packing in West Africa, we sit in on a debate between George Soros and Paul Klugman about economics and global capitalism, and we hike out to meet a legendary ecologist. Homer Dixon's personalised style of writing is engaging and informative, despite an undercurrent of Old Testament style exegesis. His account culminates with ecologically inspired systems theory. Encounters with individuals who function as wise prophets propel the narrative into contemporary scientific ecology.

Personal meetings with the anthropologist Joseph Tainter and the ecologist Crawford Holling lead to the development of his ecologically inspired systems view, 'catagenesis'. After discussing the resilience of forest systems with Crawford Holling, 'one of the world's great ecologists', Homer-Dixon was able to better understand that

> [t]he catastrophe of collapse allows for the birth of something new [. . .] the cycle of growth, collapse, reorganisation, and rebirth allows the forest to adapt over the long term to a constantly changing environment. 'The adaptive cycle', Holling writes, 'embraces two opposites: growth and stability on one hand, change and variety on the other.' It's at once conserving and creative – a characteristic of all highly adaptive systems.[21]

Homer-Dixon's most optimistic hope is that the Internet will enable the development of worldwide communities of like-minded people, 'who in the course of working together on tasks, become bound together by trust and shared values and understandings.'[22]

The work of Diamond and Homer-Dixon could be characterised as optimistic catastrophism – similar to the approach of Al Gore and Niall Ferguson, introduced in Chapter 2. This approach provides a refreshed 'road map' of human ecological problems up to the beginning of the twenty-first century. Typically, neither published account emphasises war as having been a continual ecological and social disaster; indeed a darker view of human nature might add war and military conflict as intrinsic to human society and a continual cause of ecological devastation – and certainly as tectonic as economics or energy. In the context of a systems view, war can be considered a dysfunctional kind of 'pressure release', and a major economic activity – despite the belief, at the front of every 'progressive' political activist's mind, that the elimination of war would have enormous environmental and social benefits.

Even if, in the future, outright warfare (and global terrorism) can be curtailed by international diplomacy and peacekeeping efforts, continuing social conflict seems guaranteed. Shortages of basic commodities such as food, water and energy, and the grossly unequal distribution of wealth across the planet, are a recipe for continuing conflict. Realistically, conflict and war are historical default positions for humanity under conditions of population pressure or resource shortage.

What Homer-Dixon's account adds to a twentieth century view of Earth as a complex and conflicted system, is an emphasis on two factors that expose the twenty first century side of wicked problems: the effects of 'multipliers' and 'convergence' in the process of system failure. The rising speed of connectivity of contemporary societies and 'the escalating power of small groups to destroy things and people' are the dominant multipliers.[23]

> The stresses and multipliers are a lethal mixture that sharply boosts the risk of collapse of the political, social, and economic order in individual countries and globally – an outcome I shall call synchronous failure. This would be destructive – not creative – catastrophe. It would effect large regions and even sweep around the globe, in the process deeply damaging the human prospect. Recovery and renewal would be slow, perhaps even impossible.[24]

In such a scenario it is important to realise that the way events unfold is largely unpredictable. A complex system subject to multiple stressors with the multipliers of rapid communication and terrorist acts, can fail in many ways in a potentially snowballing cascade of causes and effects. The outcome of a 'convergence' of partial failures in normal complex systems (like a failing aeroplane in flight) is catastrophic failure of the whole system. Crash and burn – no survivors.

Optimistic system theorists, such as the 'professional optimists' to be reviewed in the next chapter, place great hope in the 'resilience' of a very large system like Planet Earth. In systems theory parlance, a system can be resilient provided certain thresholds, or 'tipping points' are not exceeded. If a complex system, like Earth, can be properly managed to avoid tipping points (like 450 ppm atmospheric CO_2, or too many 'toxic loans' in financial systems) then the system can find new balances and adapt to new circumstances. That's the big hope for Earth, and that's the big gamble that is currently played out along the converging pathways of human over-population, climate change and economic growth. So far, there is still some reason to hope that the combined determination of so many living creatures to survive and live does indeed make Earth particularly resilient. For most contemporary 'big picture' systems theorists the connective power of the Internet and the global problem of terrorism provide 'X-factors' that make all predictions uncertain – although optimists always see more communication as a positive force. Optimists also tend to steer away from the 'convergent' issues associated with population growth. This is a nagging absence to which we will return.

The main point of agreement among all forecasters is that good management is the key. For that reason emphasis has been placed, in later chapters, on environmental politics as a way forward. But, first, the outer limits of good management need to be established. This brings us back to reasons why, among all other global problems, climate change, economic growth, and over-population are the three biggest elephants in the room.

WHY ENERGY SUPPLY IS LESS OF A WICKED PROBLEM

Fossil fuel supplies are certainly not infinite, but still in the ground there are: much coal; dwindling, but still indeterminate, reserves of crude oil; and large amounts of natural (and unnatural) gas. Nuclear power already supplies the majority of France's energy needs and contributes significantly to the energy budgets of many developed economies. Renewable resources are a brave new frontier, and there are many possibilities to come. Solar hot water is certainly here to stay. This brief inventory should demonstrate that even if crude oil supplies are interrupted by war or natural shortages, other means of energy supply are available and already being cultivated. The major constraints on domestic and industrial energy availability are economic, not technological. The sad fact is that our atmosphere is so polluted by the burning of fossil fuels because it is generally cheaper in the short term to burn coal in power stations, gasoline and diesel in cars and trucks, or to convert to gas in the near future, than it is to build new power stations based on renewable energy and to electrify the powering of transport. The technological means of generating energy cleanly (without resorting to nuclear power) have been available for some decades.

In other words, the supply of energy is very open to management in both public and private sectors. Countries can change the way they generate electricity, and many can change broad patterns of energy consumption. Compared with the issues of over-population, climate change and economic growth, energy consumption is an easier problem to manipulate. Political will, consumer demand, and market profitability are much more controlling in the case of energy production and consumption than they can possibly be with respect to over-population, climate change or economic growth. These latter problems are relatively intractable. The burning of fossil fuels is a direct cause of climate change, but short of quickly 'macro-engineering' the atmosphere to remove greenhouse gases, climate change will have runaway effects and cause irreversibly permanent damage. Rising populations and rising levels of consumer demand compound this and all ecological problems. There is at least one vicious cycle of cause and effect imbedded here. But all roads – whether they meander through energy issues, or food production, or water supplies – still lead back to the big three. These three, together, are the mother of all wicked problems.

There are many problems, processes, practices and issues that are part of most environmental and ecological problems. For example, the pollution of air, water and land arise from currently unavoidable practices such as the burning of coal and petroleum, the mining and refining of iron ore, and other minerals, and the unabated intrusion of suburbia into agricultural and wilderness areas. Deeply engrained cultural habits such as the use of air conditioners and private transport are also involved, but in the longer term the 'big three' problems will overwhelm any gains that can be made by changed habits and efficiencies in production and consumption. Just as all roads may have once led to Rome, the intractability of most of the ecological problems that confront us now, and into the near future, can be traced back to this 'big three'. These problems represent far more than material issues – they are deeply cultural and provide an ecological lens that reveals aspects of culture and society traditional methods of analysis have tended to gloss over. The near blindness of traditional 'left' analysis, for instance, has failed dismally to diagnose industrial society itself as the most likely agent of its own destruction – via any of the associated ecological dead ends of pollution, climate change, or human over-population. The human-centred preoccupations of the left made serious ecological critique a revolutionary activity on the left. It took the evolution of Green parties internationally to rouse the left from its deep intellectual sleep – a process that is still philosophically problematic, as will be discussed further in Chapter 8.

The main point in digging over these old bones is to emphasise the importance of new (and old) political processes in any attempts to untangle thinking about these three big issues. No amount of scientific or technological research will overcome the material dilemmas of growth that make pollution and climate change, human reproduction, and economic processes so intractably difficult. In many ways humanity is at a crossroad. Human society is now thoroughly global, and we are in uncharted waters. The social and cultural changes required to navigate forward need both political leadership and policies that may not be popular – such as using less electricity, changing dietary practices, limiting family sizes, job sharing, or controlling immigration.

THE PROBLEM OF OVER-POPULATION

Seven billion people now on Earth, or thereabouts, are already too many for a sustainable future. This level of population consumes resources at 1.5 times the planet's ability to renew them; in 15 years it is estimated that we will exceed this ability by a factor of 2.[25]

These are global figures; population growth does vary nationally and regionally. The poorest countries tend to have the largest rates of population growth, and conversely the richest countries have the lowest rates – but are boosted by immigration from poorer countries.

Current UN figures for national rates of population growth force at least one interesting qualification to conventional wisdom. Australia has a very high comparative level of immigration that counteracts an otherwise decreasing fertility, and declining 'natural' rate of growth. In 2013 the UN estimates that Australia will only rank behind the USA,

Canada and the UK as the highest net receivers of migrants, at 150,000 persons annually.[26]

In that scenario Australia will achieve a population of 41.5 million by the turn of the century. This assumes a much higher population growth rate than our near neighbours New Zealand or Indonesia, and a higher rate than that of the UK, USA, Sweden, and all other wealthy economies. This high growth rate has been quietly endorsed by recent, and current, governments (Labor and Liberal) as a necessary encouragement to continuing economic growth.[27]

Everywhere, discussions of desirable human population sizes are highly politicised. Professor Ian Lowe, an eminent Australian science policy advisor, has suggested that any opposition to migration (and, implicitly, even opposition to high rates of migration) 'is likely to be interpreted as code for a racist agenda, so educated professionals have been co-opted to the growth agenda . . . As a new electronic book by Fiona Heinrichs says, at the moment we are collectively sleepwalking into a future that looks disastrous.'[28]

The prediction of future population sizes involves uncertainties. The current UN predictions are higher than those for the previous year and appear to overturn earlier more optimistic projections of earlier downturns. For example, in 2011, Fred Pearce assumed that 'half the world's population are having two children or fewer. Within a generation, the world's population will be falling. And we will all be getting very old.'[29]

In 2013, UN figures did not support that optimism. Small changes in fertility rates can have very large consequences:

> In the medium variant, global fertility declines from 2.53 children per woman in 2005- 2010 to 2.24 children per woman in 2045-2050 and 1.99 children per woman in 2095-2100. If fertility were to remain, on average, half a child above the levels projected in the medium variant, world population would reach 10.9 billion by 2050 and 16.6 billion by 2100. A fertility path half a child below the medium variant would lead to a population of 8.3 billion by mid-century and 6.8 billion by the end of the century.

Nonetheless,

> population growth until 2050 is almost inevitable even if the
> decline of fertility accelerates.[30]

It follows that whatever gains can be made from addressing climate
change and the ecological insensitivity of current economic modelling
will be offset by increases in population. If populations increase exponentially, ecological impacts will also have to be mitigated exponentially
– if the status quo is to be preserved. The simple logic of the IPAT equation, and common sense, suggests that new technology will have to play
a major role in reducing human impacts, including mitigation of the
effects of increasing affluence. For all pro-active steps currently attempted, the amount of CO_2 entering the atmosphere is continuing to rise. We
are going backwards, despite our best efforts so far.[31]

This is global logic; different rates and problems occur nationally
and regionally. However, one thing seems very clear – the problem of
over-population will not, in the near future be dealt with by international treaty, or via education programs delivered by the United Nations.
As the UN data quoted above states so emphatically, population growth
until 2050 is 'almost inevitable'.

Human over-population is what makes the goal of sustainability, or
'no growth', so difficult to achieve. All efforts to reduce per capita rates
of carbon pollution are easily compensated by increasing populations
– particularly if increased consumption also occurs. *Everywhere,* more
population poses more ecological problems. The insatiable dependency
of development on more of everything guarantees ecological decline.
Increasing human populations appear to be sealing our fate. In summary,
the problem of human populations increasing globally is compounded
by climate change denial, addiction to economic growth, and a very
widespread distaste for population control. We have a wicked problem
that is getting more and more difficult to resolve.

As mentioned earlier, Thomas Malthus was the first to suggest the statistical inevitability of collective ruin due to over-population – because
population growth is potentially exponential, and the growth of food
supplies is only arithmetic, starvation and disease are inevitable. His

prediction, made in 1798, did not anticipate new technologies, such as fertilizers and new crop varieties, or contraception for women, and so his predictions have not, so far, been borne out. Similarly, depending on reasoning that is technologically optimistic, some demographers and commentators do not agree that over-population is inevitable. For example, the well known Australian commentator Professor Tim Flannery has remarked:

> In other words, soil carbon is a potentially potent yet an under-researched and underexploited contributor to returning Gaia to health [. . .] If such practices are combined with a shift away from the feeding of grain to cattle in feedlots (a process that wastes 90 per cent of the energy in the grain), the application of intelligence to agriculture and the wise use of marine resources, I'm certain the Earth can support a future population of nine billion. It might not be able to do so indefinitely, but it might make it possible for us to pass humanity's population peak without catastrophe.[32]

If the problems we face could be solved by such apparently simple technological shifts, we all might breathe easier – but there's a big hitch. Even if human populations stabilise by the end of the century, there's no guarantee that the planet will be a very nice place to live. Indeed, without addressing the cultural driving forces behind human reproduction, no amount of intelligent agriculture and technological innovation will guarantee a limit of 9 billion. There's something else that keeps popping up – humans have the overwhelming collective attitude that reproduction is the main purpose of life. Most religions postulate this in terms of reproduction being a sacred duty.

HUMAN REPRODUCTION IS A SACRED COW

With the scenario of climate change and declining ecologies as an existing reality, it seems very hard to reconcile future well being with increased populations. At best, larger populations just add stress to already over-stressed systems, *everywhere*. The 'most sensible' strategies require the stabilisation and eventual reduction of population sizes – locally and globally. This is true for all future estimates of population growth. As discussed, the uncertainties of these estimates, coupled with an ideology of economic growth and the demonization of critics of population growth and high immigration rates for countries like Australia, have stifled debate. Because of the unhelpful politicisation of debate, the concept of 'carrying capacity' applied to human populations remains a taboo subject. Farmers have no problem with the idea in calculating their anticipated profits from the management of herd sizes, but the subject of limits to human population sizes occupies a very different niche in popular imagination. Arguably, the subject is too closely connected with the success or failure of economies, and too closely associated with infamous past attempts to regulate population sizes through eugenics and genocide.

It is one thing to persuade individuals that there is a case for climate change, or even that growth economics is ultimately unsustainable; discussion of personal reproductive rights is an entirely different issue. The right of every human being to reproduce as they desire appears a 'sacred' right in all societies, with the single exception of China where capped family size has been 'officially' put at one child. Even this state driven policy does not change the argument: the right to reproduce is universally considered a basic (and largely unquestioned) human right. Not only is reproduction a universal right it is also widely considered to be a duty.[33]

Inbuilt social and cultural imperatives drive these assumptions. Growth economics need ever increasing numbers of consumers, churches need a continuing supply of 'souls' to save, and most individuals do not seem able to contemplate a life without their own offspring.

Dick Smith, an Australian entrepreneur and philanthropist, shocked the Australian public and political elites when, in 2011, he 'came out' and declared his conviction that over-population was a critically important problem for Australia, yet one that was hardly recognised by the country's leaders:

> Clearly it was well overdue for Australia to have a national
> population policy, but when I discussed it with our leaders,
> they were perplexed. Few of them had joined the dots on
> the myriad pressures that population growth was placing on
> the nation, and they had no idea what to do.[34]

Although he admits to being no expert, the impact of Dick Smith's
pronouncements is probably greater for that. Perhaps his independence
and self made status have bolstered his courage to say things that those
in more compromised positions have not felt able to say. On the gender
politics involved in over-population he is quite explicit:

> The unmet demand for family planning services is estimated
> to have driven up fertility rates in poorest nations by as much
> as 35 per cent. Approximately 80 million pregnancies each
> year in the developing world are unintended. Cultural and
> religious objections to adequate family planning result in 40
> million induced abortions each year, half of which are per-
> formed in unsafe conditions. This results in more that 70,000
> deaths and five million women admitted to hospital to treat
> abortion related consequences.[35]

Few people are brave enough to talk publicly about the consequences
of cultural or religious objections to adequate family planning – probably because of a justified fear of deeply held religious and economic
prejudices. Public conversation about these subjects is difficult because
they are taboo subjects, and critics are easily stigmatised – taboo and
stigma are ancient and highly effective forms of social and cultural control; even today taboo and stigma are coded (more or less subtly) into the
discourses of religion and consumerism. The sanctity of human reproduction is one subject that can unite Church, State and Business. These
globally controlling institutions have the same goal: more.

'Family planning' is a polite euphemism in itself, of course. Men (generally) are a fertility problem in all cultures, whether or not they are
bound by religious doctrine. Male dominated cultures remain a worldwide obstacle for women who might want control over the number of

children they bear. The legitimacy of the control of men and religions over reproduction and family life are still taboo subjects in all cultures – many of which are so otherwise explicit about sex and violence. In liberal democratic societies that have enshrined free speech and the protection of the law for all, the subject is politely avoided. The cost of children is easy to talk about; their right to exist is an absolutely taboo subject. In such an over-populated world it is still hard to even write such words.

But there is another subject underpinning patriarchal dominance in culture and society: the existential dilemma of non-reproductive purpose. The idea that some life might not seek to reproduce itself runs contrary to most definitions of human progress, civilization, success, fulfilment, and 'life' itself. The stigma of being 'barren', a 'spinster', old, infirm, childless, single, sexless, homosexual, or in some other way 'queer', are potent because of the 'impotence' they deride. Family life and reproduction are synonymous in all popular imaginations throughout history – the end of a family line is a tragedy and no cause for satisfaction. This has been the norm, with few exceptions; failure to reproduce is only valued when sanctioned by religions as a sign of spiritual purity, or a condition of 'professional' religious life. At best, the barren are tolerated, and only very rarely applauded.

Traditionally, the desire of a few for a 'purpose' other than that of child rearing was facilitated by monasteries and nunneries as places where celibacy could be celebrated as a noble practice (in theory). Other forms of 'withdrawal' from society for purposes of study, contemplation and artistic creation are present in all cultures but do not generally challenge reproductive purpose as a necessary end – a spiritual or creative life is certainly not always celibate. Access to contraception has broadened reproductive choice for many, but none of these 'low growth' cultural options have had noticeable effect in slowing the exponential increase of global population since the early nineteenth century. Neither have declines in reproductive rates in affluent societies (in Europe) affected this exponential growth: population growth in developing economies is overwhelming.

There is one certain psychological crisis humanity will face if populations plateau somewhere around 10 to 15 billion by the end of this century. This will be the likely collective tragedy of non-reproductive purpose. What meaning can life have if families become 'downsized' and childlessness becomes a much more common practice? The end of the world as we know it? And yet this may be the only condition under which humanity can progress beyond growth economics.

The short conclusion to this brief review is that although humanity may have mixed feelings about the desirability of human over-population, there is absolutely no disagreement about our right to breed. There is, moreover, little enough disagreement about the need to breed. This makes population growth the root cause of our current ecological crisis, the mother of all wicked problems, a multiplier of all adverse ecological impacts, and the ultimate reason why humanity will decline. Sadly, in the long run, Malthus will probably be proved right.

THE BIG THREE: AN OVERVIEW

Prima facie evidence suggests that on a global scale there are three elephants in the room: global warming causing climate change, economic growth, and over-population.

Climate change caused by global warming is the first elephant in the room. Increasing levels of greenhouse gases caused by human activity have already raised global average temperatures by approximately one degree Celsius. The science is in; without major countervailing events, average temperatures will continue to rise for some years to come. The chances of a two degrees Celsius rise, a tipping point for serious climate change, are increasingly high.

The second elephant is population growth. Approximately seven billion people on Earth, now, are already too many for a sustainable future. This level of population consumes resources at a rate greater than the planet's ability to renew them. There are many factors involved in the continuing explosion of human numbers, and the connected booming consumption rates. Proudly dominant in the rhetoric of all governments in rich countries is the logic of growth: to stay rich we need economic growth. To avoid recessions and unemployment we need economic growth. There is no apparent escape in this kind of thinking. However, even if greater productivity (which comes from new technology and higher efficiencies) is factored in, all growing economies currently depend upon population growth. The one issue that virtually no politicians are brave enough to tackle, and few citizens brave enough to even contemplate, is the need for population growth to decline.

The logic behind growth economics, and the associated pressures to pursue growth of production and consumption, is remorseless. This is true in all countries. In countries where population levels are relatively stable, such as in some Northern European countries, export earnings still come from expanding markets for goods and services that are the product of population growth in other markets (including banking services, in the case of Switzerland and other European banking centres).

Impoverished countries raise different considerations. Their low rates of GDP are often compensated by aid from wealthy countries; nonetheless, their poverty can be made worse by a combination of inability to participate in high technology industries, resource and labour exploitation by foreign owned companies, endemic corruption, and violent conflict. In these countries, large families remain the norm – driven by tradition, religion, male dominance, lack of family planning advice, and economic logic.

These challenging conditions are typical in Africa, where many countries have never undergone significant levels of industrialisation. Some developing economies, such as those of India and China, have had the benefit of industrialisation and wealth generation that has had an effect on quality of life. China is the best example – and really the only successful example – of a country determined to slow population growth and improve standards of living. But even in growing economies poverty is widespread. In the case of India it is doubtful that increasing rates of wealth generation will have sufficient 'trickle down' effect to compensate for still enormous rates of population growth. Rural poverty in India is an ever-present tragedy.

Whatever benefits increased wealth has on living standards in poorer countries, the fact remains that all economies are caught up with the logic of growth. There is no escape in the globalisation of economies. Growth economics is the third elephant in the room.

In this chapter, analysis of the prospects of future growth might also be summarised in a single strategic question: what issues are avoided because they are too hard to contemplate? Climate change, human over-population and economic growth are three obvious candidates.

How it is that humanity has reached so many 'tipping points' for a future blighted by ecological decline and social unrest is the continuing theme of this book. There are a number of relatively unexamined socio-cultural factors that explain a great deal. That fact that the complexity of the problem is so 'wicked', and apparently insoluble has been raised. The general reluctance to question the desirability of population growth has also been raised. The ideology of progress and cultural attachment to technological 'fixes' will be introduced in the next chapter and further discussed over the following three chapters; 'professional optimism' is a major contributing factor also, and will be discussed in the context of futurology and 'denial' in Chapter 4.

DENIAL

'Denial' is the most immediate explanation that will spring to many minds. If the interlocking problems of climate change, over-population and economic growth do pose a real threat to our collective futures, it seems hard to avoid the conclusion that 'denial' continues to play a major role in the mass production of perceptions about 'the future'.

It seems quite obvious that 'denial' can be developed as a devastating political strategy. In Australia the recent granting of a coal-mining license to a huge state owned Chinese corporation seems to be the desired outcome of a sustained government campaign of denial.

Not only does such a decision require denial of ecological issues caused by the burning of coal well into the future, it requires denial of economic realities. The demand for coal is softening; the market price is falling and will probably stay low if sustainable energy becomes more popular globally; the cost of development of the mine will exceed returns for years to come. What we do not see in Australia is transparent decision-making around these issues – what we continue to hear from politicians and corporate managers (when they do speak) is very effective denial that there is a problem. This is a most disturbing kind of deliberate and systematic denial. We assume that 'they' really must know because they've been told the truth by experts – we know that they know; further, they know that we know that they know. What we do hear is mumbo-jumbo about leadership. It's a disaster. At the level of political process it may be more accurate to classify such co-ordinated campaigns of denial as deception, for whatever reasons.

The long-term effects of political deception on voting publics are unclear. There are signs that many people are unhappy with the consequences of new coalmines and gas wells on water supplies and public health – but we have to wonder about the level of denial that governments are able to develop in trusting publics. This is a difficult issue because it may not be clear that there is a distinction to be made between personal psychological mechanisms and politically motivated campaigns of 'denial'.

Arguably, denial is a routine phenomenon related to the natural limitations of individual perception and awareness. At the limits of perception, the normal brain does not respond to 'slow creep' phenomena, like climate change; small changes in environmental conditions do not cross thresholds of conscious awareness. We all establish a sense of what is 'normal' and what conditions and circumstances can, therefore, be 'taken for granted'. Indeed, much everyday reality is based on limited perception and behavioural habits – thus, it may be that we forget whether we have locked the front door, or switched off the lights. We are not fully engaged with external reality – our senses are limited, our interests are selective, and our cognitive powers finite. In that context, 'denial' may simply arise as the assertion of everyday realities and 'common sense' – despite countervailing evidence such as another's observations of our individually unconscious behaviours.

Denial that arises as a consequence of 'natural' limitations of perception and awareness is, however, rather different to the kind of denial involved in much more highly orchestrated processes, such as climate change denial. Here we can find obvious social causes, such as deliberate campaigns of misinformation, vested interests, and an economic ideology based on growth and over-development.

Indeed, 'climate change denial' has given new currency to the idea of denial. In all spheres of engagement, humanity's historically destructive interactions with the biosphere – its ecologies and environments – are largely ignored in favour of growing human populations and economies. Some level of collective and individual denial seems necessary to explain how it is that our species appears to be sleepwalking into the future. The 'big three' are such a wicked problem because of the extent to which denial enables the knot to be tied, and retied, without much conscious awareness of the way life is being strangled out of humanity's future.

Denial has become a highly charged concept, with a rich recent history. 'Holocaust denial' is perhaps the most memorable recent spark, replete with associations of genocide and anti-semitism. But denial has a longer psychiatric and psychological history that can be traced back to Freudian and post-Freudian psychology. In those traditions, denial comes with many other disciplinary and clinical associations, including a general model of the 'inner' person. This model does not amount to much as a description of the connection of an individual psyche to an ecology or a planet, and has been well criticised by deep ecologists and eco-feminists as a limited description of the social relations experienced by an individual – the role of women has been particularly problematic in Freudian psychology. Nonetheless, all 'modern' western culture has been affected by 'psychology' – most obviously, all consumer culture depends on advertising and 'conditioning' that are, in effect, applied psychology. In cultures that are highly individualised, the charge of 'denial' strikes a strong chord. It seems reasonable to suppose that post–nineteenth century modernity has become a culture of denial – in particular affluent modern societies live in denial of the effects of the lifestyles we enjoy; climate change, and an underlying drive to grow and so dominate all other life forms, depend on denial.

The mechanisms of 'denial' and 'apocalypse culture' can provide some understanding of how it is that many in 'the west' continue to tolerate ecologically destructive practices. There are other more familiar individualised explanations such as greed, envy, gluttony, and ignorance, but certainly, for all possible causes, whatever hope there can be for 'solutions' and future 'progress' will depend on science. The neglected cultural importance of science will be discussed in the context of a brief history of climate science and the importance of this (and other) cultural

institutions. Hope also depends on 'progressive' politics and the availability of alternatives to 'growth economics'.

On that general basis it will be argued that developing a 'pragmatic
eco-centric position' is the only viable option for a sustainable future.
The revaluing of nature, and our relationship to it, is essential if we are
to go forward.

CHAPTER
3

GOING FORWARD

I've seen the future baby,
It is murder.

Leonard Cohen, *'Future'*.

A global ecology includes human systems as well as the physical and biological systems studied by natural scientists. Human politics and economics are, of course, paramount activities that will direct our common future, but complex global systems respond to all human inputs, no matter how rational or irrational, optimistic or pessimistic. Further, because the kinds of ecological changes that concern scientists are increasingly sensitive to human expansion, they require close monitoring. This calls for more science and increased sensitivity of politicians to findings of the ecological sciences.

However, as we move further into unknown ecological territory, where human impacts are increasingly dominant globally, we depend upon the wisdom of politicians and economists, in particular, to minimise the effects of human industry, population growth and consumption of Earth's resources. In the 'progress' of human society scientists inform, but politicians and economists tend more to steer the ships of industry and state.

In that context the future is negotiable; futurology and forward-looking commentary are uncertain practices; 'going forward' is, necessarily, a risky business. Scientific knowledge can only advise politicians and bureaucrats and, at best, be part of economic calculations. In these processes of policy formation, governance, and managerial strategizing, 'the science' involved tends to remain away from the public gaze. Politicians and managers may not always reveal how their decisions are based in 'fact', and specialist researchers do not always see their role as requiring the communication of their findings to non-specialist audiences.

Science based findings can reach larger audiences through the work of popularisers and commentators who are able to 'translate' specialised findings and present them as part of broader conversations. This chapter will introduce a number of well-known commentators who have written extensively about the future: Al Gore, Niall Ferguson, Clive Hamilton, Paul Gilding, and Roger Scruton. These authors have a multi-disciplinary appreciation − of the importance of science, technology, politics, economics and ecology in particular − and are all highly achieved 'public intellectuals' and professional consultants.

There is a rapidly increasing volume of future-oriented literature with many new authors, so there has been a necessary arbitrariness in the choice of particular authors to form an introductory sample. Their ideas are far from arbitrary in scope: their combination provides an overview of current professionally based opinion about 'the future'. It is the field of ideas so generated that is most important − what is particularly interesting is the extent to which ecological ideas and metaphors have become part of the reasoning and theory construction of these commentators. Many of the other scientific ideas raised are also highly interesting − there is a discussion of energy and thermodynamics, for example, that is long overdue in the formation of 'popular' views about climate change and the fate of heat generated by human processes. This conversation will resume in Chapter 5.

The optimism of these writers is very often, remarkable, but no greater than the discipline based futurologists introduced in the last chapter (the anthropologist Jarred Diamond, the historian Thomas Homer-Dixon, and the policy consultant Eric Knight). The next chapter will look more closely at 'professional optimism' as fact of institutional life; in the light of that chapter, and in context of the over-view of climate science provided in Chapter 5, it is fair to say that all the authors discussed in this chapter are probably over-optimistic.

'Going forward' (that is, moving towards long term best outcomes) depends on broadly based research requiring skilled personnel and well-funded programs. Government policy that is not informed by specialised research and scholarship will likely lead to a future of crisis management rather than good governance or collective wisdom. 'Going forward' also depends on governments seeking and taking advice from a full range of experts. Science, however, is particularly important for two reasons: it should provide the factual basis for decision making around the limits of bio-physical systems, and it is the cultural bastion of secular reason in the west. This chapter is more interested in the substantive narratives of science-based forecasters; discussion of the importance of secular reason will be largely deferred to Chapter 5.

Science, like most professions, is highly vulnerable to decisions by governments and private funders about levels of funding, desirable research directions, and the quality of current research. None of those decisions should reasonably be made in the absence of considered consultation with scientific communities. That consultation appears to have been largely absent from many recent Australian Federal government decisions about the funding of climate, and other environmentally related, research. In Australia, politicians and industrialists still directly challenge the veracity of climate science; other environmentally related research they merely ignore.

ONE STEP FORWARD, TWO STEPS BACKWARDS

Panel discussions on television can be highly entertaining. For those who enjoy the quiet understatement of scientists, it was 'ground hog day' again, in Spring of 2014, during a special episode of the Australian Broadcasting Commission's program *Q&A*.[1]

A carefully selected group of Australian scientists including two Nobel prize winners, the government's Chief Scientist, the latest Young Australian of the Year, and the presenter of the 2014 Boyer Lecture, had been gathered to discuss the current state of Australian science. Subjects broached included the representation of science in government, the need for elite scientists to find employment overseas, the importance of 'blue sky' research, the poor articulation of Australian science with industry, promising developments in cancer research and the need for wise leadership. Some subjects never change – except for the last question of the evening. This was about the defining issue of the current age: climate change. There was, predictably, furious agreement about the importance of that; no other issue came close. With respect to leadership, the female Young Australian of the Year (a scientific entrepreneur in the field of robotics) thought that 'big visions' were necessary to inspire young Australians. In that department, she asserted, Australian science was lacking. Her elite colleagues (all men, save one other woman) seemed less than amused, but there was no disagreement.

This was, for those who follow the vicissitudes of science and scientists, an all too familiar display of professional optimism alloyed with grim humour, youthful enthusiasm and very understated anger. The public performances of Australian elite scientists tend to convey, over the years, the same feelings about their under-appreciation. . . perhaps when scientists are chronically under-funded, there can be hope without clear vision. The scientists on that night were not professional forecasters of the type we will encounter in this chapter, but they were all leaders in their various fields, and therefore well equipped to predict future trends. Any indication of future directions in research that could be extrapolated from what was said was over-shadowed by the uncertainty they all felt about their professional security. This was very clear, even allowing for possible exaggeration.

Uncertainty about job security, government funding and public support is not limited to professional scientists. All professionals share these uncertainties. This is undoubtedly one of the driving forces behind 'professional optimism' – and indeed, all professional futurologists (and *de facto* futurologists), including politicians, pollsters, stock market speculators, economists and those particularly concerned with predicting human futures generally apply an optimistic spin. The future is, after all, a work-in-progress.

Political imperatives for economic growth continue to be the primary reason governments will not countenance ecological bad news. It does appear, however, that our current government's aversion to science extends more widely. In Australia, there have been general funding cuts across most fields of scientific research, including the downsizing of the CSIRO, one of the country's leading research organisations, and its largest[2] ; there has been the removal of key scientific representation to government; and there are ongoing threats to privatise universities – with the obvious implications this would have on research priorities. The rhetoric of governing politicians has included full denial of scientific consensus about climate change; even more alarmingly, senior politicians have ventured to assert confident opinions about the non-existence of climate change, and the state of the science.

The willingness of politicians to assert authority over professional scientists attempting to research climate change and the ecological impacts of growth demonstrates much about the vulnerability of all professional fields to political interference disguised as 'leadership'. The ability of politicians to radically affect research agendas of major institutions indicates the isolation – from audiences, voting publics, and other organisations and institutions – of most critically important research. Generally, the sciences are more institutionally secure and highly funded than other disciplines and research programs in the tertiary sector. The forecasters and commentators reviewed in this chapter are, generally, not as institutionally secure as leading scientists, and they do not have the same levels of influence over political decision making. As 'public intellectuals' these individuals may retain considerable control over the direction of their researches, but that autonomy has generally come at the cost of government funded support. But of course, the levels of control public intellectuals have over their media patrons is another matter.

PROFESSIONAL FORECASTING
– SOME CAUTIONARY REMARKS

It is possible to make some broad generalisations about issues of direction and control of research and the generation of knowledge in all fields – but particularly as relevant to the inter-disciplinary discussion of 'going forward' that follows.

Neither politics nor economics are 'exact' sciences. The direction of human behaviour is not open to the same methods and assumptions that natural scientists use in their predictive work. Indeed, none of the disciplines that study human behaviour and social processes are 'exact' or 'hard' sciences – like physics, chemistry, or biology, for example. 'Political science', and 'social science', are misleading names for activities that are far more theory driven, inherently politicised, and approximate, than may be commonly realised. Any futures their professional scribes may postulate are also negotiable.[3]

Having said that, 'human sciences', and arts and humanities, are more important to humanity's future than most natural scientists might wish. Contemporary futurology, which has become a new quasi-professional activity draws heavily on social sciences – and is part of that broad domain. Indeed, many of the public intellectuals and commentators who address Earth's future today are not natural scientists, and that is a good thing, because so many of the issues and systems we can most easily change are matters of human behaviour. We can close a factory with the stroke of a pen, but we cannot undo the climatic effects of 450ppm CO_2 so easily.

Despite the scientific obtuseness of many politicians, it has never been easier for non-scientists addressing Earth's future to be well informed scientifically. The Internet has revolutionised access and communication between specialists and the public. Well placed individuals, such as Al Gore, can access and publicise the findings of government review processes. Investigative journalists can provide current research findings regularly, and at least alert their audiences to new work presented at conferences and other research forums. There has never been more potential for communication between specialists and wider audiences. Even so, there are limits to what can be expected from clearer communication, or from sciences and other fields and disciplines that trade in 'facts'.

All knowledge and knowledge claims (including science) involve interpretation – to some extent. Authors and audiences are constantly 'at it'. In the increasingly busy processes of contemporary communication there are three major considerations that bear on the interpretation of *all* texts and messages – and particularly bear on the possibilities of futurology:

1.   All texts and authors (even scientists) have disciplinary, personal and 'cultural interests' that limit the scope and depth of ideas and research findings;

2.   The publication of research findings involves 'others' beyond individual authors who can delay and in various ways interfere with the public dissemination of information; and,

3.   All complex systems are to some extent unpredictable, which limits the certainty of most scientific knowledge – particularly climate science and ecological science.

None of these cautionary 'considerations' necessarily invalidate predictions, or postulated knowledge, or 'truths', but they do explain why all knowledge should be regarded as a 'social product' subject to correction, review and change.

The third proposition is important in the context of what has become a highly politicised 'conversation' about climate science. We can still rely on scientists, such as those on the International Panel on Climate Change (the IPCC), to provide the best available assessments and predictions. However, as most ecological scientists themselves are at pains to indicate, their findings are probabilistic – and usually only announced when very high levels of confidence can be had about their findings. Climate scientists are highly confident that the planet is warming – about 99.9% confident, yet are necessarily limited in the kinds of conclusions they can legitimately make. Once climate science is inserted into the output of other sciences, engineering, economics and politics, new orders of complexity emerge, new possibilities emerge, and our predictive power falls ...

The advent of the Internet has made the public dissemination of information easier than in days when authors depended largely on the cooperation of publishers. However, no one should assume that research findings critically important to economic security escape scrutiny from, and possible interference by, governments and other organisations whose interests are affected. Many scientists – including James Hanson, the pre-eminent US climate scientist whose work is discussed at greater length in Chapter 5 – suffer at the hands of government agencies empowered to interfere with publication processes. Large corporations employ people 'tasked' with the job of 'public relations', the monitoring of relevant research, and the development of pathways of influence. Generally, the funding of major research is a highly politicised process – all funding can be cut and influenced in administrative processes, and further, 'strategic' research can be conducted in secret, and its findings never published.[4]

The politicisation of research funding may allow more predictable outcomes in some complex systems, but in general, the greater the level of complexity, the less predictable large systems become. In the case of the global ecosystem, no one knows the details of what is to come. This is particularly obvious if the effect of human 'choice' is considered: any conventional understanding of the meaning of 'choice' allows some degree of freedom to choose – in the market place, in personal relations, in political processes, in the development of designs, or in construction projects. Choice means an unresolved future, and a future that is open to the persuasive arts. Even if choice is actually something of an illusion – in the context of beliefs and behaviours that are highly conditioned and patterned to begin with – we all act 'as if' we had choice. These choices affect the interpretations we make, the futures we anticipate, and the futures that are built.

THE FUTURE ACCORDING TO AL GORE

A major work by a figure as prominent as Al Gore merits close scrutiny. We should wonder how the personal and professional interests of a very senior, and wealthy, ex-US Democrat politician, and winner of a Nobel Peace Prize, might influence the findings of a book as apparently profound as his latest work, *The Future*? We can be confident that Al Gore is not taking money from green industry groups such as solar panel manufacturers, but we might wonder whether the history, and current political denials of the USA are 'air brushed'. We might wonder whether his optimism has been conditioned by a cultural belief in miracles and divine intervention. We might wonder whether he over-represents the interests of the next wave of technocrats.

Gore's film *An Inconvenient Truth* was a milestone along the road of climate change consciousness-raising. This film was viewed by millions in many different countries and undoubtedly served as a wake-up call to many. No one expected a recent Vice President, and genuine contender, to seriously compromise American interests – yet his message was uncompromising in many ways. We change, or we go down. However, his argument for cultural change – without disturbing the political equilibrium, and involving a strong American presence – will not be persuasive to many, including hard left warriors waiting for 'the revolution', that will destroy American capitalism. Nor will such a view be persuasive to terrorists, and other warriors to 'the right' – for the same reason. Nonetheless, Al Gore remains one of the world's most highly influential commentators about 'the future' – even though he is a part of the political establishment of the world's largest economy. We need to appreciate his analysis in that context.

In his latest book, Gore identifies six 'drivers of change': the emergence of a globalised economy and communications grid; a new balance of power; rapid unsustainable growth in population; resource consumption (particularly depletion of top soil, fresh water supplies and living species); pollution and economic output; new technologies in biology, biochemistry, genetics and materials science; and change in Earth's ecological systems.[5]

These are uncontroversial findings. Gore's optimistic take on a possible 'future' depends, however, on analogy with two major scientific theories: evolution, and the 'new' thermodynamics of 'dissipative systems' – Ilya Prigogine was recently awarded a Nobel Prize in Chemistry for his thermodynamic work about the emergence of new stable systems from unstable ones. [6]

He now joins Charles Darwin in being inspirational to commentators describing social and cultural change. Gore seems rather taken with the socially transformative potentials of this new scientific principle; but there is an ideological trap awaiting those who seek to justify particular social and cultural forms as necessary outcomes of evolution and thermodynamics – 'whatever is, is right', as Voltaire famously put it. Gore's assumption that innovative solutions to climate change, and all the problems of modern industrial societies, will 'emerge' because of the scientific laws of evolution and thermodynamics is utterly untestable. Further, the complexities of human agency and political intervention are subtler than the possibilities of random selection and equilibrating physico-chemical systems. So too, the complexities of living eco-systems appear more complex than simple description as 'evolution', or 'emergence' can allow – not that these considerations are unimportant. Therefore, the dynamic behaviours of eco-systems (increasingly incorporating human activities) are still largely unknown – but are the subject of many ecological research projects.

Another idea that will distress many is that 'the future', in Gore's view, is only possible with leadership from the USA. It is, of course, hard to imagine any other nation state that could presently compete successfully with the USA as an innovator across the wide range of the 'drivers of change' Gore describes – but we should note that change in ecological systems, even if we credit the possibilities of evolution and a new thermodynamic law, does not recognise nation states, *per se*. The future that Gore would like to see should not be seen simply as an outcome of scientific laws, or as somehow mainly guided by scientific laws, or any some other 'external' process of guidance. The sub-systems that science can describe best are comprised of matter and energy; the prediction of human behaviour and social development is not a realistic goal for the contemporary sciences, natural or social. The USA may still be a dominant world power, and an innovative catalyst and rate controller, but world powers change. It is not the logic of thermodynamics or ecological systems theory that guides economists to expect China to become the world's largest national economy within a few years; that is a prediction based on rates of economic growth, and estimates of changing balances of political, economic, and military power made largely by (non-natural scientific) experts in politics, economics and military affairs. The prediction that the United States may not remain such a dominant superpower into the future is not basically in consequence of any laws of ecology or science; natural ecosystems tend to be indifferent to designs on flags.

Conversely, however, whatever nations become dominant superpowers, the enormous consumption of energy resources and the commensurate production of energy and heat by all nations make general thermodynamic considerations critically important in forecasting the ecological future. Where does all the heat go? What range of temperatures can living systems survive? Is there a point at which the heat generated by human work exceeds the ability of ecological heat sinks to absorb and recycle excess heat sustainably? What happens when the resources needed for the growth of a society, or an empire, are not available?

These are not simply hypothetical questions. According to some historians, ancient Rome declined because it outstripped available resources:

> Rome was ... locked into a food-based energy system that left little room to manoeuvre. Without the scientific skills to make the jump to a new kind of energy system – like one based on fossil fuels – the empire was trapped in a thermodynamic crisis that exacerbated its underlying brittleness.[7]

All societies exist within 'natural' ecologies that involve human cultivation and interference, but they are, most fundamentally, ecological phenomena themselves; they are organically part of the ecologies that support them. The collapse of ecological systems that support societies can be catastrophic in their effects. As Jarred Diamond pointed out in his very timely and highly acclaimed work, there have been a number of ecological collapses that have brought societies to destructive ends.[8]

No society is immune from lack of resources, or ecological ruin; but most critically, the collapses Diamond reviews were never simply, or only,

caused by lack of combustible fuels. Ecological collapses can be initiated by such 'thermodynamic' crises, but as Diamond suggests, we need
to wonder how better management could have controlled the various
combinations of over-population, warfare, decline of trade, environmental degradation, other human activities – and fluctuations of climate
– that were associated with ecological collapses in the past.

It is tempting to assume that overarching scientific 'laws' and other
established scientific principles (such as those of thermodynamics) provide simple answers to problems arising from complex processes – like
climate change and economic growth. Indeed, modern science is a very
credible contender for providing answers to all questions that require
'facts' – but, of course, the future is not just a physical system, it is, as we
know, a much more complex system that will be highly determined by
political and economic practices.

Al Gore is not wrong in looking to thermodynamics as a source of
hope for something 'new' which might save us from the inevitability of
thermodynamic decline, and that might explain the resilience of life and
human society. The emergence of order in life and human societies is an
intriguing anti-entropic process. Prior to Prigogine's theorising of the
emergence of 'order out of chaos', thermodynamics inspired cosmologists with ideas about the inevitable decay of order in the universe. Life
and human society were brief and probably anomalous events; life on
Earth would suffer a hot death. That is still what most physicists predict
for the very long term, but that leaves life on Earth a possibility for a
long time yet – astronomers and cosmologists think about five billion
more years before the sun 'will puff itself into a red giant star and swallow the inner solar system before slowly fading to black.'[9]

Scientific debate about the place of life in the universe is far from
resolved. Even in the bleakest of views in which human life is unique
and fragile, there can be hope and optimism. For example, although
Professor Brian Cox thinks that life is certainly rare within a few light
years distance from Earth, and that life on Earth may even be unique
in the cosmos, this means that life is all the more worth valuing and
protecting. [10]

As Gore's account shows, the understanding of complex systems requires insights from different disciplinary perspectives. Single disciplines only reduce the complexity that characterise the external realities that are the objects of investigation. Economics, for example, a notoriously inexact 'science', provides a critically important mode of understanding, but can only be ecologically 'rational' if insights about declining natural resources and the degradation of the environment – that come from other disciplines – are factored into forward estimates of costs. Allowing economic ideas, alone, to actually determine the outcomes of government policy – as routinely happens – is a recipe for ecological disaster (and economic disaster).

There has always, so far, been an uneasy relationship between human societies and natural ecologies. By the nineteenth century, however, industrialisation and the consequent population growth that was expected appear to have established a new idea, formalised by Malthus –growth of human populations will encounter natural limits, or as rephrased in the twentieth century, there are 'limits to growth'. The continuing difficulty of establishing the concept of ecological limits in economic and political thought is the best, and most life-threatening, example of the uneasy place that human society occupies in natural ecologies. This problem now challenges all contemporary professions and disciplines 'going forward'.

GOING FORWARD

If any industrialised nations are to provide ecological leadership into the future, they will need a smaller carbon footprint – which is intrinsically an economic issue. The ecological impact of the USA, for example, is not simply a matter of the size of its carbon footprint – as the recent Global Financial Crisis demonstrated, the banking and finance sectors of the US economy are dominant in a global market place. The sheer size of the US economy is obvious; the global scale and complexity of connections between banks and financial products, and their disconnection from democratic governance was, however, surprising to many. Less surprising is the renewed commitment of the USA to fossil fuels to underpin and stabilise its economy. Rich deposits of shale gas have ignited a boom in gas extraction and another era of cheaper energy for US industries. This is a poorly regulated and toxic economic bonanza. Any hopes that the imminence of 'peak oil' would drive increased dependence on renewable energy sources are going up in smoke. This all occurs for economic and political reasons – 'ecological rationality' is a very minor consideration.

The USA is the world's largest per capita energy consumer and China is the world's largest single nation emitter of greenhouse gases. The high levels of fossil fuel consumption required by these two giant economies will almost certainly continue long into the twenty-first century – despite any efforts to curtail energy usage, reduce pollution levels, or change the mix of energy consumption. In that light, any perceived new bonanza of natural gas supplies in the USA can be better appreciated as a distraction from an unchanging energy industry determination (in both countries) to thoroughly exploit all fossil fuel resources – now, and tomorrow.

If current US industry and government enthusiasm for shale gas is placed in context of anticipated trends in total energy consumption, it is forecast that coal and oil will remain the dominant source of US energy well into the foreseeable future (approximately 52% by 2035). In 2035 fossil fuel consumption is predicted to account for an estimated 78% of total consumption. 'Natural gas' consumption is expected to remain constant at about 25% of the total. Over that period the small decline in fossil fuel usage (83% declining to 78%) will be due to a doubling consumption of renewable energy (8% to 16%). [11]

Even if the increasingly higher targets for renewable energy generation that many governments are currently negotiating give some cause for hope, the ongoing impacts of 'carbon pollution' are basically unknown and are possessed of great forward momentum.

Our ecological future is dependent on governments, industry, and national economies being willing to change. In the short term it is much easier to burn coal, and pollute rivers, than it is to persuade electorates of the need to modify the economy. As important as the broad brushstrokes of Al Gore may be, economic analyses that can factor in international political interests *and* ecological interests are now required in much more detail. This could amount to economic paradigm change – as discussed further in Chapter 6.

Niall Ferguson is one academic economic historian who did respond to the GFC in a more holistic way. His television series *Money* and *Civilization,* together with his recent written publications, have definite ecological sensitivities. Mainstream economics is probably the most difficult disciplinary framework of all from which to advance an ecologically informed view – and so Ferguson's work is all the more important for that reason. In *The Great Degeneration* we see Ferguson's best analysis: economies are like evolutionary systems. Economies have 'genes' stored as 'organisational memory'; spontaneously mutate; are based on competition; display natural selection; have scope for speciation giving rise to new 'species' of financial institutions; and can become extinct. He goes on to discuss the similarity between economies and complex systems in the natural world:

> All complex systems in the natural world – from termite hills to the human nervous system – share certain characteristics. A small input to such a system can produce huge unanticipated changes . . . It turns out that financial crises are much the same.[12]

This metaphoric innovation to economic theory is probably the best one might expect from mainstream economics. The fact that economic growth is now a problem in itself remains a consideration in hiding. Economics and economists have professionalised, discipline based interests in preserving the coherence and integrity of an established 'paradigm' premised on goals and assumptions about the continuing desirability of economic growth and increasing prosperity.

Besides Ferguson's efforts, it should be noted that exploration of ecological models within established disciplines is becoming more commonplace in many disciplines. The life sciences have been so engaged since Darwin, and the social sciences since the 1920s.[13]

Indeed, even within economics there have been a number of rene-gades who have attempted a more holistic approach. Herman Daly, for instance, has struggled over decades to break out of the constraints of economic modelling based on the assumption of continued growth. He has written at length on 'sustainable economics', and has gone much further than writing in metaphors (see Chapter 6).

However, arguing that particular systems – such as an economy or information technology – are 'ecological', and evolutionary (as Ferguson suggests), does not necessarily extend in any material way directly to biological eco-systems. An 'ecology' can now simply mean a complex system with 'feedback' and 'feed-forward' or refer to highly abstract the-oretical systems, or every highly mechanical non-living systems. The word *ecology* is now regularly appropriated as a signifier of complexity and interactivity in the human made systems and spaces of informa-tion technology and advertising. This 'slippage' in the meaning of a now common term is insidiously human-centred.

'Greenwash' is a good way of describing such rhetorical usage. We have, for example, the 'ecology' of information systems, 'ecology' in vir-tual worlds, the 'ecology' of marketing and sales campaigns, the 'ecology' of corporate culture, etc. [14]

Nonetheless, although there is a fine line between the creative and productive appropriation of specialist terms (by other fields, gener-al analysis and commentary) and rhetorical misappropriation; the idea of ecology is now central in the development of a global movement towards sustainability. Indeed, the development of ecological ideas has itself benefited from concepts and models that have been adopted from a number of non-biological fields, including mathematics, systems theory, computer modelling, and engineering. The idea that all ecologies have limits, for example, can be traced to mathematical calculus, and ultimate-ly the mathematics of the ancient Greeks. The development of models that can account for the limits of material supplies, limits to amounts of pollution any system can tolerate, limits to economic and material growth, and so on, define the boundaries of all ecologies, and require inter-disciplinary collaboration for their optimum development.

So although Niall Ferguson's use of ecological analogies might be considered a sophisticated form of greenwash, it is critically important that economic theory begin to appropriate ecological ideas *and* operate within ecologically defined limits. However, the incorporation of ecological ideas into any economic theory does not necessarily entail a move towards sustainable practices. A complex economic system might be called 'ecological' and quite conceivably sustain the destructive practices of coal mining and 'fracking' far longer than is good for the climate or the environment. In this sense an economic 'ecology' could remain quite insensitive to real economic costs and preserve conventional economic practices – normally elements that do not enter economic calculation as direct costs, or as measurable profits (such as air, or water quality) are referred to by economists as 'externalities'. Conceivably, an economic theory that incorporated all the ecological metaphors mentioned by Niall Ferguson in *The Great Degeneration* might externalise 'real' ecological components and still call itself an ecological approach. This is what we can realistically expect from mainstream economics that, after all, must maximise 'private' financial profits, and growth, for business clients. But at least the door has been opened towards the incorporation of material limits directly into economic calculations, as will be discussed further in Chapter 6, 'Changing Economics'.

Like Al Gore, Niall Ferguson also identifies six key change agents in his book *Civilization*. He identifies six 'killer applications', or complexes of institutions and associated ideas and behaviours, that enabled Western civilization to successfully emerge from 'the Rest': competition, science, property rights, medicine, consumer society and the work ethic. [15]

The interconnections between these two global views are very clear. It is easy to connect Gore's 'drivers of change' with the 'killer applications' that Ferguson describes as having made the West dominant. Gore's change agents are products of the innovations that made the West so successful. For instance, globalised property rights, consumer societies, and innovation based on modern science (and technology) are attributes of the global economy and global communication network that Ferguson's 'killer applications' have delivered, and the contemporary starting point for Gore's exploration of future possibilities. The systems of the twenty first century have evolved from the systems of the nineteenth and twentieth centuries. The great intellectual advance of Gore's panorama is the simple acknowledgement that the successes of Western science, industry, business, health and lifestyle have come at great cost to the Earth. Ferguson's account of 'civilization' seems airbrushed in comparison.

Gore's concerns about climate change and the ecological impacts of 'progress' appear more aligned with current scientific and technological research than Ferguson's account. Yet the cautionary pessimism that consideration of ecologically related research findings might suggest is not present. Gore's narrative, like that of Ferguson's *Civilization*, is basically optimistic and in line with conventional ideas about social progress. He acknowledges the limiting potentials of both thermodynamics and ecological impacts, but his positive reference to Prigogine's new law of thermodynamics – the creation of 'order out of chaos' – allows him to remain optimistic about future prospects even though pessimism might seem more appropriate.

Clearly, one should worry about heat retention by atmospheric greenhouse gases. In that respect, the long established laws of thermodynamics give no cause for optimism – the atmosphere, oceans and surface of the Earth are, on average, heating up. Arguably, that should further demonstrate the contention that the laws of science are indifferent to the particular wishes, or needs, of humanity. Indeed, the laws of thermodynamics, in particular, have long presented a problem for those trying to make positive narratives out of the natural laws of science. The 'fact' that all systems tend to 'run down' as disorder increases over time – striving naturally for equilibrium states of maximum disorder, and either heating up or cooling down depending on circumstances – does not inspire positive narrative spin. The possibility that disorder, rather than order, was such a fundamental principle was a concern for social philosophers as much as natural scientists. Human systems that could not be easily accounted for in terms of 'natural law' required other explanations – and social scientists provided their own explanations of order and 'social' systems.

All this was true only prior to Prigogine's thermodynamic discovery; prior to that event the development of higher levels of order in any system, without external intervention, was considered to be 'anti-entropic' and, effectively, at odds with the laws of nature. After Prigogine's thermodynamic research on irreversible processes in 'dissipative systems', audiences were eager to move on from the pessimism of worlds either running out of steam and freezing, or overheating and exploding – such were the limits of classical thermodynamics.

Following the scientific and mathematical innovations of dissipative systems and 'chaos theory', the emergence of new levels of organisation in social and cultural systems can (again) be argued to be *natural* phenomena based on *natural* laws. This is helpful to those professional forecasters who, like Al Gore and many science-oriented commentators, would avoid the theoretical snares of the arts, humanities and social 'sciences'. Yet again, optimism and the narrative of progress can open the door to a magical realm that lives forever in sunshine and good health – Oz revisited.

Nonetheless, the classical laws of thermodynamics, like Newton's Laws of motion, work for the macroscopic Earthly projects of practicing engineers, architects, town planners and builders. Whatever new levels of organisation may be currently unfolding, the first three laws of thermodynamics still enable calculations about the heating up of Earth's atmosphere to proceed, and too, calculations about heat transfer necessary in the design of buildings and industries. This is the world with limits and decline that many optimists seek to avoid and deny.

Yet, as previously suggested, the metaphoric implications of Prigogine's thermodynamic discovery are considerable. If the behaviours of particular chemical systems in laboratories are considered to be analogous with social systems, it could be said that 'revolutions' might occur because of a natural tendency for complex systems to reorganise in new and surprising ways. A complex human society way out of equilibrium because of ecological stress and other unsustainable forces might 'throw up' some game changing innovation – like pollution free energy sources. This is the kind of model Gore seems to have in mind also. It's a 'long bow'. Human societies are a long way from being controlled laboratories, or reducible to the algorithms of computer programs, or predictable in response to crisis, or 'system stress'.

In Gore's account, the possible injection of new 'natural' order from the tendency for complex systems to reorganise does not diminish the urgent need for social leadership – this is a very real consideration. With the right leadership and strategic management Gore suggests we can have 'a future' rather than a systems failure. And then, the triumphal history Ferguson describes can smoothly lift off into the future Gore would like to see.

The idea that *any* radical change can be well managed is probably optimistic from a natural scientific point of view. Systems that are unstable are not fully predictable – their behaviour can only be predicted as probabilities. The further one moves from equilibrium states the more chaotic things become. For example, the behaviour of complex systems modelled by 'chaos mathematics' can be anything but predictable – fluctuations can be quite radical, as the famous 'butterfly effect' demonstrates.[16]

The unpredictability of fluctuating systems raises great concerns for the management of complex systems. Whether 'crisis management' will be the default position for humanity adjusting to the demands of changing climates remains to be seen – but already it seems clear that natural disasters generally require crisis management. The unpredictability of earthquakes, cyclones and storms requires emergency services that can respond quickly to disasters; so far these are only episodic. If we are to avoid a situation where crisis becomes more frequent, more precautionary steps need to be taken now. In the future the question of whether we could have done things differently will always arise. Shifting away from a habit of crisis management towards the type of social and ecological planning that can be called 'sustainable' would be the most rational approach. Rationality is, however, not always an obvious source of optimism.

ANOTHER FUTUROLOGIST

The Australian futurologist Paul Gilding is optimistic. Despite a 'great disruption' as our current model of social and economic progress 'dies', things will turn around because they have to. 'The *only* choices we get to make are how and when we change, not whether . . . our criteria for success, at the personal, corporate and government levels, need to shift away from the idea, now proven wrong, that economic growth and personal wealth are the right central focus because everything flows from that. That game is over. It will die with economic growth. A new game has begun, and we get to write the rules. So there is only one question left to cover. "Where do you fit in?"' [17]

Gilding's views are typical of a new breed of management consultant – ecologically informed, commercially experienced professionals who promote ecologically inspired transformation and change for corporate workshops and team building sessions. [18]

Gilding's reasoning, like Al Gore's, is that change will definitely happen because it will be forced upon us by the progressive failure of ecosystems and related human systems. Both writers emphasise the importance of leadership – Gore is more 'top down' and does not emphasise the role and power of individual choice in the way that Gilding and many management consultants do. But both writers do have a kind of religious conviction that good will happen because it has to happen. This kind of conviction will infuriate some because it seems a positive and optimistic fatalism at a time when negative and pessimistic fatalism cannot be ruled out. Gore and Gilding are also post–Enlightenment writers in the sense that they have great faith that human reason will prevail in the long run. They may be right in being so confident that new technology and a new world order will emerge in time for there to be a future worth living, but really, nobody can predict that with confidence.

With or without faith, the emergence of the Internet and global communications technology may hold some hope. This may be a contemporary example of how new modes of human organisation do 'just emerge' from the innovative complexity of new technology. Gore, Gilding and new generations of technophiles have good reason to be optimistic about the potentials of new technologies – even if it remains to be seen whether generations of children born plugged into a screen and network will generate more sensitivity to issues of sustainability than they presently appear to manifest. But who would confidently predict the ecological engagement of future generations?

THE REALISM OF PESSIMISM

Clive Hamilton, a better-known Australian commentator, is unusual in being realistically pessimistic. His commentary on public life has been wide-ranging and always astute – quite an achievement for an academic among disciplinary specialists. As a professional in the field of public policy, his optimism has always been nuanced. In *Growth Fetish* (2003) he goes to considerable lengths expounding the idea that wealth doesn't produce happiness, and concludes:

> the central objective of a post-growth society is to provide opportunities for human fulfilment and self-realisation. Pursuit of wellbeing – which for many will require abandonment of the money obsession and rejection of the pursuit of identity through consumption – would allow the emergence of authentic (rather than manufactured) individuality and the flowering of human potential.[19]

Ten years later in *Earth Masters: Playing God with the climate*, he concludes,

> Prometheans rule. Over three centuries of advance, displaced workers, romantic poets, dismayed clerics and far-seeing ecologists put up resistance; all sooner or later were crushed. Who can hold back such a force? Yet history proves that the invincible can be thwarted and the mighty brought to heel in unexpected ways. As the Chinese proverb has it: when taken to their extreme, things revert to their opposite. Only history can answer whether the time has come; but if the meek are ever to inherit the Earth then they had better be quick.[20]

Hamilton's unfolding view has all the nuance of a post-Marxist Mason. His high regard for the myths and legends of the ancient Greeks probably pre-disposes tragedy at the expense of comedy – but the idea of cosmic *déjà vu* is not at all frivolous. There is a good fit between many of

the heroes and heroines in the narratives that unfold as news and investigative journalism and the heroes of ancient mythologies. Hamilton
never misses an opportunity to show the relevance of the ancient Greek
pantheon: Hubris, Nemesis, Pandora, Polyanna, Prometheus and, most
recently in his decades long review of the ancient Greeks, Soteria, the
goddess of safety, preservation and deliverance from harm. He is not
wrong; there are not too many archetypal stories – particularly as they
unfold in the news.

Clive Hamilton's analyses of capitalist economies and societies have
been influential on the thinking of many Australians critical of 'the
system' – including organised politics. Even further afield, younger
leftists such as Naomi Klein, hold him in high esteem. His critical determination, like that of many older leftists, is hardly optimistic – perhaps
'tragic' is not too much of an exaggeration. Without disputing his cultural importance in the diagnosis of our current ecological tragedy, it is
interesting to wonder how it is that he manages to address the issues of
ecological limits with such an appropriate level of pessimism – when so
many other academic leftists refuse to go further than endlessly blaming
a greedy and rapacious capitalism for humanity's woes.[21]

In Australia, academic left wing cultures have had a high degree of
cultural autonomy – and have dominated many networks in the disciplines of the arts, humanities and social sciences; the outputs of this
process have had little traction with liberal and conservative governments, or the captains of industry. Because the professionalism of left
academics has few 'external' clients, it tends to circle endlessly around its
core cultural issues – social inequality and social justice. Academics like
Clive Hamilton are something of an exception. Broad ranging interests, the status of high profile institutional locations, and a variety of
clients, and audiences, for 'public policy' projects makes him far more
credible as a 'public intellectual' than hide bound ideologues of the left.
Consequently, in his work a more open view of an unfolding ecological
tragedy has been possible, a view that could be described as pessimistic
optimism.

The fact that the archetypes of human behaviour represented in the
ancient Greek pantheon can appear relevant to modern life certainly

indicates that there are enduring ideas and qualities in human culture, despite the waxing and waning of empires. The ancient Greek historian Thucydides, for example, is prototypically modern in his writing – as we might assume were the ancient Greeks in their approach to life. Yet the ancient Greeks were overwhelmed by the technological and administrative superiority of the Romans (who then improved roads, water supply and sanitation). The Romans were in turn overwhelmed as an over-extended empire fell apart – and so on, through all the cycles of warfare, colonialism and system failure that have delivered the west to where we are. With hindsight it is easy to see the innovations of technology, warfare, public health and bureaucracy that enabled conquest and new empires as 'development' and 'progress'. The underlying cultures – the myths, religions and popular cultures – are less obviously 'progressive'. For instance, the ideas the ancient Greeks and Romans had about fate and destiny still survive in modern times – in and through all religions, and in and through popular cultures that always retained and cultivated earlier superstitions, and a strong sense of fate and destiny. [22]

As mythologists point out, ancient myths and legends incorporate cyclical thinking. The cycle of life, death and rebirth is a recurrent theme in all myths; all nature (and time) is cyclic. This is quite different to the idea of 'progress' and the endlessly forward movement of time. Modern capitalism has made a fetish of 'the new' and, so far, the ideas of endless growth and development are axiomatic in modern economics, many sciences and technologies, and even in the arts humanities and social sciences. Critically, the idea of natural limits has been avoided in all things 'modern'.

Clive Hamilton's fatalism, however, never rises too far above the 'tragedy' of contemporary capitalism; nor is he a revolutionary – indeed, the myths and legends of the ancient Greeks do not inspire many leftists. Nor does he see a way forward in contemporary radical politics. In that respect he is more pessimistic than most futurologists.

JUST CARRY ON,
AND BE SENSIBLE

There is little disagreement among historians and sociologists about substantive developments in the emergence of 'modern' western societies. The institutionalisation of science, medicine and law, changes in the political role of the church, the rise of secular reason and professional 'classes', technological change, an industrial revolution, the gaining of political rights for workers, the rise of trade unions, the gaining of rights for women and slaves, and the rise of secular liberal democracies are all widely acknowledged as important developments in the social fabric, often achieved at great human costs. The projects of colonialism on the other hand are generally agreed to have been highly problematic – for reasons of war, domination, exploitation, injustice, violence and cruelty.

Agreement about the necessity of progress is widely implicit in western culture today – for instance, where there are major philosophical disagreements – as, for example between accounts from the left and from conservatives – the disagreements are not so much about the broad achievements, but more about 'the system' that gave rise to them (capitalism), and the quality of 'the West' and global capitalism in contemporary times.

For example, in Niall Ferguson's account of the 'civilization' of the West, competition, science, property rights, medicine, consumer society and the work ethic are highlighted as 'killer apps'. Most left critics would hotly contest the greatness of property rights, competition and 'the work ethic' *per se*, even though these developments have been (and continue to be) main means in the successes of capitalist enterprises. Many of these critics would also point out that the roles of women, children and ethnic 'minorities' are usually airbrushed in conservative and liberal historical accounts – the 'individual' assumed (and its feelings, perspective, rights, reasoning and sensibilities) is usually a heterosexual, white, European, adult male.

These ideological differences lead to very different accounts of ecological decline: on the left, capitalism is seen as the root cause; on the right, ecological decline is rarely analysed in any depth, but when conservative politicians do address the subject they have tended to either deny the phenomena as real, or assert that everything can be explained as natural variations, or natural cycles. Right wing explanations of social and cultural 'decline' have conventionally relied upon the loss of 'traditions' – such as observance of 'correct' religion, or acknowledgement of the cultural and physical supremacy of particular races. Understandably, it is hard to persuasively connect ecological decline with those ideas, but we can be sure such efforts will be made in the future.

Generally, conservatives appear more interested in tradition and order than in progress, *per se*. Progress and 'progressive' attitudes, however, are not unambiguously positive as a way forward. This will be discussed at greater length with respect to the history of science in Chapter 5, but there are other examples. The human rights and freedoms that are emblematic of modernity and progress, for instance, cannot be understood as 'absolute', or without intrinsic conflicts and tensions. Freedom of expression, or 'the right' to free expression, can allow race hatred, or be defamatory. Less obviously perhaps, human freedoms to consume, pollute and decimate ecosystems are clearly not in the best interests of economic or ecological sustainability. Some constraints on human freedoms are obviously necessary. It is the way these constraints are theorised, and realised, that separates different political and philosophical positions, not so much the idea of constraints, *per se*. This extends to the 'natural' limits that were raised in the first Club of Rome report, and that are problematized by the 'endless growth' of economies and their material expression.

Nonetheless, our habits and traditions are a common heritage, whatever our attitudes to them may be. It is commonly assumed that much wisdom is sedimented in 'old ways' of doing things – older people, old achievements, old records and old wars are often ritualised and afforded reverence. Indeed, everything that is 'new' incorporates the past. Language, emotions, habits and patterns of thought in individuals and groups express the past as much as they might look to the future. Many traditional ideas and practices remain in all contemporary cultures – and are celebrated in conservative politics.

From an ecological perspective, some old habits have become very problematic: inflexible dietary practices, unsanitary waste disposal, the use of fossil fuels for energy production, and in general, the casual (and determined) pollution of air, water, and land, create problems for us all. These are not the traditions conservatives have in mind. Yet we might wonder what ecological wisdom there is in some of humanity's oldest traditions and values – for instance, whether traditional practices and values have some positive potential in constraining freedoms, or natural human inclinations towards self-indulgence and hedonism?

It would appear that some of the strength and persuasive power of professions comes from regard for social practices and values that have stood the test of time. The best example might be the traditions of the law that bestow rights and freedoms on the individual, in the context of countervailing rights of others. Other conservative favourite institutions, such as family and church, seem difficult to comprehend as positive ecological forces. Nonetheless, before dismissing tradition and ritual as unworkable, reactionary, or just a recipe for the intensification of class warfare, it might be prudent to, at least, consider some of the ideas that have been recently proposed as a 'conservative' approach to environmentalism. However, as mentioned, it is rare for conservatives to address the subject, and even rarer for them to write reasoned treatises. It cannot be surprising that the ecological potentials of conservatism are not well known.

Roger Scruton, the British conservative philosopher, is puzzled:

> There is no political cause more amenable to the conservative vision than that of the environment. For it touches on the three foundational ideas of our movement: trans-generational loyalty, the priority of the local and the search for home. Conservatives resonate to Burke's view of society, as a partnership between the living, the unborn and the dead; they believe in civil association between neighbours rather than intervention by the state; and they accept that the most important thing the living can do is to settle down, to make a home for themselves, and to pass that home to their children.

Oikophilia, the love of home, lends itself to the environmental cause, and it is astonishing that the Conservative Party has
not seized hold of that cause as its own. . .

The sad thing is that the Conservative Party has said so little
to clarify what is at stake. Why do those old-fashioned words
like trust, settlement, beauty and home so seldom pass the
lips of those who are now, nominally at least, in charge?
And why is the agenda still set by those for whom climate
change, renewable energy and global warming define the
problem, and for whom the favoured solution involves the
total destruction of the things we love?[23]

'The things we love' (including loyalty, home, family, the Church and
God) are organically part of the foundational ideas of the conservative
movement – as defined by Scruton and other conservatives. This love is
only accidentally about the environment – which may explain why his
environmental views have not excited too much support, even among
fellow conservatives. His views are still worth inspecting, not least because
they so clearly expose reasons why being excessively human-centred is
increasingly problematic.

In his book *Green Philosophy,* Scruton is usefully programmatic. He
outlines a broad conservative approach to environmental politics –
which involves the interplay of market economies, citizens who care
for the environment, the traditions of family and local communities, the
rule of law, and all the other institutions of modern societies, including
publicly funded science, industry, and new technology.

The North American Professor of Law, Jonathan Adler, also attempts
to be programmatic in his criticisms of past conservative attitudes to
environmentalism. His five point program is very similar to Scruton's
approach:

1.   'First do no harm';

2.   'Green' through growth;

3.   Promote and protect private property;

4.   Make the polluter pay;

5.   Decentralise decision-making.[24]

Modern conservatives do struggle with economics. There are just too many competing variables: traditional establishments and institutions, modern secular democracies, large corporations, 'nouveau riche' middle classes, survival-oriented small and medium sized businesses, and unionised working classes make a volatile mix not particularly united by respect for aristocrats, priests, theologians or aesthetically oriented philosophers (like Scruton). How to minimise government intervention, while preserving traditions, does not translate easily into economic policy – or environmentalism as found in most contemporary environmental organisations, and Green political parties.

Conservatism is rooted in 'old-fashioned' ideas. Yet the world has dramatically changed over the last few centuries. Societies and cultures have changed, and ecological limits have intruded into all aspects of human activity, whether or not humans are conscious of the fact. The world has become complex and fragile; all sectors of societies (and economies) are more closely bound by globalisation than even Marx could have appreciated.

It is not just conservative ideologies and governments that struggle to comprehend a changed world. No governments have been able to manage the diametric opposition between growing economies and the declining ecologies that support this growth. Humanity is becoming 'the problem' and this is a challenge no ideology so far has been able to countenance.

The 'conservative' and 'neo-conservative' governments led by John Howard, Margaret Thatcher, Ronald Regan and two generations of Bushes – to pick five prominent examples – were divorced from the basic problem of growth versus the environment. They demonstrated that when modern societies allow market forces to be dictated by large corporations, the inevitable outcome is a very high rate of environmental devastation – environmental regulations and measures that might protect the environment are regarded as 'external' costs to be minimised and 'collateral damage' best 'swept under the carpet'. At the same time the costs of wages and human welfare were also regarded as costs to be minimised – resulting in record profits for corporations and very dissatisfied workforces. These styles of government were eventually voted down, but not replaced by governments with an inclination to solve the basic contradictions of economic growth and ecological decline.

While it has been argued that all ecologies function best when left alone (like 'free markets'), this is only an optimal solution when there is species diversity and ecosystem complexity. When population overshoot has occurred – in the case of humanity on Earth – and one looks to avoid the excesses of a population crash (as normally happens in free range ecologies) then complex management strategies have to be initiated. This is the reality we face on Earth today. Further, if governments do not heavily regulate the 'business as usual' approach of mining and energy generating industries, for example, there can be little doubt that the environmental damage that will continue to occur will be utterly irreversible. The recent poor responses of Union Carbide, Exxon, Shell, BP, and Tepco, to the creation and management of environmental disasters illustrate this point eloquently.[25]

Certainly, in all those cases new balances have been struck, and markets have continued to operate – but life in all the environments affected by those environmental disasters has continued in very diminished ways. At the moment these are isolated disasters, but we should be very concerned. The sum total of such continuing disasters could add up to something far bigger than the individual parts.

The efforts of large energy corporations to maximise their own freedom to act in remote and often pristine environments – with minimal government regulation – is at the centre of the life and death struggle green organisations around the world have with rapacious large corporations and ecologically destructive 'free markets'. For conservatives the main 'new' issue must be for how long the 'freedom' to create economic wealth in relatively 'free' markets can continue to cause extensive environmental damage..

Scruton's ideological approach seems the epitome of philosophical reason, and there is no doubt that he is lucid in the development of many of his arguments. And there is certainly something proto-typically ecological in conservative lines of argument – after all, survival of the fittest, free markets, and minimal government intervention do favour the strong and ruthless. Yet, in a rather extended book, after a very long and careful review of the silliness of most of the beliefs of radical activists, Scruton's best suggestion is that we all should practice care for our home (or 'oikophililia'). Among other things this requires 'actively handing on to the next generation all that we have by way of knowledge and competence, and imbuing our successors with a spirit of stewardship that we also, in our own actions, display.'[26]

As a serious program of thought and action Scruton's book is minimalist. We should do a lot of things, but we don't – and the worry is that we won't. That situation deserves better analysis. There is something quite chilling in the relaxed attitude that comes from his clear thinking. Perhaps the youthful recipients of our best efforts won't get it either (that is, love for the old ways, and personal responsibility for stewardship of the commons). Maybe they've already been rewired into the new natural order of cyberspace.

The future prospect of capitalist economies working within naturally defined limits – to growth, to pollution, to population sizes – will provide great challenges to contemporary conservative (and liberal) thought. It is hard to imagine that any of those limits will naturally emerge from free markets under the minimal constraints of small governments.

DOING SOMETHING

Sifting through the work of professional scientific and popular writers who confront our ecological crisis revealed at least four broad avenues of approach. The first two avenues arose together in recent history as extremes in an ecologically focussed and oppositional 'green' social movement – discussed at greater length in the Chapters 7 and 8. The one extreme emphasised lifestyle change as the basis for sustainability; the other emphasised radical political action. The third line of approach arose later, over time, as a professional reorganisation of many sciences in response to perceptions of an ecological 'crisis'. From the mid-1980s there has been a slowly increasing 'wave of association' in university systems as individuals and small groups were encouraged to form larger research groups and organisations and to also function in larger Schools and Faculties. This aggregation stimulated the emergence of the new disciplines of environmental science, ecology and social ecology, inter-disciplinary environmental studies, and research centres, and smaller groups devoted to climate change and other ecological 'hot topics'. As advocates of responsible change, this third line of development is typified by scientific ecologists – who, as a professional group, tend to recom-mend scientific and technological solutions, and reform of agricultural and industrial practices.[27]

Most contemporary popular 'experts' synthesise two of these three types of action into an ecological 'fourth way' – they do not generally endorse radical political activism, and avoid 'hard left' activism. That is reflected in the positions expressed by those reviewed here, and in the positions of many commentators referred to in later chapters – Chapter 5 goes on to introduce two scientists who have become perhaps the most famous ecological public intellectuals: David Suzuki and Davis Attenborough. In all these cases, it is noteworthy that most ecological synthesisers who are also public broadcasters, 'public intellectuals', and journalists inevitably fall short of recommending individuals take radical action that might change consumption habits and the practices of 'big' agriculture and industry – even though, in various ways, they all demon-strate some loss of faith in the ability of current political structures to bring about change. Al Gore, for example, writes and talks about the natural emergence of new structures, and processes, which might save the show (and preserve the American way). He, along with those other public broadcasters, is still a strong voice for change. That lack of overt 'public politics' might appear puzzling, but we cannot expect them to advocate the destruction of the very systems that allow them to speak. As broadcasters they are voices, and leaders, but not substitutes for bigger political processes.

For various reasons there is a limited range of views presented in mainstream publishing about 'ecological crisis'. Over the last couple of decades, for the most part, those perspectives that are critical of indus-try, large agriculture and governments, are 'left of centre'. Writers and commentators further to the right, such as Roger Scruton, are rare

– undoubtedly being preoccupied with negating the radical views of 'greenies', but reluctant to engage publicly with such divisive issues. There is, however, a steady increase in 'technophilic' commentary that looks forward to an Anthropocene epoch – in which humanity will have radically transformed Earth's eco-systems.[28]

However, some audiences and programming are becoming more discriminating about technological solutions. Stephen Hawking's enthusiasm for transformative scientific and technological innovation, for instance, is noticeably qualified by ecological concerns. His recent television series 'Brave New World' (Channel 4, 2014) combines human and ecological concerns in a way that almost makes the future seem positively alluring.

Most 'ecological crisis' literature does not endorse the environmental policies of major parties anywhere. Generally, critics have understood that party politics may be part of the problem, for all the reasons that will be discussed in later chapters – most basically, major parties have to be perceived as effective economic managers, and this, to date, has ruled out changes that would reduce the profitability of large corporations and whole sectors of industry. [29]

Ecological crisis writers are often either explicitly, or implicitly, supportive of Green parties. David Suzuki, for example, has often endorsed Green parties as seriously progressive and sees political leadership as a major issue. On the other hand, Clive Hamilton, in Australia, has in the past personally dis-endorsed his local Green parties and recommended the formation of a new political party to move on from the failure of social democrats and the left to make much of a difference. 'Downshifting', and the politics of wellbeing, seems the most promising avenue of change in his analyses. Currently Green parties do not appear on his political agenda, probably because of a perception of them as overly ideological and narrow in appeal.[30]

WHAT CAN BE DONE?

'Going forward' is a reassuring phrase. It lacks the momentum and confidence of 'progress', but is sufficiently optimistic to satisfy most 'spin doctors'. When the forward gaze of public scientists and other futurologists expresses questionable optimism, 'going forward' is much easier to say. Hopefully, all professionals will eventually go forward, leaving unbounded progress behind as a relic of outmoded optimism.

If that is to occur, progress will have to incorporate limits – and 'going forward' will take bearings from sustainability. 'Growth' under such circumstances might become a more abstractly measured phenomenon: first relating to parameters of a 'steady state', and eventually becoming an idea associated with a less enlightened time. That would require the discovery that economies and ecologies were only able to be finite.

Today such dreams take shape as a critique of a way of life that has become separated from limits to growth – and more fundamentally separated from organic connection to other life forms and their ecologies. Undoubtedly analysis that has been critical of modernity and capitalism has paved the way for sober reflection, but as this book argues, much more in the way of radical critique is required. The best way forward will be to 're-centre' our understanding of what it is to be human as an Earth-centred understanding – or as later chapters put it, an eco-centric view is required. This is a view that involves limits.

If the ultimate limit, global catastrophe, is too challenging for everyday conversation, the general idea of 'limits' should be easier. Anybody who was taught introductory calculus will remember that the mathematical idea of a *limit* requires an exercise of imagination to think of numbers and axes that are infinitely large and long, and distances that are infinitely small. At the same time, *limits* enabled smooth curves to be drawn and wonderful shapes and surfaces to be conceptualised. By extension, limits have come to define boundaries for the behaviour of mathematical and mechanical systems – even 'chaos mathematics' has its limits.

These are relatively abstract and psychologically comfortable ideas. When translated to life, environments and ecological systems the idea of limits becomes much more threatening to the whole edifice of global consumption – and conventional ideas of growth, progress and professional optimism. It is no wonder that the 'Club of Rome' has been demonised for its bravery in publishing and pursuing *The Limits to Growth* in 1972. It is still asserted that those researchers in that club are really a secret diabolic cabal dedicated to the destruction of the West. It is time to try again: there are limits to growth, and they will be discussed in all the material that follows in this book.

Forward movement can be a deceptive sensation. Einstein revolutionised physics with the idea that movement in any frame of reference can always be considered in a relative way. Backward motion in a forward moving train can be measured either in the train or outside the train – the results depend on the choice of a particular frame of reference. Analogously, forward motion for an economist can be a retrograde step for an ecologist or an environmentalist. The idea of limits for living systems challenges all the old frames of reference. 'Progress', 'professional optimism' and even 'going forward' are now all increasingly problematic ideas in any ecological frame of reference.

With or without Green politics, all serious ecological commentators agree about the importance of personal action, and that we, 'the public', should look more closely at our consumer habits and consumption patterns. Market economies depend on the purchase of goods and services. We can individually make choices that affect the supply side – food, energy consumption, waste disposal and all the other ingredients of life styles are negotiable. About that, all sides of politics now furiously agree. In that respect the early examples set by alternative life-stylers and hippies have been more successfully mainstreamed than the 'radical' politics of Green parties.

Reason and argument can lead us to recognise the inevitability of ecological decline, but accepting the inevitable and going on from there is not simply a matter of applying further reason. We can have some solace in the fact that science, secular reason, and the optimism of professionals are still being recruited to the task of saving a viable global habitat. But this is not sufficient. Political will, rising from a popular demand for change, remains absolutely necessary – and in the West we have the advantage of democratic institutions of governance, imperfect as they may be.

In the changing fortunes of nations and empires, individuals have always had limited choices in what they could do, and how they might best survive. Today the stakes are higher, and the need for citizens to become more engaged with ecological and environmental issues has never been greater. It also happens that citizens in democratic societies have never before been so empowered by new communication technology and political freedoms — such as free speech, and the right to organise and protest. Science, technology and cultural analysis have never had such active potentials to engage with the intellectual and political challenges that confront humanity. We may not be able to predict what the next 'level', 'stage' or 'phase' of development will be, but it may be helpful that optimism can come so readily to many. More important though, and probably as never before, it is time for humanity to take a collective deep breath.

> We are but a small, shining cog in the big wheel of life on Earth. And as shining and fascinating as we are, we need the humility to recognise that fact, because in the end, the Earth doesn't need us.
>
> But we certainly need it.
> *David Suzuki* [31]

CHAPTER

4

PROFESSIONAL OPTIMISM

The trouble with the world is that the
stupid are cocksure
and the intelligent are full of doubt.

Bertrand Russell

Despair would seem a rational response in a world without hope. One would anticipate that the apparently hopeless ecological situation we are facing would generate far more despair than we currently see. Yet, in a world full of hope there is little room for despair – and certainly, the orientation of public life in many countries is well away from despair.

Hope arises spontaneously as a response to all manner of challenges. Hope enables us to start a new day with optimism and good cheer. It may not matter what the object of hope is – hope just needs to be there. And optimism can sustain all hopes. These are our common experiences, and the threads that weave through most novels and biographies.

This chapter was first intended to be a discussion of the ways despair and related emotions are produced and manipulated. What quickly emerged in the research and writing of the chapter was that despair is usually avoided as a topic of conversation because it produces such unsettling emotions. Optimism is an antidote, and this is the feeling that is most easily injected into the texts, narratives and conversations that support life, society and culture. Evidence of this will be produced from some of the narratives and pronouncements of individuals who have had significant public impact on the issues of ecological decline and climate change. Optimism, and its normalisation in social institutions, quickly became important in understanding both denial and the resilience of modern institutions.

Because optimism, hope, and despair, can be driving motivational forces common to us all, it is important to recognise that there are many social and cultural processes that produce and control these feelings. All forms of training and 'discipline' produce patterns of thought, emotion, and behaviour. Family life, school, work, sport, recreation, and peer groups all provide individuals with training and education; beliefs, values, and 'appropriate behaviours' are acquired, in various ways, over a lifetime. Through these processes we learn a repertoire of roles and come to identify with various attributes of gender, nation, age and religion – among other defining cultural traits. In short, we are all 'socialised' and learn what it means to be 'human' and a member of a particular culture. Many of these patterns are relevant to understanding why and how humanity has arrived at a point of ecological crisis; very often, our relationship to other life forms is the most casual and accidental process in all these different kinds of socialisation.

Hope and optimism are basic behavioural 'tools' in all processes of socialisation, ensuring the general success, pleasures, possibilities, and endurance, of socialising agencies. Hope and optimism are, therefore, apparently 'natural attitudes' to find in professional training processes. However, when these attitudes are inappropriate they can deflect attention away from problems – and when these problems are as dire as climate change and ecological collapse, hope and optimism become particularly problematic. The compulsive optimism of professional forecasters is a focus of this chapter.

There are other reasons why optimism is such an important feeling and general orientation. Growing economies depend on optimism: consumer confidence depends on business having optimistic forward outlooks – and vice versa. Politicians, educators, advertisers, and all those trying to sell a message, benefit from positive attitudes. Optimism is the necessary default position for individuals and organisations. Optimism would appear to be in the genes of modern western economies and societies.

For good reasons then, the more extended topic of the chapter became optimism and its institutionalisation in the most secure and reliable parts of society and culture, the professions – and the way optimism may also be disabling effective action in professionalised organisations and cultures.

Communication and semantics are important to any investigation and analysis. Here the concept of 'institution' has been introduced as a way of referring to some of the big social and cultural patterns that create our realities and experiences. Politics, the law, religion, education, health, and even families, are today commonly called institutions – although the family is not a public institution based on paid occupations and professionalization like other institutions dealt with in this chapter.[1]

These 'parts' of modern societies have long traditions and bodies of specialist knowledge that give them particular weight or 'status'. The 'peak' occupations that constitute them, and represent them, are usually referred to as 'professions', but really there are many other jobs that help support institutions. Today many established occupations refer to themselves as 'professions' offering professional services provided by professionals – the word inspires confidence.

This confidence is reflected in the evolution of language used to describe a new occupational stratum of 'professionals' that has steadily emerged over the last several centuries – roughly coincident with the emergence of 'universities' as providers of specialised education for future professionals. Over time universities developed *disciplines* housed in faculties, schools and departments to provide specialist education – first for lawyers, doctors and teachers of the arts and humanities, then for scientists, engineers, architects, and more recently for specialists in the 'social sciences' – such as economists, geographers and sociologists – and many

other 'new' specialist occupations including business studies, accountancy, nursing, information technology, journalism, music and art.[2]

In the process of 'professionalisation' *masters* and *apprentices* became
supplemented with *experts, expertise, students, cadets, boffins, professors and
doctors.* *Guilds* ceased to monopolise highly skilled occupations (many
became *trades*). *Institutes* emerged from the shadows of more august references to the institutions of church, state and family. The title *Institute*
is still used to describe particular organisations with professional or
semi-professional claims – for example, the 'Institute of Architects', and
the now antiquated 'Mechanics Institutes', and 'Institutions of Arts and
Sciences'.

With the help of sociologists, the word *institute* has been reassert-
ed with a new theoretical weight. In an interesting twist, the word has
been expanded slightly to refer to more than the clubs and societies of
increasingly confident 'professional classes'. To sociologists, *an institution*
now also refers to a more abstract notion – established *patterns* of thought
and action. These could be the family, gender, the law, education, health,
or almost any other social and cultural formation, including optimism.
Institutionalisation is, then, a shorthand way of referring to all the processes involved in the forming of such patterns.

Institutions survive because they have the magical effect of resisting
change. Yet institutions can at the same time preserve outmoded traditions. Indeed, one of the main reasons sociology became such a popular
discipline in the cause of intellectual radicalisation in post-1960s western societies and culture, was because of the critical insights sociologists
were able offer about many institutions. Traditionally based institutions
of family, religion, education, health, and government were increasingly
described by them in terms of inequalities and injustices due to social
class, gender, race, and ethnicity. These new perspectives became part of
the cultures of 'new social movements' and social commentary that was
able to be much more critical of the social status quo. Post-1960s radicalisation extended well beyond conventional social institutions – the
relationship of humanity to the whole of nature (that is, 'the cosmos')
was also part of a cultural revolution that questioned all established order.

Nonetheless, this chapter attempts to be upbeat about the enabling and progressive potentials of the professions. It is the very optimism of all the professions (and institutions) that has provided a starting point for an analysis that concludes with a 'newer', greener political and philosophical position. This position will be cast as 'progressive', however, the weight and inertia of professions and professional organisations are not automatically 'progressive'. Not only sociologists, but any critic of traditions and 'establishment' values would point out that the freedoms and opportunities we all commonly enjoy in the west have been gained despite opposition from church, state, family and all hierarchical and patriarchal institutional traditions.

It is important to recognise the enabling role that social institutions, and the professionals who define them, can play in mitigating climate change - and the other components of the big three: over-population and economic growth. The specialised knowledge that can affect these cultural gridlocks is controlled by professionals and related institutional practises. At this stage of our planetary ecological crisis it is quite counter-productive to view social institutions as only counter-revolutionary, or stiflingly conservative. In later chapters an argument about the need for a 'radical centre' will be explored. Optimistic, pessimistic or ambivalent, professional knowledge is one of the keys to a happier future.

It is also important to recognise the inevitable emergence of new intellectual and emotional habits. Climate change denial is one such new 'institution'. More science and greener political analysis is the pathway that will be promoted to deal with climate change denial and the interconnected tangle of 'the big three'.

Whether optimism can be described as an emotion, attitude, or feeling may worry professional psychologists; I have opted for optimism being an 'attitude' that has become institutionalised in the texts and activities of professions. Optimism and its opposite, pessimism, are two of the most basic attitudes acknowledged by psychologists, social psychologists and philosophers. By consensus, optimism functions as a way of sustaining hope.

All terms that refer to 'inner states' are ultimately difficult to define because they are 'subjective' and therefore hard to measure 'exactly'. Thinking, feeling, emoting and having attitudes are, therefore, hard to define in ways that can satisfy all different professions with a special interest in such ideas and states of being. Therefore, I have opted for a dictionary definition for attitude as being 'a settled way of thinking or feeling about something'.[3]

One of the major points I wish to make in emphasising that inner states and feelings are produced and sustained in social processes is that the conventional idea of institutions being 'patterns of thought and action' misses the way that feelings and emotions are part of, if not the major 'victim' of, any process of institutionalisation. In modern societies, one of the major 'disconnects' that so readily permits the destruction of non-human worlds derives from learned difficulties humans have with 'feeling into' or 'empathising with' non-human realities. This is not simply about the lack of emotional 'connection'; there is the question of how this disconnect is socially and culturally sustained. This requires a multi-disciplinary approach to the institutionalisation of human *feeling*.[4]

PROFESSIONS

The professions are synonymous with 'modern' societies – and evolved from skilled activities that were important in all ancient societies. The oldest professions emerged from crafts and guilds that were able to exercise some levels of control over occupational recruitment, training and practice. Lawyers, herbalists, doctors, teachers, builders and various crafts persons, and other skilled workers, gradually attained levels of occupational autonomy that facilitated the eventual rise of the 'middle classes' and the development of market economies. These changes required new intellectual freedoms. By the eighteenth century in Europe what some social philosophers have referred to as the 'project of enlightenment' was occurring. This involved the 'enlightenment' of secular reason and an increasing commitment to social justice; increased levels of intellectual freedom became socially acceptable and transformative of major institutions including the law, government and banking. By the nineteenth century the idea of 'progress' began to emerge as a scientific and philosophical concept. These changes also encouraged scientific research and the eventual professionalization of scientists – however, only by the late nineteenth century was science becoming an occupation with discipline based professional associations and paying clients.

Arguably, this project of enlightenment is the beginning of western modernity and the philosophical foundation of all modern professions. The separation of church and state and the 'scientific revolution' in sixteenth century Europe are other key historical developments in a complex process. Modernity and the professions have been a long time in the making. [5]

Today the idea of progress is the most easily contestable component of modernity – but this tends not to worry many professionals. Their training and commitment requires and delivers positivity – this is the bankable public face of all the professions. Unsurprisingly perhaps, most professional training is not highly 'philosophical' or historically informed; nor is it environmentally or ecologically involved. Professionals most need to be pragmatic and able to engage with the specialised needs of their professions. Any legitimation or promotion that professionals may have to engage does therefore rely on some ideals of social progress which are implicit – it is nonetheless widely understood that social progress is perhaps the highest secular goal of professions, loosely understood as 'doing good' while 'moving forward' in other ways.

The idea that 'progress' in society and culture is straightforward, or automatic, cannot be assumed. The great cultural contribution of 'new social movements' in the western post-sixties era was an increasingly common knowledge that history is about continual warfare, inequality, and injustice – all concurrent, and in tension with other more progressive developments (such as technological innovation, organisational support, organisational and institutional accountability, and perhaps even 'nation building'). [6]

Of all the occupations in any society, the professions are an important sub-set. Professionals are normally highly trained to be competent problem solvers in a range of fields that provide essential services to industry, commerce, governance and many other fields of activity.

Professions can be distinguished from any other job or occupation by virtue of lengthy training process that occur in organisations providing tertiary education, and by their established social worth. [7]

We may confidently assume that there will continue to be a combination of *professional* scientists, technologists, economists, forecasters,
politicians and administrators at the forefront of climate change mitigation and global ecological repair and maintenance. This is a very good
reason to look more closely at the general 'tone' of professional discourse
– because we should wonder whether the enthusiasm, optimism and
other feelings that are systematically produced in professionals might
have unanticipated and, perhaps, undesirable consequences. For instance,
apart from 'simple' conflicts of interest, it seems most important to be
wary of professional discourse becoming 'greenwashed' by optimism –
this particular concern is a recurrent theme in chapters that follow.

As already suggested, the most basic elements in 'the tone' of all professional discourse are ideas about progress 'doing good', objectivity, and
optimism – these are the philosophical elements that inspire confidence
in clients and the good behaviour of professionals. These elements are
often explicit in the codes of ethics upheld by professional associations:
all emphasise service and moral behaviour – professionals should be
good citizens as well as competent. [8]

Doing 'good' is of course socially defined, and it would be naïve in
the extreme to suppose that, in practice, professionals (and professionalism) are entirely objective or 'value neutral' – even if we assume that
all problem solving is best served by 'objectivity'. It is noteworthy that
all occupations have a 'promotional' side to their activities – which is
important for success in competitive market places, recruitment, identity
formation and maintenance over careers that may be very long.

Underlying these moral and ethical undertakings, however, are more
fundamental 'epistemic' attitudes that follow from the problem solving methodologies employed in the disciplines that provide knowledge
and technical skills for their practitioners. With the exception of the
clergy, this boils down to a commitment to 'objectivity', 'value neutrality' and other ideals inspired by science and art – such as 'universalism'
in the case of scientifically based professions, the goal of healing in the
case of medicine, or aesthetic considerations in the case of architecture. It might appear that professionals ought be, at times, conflicted by
the different priorities that such a complex mix of ideals and standards
demand. Economists, for example, might be conflicted by the competing

demands of maximising the profitability of an organisation, obeying the law, serving the community and protecting the environment. All professionals juggle most of these different demands with strategies that evolve with experience. For any conundrum, however, optimism is a particularly winning attitude.

The addition of an ecological crisis makes any lingering thoughts about the inevitability and linearity of progress even less persuasive. Indeed, what this chapter will celebrate as the triumph of science in the west can, hopefully, be read in a more nuanced way. Although science, and scientists are a major source of hope in this new age of ecological decline, whatever success can be discerned in the prosperity, institutional stability, and creative vitality of the west is now over-shadowed by 'our' failure to make adequate plans for ecological decline, and most likely the social and cultural decline that will follow. This is not the view of most professionals who are public intellectuals, or published commentators – some of whom are reviewed below in this, and following chapters. Most are optimistic. Public scientists are often the most optimistic because their belief in reason and scientific method is pretty much absolute (despite other religious beliefs they may have). They also tend to avoid being seen as political in any overly demonstrative way.

PROFESSIONAL OPTIMISM

The optimism that is such a defining attitude of professionals and professional behaviour derives largely from competence – from both success in practice, and public perceptions of competence. Occupations that maintain the smooth functioning of societies are widely perceived to be important, and a professional's cognitive orientation of problem solving is widely respected. Ethical standards that protect rights of clients and the autonomy of professionals also provide security to professional occupations – normally, professionals have the protection of the law and the positive estimation of their clients. Further, the activities of professionals contribute to general economic growth and the individual wellbeing of their clients. These are all established and, usually, comfortable arrangements. The main source of disquiet for professionals comes from economic and reputational failure in market places. However, unhappiness about the environmental impacts of professions is not, so far, a major concern for established professionals, or professional associations.

This is evident in codes of conduct and ethical standards presented in tertiary training, in the articles of professional associations, and in the attitudes and behaviours of practising professionals. For doctors, architects, lawyers, engineers and scientists whose education and professional accreditation was completed in Australia before about 1990, care for the environment (including ecological awareness) was treated as *external* to the profession – insofar as it was the responsibility of *others* (government agencies, environmentalists and Green parties) to actively care for the environment. Individual professionals might pursue their own religions or political agendas (so long as these are not in conflict with professional expectations), but environmental concern was universally understood to be a *private* matter. After that date, long established professional associations became more concerned about environmental and ecological decline but, with the exception of architects, still operated with traditional assumptions about their designated roles – care for the environment was still *extra-curricula*. However, in a slowly evolving division of specialist expertise such traditionalists could now assume that there were *others* (such as environmental scientists and engineers) whose job it was to care for the environment and enforce environmental legislation.

Environmentally and ecologically focused professionals may be an exception to this rule – but this does not extend to the vast majority of other professionals who, in their work as professionals, are not obliged to take an ecologically pro-active stance. Some professionals might well object that they 'really are' concerned about ecological matters – which is undoubtedly true. What this exposes is the very real difference between 'public' and 'private' spheres of individual behaviour. Generally, professional behaviour can be classified as being in the public domain – much the same as all occupational behaviour. It is the behaviour of individuals *as professionals* that is the focus of this chapter – along with other patterns in collective thought and behaviour identified as 'institutions'. In the end, it is the public face of individuals and organisations that can be the most legitimate focus of organised politics and the law. What individuals do in 'their own time' is hugely important to the success or failure of political parties, social movements and global ecology, but it is what individuals are obliged to do as part of their work that will continue to have large negative ecological impacts. This is another reason to look more closely at professional cultures.

Nor do any personal environmental and ecological concerns appear to negate the positive and optimistic outlook of most professionals. This derives from longer and deeper cultural traditions. In particular, the cultural inheritance of secular reason, science, the rule of law, and secular liberal democratic institutions of governance provide a very secure foundation from which individual professions in many countries are able to operate as custodians and purveyors of specialist knowledge and developed skills. Established career paths and relatively high levels of remuneration add to the picture. Most fundamentally, professions are at the heart of capitalism. Economics, politics, trade and manufacturing are all professionalised domains. So, too, health and social services are professionalised; and the military. . . and even sport. Success is a common ambition; growth and development are everywhere. It is easy for the professions, and professionals, to be optimistic; in fact optimism is required. Forward movement depends on it.

These social circumstances do not encourage desperation about environmental and ecological 'externalities', or desperation about the apparently intractable contradiction between economic growth and sustainable ecology – which will be dealt with at greater length in Chapter 6. Our highly specialised division of labour focuses on solving definable problems and making a profit within restricted settings. There have been few economic or political incentives for environmental anxiety.

Even when professional biologists become public broadcasters with a popular mandate to talk about the 'big picture', their success has depended on an ability to remain optimistic, or at least 'up-beat' about declining situations. Audiences will listen to programs that make them feel good or confirm their basic prejudices. Bad news is very hard to sell or mount as a platform for advertising.

Optimism exudes from much of the cultural apparatus of contemporary western societies – often characterised as 'modernity'. Although one could suppose that some early modern art, literature and music seem anything but optimistic, there is always a remorseless forward movement implicit. As many commentators have pointed out, capitalism is all about the destruction of the old and the emergence of the new – so much so that novelty and innovation have become a fetish. Among any of the ruins of old buildings, lost jobs and displaced lives created by 'new development', there is not only despair – optimism, hopes and promises are always part of endless narratives of 'progress'.[9]

CRISIS OF INSTITUTIONS?

The proposition that capitalism (and the west) is 'in crisis' has been presented by left activists and theorists since the time of Marx. In this view class conflict and ever increasing economic inequalities constitute an ongoing crisis in all capitalist societies. The only economic beneficiaries of this state of affairs are 'ruling class' capitalists and those in the middle class whose wealth can increase – but really nobody benefits because everybody fails to realise their 'full' (or 'revolutionary') potential. All are 'alienated' except those who understand history and the revolutionary potential of the working class – that is, those radical leftists who constitute the 'vanguard' of the people. The crisis is considered to be political and economic in origin – and all the institutions and occupations that support capitalism (and the west) are supposedly complicit in creating and supporting such a general crisis.[10]

In the general model that inspires modern leftists, all the institutions of state, and allied professions, experience individual crises arising from the contradictions and tensions of the capitalist system. In various ways, all these institutions and organisations are necessarily oppressive, repressive and ideological; they are intrinsically exploitative and de-humanising; they alienate humanity from nature and society; they will be instrumental in the inevitable collapse of 'the system', and be swept aside in revolutionary processes.

Roughly concurrent with the perception of that crisis, the conservative side of politics and society perceived a quite different, but equally world-shaking crisis – the decline of traditional institutions caused by modernity. Industrialisation, scientific and technologically driven 'progress', the empowerment of working people and women, and the rise of mass media and popular cultures were all perceived as having major negative effects on the traditional power and authority of churches and aristocracies in western societies. For conservatives a changing class structure, in conjunction with modernising cultures, represented a crisis of religious faith, a loss of family values, and a general erosion of traditional values.

Neither of these views of 'a crisis' registered a declining global ecology; nature was, until about 1950 (and the increasing stridency of environmentally focussed social movements) simply assumed to be infinite, inexhaustible, God given, and 'there for the taking' by all.

In that broadly critical context the proposition that there is a 'crisis of institutions' is not new or surprising. From the left we have been told that organised politics, the law, the police, religion, and the family, are basically repressive and controlling of society and individuals. From the right, we have been told that loss of respect for the traditions of class, monarchy and religion will cause the breakdown of society. Naturally enough, there has been a steady movement away from the perceived extremes of these views towards more neutral ground in the 'centre'.

The view that capitalism must fail because of its 'internal contradictions' – still prevalent on the academic and political left, deserves particularly close scrutiny because it has become a institution in its own right, obliging generations of students and critical commentators to 'bend the knee' to an official line that is in reality unfounded – capitalism survives as a robust, if flawed, globalised political and economic system. That is an awkward reality for all 'old fashioned' leftists who still take grim pleasure in all signs that 'the system' is in decline. It is also an awkward reality for many generations of students and radical politicians who have been schooled in 'broad left' thought that basically never accepts the existential reality of capitalism 'now and later' – in the sense that capitalism will be the economic system that determines our ecological future in the next few decades.

In a modern and globalised capitalist system science is, nonetheless, a resilient and vitally important part of a secularised 'world view' that is supported by optimistic professionals. This cultural achievement should be celebrated as a relative triumph of 'truth' over superstition, yet it is probably a source of private anxiety for conservatives who believe in the creation story, or other religious myths of origin. Science is also not welcomed by many others whose interests are compromised by 'the truth' – about the health and safety of working people, about climate change, about the degradation of habitats and environments, about the nutritional value of highly processed food, and so on. For those on the left science has been a mixed blessing: in the service of capitalism, science is problematic because it can work against the interests of working classes, women, 'minorities', and all others exploited by capitalists; in the service of 'progressive' state organisations it can be part of technological development and the provision of health and services to all. It all depends on who you are, and where you are.

Neither of these ideological extremes ('left' and 'right') may sound particularly plausible, yet they remain influential in different social circles that are international and connected to organised politics and other professionalised spheres. The narratives of 'the left' are, in comparison to those of 'the right', much better articulated and often persuasive – however, in a world that has become so globalised, and so blighted by the effects of over-development, new forms of social criticism that are much 'greener' need to evolve if we are to have a future rich in opportunity. Later chapters that are focused on political processes give a more detailed account of the effects of contemporary left political thinking on the formation of Green parties in Australia and the need to abandon 'old left' ideologies in the progress of green politics. The narratives of 'the right', whilst being perennially important, are not given quite the same attention, but they feature strongly in consideration of opposition to science generally, opposition to climate science in particular, and forthcoming analysis of the growth of populations and economies. It should become clear that neither left nor right are sufficiently supportive of science either ideologically or through practical political processes, nor are they able to contribute positively to any ecologically based futures.

This section is an exploration of concerns of the political and academic left that any optimism about the future trajectory of capitalism is unfounded because of a 'crisis of institutions' – in Australia, and elsewhere in the west. Claims of this nature relate particularly to the ideological view that capitalism must inevitably fail because of its internal contradictions – and avoid the point that industrialisation, over-development, and over-population will pose increasingly major threats to human welfare. These pressures, rather than the traditional 'contradictions' (of class warfare and private property) will be the causes of future crises. Not only will economies struggle to deliver growth under such conditions, all our institutions will struggle to build forward looking and optimistic societies. There is, indeed, a crisis developing in the institutions of modern societies as they struggle to deliver sustainable outcomes to societies that are increasingly over-populated, over-developed and polluted. Further, it is unsurprising that, in critical circles that are 'left of centre', it has become unfashionable to reflect positively on the ways that social order and public confidence are generated and supported. Any support for the 'status quo' is seen as the particular concern of political conservatives, 'neo-cons', and all those committed to resisting change.

In general, there has been an almost automatic reflex for left intellectuals and activists to find a crisis in every institution and organisation of capitalist society. These claims have been so insistent that perhaps we should wonder whether there are valid reasons to support the idea of an institutional crisis in Australia. Here the thoughts of a past-leader of the opposition, Mark Latham, will be considered as a starting point for further analysis. In his 'broader' left view of class conflict, the political relevance of a declining working class, and the emergence of a strong 'middle class', to understanding voter behaviour is present, as is the problem of political disengagement by voting populations. Also present is the 'old left' view that there is a crisis in Australia's institutions.

Nonetheless, it is unsettling when public figures as eminent as a past leader of a large political party begins to describe a 'crisis of institutions'. Latham, sensitised by allegations of abuse in the Australian army, State police forces, corporate Australia, trade unions, the Catholic Church and the mass media writes,

Almost without exception, old institutions in society have become more inward looking, more resistant to public scrutiny and accountability . . . These recent controversies have added to a longer-term more disturbing trend in civil society: a loss of connectedness – the social habit of belonging to collective organisations and trusting in other citizens.

Mark Latham is most exercised about 'the changing nature of power and public trust' – and few would argue that professional politicians and all the other professionals he refers to above (senior soldiers and police, business leaders, trade union officials, priests and journalists) have sunk to low levels of social esteem in many countries. He is, nonetheless, still optimistic about the future of 'the people' and 'class struggle' because he detects that

With the rise of mass higher education, the naivety and helplessness of earlier generations has dissipated. In their formal qualifications and knowledge, fewer people feel inferior to the political class. They have the skills and confidence to match it with anyone. In their daily lives, they want to make decisions for themselves, ending their reliance on institutional power . . . the people . . . have moved on to a new world of self-reliance and institutional distrust. [11]

The skills and confidence he refers to do, of course, come about because of the contributions of other institutions and professions. Arguably, a firmer application of existing laws and sanctions through processes like the Independent Commission Against Corruption (at state and federal levels) would help better deal with political corruption – a subject that politicians and ex-politicians like Latham tend to skate around – even though corruption is the main thing that 'the people' object to in their cynicism about organised politics. It should not, therefore, be surprising that membership numbers of political parties are low. Nor should it be surprising that membership of unions is at a low ebb – they too are often perceived as corrupt, and dominated by bullying men.

Latham's main argument about loss of connectedness can be seen as very myopic – politicians and other over-institutionalised professionals tend not to see too far beyond their known worlds. There is much countervailing evidence for the emergence of different forms of connectivity – people are electronically networked, they join sporting clubs, they are audiences, many have a sense of belonging to social movements . . . and they still work, mostly live in families, and recreate with others. Tribalism is still very evident – most basically, everyone still can find 'us' among 'them'. Individuals still construct identities in social processes, no matter how radically different the cultural raw materials are becoming. Social connectedness, indeed 'civil society', still operates within older social structures.

However, in many countries there is a loss of confidence in public institutions that may be a more serious loss of 'connectivity'. There are many contributing causes for this. There is the perception that politicians and senior corporate figures in banking and finance, in the energy and mining sectors, in chemical industries and in other industries that pollute appear to exert strong influence on the political process; the law and politics often seem weak and other institutions – such as religion and education – do not seem capable of reforming a moral compass hijacked by mass media and mass culture (including an uncontrollable Internet). Most institutions are still dominated by men – 'boys clubs' are ever-present obstacles to career success for women, in nearly all occupations.

Despite a long history of concern with many of these, and other issues related to 'the crisis of capitalism' perceived from the 'broad left', the root causes of a global *ecological crisis* have been very neglected. That is, growth economics, over-population and pollution are not widely considered by those on the left to be a symptom (or cause) of institutional failure, crisis, or even weakness, in all, or any, institutions, professions, and other occupations.

It would seem that any new political empowerment of 'the people' observed by Mark Latham needs to better address the social implications around ecological decline and climate change. The loss of connectedness he refers to is more fully what Karl Marx originally referred to in describing the 'alienation' of all people under capitalism – a disconnection from both society *and* nature. Marxism never did overcome its obsession with human society being independent of 'nature', but Latham might find refreshment from a re-reading of the younger Marx; he might develop a greater sympathy for not only the Marxists in Green parties, but for the whole Green project of making society more ecologically sustainable. Certainly, Latham's observation that 'class struggle still exists, not in the workplace, but in popular perception that Australia's political class is undermining the public interest' is intriguing – albeit guaranteed to stimulate contempt from theoreticians of the left. Mark Latham's book (perhaps unintentionally) demonstrates the idea contained in the title: 'the political bubble'.

When a former leader of the Australian Labor Party refers to a 'crisis of institutions' we can assume that he has come from left ideological traditions. However, we can also assume that that leaders of all political parties are embedded in the institutional structures that many on the left (and the 'hard left', in particular) have come to hate, and that those on the right have come to regard as weak and over-liberal. We might also assume that any general crisis that is observed and reported 'from above' will probably be limited in scope and self-serving.

In a long and remorseless critical onslaught from the left, the positive side of the subject of social order has been neglected. However, Australian conservative and liberal commentary has been more reactionary than coherent, and cannot be said to amount to a clear ideological position, other than advocating 'small government' – which usually means a free reign for business interests. It is likely, therefore, that any formulation of a radical middle ground will find itself mostly in public discourse with the left and centre left of politics and philosophical analysis. [12]

Further, if the views of Mark Latham are assessed in that light, and 'the optimism of professionals' considered as a natural consequence of the enduring 'successes' of capitalist societies, there is less reason to insist that our institutional arrangements are a terminal failure.

Nonetheless, if one were able to have followed in the footsteps of the left, since at least the time of Marx, capitalism and the institutions and professions which support modern society (as we find it today in the west) would have been long dismantled in processes aiming at 'flatter' social structures, the redistribution of wealth, social inclusion, and 'the withering away of the state'. At least, that's the 'official' view from the left.

As an alternative path of criticism, the general political, economic and social criticisms that have come from the left – as noted above – largely ignore an ecological crisis that is occurring for reasons other than polit-ical and economic exploitation and social inequality. These social issues may be relevant, but as 'obsessions' of the left they have become prob-lematic in the way they marginalise environmental politics. This building political crisis is the subject of later chapters.

Closer inspection of our institutions also reveals ecological exclusion to be endemic – not that close inspection of any institutions is encour-aged or easily achieved. Mostly, our leading institutions are not obliged to declare a position on subjects as threatening to the whole system as climate change, or social inequality. With the partial exception of science and philosophical critique, our institutions are carefully managed by pro-fessional elites to support what is perceived as the 'status quo'. These management strategies are well served by the legal, financial, occupa-tional and educational autonomy enjoyed by leading institutions and professions.

As a result of this autonomy, general knowledge of institutions and professional cultures is quite superficial. This is to be expected because knowledge of the Westminster system of governance, the banking system, taxation, the legal system, health matters, and climate change, for example, is mediated by professionals who have an interest in restrict-ing information flow to clients and publics – who in turn often do not have the time or interest to known 'the details'. That is the whole point of a division of labour with specialised professions. Such systems are mostly not about the distribution of knowledge; they are generally task oriented. The 'success' of professions also often has the unintended consequence of concealing systemic problems from public view – which coincidentally, makes any claims of 'crisis' harder to sustain.

Well placed as the suspicion that professions cannot be altruistic may be, the one institution and profession that should be distrusted least is science. All optimism about a prosperous and healthy future will come to nought without science. The only fundamental cultural process (that is, institution) that does not back away from the very 'inconvenient truths' of climate change and ecological change remains science and scientists – generally speaking. The deepest levels of optimism require knowledge that is securely founded. This is not to say that science and scientists should be immune from public scrutiny, or that the history of science and its extensions in industry and new technology are necessarily positive. The most general point to be made is that science, economics and politics, are of such importance to our collective wellbeing that they need far more critical scrutiny. The adequacy of these three fields to be custodians of our ecological futures is what is at issue.

Climate change needs to be an area of research concentration among natural scientists – everybody needs to be persuaded by scientific facts. What may be less obvious is the systematic, politically driven, downgrading of scientific research in Australia with particular attention to those fields most likely to provide 'difficult' information about climate change. More broadly, genuine concern for the health of the natural sciences (and indeed most areas of Australian academic life) is largely restricted to scientific communities and some university vice-chancellors. Science has been submerged in the noise of modern societies.

Politics and economics are other spheres that are deeply troubling, for different reasons – and all raise ecological concerns, as discussed at length in following chapters. The reluctance of our leading institutions to play a critical and pro-active role in addressing the problems of climate change and ecological decline is surely indicative of an *impending* crisis in all institutions – notwithstanding the optimistic spin of most professionals.

THE IMPORTANCE OF SCIENCE AND SECULAR REASON

The social and cultural role of science is fundamentally important to any understanding of contemporary institutions. It is particularly disturbing that the general authority of science has been undermined in a decades long assault by extreme religious organisations and by conservative economic and political forces – climate change denial is only the most recent episode in a much longer counter-offensive by those often united forces. This assault on science and scientific reason is the most profound crisis that all institutions, and particularly western institutions, will face in the coming decades.

There are many reasons to be concerned about the undermining of science in contemporary societies. Indeed, science has come to underpin modern societies – because, of all types of knowledge and belief that find expression in the west, science and scientific reason contribute most to the quality of life and freedoms we enjoy. Science and scientific research have contributed mightily to improved standards of living and quality of life around the world, and to intellectual freedoms that many in the western world may take for granted. The material contributions of science are easily demonstrated; the importance of 'scientific reason' may be less widely appreciated. The idea that 'evidence' is fundamentally important to all forms of reason is obvious enough (and helps avoid some of the worst effects of authoritarian rule, generally) but the acceptance that religious authority should be limited in governance and daily life is a particularly important achievement in western societies. It is this 'secularisation of reason' that is so important as the basis for government, and cultural freedom in the west.

Even though contemporary western cultures may often appear anything but reasoned or progressive, their deeper levels of tolerance need to be appreciated positively. It is significant that the apparent chaos and bizarre juxtapositions of advertising, apocalyptic culture, sporting cultures, and all the other weird excesses of mass media cultures, arise from a professionalised division of labour which, generally speaking, is 'scientised' – that is, based on science and permeated with ideas and methods derived from science. This allows the cultural pervasiveness of science to be now largely taken for granted – such that the upfront impacts of media spectacles and the routine demands of daily life do not occur as anything like a series of scientific facts or the outcome of experimentally based knowledge.

The most persuasive argument for the resilience of the cultural authority of science comes from the universally acknowledged successes of modern medicine: almost everyone will take basic advice from a doctor. Science based medicine (and secular reason) is generally the first refuge sought in cases of illness and physical mishap.

It is worth repeating that it is not just science that stands between civilization and superstition and other irrational authoritarianisms. 'Secular reason' is an even more profound and important cultural and social achievement – 'secular reason', as already mentioned, is reason that does not depend on the ultimate authority of God, or gods, for its persuasive power and legitimate authority. Even the banal 'common sense' of Australian everyday life is strongly secular, or non-sectarian – because conversation in any pluralist society requires some relatively neutral, 'common ground'.

As influential as science has become, its success is likely the product of cultural environments where secular reason could allow thought (and experiment) freed from religious constraint. Science does best in tolerant cultures – the historical flowering of science occurred in societies and cultures where the control of priests was either relaxed or avoidable. [13]

Secular reason is most obviously expressed in many modern political systems. Arguably, secularism has been a pre-condition of all successful democracies – but not all secular governments are western democracies. Communist societies such as China and Cuba are strongly secular; military dictatorships are also often secular. The secular governments of the world have a 'separation of powers' in which Churches cannot play a formal role in government. This is a very good way of avoiding rule by popes, priests and untestable private religious revelation. Secular governments do not necessarily dispute religion, they merely disqualify them as political masters.

We might note here that science and scientists have a challenging relationship with religion, since no science depends upon theological assumptions. Individual scientists are not necessarily atheists, but in their work as professional scientists they generally do not express theological arguments.

It is, however, the 'liberal' democratic variety of secularism that provides the main political and cultural context for this book – largely because these political arrangements provide the greatest autonomy and freedom for all the different institutions that are important in the cultivation of 'progressive politics' and eco-active societies, but also in part because the main setting of the analysis of Green politics in the concluding chapters is Australian.

The optimism of professionals springs very largely from the material successes of science and scientific research. The oldest, practically focused professions – medicine, engineering, and science itself, are thoroughly based in, and legitimated by, scientific knowledge and methodology, and all demonstrate secular reason. Architecture is more of a hybrid affair, but its aesthetic concerns are grounded in science and engineering. Education makes science and mathematics a compulsory foundation for the instruction of all children. All the more recent professions – and what established occupation is not today a 'profession' – are at least grounded in secular reason and axioms of basic logic.

The profession of law is a paradigm case that demonstrates the role and importance of secular reason in modern western societies – and where science and reason can be at odds with the traditional legal practices of indigenous cultures, secular reason and science are still active principles in practice. Even the clergy – arguably the oldest profession – has to struggle with Darwin and atheists. Bishops, cardinals, archbishops, and popes, all have to be somewhat in touch with the findings of modern science and recognise rights of 'non-believers' and agnostics. There is nothing quite so embarrassing as an archbishop who doesn't realise that Neanderthals are actually extinct. [14]

Most established 'trades' are professionalised and reliant on new and old science – buildings need to survive and have 'the services' of water and electricity – courtesy of ongoing research; building materials are products of scientific research. New trades and services in the information technology sector are dependent upon science based research and development – and so on.

In summary, the basic security and quality of life that Australians enjoy (for example) is not simply because of a secular, liberal democratic system of governance. It also depends on established institutions and healthy professions. In particular, Australia is well and truly built on the secure foundations provided by thoroughly 'scientised' professions, trades, and skilled workers that look after our health and wellbeing. The triumph of reason that modern science represents also guarantees the viability and plausibility of many other cultural practices and institutions in Australia. For instance, the creative arts and tertiary disciplines in the arts, humanities, and social sciences, are all buttressed by science and secular reason. Even when a discipline such as sociology can promote postmodernism, or the need for 'male reason' to be transgressed by poetry and play, communication will eventually resort to secular reason after the poetry or abstract expressionism. It is not enough to be creative – some level of rational discourse must follow. Such is the joy of a modern pluralist culture. Anything is possible, most things are permissible, but it is not cool to be totally unreasonable – the law, and psychiatry, take a dim view of that. Under these social and cultural conditions it is easy to appreciate 'the optimism of professionals': despite most countervailing forces, reason can prevail.

Science and secular reason do not depend on any particular emotions – there is an obvious and well-practised difference between reason and emotion. Nonetheless, no human activity can be understood without consideration of the emotions and feelings that are present in individuals and organisations. Optimism, for instance, is part of the fabric of all professions – it is institutionalised, and a now problematic component of futurology, as will be described in more detail below, and in following chapters. Indeed, there are many obvious cracks in our cultural foundations that challenge the possibilities of optimism. In many ways optimism functions as a compensatory attitude in worlds that are complex, troubled and uncertain. General uncertainty about social order and the cultural role of science require optimism as a cultural counterbalance and necessary motivation for positive behaviour. It can now be argued that optimism has now become a symptom of a much wider *impending crisis* in a number of institutions.

This perception of an impending crisis provides an important and necessary context for any understanding of the way optimism plays out in professionalised discourse (in Australia and most other societies). The perception of a more immediate crisis in the credibility of science, coupled with the natural distrust conservative governments have of 'free thinkers', also helps understand why professional scientists continue to so value their autonomy, and why they continue to be so publicly a-political.

THE POSITIVE VIEW OF
PUBLIC SCIENTISTS

Tim Flannery is an optimist who, in his books, is politically reticent. This is despite Australian scientists experiencing declining levels of government funding, and strong government resistance to ideas of climate change and ecological decline due to industrial and mining impacts. Like many other eminent scientists who do speak and debate in public forums, Professor Flannery is able to be measured and determined about the role and possibilities of science. Flannery, who is a biologist and anthropologist, has observed a collective failure to protect Australian native species, and yet is still able to strike an optimistic note about the way forward:

> Quantify the problem, devise a plan to deal with it based on sound science, and report on outcomes. And keep the politics out of it. That is the approach required if Australia's magnificent natural heritage is to flourish into the future. [15]

The more recent loss of the independent (but government funded) Climate Change Commission – of which Flannery was Chairperson – and the loss of a Minister for Science, and the downsizing of the CSIRO (Australia's peak independent research organisation) may have severely tested Flannery's political reticence, but we can be sure he remains optimistic.

All professional scientists are optimistic about the value of more research and more scientific knowledge. Whatever other beliefs scientists may have – and these include traditional religions (such as Christianity, Buddhism, Hinduism and Islam), mysticism, 'new age' approaches, agnosticism, and atheism, and various political beliefs – all scientists believe in the power of reason, or rationality.

Sir David Attenborough certainly thinks so: 'can our intelligence save us? I hope so.' His enormous authority as a popularly acclaimed spokesperson for Earth's ecology is thoroughly scientific. Despite all the challenges that human neglect, abuse, and over-population have delivered, his unflagging enthusiasm for the beauty and joy of the natural world is based on the cultural power of a scientific approach: 'understanding the natural world is crucial to all of us.' Despite his stoic a-political public stance (the necessary objectivity of a scientist), his deeper belief clearly is that the knowledge of science should be applied politically – all politicians should take note, and act accordingly. His message, oft repeated, is that humanity needs to think rationally, plan, and change behaviours: 'we're at a crossroads.' This is about as a-politically political as public scientists generally can be – his deepest hope is that reason can prevail.[16]

Attenborough's appeal for change is basically practical and ethical in the sense of the western 'liberal' tradition of valuing 'the common good' – but in an expanded ecological way. The best interests of 'all' includes humans, animals, plants and their ecologies . . . locally and globally.

Making changes, in this view, can be quite consistent with science's empirical method – its goal directed, theoretically informed, experimental approach. Any changes we might make will always be experimental to some extent – but monitored scientifically, and managed astutely, something sensible can always be done. In the case of managing wilderness areas, this may even mean a management strategy as simple as keeping human impacts to an absolute minimum.

It is encouraging that many well-known contemporary commentators writing and speaking about planetary ecology, and the way forward, are surprisingly upbeat. So, even though climate scientists are increasingly disturbed (and possibly pessimistic) in the context of continuing political and media capitulation to the logic of economic growth, most professionals (and others) have not surrendered. As already mentioned, all professions, including science (in all its institutional forms) are, in one way or another, committed to belief in 'progress' as a force for social, cultural and political good.[17]

Public intellectuals who have been prominent spokespersons for planet Earth have, over the last few decades, tended to be scientifically trained.

David Attenborough and David Suzuki were among the first public broadcasters to draw serious attention to the great beauty of our planet in a new context of global ecological decline. The fact that they were both male English speakers with scientific backgrounds gave automatic authority; but both were, initially, hamstrung by the built-in resistance of popular science broadcasting to 'politics'. Today these two old men deliver a clear message about the perils that confront the Earth: scientific knowledge is not enough, in itself, to save the planet. Scientific knowledge is critically important, but it needs to focus the political process to a far greater extent than we currently see. These two men have fought long and hard to gain, and retain, credibility with audiences and broadcasters. In an era with mass audiences more partial to entertainment than eco-politics, the continuing success of both men to communicate a sobering message is remarkable.[18]

It is hardly surprising that scientists have led the way in publicising the perils we face. Scientists are best placed to deal with the usually (and sometimes deliberately) ill-informed rhetoric of politicians, industrialists, and other business people who have commercial, rather than ecological, objectives. As argued, science today is authoritative as a form of knowledge. Mass audiences accept this, as do most other professions and occupations. The opinions of priests and politicians can be decisively important in certain contexts, but courts of law will actually pay scientists for expert advice. They tend not to recruit priests, politicians, or philosophers as reliable experts. While scientists are generally constrained by their role as objective and impartial champions of truth, when they do speak publicly, their pronouncements have all the more weight because of this general perception of impartiality. Even when individual scientists are revealed to be partial by being, for example, in the service of cigarette companies or polluting energy companies, their partiality is still 'haloed' by the science they profess.

Biologists, in particular, have played an important historical role in the development of public ecological discourse. Rachel Carson, who spoke out about pesticides in 1972, was a professional biologist, as is David Suzuki. David Attenborough was first trained as a biologist, and is a life-long naturalist. Tim Flannery, now head of Australia's Climate Change

Commission is a biologist, anthropologist, and naturalist. Medically trained biologists (doctors) have also been prominent in defence of Earth – in Australia Bob Brown and Helen Caldicott are famous for their work (in Green politics and anti-nuclear activism). Today many other scientific disciplines contribute to public discourse about ecology and the fate of Earth. Many scientists work long hours doing science, collaborating with co-researchers, peers and students, writing papers and reports, going to conferences, appearing on television to debate sceptics, industrialists and politicians. Generally, it would appear that scientists whose work involves global systems tend to be most outspoken about the ecological problems that confront us. After all, they are more exposed to the facts of a declining planetary ecology. And consequently many of these scientists are far from optimistic – so despite the cultural conditioning of professional optimism built on an ideology of progress, some scientists are beginning to show signs of desperation.

The chemist, James Lovelock, and the climate scientist, James Hanson, are two good examples whose work will be more closely reviewed in Chapter 4. As committed ecologists, neither of these scientists could be described as particularly optimistic about the future of humanity. Whether one sees Earth as intelligent and capable of goal directed action, as does Lovelock, or whether one sees Earth as a highly complex system comprising life and matter and more simply a matter of physics chemistry and biology, as does Hanson, a positive outlook for humanity is not guaranteed.

Climate scientists are not typical professionals. Most other non-scientists are optimistic, even those whose job it is to predict the future. Very few are quite so pessimistic as to assume that there is no hope that Earth's ecology can recover. Al Gore, for one, has recently written a large book titled *The Future*, in which he concludes that human civilization has reached 'a fork in the road we have long travelled'. One path leads towards a disaster fuelled by 'the destruction of the climate balance on which we depend, the depletion of irreplaceable resources that sustain us and the degradation of uniquely human values'. The other path leads to 'the future'. [19]

It might be surprising that most published future oriented material is positive in outlook. The most authoritative public broadcasters who deal with ecology and the future always hold out some hope that leadership, research, innovation and public education can see humanity through an impending crisis. David Attenborough, Al Gore and David Suzuki, for example, see serious dangers ahead, but remain upbeat. The next chapter outlines the viewpoints of some other better-known public commentators; the chapter that follows wonders how, why, and whether they can continue to be so optimistic in the light of current climate science, and the spotty record of science applied as new technology.

5

SCIENCE TO THE RESCUE?

Science is the one human activity that is truly progressive.

Edwin Hubble, *Realm of the Nebulae*, 1936

Science enjoys a very high status in modern cultures for good reasons. Science gives us reliable knowledge about the world and facilitates improved standards of living. Science also defends against risks and adversity. At times when the prosperity, health and safety, and general wellbeing of whole populations are threatened – by epidemics, natural disasters, war, and now climate change, scientists are expected to play a leading role as problem solvers. However, when the findings of scientific research threaten the commercial viability of particular industries, and the lifestyle habits of millions, major conflict can be expected. This chapter both presents major research findings that have placed many people on a state of high alert, and addresses the undermining of science by climate change denial.

In rejecting the findings of climate scientists, 'denialists' strike at more than a few scientific facts. Because most denialists are non-scientists, their offense strikes at traditions that are even more ancient than the historically recent event of 'science' (which can be traced back to the ancient Greeks and the formalisation of 'reason'). Climate change denial offends deeply held beliefs about the importance of telling the truth, and about truth itself – particularly when lives and futures are at stake. Telling the truth is something most cultures value extremely highly, and always appear to have done. In a modern secular world, science is the 'truth sayer'.

If one can speak of 'modern myths', then science certainly qualifies.[1]

Like a hero of old, science is wise and powerful; its accomplishments are extraordinary. In this mythological appreciation – generated widely by popular culture – when big problems arise in science's material and cultural domain, all eyes and ears turn towards scientists. They, rather than politicians, economists or journalists, are expected to do the research and 'tell the truth'. And, in conjunction with technological fields that are more practically and commercially oriented, science (and scientists) are assumed able to come up with 'solutions'.

Understanding that science is deeply coded into the DNA of Western societies as modern 'myth' – and therefore as a source of fundamental values and cultural legitimation – helps explain the depth of shock and horror inflicted in some by 'climate change denial', but also raise questions about the apparent complacency of others with respect to the activities of 'denialists'. If science is such a fundamental cultural value, how is it that governments can, with such apparent ease, ignore the findings and protestations of so many eminent scientists about not only climate change, but many other issues that affect public health and well-being? The broad approach taken here assumes rather that climate change deniers are not the only ones 'in denial'. The problems raised by climate change go far deeper than merely questioning 'the truth'. Climate change challenges many of the comfortable assumptions of citizens of wealthy countries, and threatens to de-stabilise Earth's eco – system. That is enough to drive most people into a state of denial, and to encourage the cultural excesses of 'apocalypse culture', and over-consumption.

Even if there is a collective psychic need for modern myths – including religion and science, as some mythologists have claimed[2], it is also critically important to de-mystify science and scientists in order to assert the realities of the threats posed by climate change and its social causes. Only by better understanding the work of climate scientists, and all scientists, can there be any real hope of preserving decent living standards for future generations. Scientists are not the only occupational group necessary for the creation of ecologically sustainable futures, but they are essential.

Climate change, and the contemporary saga of climate science certainly tests any mythological assumptions about the powers of science. To begin with, scientists do not have a fully adequate knowledge of climate change or ecological decline – more research is desperately needed. And, even with the disturbing research findings already available, scientists are still struggling to bring the problem of climate change into the frame of politicians, industry, corporations and economies – to name a few of the 'key players' in our planet's future.

The power of scientists to directly intervene in the governance of societies has always been limited. Scientists have had the patronage of monarchs, governments, and the rich and powerful but they have never held the reins of power. Generally their political role has been advisory and their command of technological innovation limited by financiers and commercial considerations. In that respect scientists function like other professionals as part of institutional arrangements that have not changed greatly over the recent centuries.

In these arrangements the limited powers of scientists are compensated by high social status. Thus research scientists may struggle to secure funding for their projects, but the general importance of science is part of popular culture. Science and scientists may dominate many university structures, but universities and other research organisations are dependent on governments and other patrons; the political power of individual scientists is generally confined in particular organisations and by the conditions of their employment. Governments and industry may starve scientists, but in the process they keep scientists 'on tap'.

It is unrealistic to expect 'science' to prevail in a world with so many powerful countervailing forces. Science has its own limits – as one institution among other institutions, and as a kind of knowledge that can never claim to know the 'absolute truth' and that is, therefore, always open to change. Science is not singular – it is not a unified field of knowledge, occupation, or 'profession'. The occupational structures of science are varied, and the job security of scientists not often guaranteed. The number of scientists available to perform frontline research on climate change and ecological problems is limited. The organisations that might employ them are limited. Their resources are finite and not equal to the tasks required. Subjects like ecology and climate are difficult to theorise, model and measure. In short, science is not all-powerful – even though it is the most reliable form of knowledge.[3]

These qualifications about the powers of science are important because those who believe in the redemptive power of 'truth', and cling to comforting myths about the powers of science, might blame scientists for not doing enough, if and when the world becomes a much less comfortable place. Scientists would be the least likely culprits – the machinations of their government and corporate sponsors would be a better place to start.

CLIMATE CHANGE DENIAL

I have found climate change denial shocking for its direct attack on the credibility of science – of climate science in the first instance, but also on the whole field of science. Such denial is particularly shocking because it also challenges the methodological basis of science: careful observation. When such denial disputes now apparent changes to the climates of many countries, including one's own, and when these changes are backed up by meteorological and other climate data that is readily accessible, and reported in the media, such denial seems more like brazen stupidity. There is abundant evidence to prove global warming, and the increasing frequency of extreme weather events; this data covers the average temperatures of the Earth's surface, atmosphere, oceans, and weather events such as cyclones, storms and droughts. Also implicated are melting ice, rising sea levels, and bush-fires. There is other less weighty data available about increasing irregularity in the flowering of plants, and the behaviour of animals, which appears to be climate related. If all this data does not qualify in some minds as 'climate change', it should at least count as evidence for 'climate de-stabilization'. However the data is categorized and named, it is disturbing and cause for alarm.

Climate change denial is not just a personal philosophical option in open societies. It is also a concerted program of opposition deliberately mounted: to discredit climate science by whatever means are available; to question the motives of climate scientists; to discredit these scientists if possible; and to use the journalistic requirements of 'balance' in reporting to allow very fringe oppositional climate science more traction than it deserves. Climate change denial is a well-financed international network involving prominent individuals, and less prominent organisations.[4]

Denial can be difficult to isolate, whatever the object. Denial can be expressed as barely articulated opposition, or mild antagonism, and can be just a matter of personal belief. However, denial becomes socially problematic when what is being denied leads to violence, oppression, poverty, or death – as can be claimed, for instance, about the treatment of women in many countries. Climate change deniers can be very stubborn and subtle – just like some men who deny being violent and sexist. Organisations of deniers can be even more stubborn and subtle – evidence suggests a highly covert side to the social organisation of 'denialist' individuals and organisations.[5]

Not many countries have governments brazen enough to have a history of open opposition to the findings of an international consensus of climate scientists and allied scientific specialists, but Australia has become one such country. Although the passage of time has seen opinions moderated and policies qualified, Australia's political and business elites – their policies, practices and rhetoric – provide good evidence for continuing climate change denial.

The strongest statement about climate change denial comes not from measurement of individual numbers and economic support for 'denialist' organisations, but from climate scientists themselves. The truly extreme nature of climate change denial is exposed when we consider the proportion of climate scientists that is convinced that human activities are significantly changing global temperatures. Researchers studying the publications of climate scientists – their individual output and citations by other climate scientists – report the level of consensus on that basis to be 97-98%. Yet climate change denial has become institutionalised in current lifestyles and rumbles through all the institutions of society.[6]

Climate scientists, ecologists, biologists and other scientists dedicated to knowing more about the future of life on Earth, find themselves in a precarious situation. As professionals, they believe in the power and value of knowledge – science is a steady march forward towards 'truth', or away from error. In this view science, more than any other form of knowledge, embodies 'progress'. Taken to a technological extreme, science can even lead the way into a new 'anthropocene' era where everything will be 'man made'. Climate change, in this view, is just another problem to be overcome in a centuries long project to completely master the natural world, including the climate.[7]

As realists and careful observers of the natural world, however, scientists are confronted with the prospect of imminent uncontrolled global warming, more extreme weather events, collapsing ecologies, and all the negative impacts of expanding human systems on a finite planet. Dreams of controlling the weather, let alone climate, do not yet have much scientific traction – even accurately predicting the weather is still well beyond the power of the best computer models. There are easier options available, and other considerations to be exhausted, before mad dreams and schemes can intrude on what is still quite a human friendly planet.

CLIMATE SCIENTISTS – A THREATENED SPECIES

Climate scientists and ecologists might be compared to the canaries coal miners used as an alarm system. These scientists are still singing in the data mines of modern science, but their songs are becoming much bleaker. The gases and toxins that threaten them in the atmosphere, soil and water of Earth are not the only sources of harm. They have also suffered abuse and scorn directed towards them from professional 'climate deniers', and other staunch defenders of the resource extraction industry, fossil fuel based industries, and the 'business as usual' model. Most critically, many suffer from lack of funding and secure employment.

Singing scientists may be somewhat rare for other reasons: their socialisation as professionals discourages popular engagement. Tim Flannery was quoted earlier because his words typify the standard a-political attitude that most successful public scientists have. That is, as far as possible, the need to keep scientific research 'at arm's length' from the manoeuvrings of politicians. In this view scientific researchers should have a high level of autonomy, because ultimately the 'truth' about the behaviour of natural systems (whether sub-atomic, ecological or inter-galactic) is not political and should not be thought of as open to 'steering' by non-scientists. This attitude is typical among scientists and helps explain why climate science is not better known.

In fact, the pressures that many ecological scientists have to endure come from far more than the 'internal' demands of producing good science (and these include administrative and economic pressures). There are also other interested 'stakeholders' who may not be scientists but have much to gain from the outcomes of scientific research. Farmers, graziers, miners, industrialists, developers, builders, café proprietors, and politicians: every conceivable occupation and economic activity is effected by the outcomes of scientific research. Some lobby scientists directly, and attempt to influence goals and outcomes. Others lobby scientific organisations and governments. It is no wonder that most scientists should prize their autonomy and perpetuate the values of objectivity, value neutrality, and social detachment. Whether or not these ideals are 'real' or ideological in the practices of science is less important than the survival of good science and the relative autonomy of the organisations that employ scientists.

The protection of scientific autonomy is also important because scientists, more than ever, need to play an advisory role in expert panels in parliamentary committees on the basis of their ability to provide independent, objective advice – scientific research is still the 'gold standard' for evidence – based decision making. Our future depends on the ability of governments to take advice that is as objective as possible about the condition of the environment and the availability of natural resources for economic exploitation.

But autonomy is only part of the social equation of science. Accountability is also part of the 'contract' of publicly funded science – the public have a right to know about the research their taxes are funding. This also extends (arguably) to that part of the private sector, which is subsidised from the public purse (in various ways, including tax breaks for research and development). Further, because the effects of private research so often impact upon 'commons' such as the quality of the atmosphere, water and land, 'the right to know' becomes 'a need to know' about all research –public oversight and access to private research needs to remain enshrined in law; environmental protection and public health should always trump commercial interests. Public access to government committee findings may be problematic in some circumstances – but public access is a foundation principle for all truly democratic societies.

One unavoidable consequence of 'public access' is that science and scientists (in all societies) are vulnerable to political interests – science is steered by various 'external' forces. Indeed, as a modern social institution, science is intrinsically political, and scientists themselves often play politics. At the same time, we rely on the objectivity of scientific knowledge as a corrective to bias, corruption and falsehoods – although goals of research may be set externally, research findings are prized because they transcend the limitations of particular interests. Science is, therefore, a high cultural value *as well as* an activity of great economic and ecological importance.

Understanding the social nature of scientific research is vital for a balanced assessment of the possibilities of climate research. Critically, output, as tested and peer reviewed knowledge, is only one process that affects ecological outcomes. The funding of climate science and ecological research, recruitment processes of scientists and support staff, the influence of the particular interests of employing organisations (for example, corporations with an interest in climate change denial, or governments and universities with more general interests) are all social processes that influence the possibilities and eventual outcomes of scientific research.

Even allegations of fraud and other mischief in the conduct of research are processes that potentially affect the conduct of future research.[8]

Ecological heroes of public broadcasting such as David Attenborough and David Suzuki would agree about the general reliability of science and the importance of research that can deliver objective 'facts' – and would add that the worlds of science are intrinsically fascinating, a source of wonder, and often very beautiful. Undoubtedly these cultural values inspire most professional (and amateur) scientists and motivate many scientists to keep going in the face of concerted criticism, and subterfuge. Most scientists are not, however, blindly optimistic about the profession of science and its broader management. For all optimism about the integrity of scientists, and scientific knowledge, scientists are only human and fallible. There are many documented cases of scientific misconduct and fraud. [9]

It is fortunate that peer review is such a highly valued principle, and such an effective corrective process in the conduct of science.

Scientific fraud is fascinating in that it tests the strength of the professionalism of the research done. Generally, there is little incentive for deception in science. International peer review and the standard methodology of science make fraud extremely difficult to sustain – experiments need to be repeatable, involve testable theory, and withstand the scrutiny of scientific peers. Also, the development of reputations is usually a highly scrutinised process.

The worlds of politicians and politics are, by contrast, quite distant from the intellectual projects of science and scientific methodology. Often there is a great gulf between the production of scientific facts and their incorporation into public policy. One could say that, like religion in modern societies, there is a 'separation of powers' in the conjunction of science and politics in liberal democracies. Further, in practice, politics and the making of public policy is not a simple exercise of scientific logic, or even common sense. Nor are these practices dependent on the impartial application of available scientific knowledge. Most often decisions about where, when and how funding should be applied, or whether particular projects should be developed, or how complex social issues should be negotiated to avoid conflict, social dislocation, discrimination, and other negative outcomes, exhibit 'fuzzy logic'. That is, issues are not simply about an application of the scientific 'facts' or reason – they also involve compromise and negotiation between different positions and interests, and collective thought in committees, working parties, and other informal processes. Evidence based decision-making and transparency are only 'best practice'. The reality is usually fuzzy logic, negotiated decision making with some dissatisfied 'stakeholders', and political point scoring that progresses interminably. Ideally, however, politics is the negotiation of 'best outcomes' from facts presented.

CLIMATE SCIENCE – AN INCONVENIENT REALITY CHECK

Climate science is still the best corrective to disbelieving rhetoric from governments, industry and conservative commentators. The startling fact is that anti–climate change propaganda has been so apparently influential, despite the best efforts of scientists to inject facts into the mix. It is tempting to conclude that this is an example of how successful capitalists are at hoodwinking the masses with clever ideology. There may be more than a grain of truth in this simple conclusion; certainly the possibilities of speaking the truth are limited by the vested interests and overt policies of broadcasters and publishers. The pursuit of advertising dollars and good returns to shareholders are powerful incentives to air brush any 'inconvenient truths'. However, the history of climate science is not just about the struggles of heroic scientists to reveal the truth about a changing climate – in a broader context of greed, self-interest and wilful ignorance. Scientists have been, and still are, conflicted and 'contrary' about many issues in the broader political *and* scientific context of climate science. Scientists have different political beliefs and disagree about *unproven* theories, methods and applications. Scientific knowledge is culturally unique, however, in being the most objective kind of knowledge available. When compared to other kinds of knowledge (and their social fields) science is the least ideological, and scientists the most difficult of professionals to 'steer'. This last point is very clear from consideration of the work of pioneering climate scientists James Hansen and Jim Lovelock.

The account of current climate science here is not intended to be comprehensive – that would require a much longer and more specialist treatment. Fortunately, the International Panel on Climate Change does publish regular and lengthy summaries, and in Australia we now have an 'independent' Climate Change Council dedicated to providing information to the public. In addition to the provision of a summary of recent findings of the IPCC, this section provides an introduction to the work of James Hansen and James Lovelock, who provide two strong and contrasting views about climate change. Other details have been sketched in, as appropriate.

One of the biggest challenges climate science poses to other scientists, policy makers in government, and those affected in the public and private sectors, is that climate science needs to be 'holistic', like all ecological research. Because of their complexity the study of any natural system requires the input of many disciplines, or 'multi-disciplinarity'.[10]

This can raise administrative problems for universities and other research organisations that have to co-ordinate the contributions of established specialists – a major reason why many ecological and environmental research projects struggle to become established.

The chemist, James Lovelock, and the climate scientist, James Hansen, are pioneers of multi-disciplinary holism in climate science. Both have written books and participated in public and private debate with politicians and other scientists. As pioneers of a science based approach to Earth as a complex global system, they deserve particular acknowledgement for their iconoclasm (intended and unintended). Both have sought to apply specialist knowledge to global problems and in the process encountered much resistance from scientific and political establishments. Scientific disciplines cannot remain in splendid isolation if they wish to solve global problems, however it takes individuals of special talent to be productive against the grain of entrenched specialist interests and the political and business elites they protect.

Lovelock and Hanson stretch the envelope in different ways. Lovelock's holism attributes intelligence to Earth and is too mystical for many scientists. Further, despite his acknowledged brilliance, Lovelock has made a career as a scientific non-conformist – often self-employed, a multi-disciplinarian and inventor, he has operated more like a successful eighteenth or nineteenth century 'amateur' than a modern professional scientist.[11]

On the other hand, Hansen's dogged commitment to the disturbing facts of climate science is too pessimistic for those who believe in the adaptability of system Earth. Both scientists have endorsed nuclear energy as the best option for future energy supplies, despite present risks and unsolved waste storage problems. Needless to say, their pro-nuclear positions have alienated them from most environmentalists. Nonetheless, primarily because of humanity's commitment to fossil fuel usage, neither Lovelock nor Hanson see a future Earth that can be a happy place for humans. Many scientists have similar views about the future potential of nuclear energy, while being highly critical of continued reliance on fossil fuels as a major global energy source. Most scientists, however, are absolutely convinced that the science about climate change 'is in'.

In the light of what is known just about the global carbon cycle – for instance, about atmospheric greenhouse gas concentrations, ocean salinity, acidity and temperatures, and land based carbon production and sequestration – it is extremely challenging to contemplate the extent to which climate change continues to be downplayed. For instance, in 2007 350 ppm CO_2 emerged as a good and possible target for atmospheric CO_2 concentrations. In that year James Hansen had suggested to an academic meeting in San Francisco that 350 parts per million of CO_2 in the atmosphere was a safe upper limit to avoid a climate tipping point.[12]

In response Bill McKibbon founded '350.org' as an international non-governmental environmental organisation, in 2009.

Today, the atmospheric concentration of CO_2 has exceeded 400ppm, and there is no reason to suppose that this concentration will not continue to go considerably higher over time. According to some climate scientists, even if carbon pollution continues at current rates of increase (which assumes major abatement in the future), global warming in excess of 2^0 C (i.e. global surface temperature changes) is guaranteed, possibly as soon as the middle of this century. [13]

There is an even greater wake-up call than this sombre prediction for life in the mid-twenty first century. Most official published estimates of rates of warming, melting, and acidification of the oceans have been conservative estimates. This has the effect of minimising public alarm and buying time for the continuation of growth economics – at the expense of ecological 'externalities'.

Even conservative analysis is sobering: '[i]t is virtually certain that there will be more frequent hot and fewer cold temperature extremes over most land areas on daily and seasonal timescales as global mean temperatures increase. It is very likely that heat waves will occur with a higher frequency and duration. Occasional cold winter extremes will continue to occur.' [14]

The IPCC are very careful about what they predict for sea level rises: '[t]here is very high confidence that maximum global mean sea level during the last interglacial period (129,000 to 116,000 years ago) was, for several thousand years, at least 5 m higher than present, and high confidence that it did not exceed 10 m above present.' [15]

Future sea levels will be highly affected by the extent to which the Greenland ice sheet, and other land ice, melts.

Economic success, however, remains the highest priority for large businesses, and this is currently understood to mean that economies must grow. This in turn requires ever-greater supplies of energy and other natural resources, right now. This guarantees ever-greater amounts of carbon pollution – even if major abatement programs reduce rates of pollution (which is not currently happening). Flawed as this logic is from an ecological point of view, the assumption of endless growth informs economic principles that rule global capitalism. Either the economic ship is too big to turn around, or in the spirit of optimism, we don't know something the apparently complacent captains of industry and government do know . . . or something else is happening, such as collective inertia caused by self-delusion and denial. Or, all of the above are happening, and more . . .

Whatever . . . climate change science, and its reception, exposes much about the inner workings of public and private sectors in modern societies. Close inspection of the production of the science is one way of sharpening focus on the tangled webs that connect different parts of the puzzle confronting those trying to make sense of past, present and future. Later chapters will look more closely at the economics and politics of the situation. We are fortunate to have some 'insider' accounts, by scientists, of the way science interfaces with governments, and of its potentials to raise public awareness. The published work of James Hansen is particularly revealing of the tensions and conflicts involved, but the work of all the other 'public scientists' referred to in this chapter (such as James Lovelock and Tim Flannery) can also be read as an account of this interface. Hanson is particularly candid.

The work of Hansen and Lovelock is disturbing to the *status quo*, inside and outside of science. Each scientist presents a challenge to the conventional modelling of climate and climate change. Each accepts climate science to be a multi-disciplinary activity driven by the need to be able to understand global climates. That is challenging enough for scientists used to careers and controls deriving from a scientific division of labour based on single disciplines. The slow, complicated, and largely voluntary machinations of the IPCC, however, underline the difficulties of large-scale multi-disciplinarity.

Both Hanson and Lovelock see science as part of a larger collective exercise that obliges scientists to be political – in the sense of engaging with others to better steer science and to raise public awareness of the dangers of climate change (paramount among other pressing concerns). Hanson is ultimately concerned with the kind of world his grandchildren will inherit. He is not prepared to have the clear implications of climate science buried in government committees with vested interests. That orientation made him a dangerous maverick inside and outside of scientific establishments. Lovelock is a maverick for additional reasons – 'pan-spiritualism'. His idea of scientific modelling goes beyond 'normal' science. He postulates that Earth is capable of intelligent, self-interested behaviour. This has made Lovelock (and his 'Gaia Hypothesis') an enduring primary source in 'deep ecology', but rather isolates him on the fringes of 'respectable' science. The popularisation of the idea that Earth is a big self-regulating system does, however, owe much to the tireless work of James Lovelock. That idea, shorn of mystical implications, has also been a great stimulus to *holistic* scientific research.

HANSEN ON CLIMATE CHANGE

In 2001 James Hansen was not successful in persuading the US Vice-President's Climate Task Force of the need for action on climate change. In two sessions Hansen, and others, presented fairly compelling data about climate change to a group of six cabinet members, the national security advisor, the EPA administrator, and Vice President Cheney, the Chairperson. In Hansen's account of one of the debates about the reality of climate change, Richard Lindzen, a canny climate sceptic from the Massachusetts Institute of Technology, was able to deflect the weight of Hanson's evidence by impugning the authority of just one place of publication of data: ' "The reference you have given, MIT Tech Talk, is basically a newspaper.' Turning to the cabinet members, he added, "You all know how accurate newspaper quotes are." There were a lot of nods and chuckles ... Lindzen had won the point.'[16]

No directives were subsequently issued by government to big CO_2 polluters; business continued, 'as usual'.

Two years later, in 2003, with the weight of more evidence, more research, and more peer reviewed publications, another briefing of the highest decision making committees in the USA was again deflected into the vast inertia of government bureaucracy and Machiavellian politics. This process continues a decade further on. Scientists and scientific bodies such as the IPCC continue to become more alarmed and issue dire warnings, and politicians continue to deflect these concerns in favour of political popularity and industry donations to political party fund raising.

James Hansen is regarded as one of the world's leading scientific researchers of climate science. He, and James Lovelock were among the first eminent climate scientists to both predict climate change, and go on to actively campaign for political and cultural change. These efforts can be traced back as early as the late 1970s. [17]

Hansen, particularly, regards public education in basic science as critically important – in his view the best antidote to climate change denial is a scientifically informed public. Although progress has been slow, Hansen has gained an international audience. His book, *Storms of my Grandchildren*, first published in 2009, should be regarded as a classic in popular science publishing, not least because it is a hard hitting expose of the politics of climate science – it is also a relatively advanced technical introduction to contemporary climate science.

Hansen's 'insider' account exposes the resistance of political and scientific establishments to inconvenient climate science. The book describes expert committee processes and public relations activities dedicated to the avoidance of scary science. The idea that elites within these establishments might be committed to the fullest exploitation of fossil fuels possible is clearly not a conspiracy theory concocted by leftists and mad ecologists. Hansen details his encounters with senior politicians and policy makers in numerous committee hearings that left him frustrated and outraged – but hardly speechless. His story demonstrates the great inertia of US government and industry, and the near criminal behaviour of public officials charged with managing the flow of information.

The need for a shift in public awareness of the scientific issues involved in climate change is essential. We can assume that increased public knowledge decreases the likelihood of reflex reaction that comes from ignorance and fear. We can also assume that increased public awareness makes the committed opposition of interest groups more difficult in the face of facts that are widely known. On the basis of Hansen's portrayal of US government processes, however, we would be foolish to assume expert committees and public relations departments keep the US public well informed. [18]

It is doubtful Australian governments are any more transparent or informative in their deliberations about climate change and related issues such as carbon abatement and the mining of fossil fuels and coal seam gas.[19]

The level of engagement with the science, and with simple logic, that Hansen and other climate science advocates bring to bear should be a revelation. One wonders what it takes to persuade voting publics that even though scientists are not immune to error or even fraud, a scientific consensus is about as reliable as it gets. Yet the spin goes on.

Hansen's book deliberately confronts the main difficulty scientists face trying to translate complex science into publicly accessible accounts – the choice of language and concepts comprehensible to audiences that may not have tertiary level training in science. He accepts this is not his strong suit, but his sincere efforts make the book all the more important: his account has certainly not been dumbed down or subverted by the demands of populism. Still, it takes intellectual work and a level of courage for any reader to engage with new ideas that are actually bad news.

In Hansen's view there are a number of general scientific issues about climate change that need to be widely known. These involve the importance of knowledge of basic science, the difficulties of measuring key variables in large systems (e.g. temperature and concentration), and better appreciation of the ideas of error, uncertainty and probability. Knowledge of more complex concepts such as *climate forcing* and *climate sensitivity* is also important; indeed knowledge from any relevant new scientific field is also on his agenda. For instance, palaeoclimatologists measure atmospheric gas samples trapped in ice cores to give good estimates about atmospheric conditions and climates as far back as about 420,000 years. This new research provides important data for arguments about trends in climate change and correlations between CO_2 concentrations, surface temperatures, and atmospheric temperatures.

Broad-ranging scientific analysis has enabled Hansen to make a very plausible case for the urgent reality of climate change. Some of the lesser known, but critically important findings he reveals include:

- It is most unlikely that there will be another ice age soon: '[h]umans by rapidly burning fossil fuels have caused global warming that overwhelms the natural tendency toward the next ice age'.[20]
- Scientists are confident that greenhouse gases are a cause of global warming: between 1750 and 2000, the only chemical agents that can reliably be said to have positively increased surface temperatures

are CO_2 and other greenhouse gases (N2O, CFC's, and methane). The uncertainty of measurement of all other *climate forcing* agents exceeds, or roughly equals, their postulated effects. The other significant variable forcing agents include ozone, black carbon aerosols, reflective aerosols, aerosol cloud changes, land cover, the sun, and volcanoes. [21]

- Climate science is hindered by lack of measurement of fundamental systems and processes: for instance, lack of appropriate instrumentation (in the form of small satellite measuring systems) means 'we still do not know the aerosol climate forcing or how it is changing.' Special interest groups have dictated the deployment of large satellite systems (which do not provide appropriate data). [22]

- US Government and industry predictions about future energy consumption are unreliable: predictions made in 1975 about energy consumption rates up to 2005 were approximately 100% inaccurate. [23]

- Thermodynamic modelling of Earth's energy systems gives us the most reliable indicator of future climate change: Earth's *energy imbalance*. This must be reduced to near zero for the climate to be stabilised. Even though the present imbalance is small (approximately 0.5–1 watt per square metre), this constant net gain of heat is sufficient to cause disastrous climatic effects. [24]

- Earth's energy imbalance is deposited almost entirely into the ocean: '[t]his means that the single most important geophysical measurement is change of ocean heat content'. [25]

- Optimism about the capacity of natural terrestrial carbon sinks is unrealistic: although measurements of Earth's carbon cycle indicate that atmospheric CO_2 continues to be absorbed into terrestrial sinks, any hope that that these sinks will continue to act as a stabiliser of CO_2 emissions 'is dependent on the assumption that fossil fuel emissions will decline'. [26]

- 'Clean coal' is 'a diversion that the coal industry and its government supporters use to allow dirty-coal uses to continue: there is no need to debate whether carbon capture and sequestration is realistic. The science demands a simple rule: coal use must be prohibited unless and until the emissions can be captured and safely disposed of'.[27]

These eight 'headline' conclusions are a tribute to the depth of Hansen's research: none of his substantive findings have been invalidated by more recent research – as shown by the latest findings of the IPCC listed below. If anything, the passage of a just a few years has only underlined the foolishness of allowing economic markets and short-term political horizons to so fully dictate government responses to climate change.

The pressures on scientists to not engage in popular communication about subjects as critically important as climate change are consider-able. These pressures arise from within scientific communities (whose core business involves scientific professionalism undistracted by unruly publics) and from without, where other professions, governments and media depend upon a well-regulated output from scientific establish-ments. Hansen's book is a fascinating account of these pressures – as well as his best efforts to remain true to the science. He is blunt about external politics but more muted about politics within the scientific community. For instance, he refers to 'scientific reticence' as a hindrance to communication with the public: 'One factor in reticence may be "behavioural discounting" – concern about the danger of "crying wolf" is more immediate than concern about the danger of "fiddling while Rome burns". In other words, a preference for immediate, over delayed, rewards may contribute to irrational reticence even among rational sci-entists.'[28]

In 2009 Hansen was able to remain optimistically pessimistic:

> The gap between public perception and scientific reality is now enormous. While some of the public is becoming aware of the existence of global warming, the relevant scientists – those who know what they are talking about – realize that the climate system is on the verge of tipping points. If the world does not make a dramatic shift in energy policies over the next few years, we may well pass the point of no return.[29]

When this happens, the sensitivity of the global climate system to temperature forcings by greenhouse gas concentrations (alone) will bring on runaway climate change.

THE INTERNATIONAL PANEL ON CLIMATE CHANGE IN 2013

The IPCC released their Fifth Report in March 2014. This Report includes data from 2013 and is the most comprehensive and reliable assessment of climate change science so far. The historical part of the data is based on measurements from field data, and the predictions about future trends are made using the best available computer modelling techniques. The confidence with which future projections can be made can never be absolute – but the extracts from the Report listed below are conservative estimates and highly reliable, being a product of 'best practice'. The confidence levels are described in detail in both the Summary for Policy Makers (from which the findings listed below are extracted) and in the full report – statistical details have not been included below, but the contributing scientists are highly confident about current data. Their confidence about forward projections is limited by the unpredictability of future human responses, and the unpredictability of Earth's natural systems. Various scenarios have been calculated.

EXTRACTS FROM THE IPCC'S FIFTH ASSESSMENT REPORT

Warming of the climate system is unequivocal, and since the 1950s, many of the observed changes are unprecedented over decades to millennia. The atmosphere and ocean have warmed, the amounts of snow and ice have diminished, sea level has risen, and the concentrations of greenhouse gases have increased . . .

Ocean warming dominates the increase in energy stored in the climate system, accounting for more than 90% of the energy accumulated between 1971 and 2010 (high confidence). It is virtually certain that the upper ocean (0−700 m) warmed from 1971 to 2010 . . . and it likely warmed between the 1870s and 1971 . . .

Over the last two decades, the Greenland and Antarctic ice sheets have been losing mass, glaciers have continued to shrink almost worldwide, and Arctic sea ice and Northern Hemisphere spring snow cover have continued to decrease in extent (high confidence) . . .

The rate of sea level rise since the mid-19th century has been larger than the mean rate during the previous two millennia (high confidence). Over the period 1901 to 2010, global mean sea level rose by 0.19 [0.17 to 0.21] m . . .

The atmospheric concentrations of carbon dioxide, methane, and nitrous oxide have increased to levels unprecedented in at least the last 800,000 years. Carbon dioxide concentrations have increased by 40% since pre-industrial times, primarily from fossil fuel emissions and secondarily from net land use change emissions. The ocean has absorbed about 30% of the emitted anthropogenic carbon dioxide, causing ocean acidification . . .

Total radiative forcing is positive, and has led to an uptake of energy by the system. The largest contribution to total radiative forcing is caused by the increase in the atmospheric concentration of CO_2 since 1750 . . .

Human influence on the climate system is clear. This is evident from the increasing greenhouse gas concentrations in the atmosphere, positive radiative forcing, observed warming, and understanding of the climate system . . .

Human influence has been detected in warming of the atmosphere and the ocean, in changes in the global water cycle, in reductions in snow and ice, in global mean sea level rise, and in changes in some climate extremes . . . It is extremely likely that human influence has been the dominant cause of the observed warming since the mid-20th century . . .

Continued emissions of greenhouse gases will cause further warming and changes in all components of the climate system. Limiting climate change will require substantial and sustained reductions of greenhouse gas emissions . . .

Global surface temperature change for the end of the 21st century is likely to exceed 1.5°C relative to 1850 to 1900 . . . [under some scenarios] it is likely to exceed 2°C . . . Warming will continue beyond 2100 . . . Warming will continue to exhibit interannual-to-decadal variability and will not be regionally uniform . . .

Changes in the global water cycle in response to the warming over the 21st century will not be uniform. The contrast in precipitation between wet and dry regions and between wet and dry seasons will increase, although there may be regional exceptions . . .

The global ocean will continue to warm during the 21st century. Heat will penetrate from the surface to the deep ocean and affect ocean circulation . . .

It is very likely that the Arctic sea ice cover will continue to shrink and thin and that Northern Hemisphere spring snow cover will decrease during the 21st century as global mean surface temperature rises. Global glacier volume will further decrease . . .

Global mean sea level will continue to rise during the 21st century . . . the rate of sea level rise will very likely exceed that observed during 1971 to 2010 due to increased ocean warming and increased loss of mass from glaciers and ice sheets . . .

Climate change will affect carbon cycle processes in a way that will exacerbate the increase of CO_2 in the atmosphere (high confidence). Further uptake of carbon by the ocean will increase ocean acidification . . .

Cumulative emissions of CO_2 largely determine global mean surface warming by the late 21st century and beyond . . . Most aspects of climate change will persist for many centuries even if emissions of CO_2 are stopped. This represents a substantial multi-century climate change commitment created by past, present and future emissions of CO_2 . . . [30]

None of the IPCC's findings in 2013 contradict the summary extracted from Hansen's 2009 book, or his early warnings in years prior to that – including his major worry about the contributions of aerosol particulates to greenhouse warming. Aerosol contributions to warming are still unable to be adequately modelled.

It is important to note that the findings of the IPCC are the result of collaboration between thousands of scientists. The agreement represented in the Reports, and in the summary extracts listed above, is therefore *necessarily conservative*. Nonetheless, the major finding announced above – hedged by the uncertainties and unpredictability of weather – is that we can confidently expect weather to become more 'extreme' *everywhere*. Undoubtedly this is mostly human caused – '[i]t is extremely likely that human influence has been the dominant cause of the observed warming since the mid-20th century'. Warming is the main cause of climate instability.

Much of what follows in this book is an exploration of the possibility that humanity can undo a complex knot of related life threatening problems. Climate change is only one of a number of ecologically related stresses that can be relieved by human intervention – others include human over-population, destruction of habitat, and prioritization of economic growth. First, however, some consideration needs to be given to the possibility that things will most likely sort themselves out (positively), without divine intervention, but definitely because there are forces greater than those of humanity alone involved in the unfolding of Earth's future.

The closest science has come to endorsing this possibility might appear to be the proposition that Earth is a self regulating system, with considerable powers of recovery. For many years (since the late 1970's) deep ecologists and large numbers of Green Party supporters have argued that James Lovelock (in particular) had scientifically demonstrated that Earth was a complex self-regulating entity that was alive, sentient and intelligent. If so, perhaps we might not need to worry so much about the consequences of human actions: Gaia will prevail in the long run.[31]

LOVELOCK AND THE GAIA HYPOTHESIS

Lovelock's Gaia Theory is fascinating and plausible, but is it testable? All his writing about Gaia is supported by scientifically based ideas, yet, like Darwin's proposition that 'the fittest survive', it is hard to imagine what a successful refutation might be. As suggested below, perhaps the end of all life would be the strongest refutation of the hypothesis of a planet capable of manipulating conditions to suit life. In any case, Lovelock's writing seems too close to mythology, or ideology, to draw much public support from scientists. That is not to say he is wrong.

Lovelock is still famous for bringing the mythological idea of Gaia close to the realms of 'normal' science. In his view, Earth (or Gaia) is:

> a self-regulating system made up from the totality of organisms, the surface rocks, the ocean and the atmosphere tightly

coupled as an evolving system. The theory sees the system
as having a goal – the regulation of surface conditions so as
always to be as favourable for contemporary life as possible. It
is based on observations and theoretical models . . . [32]

This is not all that Lovelock has to say in definition of Gaia. He also
says that Earth is alive, is intelligent and 'wise' – as expressed in the evolution of human intelligence.[33]

The idea that Earth is alive is not a new idea, but it is radical coming
from a scientist. The granting of sentience and goal directed behaviour
– 'intelligence', perhaps even wisdom – can be found extensively in the
writings of 'deep ecologists', and in the prior discourses of mystics, alche-
mists and tribal peoples. Lovelock's proposition that Earth is intelligent
is definitely not original – what is original is Lovelock's twentieth (and
twenty first) century synthesis of science based arguments to support the
idea. It might be surmised that Lovelock's views have been so influential
because of his scientific status – but this is a status well deserved. Among
his many contributions to atmospheric science and related fields, he
invented a device to more accurately measure ozone concentrations [34] as
part of his commercially viable career as writer, researcher, independent
scientific consultant, and problem solver.

Lovelock's advocacy of nuclear power has, however, placed him firmly
at odds with the anti-nuclear core of most deep ecological philosophy,
and Green political and philosophical positions – all of which are fundamentally opposed to the use of nuclear power as a 'solution' to global
warming. Indeed, the threat to future generations, and ecologies, from
unsolved issues about safety, waste disposal, and weapons proliferation
do make current nuclear technology an overwhelming problem for any
eco-centric position. Nonetheless, Lovelock, like Hansen, is so alarmed
by climate change and the passing of various ecological tipping points
that he is resigned to the prospect of a very hot planet and a vastly
changed ecology (with, or without, increasing uptake of nuclear power
technology). In that respect climate science functions as a common
ground for individuals with very different political views and assumptions about the prospects of new technologies, and science.

Lovelock is also infamous for his stubbornness about the non-threatening nature of CFC's – because they are relatively inert chemicals, he assumed they could not interact with ozone molecules in the atmosphere. This view is now discredited. [35]

Lovelock thinks humanity has a special role on Earth – we are the brains of the outfit, as it were. In his version, if humans choose to introduce a new mass technology such as nuclear power generation, then this is simply a manifestation of the intelligence of the whole – and conversely, if poor technological choices are made, this is because collective intelligence is insufficiently high. In Lovelock's view a climate saving technology, like nuclear power, is not inevitable, but highly likely because Gaia is intelligent. In any case, there are choices involved – which returns us to a rather familiar (and irrefutable) position: the right choices will deliver us to a more intelligent future, while the wrong choices will lead us downhill, as it were. What is not clear is how the more intelligent path can be revealed. This does not seem to be a matter easily resolved by the production of more science. Wise choices need to be made, which in delightful circularity, returns us to the agency of Gaia.

One could argue that the facts of ecological decline demonstrate something quite different: that humanity is short sighted, reckless and terribly destructive. Perhaps the collective 'intelligence' of a increasingly large human 'whole' can be less than that of its constituent 'parts'. This may not be a welcome idea, but we need to remain open to all possibilities. Systems theory certainly indicates that increasing size and complexity can lead to dysfunction in any system; archaeologists and historians find evidence of decline of empires due to over-complexity and (or) climate change – as further discussed in the next chapter; sociologists and psychologists have noted the abilities of crowds and mobs to demonstrate herd-like behaviours, or more chaotic violence; war and conflict appear a 'normal' part of geopolitics. As even Lovelock would doubtless concede, there is much countervailing evidence against the proposition that collective 'intelligence' is evolving.

There is, however, a less anthropocentric approach to the Gaia myth, as expressed by most deep ecologists: Gaia locates humanity in the vast world of 'nature'. Humanity does not transcend the whole by being the highest intelligence of Earth. Variants of these arguments have been examined by theologians concerned, since at least the time of Thomas Aquinas, to establish the omnipotence of God and the necessary subservience of humanity. Humanity is only part of a much bigger and more complex 'whole' – if there is a higher intelligence it certainly transcends humanity. A similar (non-theist and non-religious) view appears to be the position historically advocated by mythologists such as Carl Jung and Joseph Campbell. This latter view resonates more with indigenous traditional views.

Any version of the Gaia hypothesis is difficult to refute. Even though its scientific plausibility comes from the simpler proposition that Earth is a complex system, the extended idea that this system is intelligent is more difficult to assess. The Gaia hypothesis appears not to be open to scientific refutation and may be more akin to mythology – and, like Marxism, extremely difficult (or impossible) to refute empirically.

Toby Tyrell, an oceanographer, has concluded that Lovelock's version of Gaia is not at all well supported by science. For Tyrell, Lovelock's hypothesis depends upon three main arguments:

(1) *That Earth is an extremely favourable habitat for life;*

(2) *That life has greatly altered the planetary environment, including the chemical composition of the atmosphere and the sea; and*

(3) *That Earth's environment has remained fairly stable over geological time.*

Tyrell suggests that the inability of life to control ice ages and the nitrogen cycle are a refutation of (1). The second argument he thinks is correct, although there is an equally plausible hypothesis, 'the coevolution of life and planet . . . life and the environment influence each other but with no requirement that the outcome improve or maintain Earth's habitability.' Argument (3) 'is contradicted by evidence for climate cycles punctuated by ice ages. We also have evidence of long-term variations in the concentrations of the major ions in seawater, and of snowball / slushball Earth events, when our planet may have completely frozen over. There is also the great oxygenation event itself which caused a mass poisoning of anaerobic organisms . . . My research led to a clear outcome:

that the Gaia hypothesis is not an accurate picture of how our world works.'[36]

Unfortunately for Tyrell's argument, life and Earth are still together, despite ice ages and other events, which may have driven life to near extinction. In Lovelock's 2009 definition (quoted above), his Gaia hypothesis only requires the regulation of surface conditions 'so as always to be as favourable for contemporary life as possible.' There is plenty of wriggle-room there – we are not dead yet.

Most scientists are quite 'positivistic' in the sense of wishing to clearly separate the discourses of science from those of philosophy and other more interpretive cultural spheres such as religion, politics, economics, and sociology. And they tend not to speculate about issues beyond their specialist interests. This is despite the historical examples of physicists of the standing of Einstein, Bohr, Heisenberg and Schrodinger engaging with the disciplines of philosophy (and religion) in the early twentieth century and the contemporary examples of Stephen Hawking and Brian Cox. There are many scientists who do not hesitate engaging with the most profound philosophical issues, but most contemporary scientists do not. Most do not have media attention because of their engagement with popular broadcasting and are more institutionally specialised in their communications. Yet overtly philosophical or not, leading physicists today have become increasingly more positivistic – in the light of the great cosmological advances of astronomy, and the success of quantum physics in providing a 'standard model' of great explanatory power. Physicists of the stature of Stephen Hawking are convinced that physics (and mathematics) can provide a unified theory of everything. [37]

This does not leave much room for the quasi-metaphysics (or irrefutable reasoning) of Lovelock. Hansen, with his apparent obsession for scientific detail, is much more acceptable to scientists – except for the politics. Because of his unwavering personal integrity, Hansen, like Lovelock, enjoys a 'maverick' status in policy circles. Both scientists have done pioneering 'consciousness raising' work, but the heavy lifting required in international policy making now requires other more conventional methods, such as lobby groups, political party initiatives, and mass protest. The impact of the IPCC – a massive, largely voluntary effort, by thousands of scientists contributing over a period of years to assemble a 'consensus' summary – on public awareness has been considerable, but only limited on governments and industry which can still postulate inadequacies in 'the science'. They can point to levels of uncertainty in data about global systems, the long time frames required for collaboration and publication, inability to accurately predict long term weather patterns and climate, and apparent inconsistencies across different scientific fields. Such doubts are convenient to many in governments and industry who are committed to a 'business as usual' scenario; change is generally not desirable and will be strenuously resisted, as the following chapters elaborate.

There is one other disturbing proposition that is consistent with climate science, scientific ecology and deep ecology: Earth is indifferent to the dominance of any particular species. Whether or not humanity thrives or survives in the next few centuries is not ultimately important or even relevant to the basics of science, systems theory or deep ecology. Life will likely continue; ecosystems will adapt to new conditions. Life is very adaptable – extremophile bacteria survived 'snowball earth', and continue to survive in conditions of extreme temperatures, acidity, salinity and pressure. Human beings, however, are not so adaptable.

For those who prefer fairy stories, Lovelock has a more optimistic conclusion:

> As a planetary intelligence we have already shown Gaia her face from space and let her see how truly beautiful she is compared with her dead siblings Mars and Venus. We could have a future in communion with our living planet to make her strong again and able to counter the disabling impacts that are due.

> Thinking this way, how could any one be a pessimist and imagine that the global heating crisis is the end for us or even Gaia? We will probably both survive and from our descendants could evolve the wiser species that could live even closer in Gaia and perhaps make her the first citizen of our Galaxy.[38]

THE ANSWERS WE ALREADY HAVE

Science is highly important for the possibilities of modern Western societies and culture. It is intrinsic to the success of professions and, considered historically, has been deployed by them to encourage a (necessary) optimism about the future of humanity. New knowledge about climate and the health of Earth's ecologies will largely come from the systematic observations, field work and laboratory experimentation of scientists. New technologies with low ecological impacts and possibly globally therapeutic effects will be spawned by scientific research. And yet science and scientists have limited powers in our present ecological crisis – economics, politics and traditional cultural practices continue to be controlling. Often when the wisdom of simpler lifestyles is examined more closely for solutions to modern problems, their science and technology is very simple, and tested in traditional practices. More science is always good, but it would be wrong to credit modern science and scientists with too much. Civilization is a very big program.

Left unchecked, the simple logic of growth economics will push all ecologies to the breaking point. The countervailing necessities of reducing population growth, lowering global consumption rates, cultivating local economies, developing ecologically sustainable energy sources, providing habitat and wilderness areas for the sustenance of biodiversity, and changing dietary practices, all require changes to established patterns of individual consumption and processes of production of goods and services. Many of these measures do not require new science or new technologies so much as the simple determination to change, and co-ordinated social action.

Despite political, economic and cultural obstacles, it is still possible to take a somewhat optimistic view. There are some encouraging signs. For instance, most of the professional commentators reviewed so far would agree that the major steps needed for ecological sustainability would include:

1. Stabilisation and slow reduction of global human populations;

2.   Shifting to low growth and ultimately no growth economics –
     that is, 'sustainable economics';

3.   Major development of ecologically sustainable energy produc-
     tion – this means phasing out the large scale burning of fossil
     fuels;

4.   Increased development of industries that are more efficient and
     less polluting;

5.   Major development of sustainable agricultural practices linked
     to sustainable dietary regimes – this means reducing consump-
     tion of meat and fish, and reducing use of pesticides;

6.   Active choice by populations for lower levels of consumption,
     recycling of waste, and less use of private transport;

7.   Minimising the transport of goods in communities and
     economies;

8.   Institutionalising the importance of ecologically directed lead-
     ership – this means being obliged to use the advice of scientists
     in governments, and in coalitions of governments and private
     enterprises.

These eight points summarise practical suggestions made by environmentalists, eco-activists, Green parties, various professionals, and many
others since the shocking findings of the first 'Club of Rome' report
in 1972.[39]

There is little doubt that these steps, if taken, would deliver a more
sustainable outcome, and pull humanity back from the brink of irreversible decline. Even if catastrophists are right to claim that irreversible
ecological tipping points have been exceeded, the points listed are still
the best that can be done.

Most of the ideas listed had been well canvassed prior to 1972 – in
the more scattered literature and informal networks of the 'alternative
lifestyle movement', and prior to that in the practices and beliefs of
people living simply and in isolation from cities – since time immemo-
rial. Arising out of these long and slow waves of ecological discontent,
the cultural revolution of the 1960's turbocharged the idea that there

was something positive to be gained in 'dropping out' and 'getting back to nature'. In Europe, the USA and Australia there was an outburst of communal living experiments generally based in the belief that 'straight' society was alienated from nature and the cosmos. Living an alternative lifestyle became part of sub-cultural identities that often rejected traditional religions in preference for spiritual experimentation. The material and technological aspects of these counter-cultural experiments were in general 'low tech' – science tended to be more interesting for its cosmological implications than its technological potentials. Investigations into 'alternative' energy sources were somewhat exceptional in being driven by the scientific and technological expertise of many individual innovators and groups – such as the Findhorn Foundation, which continues today.

Many of the items in this list of *things we already know to be good ideas for the health of the planet* can be very 'low tech', and require little further research. In the case of solar energy technologies, for example, the effort required today is mostly about the application of existing knowledge and technologies, and the development of government backed economic incentives for new industries. That remains a highly political step, more controlled by the imperatives of growth economics than simple common sense.

With the exception of the first and the last items on the list (about population reduction, and scientifically advised leadership from governments and industry), the average hippy from the 1960s onwards would have regarded all the other items as 'no-brainers'. If a hippy from Haight-Ashbury, or London, in the late 1960s, could have listed off most of 'the things that need to be done' to save the planet, why hasn't such wisdom become more mainstream?

The obvious answer to that question is that, in general, given other available choices, people have chosen to not live communally; most people like the security of nuclear families and more intensively technological pathways that can deliver health, wealth and personal security. People prefer not to share too many basic commodities. Many modern eco-activists also do not want to return to communes, or the cave. They believe that ecological sustainability is achievable without going to

extremes of economic hardship, communal life, or political despotism –
as the following chapters confirm.

There is, however, one other consideration that often escapes activists
and analysts in wealthy countries: ecological impacts in the developing
economies of China, India, Africa and South America are likely to be
increasingly enormous. It is well known that there is a strong negative
correlation between affluence and population growth. As populations
grow and consumer demand rises and peaks in all these developing
economies, the principled efforts of wealthy countries to limit greenhouse emissions, and other pollution, consumption, and so on, will be
swamped by the sheer volume of adverse impacts from these new hot-
spots of growth – this is the subject of the next chapter.

Science and technology will remain part of an ongoing dialectic
between progress and regress, development and destruction, and all the
secular equivalents of the perennial struggle between good and evil, but
in themselves cannot possibly 'save the day'. 'Going forward' requires
the greening of all other institutions and a much better appreciation of
the obstacles that can prevent 'progress' from becoming an ecologically
defined ideal.

6

CHANGING ECONOMICS

There's much about business I don't understand. I still can't see how you guys bought eggs for seven cents apiece, sold them for five cents, and made a profit.

Yossarian, in Joseph Heller, *Closing Time*. Harper Collins, 1994, p.379.

We can't pursue environmental improvements at the expense of economic progress.

Tony Abbott,
Sydney Morning Herald,
5 December, 2014, p.5.

The painfully slow realisation by most professional economists that economies have material limits is not just the result of an unhealthy obsession with profit maximisation. Neoclassical economics – the dominant 'conventional' approach – has major difficulties confronting a future that will be increasingly absorbed with issues arising from declining stocks of resources, global pollution, and a driving need for limits to growth.

Climate change exposes all economies to increasing costs, as revealed in a number of major government sponsored reports. However, climate change will not be the only global ecological crisis the world's economies will have to confront – as discussed in Chapter 2, population pressures (alone) will guarantee serious problems with the supply and maintenance of stocks of natural resources. There are many ways for global systems to suffer major setbacks, damage and decline. Many of these possibilities are unpredictable. Climate change is, however, upon us, and can provide useful benchmarks for the kinds of global system issues we will inevitably deal with in the future.

The inability of conventional economic approaches to seriously engage with the problems of ecological decline, and inevitably declining resource stocks, is not just an economic problem. It is also, overwhelmingly, a political problem – the closing chapters of this book are about the present and future importance of green politics. However, economic analysis remains a key driver of all national strategies. Who could forget Bill Clinton's immortal campaign line '[it's] the economy, stupid'? In that light, this chapter raises the possibilities of a quite different approach to economics – 'ecologically sustainable economics'. This is an economic perspective urgently required in an era of climate change, exploding human populations, and cultures obsessed with the imperatives of economic growth and consumption – that combination is on collision course with ecological limits.

Drawing on recent work by economists, this chapter is an ecologically concerned critique of neoclassical economics. Ultimately the shape and content of any 'new economics' can only develop in concert with changing patterns of consumption, production, and changed ideas about human wellbeing, economic activity, and 'economic reason'. Such mass changes depend, in turn, on cultural changes of the kind to which this chapter (and book) is intended as a contribution. Progressive adjustments to existing economic practices also need to be driven by parliamentary means and public demand. Clearly, the development of an ecologically sustainable economics is very much a work in progress.

THE STERN REVIEW

Commissioned by the UK Treasury in 2005 and published in 2007, the Stern Review is widely acknowledged as a benchmark for all economically based government policy analysis of climate change. The Stern team, coordinated by Sir Nicholas Stern, included twenty two others, led by Siobhan Peters. The team sought submissions, conducted literature reviews and performed original research. The Review's acknowledgements section is fully two pages, crediting many academics and researchers, British government departments, non-government organisations, business people, and representatives of thirteen countries, and the European Commission. By any measures the Review was a big and highly credentialed process.[1]

The Stern group are particularly memorable for three general conclusions: that the figure of 1-2% of global GDP is a good estimate of the ongoing costs of sensible reduction of greenhouse gas emissions[2] ; that some discounting of future effects is basic in conventional economic analysis of climate change; and that there can be no global solution to greenhouse gas abatement without the participation of developing countries.

Economists and policy makers continue to differ about details, but the general analysis of the Review is both consistent with neoclassical economic theory and anticipated major issues that have dominated subsequent international climate change forums. In their analysis it is clear that economic outcomes are affected by government interventions (in the form of regulations, taxes, social policies and other political interventions), but that market forces and the assumption of individual self-interest define consumer behaviour and economic logic – this is the essence of neoclassical theory.[3]

It follows that the implications of those three major conclusions of the Stern Report are somewhat reassuring, when they really shouldn't be. What is so disturbing about standard economic analysis is the assumption that economic forces, with a bit of help from governments, are able to solve all future problems. While it is important to recognise the positive strengths of a conventional approach, such as that of the Stern group, it is just as important to recognise its fundamental limitations. A strong empirical basis, a firm grasp of market fundamentals, and descriptive accuracy are positive assets in any conventional approach – yet the future role of declining stocks and resources, and the negative contribution that any economic analysis that presupposes unending growth ultimately has, make conventional economic analysis intrinsically problematic.

The great contribution of the Stern Review is its demonstration that the mitigation of climate change is economically rational *now*. It is clear that action now will have greater benefits now than later – despite uncertainty about the numerical value of the rate of discount to be applied[4], or any reservations about the future impact of developing economies on the economic logic of action *now*.[5]

This conclusion about the immediate need for deep cuts to emission levels has been repeated in other subsequent government reviews. For instance, in Australia the review conducted by Professor Ross Garnaut came to very similar conclusions.[6]

The possibly dampening effects on global economic growth of even the reportedly modest Stern Review estimates of the costs of adequate carbon pollution abatement, in conjunction with uncertainty about the appropriate discount rate to apply in economic modelling, continue to worry many economists. This fact – despite any countervailing assurances about the positive effects of healthier ecologies, greater efficiencies, or the economic contributions of growing renewable energy production and other green manufacturing enterprises – exposes the core weakness of conventional economic modelling. That is dependence on continuing global economic growth of greater than 2 per cent per annum, and, coincidentally, the continuing growth of human populations. Another important limitation exposed by all reviews and policy analyses of climate change is that positive ecological and environmental outcomes will depend on strong actions by governments. Economic analysis can only go so far; economic rationality can be always trumped by political rationality (or political expediency) – and, so far, governments worldwide have not been sufficiently pro-active to make any significant change to rising rates of pollution by greenhouse gases.

Possibly because the commissioned Review reads like an economics textbook, Sir Nicholas Stern published his own more personalised account in *A Blueprint for a Safer Planet* (2009).[7]

His declared reason for writing the follow-up was that the earlier Review was too conservative. Thus, in his own book Stern is quite clear about the need for deep cuts to emissions:

> In the Stern Review, costs were based on an upper limit of 550 ppm CO_2e; the science now suggests this is much too risky. We should see 500ppm CO2e as a more acceptable ceiling, revising as necessary, probably downwards, as we learn along the way [...] the 500ppm target path involves cutting current levels by more than half relative to now [2009] and around a half relative to 1990 or 2000 (which for world totals were fairly close).[8]

No doubt, governments and the international community will continue to generate more economic reviews of the impacts of climate change and the kinds of policies required to address a growing problem. Just as certainly, governments will avoid the fact that conventional economic logic cannot escape a declining situation: global encroachment of ecological limits for human and non-human species, in conjunction with economic models dependent on growth, will lead to disaster, sooner or later. What is, therefore, even more urgent is the development of a political appetite for more thorough reviews of the premises of conventional economics – particularly those relating to growth and the production of sustainable ecologies. This is not a new idea – many people are already engaged with networks and projects related to 'sustainable economics' – however, not many others have been carried along by these new visions. What follows is a middle ground critique focused on the out-dated logic of neoclassical economics, and related assumptions about the nature of global capitalism. This is, indeed, a kind of political economy – but one that can hopefully deliver a radicalised middle ground and not the old clichés of left and right. Changing economics is, without doubt, a very difficult challenge to everything.

THE IMPORTANCE OF
GOVERNMENT INTERVENTION

It was government intervention that prevented a global financial crisis in 2008-09; 'quantitative easing' and other forms of government stimulus worked to stabilise economies. That government intervention in economies can be necessary is a big lesson for all those who still believe in the absolute freedom of the 'market place' and small government – or 'laissez faire' economics. The success of central government interventions in averting a global economic depression is a strong sign that governments can and should regulate economies.

The last global financial panic was caused by lax regulation of banking sectors' pursuit of unsustainable profits. All major players agree that fiscal mismanagement was the cause. Arguably, any future global crises caused by more tangible meltdowns, such as unpredictably bad weather leading to global shortages of basic commodities like food, water and electricity, will be harder to deal with, but governments will have to intervene again to repair infrastructure on a large scale, provide food and energy, and do their best to deter future recessions and depressions.[9]

Fortunately, governments can plan ahead. The economic debates of the day now concern the extent to which governments and taxpayers are prepared to invest in planning models that will necessitate government intervention. Such 'conversations' are a great advance on nothing much being done at all – which roughly characterises the twentieth century. It may have taken a large number of toxic spills, a nuclear meltdown or two, water shortages, and now increasingly obvious climate events to force our habitat onto the political agenda, but now there is at least some agreement in many political parties, in governing environmental portfolios, in think tanks, and in some environmentally focused private sector companies, that environmental issues are here to stay, and that they are going to cost money – and that governments will have to be more environmentally pro-active. The translation of this recognition into policies that work for for bio-systems is proving more difficult – particularly for politicians with 'non-environmental' portfolios, or ideas of relevance defined by the demands of 'winning' (pre-selection, or the next election), or those with the great desire to stay out of trouble and away from overly contentious issues. Hard decisions and the rethinking of basic assumptions can be deferred for a long time, but the ecological penny has dropped.

If major crises resulting from climate change are to be modified, there is little serious disagreement that governments must act to encourage sustainable energy pathways, legislate to reduce pollution, and encourage ecological education and research. Governments must also play a role in discouraging over-consumption and over-development. Improved living standards should not be at the expense of ecological viability. This requires cultural re-programming – and it is imperative that politicians take some responsibility for leadership. It is not reasonable to expect professional educators, or the private sector, to do all the heavy lifting; they may have the motivation, but often may lack the financial means. So far, most politicians are reluctant to disturb the status quo of 'business as usual'.

Many economists, policy makers, and private sector consultants are convinced that steps can be taken to move away from economic models requiring high growth and high consumption while still generating suffi-cient revenue and profit to provide basic infrastructure and employment. Historically, these views have been strongly influenced by Marxist polit-ical economy and more recently by 'dependency theory' that is critical of western capitalist ideas about 'development' and 'underdevelopment'. The main thrust of these views is that it is not economically rational to create poverty by increasingly concentrating wealth in the hands of very few – governments should intervene in economies to re-distrib-ute wealth and provide basic services for all. All successful economies depend on high levels of public participation; high levels of unemploy-ment discourage consumption. Few could argue with that logic on any moral basis, but 'free marketeers' remain unconvinced about the need for governments to provide much in the way of welfare benefits, health care, or the basic infrastructure of roads, railways, clean water, electricity, and other 'basic' services. However, none of these positions and debates have expressed economic analysis in terms of ecological rationality. It is only very recently that ideas about 'sustainability' and the costs of carbon pollution and climate change have emerged out of the shadows of Marxist economics.[10]

In any case, the best stimulus to contemporary post-Marxist theorising of 'sustainable economics' has been the recent global slowdown of economic growth. Even the booming economies of China and Brazil are predicted to slow into the future. Lower rates of growth now define the contemporary reality of economics – all 'wealthy' economies are adjusting to that downward trend. This global contraction is probably more than just another 'correction' on the path of ever growing economies, because it derives from a structural principle of all modern economies: the financing of public infrastructure and services by governments borrowing money and thereby creating both public and private debt. It is becoming apparent that we are living on borrowed money.[11]

There was a major shift in economic foundations mid last century. Booming economies encouraged everyone to borrow. Debt was sold as the quickest path to private and public wealth – as it was under conditions of steady economic growth, because debts could be guaranteed by future earnings, and interest payments serviced using profits generated by economic growth. Unfortunately, when economies slow and jobs are lost, some are unable to repay loans, or pay interest on loans – currently the Greek economy has become so indebted that unless unpopular 'austerity measures' become a new norm in Greek life, the European Central Bank will not lend more money to enable the Greek government to make interest repayments on existing loans.

In all economies the growth of public and private debt continues as the new condition of economic growth. All this is borrowed from the future. There is very little disagreement that, collectively, western economies are living beyond their means. Some are convinced that we will never be able to repay our debts because the days of continuing economic growth are numbered – if for no other reason than the costs of climate change and other environmental 'externalities' will unavoidably depress all future economies. We may face eviction!

Nonetheless, it is the unsustainability of globally high levels of public debt that may be the trigger for a new era of ecologically sustainable economics. At present, however, economists assisting with government economic policies are only just coming to terms with the idea of a global economic contraction. So far conventional economic models are still holding up, or are perceived to be, because fluctuating rates of growth are accommodated in conventional economics. They are already part of business models that assume the 'boom and bust' cycles of capitalist economies. They suffer 'corrections', 'recessions' and 'booms' and 'busts' with some regularity, allowing the term 'business cycle' to indicate order where there is mostly guesswork. Markets are said to be inhabited by 'bears' and 'bulls'. The 'bust' phases of capitalist business cycles are hardly desirable. High unemployment and poverty are conditions that modern economic modelling seeks to avoid, yet, so far these are unavoidable conditions of 'cyclic' economic growth in all economies – in which governments (and national 'reserve' banks) are highly influential in their ability to regulate markets and affect growth through the interventions of legislation, fiscal stimulus, taxation, and reserve bank interest rates.

Growth is the fundamental goal of all modern economies. Contemporary economic wisdom has it that a growth rate more than 2% of GDP, and being 'out of recession', is cause for some celebration.[12]

Anything less than positive economic growth – that is less than zero – is however, officially, a 'forbidden' zone. The political consequences of 'deflation' (or even 'stagflation') are considerable – no 'peace-time' governments survive major economic decline.

Even a globalised capitalism does not appear to have softened this economic cycle; therefore, for various reasons, known and unknown, governments are sometimes forced to intervene strongly in market processes to avoid system failure and an event as dire as 'The Great Depression'. The fact that economies decline with unpredictable regularity is probably why all governments are very wary of increasing public expenditure on pollution abatement and sustainable energy production, or curtailing environmentally destructive mining, logging and farming. The immediate effect of any such intervention would be loss of revenue, loss of jobs and declining share prices – the flow on effects could be major for small economies dependent on primary industries, and for incumbent governments. The consequences of a government leading an economy into recession because of too much spending, and too much debt, is something all Treasurers and their advisors seek to avoid. This limits the amounts governments are willing to invest in research, development and low yield investments – such as solar energy farms. This is true beyond all political ideologies: governments are pragmatic. On the rare occasions when they are not, they tend to be short lived.[13]

The success or failure of political parties as 'economic managers' remains the dominant theme in Australian (and western) political campaigning and looks set to remain so for some time yet.

REINVENTING CAPITALISM

Nonetheless, capitalism has survived, despite its flaws. Some would say that as a complex system of economic, political and social management, capitalism has gone from strength to strength, becoming a global economic system that may even be capable of economic sustainability.

Contemporary corporate capitalism, wherever it is found, has major flaws. As its many critics have pointed out, it has not, and probably cannot, deliver full employment, economic equality, social justice, or ecological sustainability. Wealthy men and large corporations dominate, patriarchal institutions still control, and the earth is plundered in the name of growth and economic prosperity. Only the countervailing forces of secular liberal democracies have prevented the worst excesses of an economic and political system designed to deliver profit and growth. But capitalism is enigmatic, contradictory and changeable.

The continuing survival of some form of international capitalism and market-based economies seems assured. The historically competing idea that capitalism might be 'overthrown' in favour of socialism or communism has become a rather quaint idea, signifying the failed aspirations of many generations of committed leftists. Most political activists now seek to reform capitalism rather than destroy it through violent revolution – social conditions have changed mightily since the nineteenth century when working class revolt was a much more realistic proposition. Today working classes and trade unions are much smaller, and in countries like Australia, more 'aspirational' than fed up, precisely because of the wealth that capitalism has generated.[14]

But is there a single entity called capitalism? This popular simplifi-cation needs to be qualified by a complex history, and an evolution of different types of capitalism within a now global economic order. In fact, there are many different forms of capitalism, each a product of particular social circumstances. Markets, trade, money and private prop-erty are ancient social practices, but most economic historians agree that 'modern' capitalism arrived with the innovation of banking, detailed bookkeeping and the ability of entrepreneurs to organise themselves economically, politically and legally into large firms. These processes of adaptation to changing social conditions are ongoing, and it is this ability to change that gives capitalism its resilience in the face of adversity and system failure.

The idea that there is 'good capitalism' and 'bad capitalism' sums up much of the contemporary economic debate. On that basis, William Baumol and his colleagues categorised four types: state guided capitalism, oligarchic capitalism, big-firm capitalism and entrepreneurial capitalism. The first two types can be seen as 'bad' insofar as they lead to economic stagnation. The last two are better because they can deliver growth. The optimal version according to this view, which roughly characterises 'the west', is focused on an entrepreneurial capitalism, facilitated by big-firm capitalism (or 'corporate capitalism').[15]

Dismissing all capitalism as 'bad', which has been the reflex reaction of the political left, is unhelpful in an era dependent on international co-operation, global trade and international consensus about the need to address climate change in a co-ordinated way. Distinguishing between different types of capitalism is important if improvement of current prac-tices is desired – the basic position in this chapter. Changing assumptions about the necessity for growth may radical for contemporary practice, but clearly desirable, and possible, as Baumol *et al.*, and other more radical economists, such as Herman Daly, show; factoring in increased govern-ment intervention is far more conceivable, and seems unavoidable, in all practical scenarios.

Forward thinking economists, like Tim Jackson, see some cause for optimism despite economists' growth oriented celebrations of the cur-rent world order. It emerges, in the account of Baumol *et al.*, that not all forms of capitalism have to be based on growth. Further, ecological considerations are just not factored into most economic equations. This, Jackson goes on to show, can be remedied by adjusting macro-economic formulae to include ecological considerations.[16]

The 'factoring in' of ecological considerations seems the only way to go if sustainability, within some version of neo-classical economics, is to be possible. Some concrete suggestions will be made in the conclusion to this chapter.

The repeated identification by professionals (in various fields of expertise) of flaws in the dominant economic paradigm should give encouragement to economists seeking change. Well-reasoned critique is, however, only part of the opposition to contemporary modern economic thought. A very loud, and formulaic, part of the opposition originates from generations of Marxist political economists, and their followers, who have assumed, simply, that capitalism will inevitably decline because of its internal 'contradictions'. Hopefully that chorus of complaint can respond to new waves of ecologically influenced reason. The call, repeated here, is that economic theory should adjust to low, or zero, growth, and factor in sustainability – without reviling economic practices that remain entrepreneurial in inspiration. This will require a disciplinary revolution. The drastic alteration of neoclassical economic theory is, however, far more likely than the overturning of international capitalism – as demanded by generations of Marxists and revolutionary socialists. Any radical revaluing of ecologies, government policy and consumer behaviour obviously amounts to profound social and cultural change, but does not require the abandonment of markets, money, banking or private property.

There is a transcendent hope embedded in the thoughts of many forward thinking theorists of capitalism: evolution. If Darwinism is cross-pollinated with cybernetics and a new thermodynamic law, and a pinch of old fashioned faith added, a new form of capitalism will 'emerge'. In other words, the smart money is on capitalism being such an intelligent system that it can learn from financial crises; an intelligent capitalism can evolve into a more resilient and productive system. Anatole Kaletsky calls this 'Capitalism 4.0':

Once we recognise that capitalism is not a static set of
institutions, but an evolutionary system that reinvents and
reinvigorates itself through crises, we can see the events
of 2007–09 in another light: as the catalyst for the fourth
systemic transformation of capitalism, comparable to the
transformations triggered by the crises of the 1970's, the
crises of the 1930's, and the Napoleonic wars of 1803-15.[17]

An evolutionary view of capitalism can, however, also be the default
position for 'business as usual' – in which everything really stays the
same. Ecology, left largely to the mercy of 'free markets' and 'free trade',
slips over the horizon again; climate change might intrude as the costs
of carbon trading, or carbon sequestration, or inclusion of renewable
energy quotas . . . and never ending growth can proceed, as normal. It's
a miracle.

Evolution is very much on the agenda for 'progressive' politics and
economics. This idea, complete with anti-entropic assumptions about
the possibilities of the next phase, is a widespread constant in contemporary futurology, 'think-tanks', and 'technobabble'. Economic evolution
is a central theme in the ideology of contemporary global capitalism.
It is present in the writings of Al Gore, Niall Ferguson, Joseph Steiglitz
and most other public intellectuals who gain the endorsement of major
political parties – particularly those who identify themselves as 'progressive'. Enthusiasm for evolutionary capitalism can easily translate to suit
conservative political views, because evolutionism is ultimately untestable. All change is, potentially, 'evolution' and need not prescribe anything
specific about social justice; 'evolution' can be seen as close to 'the law
of the jungle' – that is, lawless and brutal. Social and economic evolutionism is easily represented as the progressive essence of 'laissez faire'
capitalism: 'survival of the fittest' in 'free markets'.[18]

Nonetheless, it is possible to think in realistic terms that are other than
those of endless growth. And, contrary to the dominant paradigms of left
political economic thought, it is certainly possible to think that social
injustice is not the only cause of ecological decline.

Modern economics is, however, a notoriously closed field of endeavour:

> No other field in the social sciences and humanities comes
> close to economics in its combination of theoretical uniform-
> ity and technical uncertainty [. . .] A degree in economics
> thus implies a capacity to solve artificial analytical problems
> and not an ability to understand everyday events and phe-
> nomena in the economy.[19]

Thus, even if economists are willing to take up new ecological considerations, the field of economics is highly resistant to 'paradigm change',
or radical change to basic assumptions. Yet, this is what the search for
'sustainability' in theory and practice requires. In order to find a way forward it will be necessary to find a way for neoclassical economic theory
and the myth of endless growth to integrate both a re-valued nature and
a reduction in the availability of natural resources. That may entail the
end of neoclassical economic theory: can there be an ecologically sustainable neoclassical economic theory?

Mass demand for economic change is, however, not established. The
changing circumstances are so potentially dire, and the forces oppos-
ing economic change so veiled, that change will most likely be driven
by 'external' imperatives – specifically, ecological decline, the changing
views of other professionals, shifts in consumer demand, and 'popular'
social movements. The needs of capitalist clients may yet turn out to be
more productive than appeals to 'common sense' or 'good' economic
theory. Establishing the profitability of alternative methods of energy
generation and green manufacturing, for instance, would certainly help
to drive change. The expansion of green energy technology would allow
ecological considerations to be factored into economic models – and
at the same time change consumer behaviour, and possibly encourage
governments to prioritise carbon-trading markets.

WHAT IS AN ECONOMY?

Increasing levels of government debt, periodic crises, economic contractions, inflation, high levels of youth unemployment, perpetually inadequate infrastructure, steadily shrinking natural resources, unhealthy ecologies, global warming. . . . there is a litany of complaint that can be described as economic mismanagement, but we should wonder whether the problems of modern economies run deeper. As we have seen, many natural resources, such as clean water and air, are becoming increasingly precious – yet they struggle to enter economic calculations. Further, economists and the discipline of economics seem isolated and unable to grasp that an economy is part of a highly complex and interconnected network of social and natural systems. Economies are becoming increasingly fragile because so many of these 'other' systems are encountering natural limits which are re-incorporated into economic processes. In short, economic theory has become over-institutionalised and will be a prime suspect in any future 'crisis of institutions'. Under similar circumstances any discipline would doubt its basic premises and assumptions.

The modern idea of 'an economy' encompasses two spheres of activity: market economies and government economies. As defined by professional economists, this is a restricted field concealing a great deal of activity that is still economic – in the sense of requiring labour, generating wealth and value, and being processes of exchange. The main excluded zones are household economies, unpaid community economies, illegal economies and natural economies – that is, in the last case, all the unpaid 'work' performed by animals, plants, and other components of the natural ecologies and geo-systems that support all life. Both market economies and government economies involve the circulation of money and other forms of capital and require banks and financial institutions. This economy is reported, scrutinised, taxed and planned. The other economies are informal, less regulated, and much less discussed. But they do generate wealth and value, require work, and are most often processes of exchange. Conventional economic relations are, by definition, based on the exchange of goods, services and labour – usually mediated by money. Of course, not all processes of human exchange are considered economic. Intimacy, friendship, love, and caring are not usually monetized even though they are valuable and basic to wellbeing. They are also basic to healthy communities, along with household economies, voluntary community work and natural economies.[20]

The exclusion of so many sources of value to humans as 'non-economic' has stimulated feminist economists to consider contributions from the household and non-monetized community as economic, in a new sense. Riane Eisler, for example, has written about 'caring economics' in an effort to overcome the domination and exploitation taken for granted in conventional economic theory. The idea that caring is economic only makes sense in the context of an economic paradigm that values the work of caring in the creation of 'wealth', defined in broader terms than money. She argues that economic theory needs to be transformed by empathy, responsibility and concern for human welfare.[21]

Economics that emphasises partnership and caring, many feminists think, could transform society and culture. The role of 'women's work' in reproduction, nurturing, partnering and 'caring' could become much more prominent at a time when the 'masculine' orientation of all cultures is widely appreciated as a cause of violence, domination and inequality. Necessary as this may be, there are two other fundamental problems that will remain, even if humans all care more: the ecological impacts of population growth, and eventual economic decline caused by the resulting depletion of resources. Both issues involve deep problems to do with 'nature'. First, because growth in populations is biologically 'natural' it is difficult to question the rights and rationality of human reproduction; attendant on this fact is the perceived need for economies to grow. Second, the intrinsic value in natural processes – such as the growth of crops, the growth of herds and the geological 'growth' of ores, fossil fuels, and gemstones – has always been appropriated by humans as essentially 'free', or freely available. Humans may incur costs along the way, but, figuratively speaking, don't pay Earth anything. From a commercial point of view, Earth is just a 'source' of wealth and a 'sink' for human waste. The fact that Earth is finite and at risk from 'unsustainable' human practices has only become a commercial issue in the last few decades – as pollution becomes a global problem for human health and agriculture, as some resources show signs of running out, and as some governments apply taxes and market based schemes to reduce carbon pollution.

Many radical economists are well aware there are other economies that fundamentally shape human society, and have sought to include considerations that modern, professional economists cannot. The earliest modern radical economic school of thought was Marxist 'political economy' which provided a major critique of all capitalism – from top to bottom. Marxism is, however, fundamentally human centred, masculine, and, in a very basic sense, anti-ecological. Marxist economic theory is centred on the assumption that human labour is the source of all economic value and that, ultimately, human values always transcend non-human values. In that respect Marxists, and many other leftists, remain very conventional. As explained in subsequent chapters, this criticism is still relevant because Marxist economic ideology is are either smuggled into ecological politics, or overtly asserted as foundational to ecological politics and philosophy.[22]

An economist employed by government, industry, or large to medium sized business cannot charge costs for most conventional 'externalities' – such as pollution, or community health and wellbeing. These considerations can arise in programs of taxation, or other government fees and charges, but governments in market economies tend to avoid them; environmental 'commons' are most valuable to governments and business when they are free. Economists, budgets, forward estimates, and business plans seek to minimise costs in competitive market places. All the 'other' informal economic activities listed earlier are present, but do not control the behaviour of markets, businesses and governments – so far.

It might be argued that capitalism is such a resilient economic mode precisely because it does exclude some economic activity as 'informal'. The exclusion of household economies, unpaid community work, and even illegal activities, from formal recognition in government accounts and most business models means that much activity can proceed untaxed and unscrutinised by governments. All these 'informal' activities, including the exploitation of 'natural capital' in untaxed and unscrutinised activities, form a huge reservoir of 'informal capital', unacknowledged in formal accounting, but necessary for the forward momentum of economies that must grow. Hypothetically, it is the circulation of capital, including all forms of exchange, that provides the resilience of capitalism. Continuing ecological decline makes the issue of informality more important than ever.

Once the natural support for all economies, formal and informal, is seriously threatened it is obviously necessary to address economic fundamentals with radical intent – our collective prosperity, and perhaps our very survival depends on the natural world remaining valuable – in formal and informal terms. In the material that follows the current inadequacies of neoclassical economics will be examined with the objective of establishing more sustainable economic models, and modes of economic activity. This project has been of concern to many for decades; the problems are huge and achievements limited. Failure to change the main game should be no deterrent – in so many ways it is all about the economics.

However economics are transformed, the account that follows assumes that 'capital' will remain valued in monetary terms; markets will remain – humans will continue to exchange their labour and goods in markets of some form or another. It is much more realistic to hope that certain 'natural' things and processes will just become formally valued (and even 'commodified') in ways that can become part of market processes. There is not time to wait for money to be abandoned, or for some wholly new processes of exchange to be quantified, agreed upon, and adopted by all.

GETTING OVER NEOCLASSICAL ECONOMIC THEORY

Current economic orthodoxy is termed 'neoclassical' and builds on a 'classical' economics that established the importance of 'free markets' and minimal government intervention in the economic affairs of capitalism. After the great depression and the various boom-bust cycles and recessions that followed, current economic orthodoxy is reconciled to the importance of government intervention at critical times. The heat in most debates about economic policy is generated by differences over appropriate levels of government intervention and taxation. At the extreme, Tea Party followers in the USA would leave health cover and the provision of roads and services entirely to the private sector. Their guiding ideal of *small governments and totally free markets* is clearly a very simple idea about how capitalism ought to work – it leaves human welfare, and all social processes to be addressed by market forces alone. Opponents point out that free markets cultivate social inequality, and are indifferent to human and non-human suffering; further, no markets are ever actually 'free': if governments don't regulate them criminal organisations, or armies, will.

If capitalism has its critics, modern economic theory also has its critics. Most fundamentally, neoclassical economic theory assumes that all individuals are selfish, but rational – and therefore will act rationally in their own interests (as far as they are able). This belief has attracted the ire of all those who believe that society benefits enormously from cooperation and egalitarian ideals. The criticism is based upon the sociological 'truism' that if we are by nature social creatures (and not atomistic individuals) qualities other than selfishness are necessary to explain social cohesion. Collectively defined attitudes and behaviours such as altruism, loyalty, team play, and caring come naturally – the default position for human life is not 'nasty, brutish and short', but social.[23]

The belief that people ought to behave for the 'common good', whether based on religious or secular arguments, probably goes back into the mists of time; the idea that we are social by nature only gained real impetus in modern times. Only by the late nineteenth century had a fully sociological view of the individual in society emerged in European and North American philosophical cultures. The now commonplace idea that societies are more than the sum total of individuals that constitute them had finally emerged – with sufficient certainty and status to allow the establishment in universities of a new academic discipline, sociology[24], and to eventually popularise collective ideals in language and mass cultures.

The academic development of sociology marks an important moment in the development of views that are able to be thoroughly critical of the assumption that 'economic man' is a selfish individual, and that this is an irreducible human condition. We now understand that individuals are born into social relations, language, values, rules and laws. Individuals are socialised and 'encultured' and are social by nature. Our personal realities are constructed in society, and by society. This includes our understandings and experiences of what it is to be in nature, and of nature – and what it means to be 'economically rational'.[25]

This 'social construction of reality' indicates human perceptions and ideas are open to change. To some extent we can, in a secular society, choose to change; and this is why it is so important to value popular political processes. They may be uncomfortable and disconcerting, but contemporary western societies, in particular, have gained the ability to vote in change without going to the extremes of violence. Indeed, legislation in constitutions and civil laws of the ideals of freedom of speech, belief, and the right to vote, is historically recent and far from being a universal cultural standard. The idea that we ought not be selfish individuals for reasons other than theology is still emerging, to various degrees, in the constitutions and laws of all countries. It is probably more accurate to describe this 'secular' cultural process as being just as much a triumph of human rights forced by social movements over long periods than (simply) an achievement of human reason. Only with the decline of religious power and the rise of the modern secular state, in Europe and the United States, did it become possible that such ideas about freedom, rights, and change could become part of popular cultures.

Nonetheless, modern 'progressive' (but still orthodox) economists – like Joseph Steiglitz, Nicholas Stern, Tim Jackson, and the Australians Ross Garnaut and Ross Gittens – still struggle with the competing demands of a 'common good' that can maximise the interests of selfish individuals. This is the defining social problem of all modern economics, and all of the institutions of liberal democracies. The rule of law, public bureaucracies, police, armies, churches, and all other guiding organisations and cultures of modern societies – including science – struggle with the competing demands of individual self-interest and collective obligations. Selfishness is not, of course, restricted to individuals, since all groups and all organisations (public and private) have their own self-interests that may put them on a collision course with 'the common good'.[27]

An ecological crisis 'ups the ante' for these established dilemmas. Now another collective interest has emerged to challenge human society in very fundamental ways. An ecosystem, of which humans are only part, raises big issues concerning rights, responsibilities and ethical behaviour – because the transcendence of human interests cannot be taken for granted. Conventional human-centred ideas about reasonable behaviour and the interests of personal survival need rethinking and qualification in personal behaviour, in institutional norms and values, and in legislation and constitutions. All eco-centric ideas are particularly challenging to conventional economic and legal ideas – particularly moves to grant more autonomy to non-human entities.

In the confined world of conventional macro-economic theory there can be little reason to celebrate the instalment of the costs of environmental damage into national accounts. Without changing the ground rules, the relevant adjustments cause big headaches. The best an ecologically concerned, but still conventional economist, such as Professor Jackson, can suggest is a 'production function' that can include costs of capital, labour and energy (including alternative energy) and costs of pollution taxes. The factoring in of 'investment strategies' that involve the protection of ecosystems may be necessary, but such calculations are still a 'work in progress'.[28]

Ecologists would hope that economic simultaneous equations can stretch further than that, and fairly soon. They would also hope that the idea of natural limits might intrude more directly – the analysis of the first report of the Club of Rome was so devastating precisely because naturally arising (but socially caused) 'limits to growth' were the eventual cause of system collapse.

Tim Jackson's work is important because for some economists it is 'state of the art' as far as an ecologically sensitive (and 'low growth') neoclassical economics are concerned. It is also important because it is unlikely that conventional economic theory, policy, and practice in business, is likely to change much further in the near future. Jackson does global ecology a great service by at least attempting to 'price in' some ecological costs of production and attempting to allow for longer-term ecological investment strategies. Imperfect as standard economic practices may be, neglect of market mechanisms and trading schemes for pollutants, the realistic pricing of scarce resources such as water, and neglect of the need to factor in the costs of protecting ecological resources, could prove catastrophic – and very expensive.

One can sympathise with professional economists who do see paradigmatic problems looming. New theory, starting with changed assumptions about growth and the value of ecological 'externalities', will be very challenging. New economics may not seem much like old economics. For example, in reviewing Tim Jackson's work, Robert Hoffman suggests, 'it is unlikely the new economic theory will be a macro economics at all: [r]ather the new economic model will have to be pragmatic in the decomposition of institutional space and its links to the underlying biophysical space.'[29]

Much current discussion of economic theory and different 'models' concerns the nature of capitalism and how it ought to proceed. However, much of the criticism from the left about future directions of both capitalism and economic systems still proceeds as if economies really were disconnected from environments and ecologies. The 'creative destruction' of capitalism provides a good example of an idea whose trajectory from nineteenth century discourse about the human tragedy of development and progress has terminated in 'high left' debate about the continuing relevance of Marx. This is an analytical world so dominated by humans that the non-human world continually 'melts into air'.[30]

In David Harvey's otherwise brilliant retake of the left in *The Condition of Postmodernity*, the 'compression' of space-time' is the answer to all questions about the meaning of modernity and postmodernity. 'All the Enlightenment imagery about civilization, reason, universal rights, and morality were for naught.' The real spirit of capitalism (creative destruction) can be found in a lineage descended from Goethe's *Faust* – running through Weber's 'iron cage' of bureaucratic rationality and Nietzsche's perception of energies that were 'wild, primitive and completely merciless'. This bleak view leads, in Harvey's analysis, to another now quaint nineteenth century idea, 'becoming'. Hegel thought becoming was a fundamental idea, as did Marx, Heidegger and generations of post-Marxists. Unfortunately, becoming more ecologically integrated has always been equated (by left and right) with an undesirable loss of reason (and faith). If *becoming connected* amounts to anything less than a celebration of human rationality and human interests, the left have always, in effect, turned right.[31]

No matter how hard the academic left has tried, right to the point of distilling the essence of nineteenth century post-enlightenment thought, nature and the environment continue to fade into the background. It is a truly remarkable cultural phenomenon that the near terminal decline of global ecology caused by the bulldozing development of modernity can continue to be hidden in the suffering of the underprivileged.

The limitations of neoclassical economic assumptions have been the subject of considerable debate, even though focus on economic theory has usually been dispersed in broader criticisms of 'capitalism'. Control of societies by markets, commerce, consumption, economic reasoning, and profit taking has particularly outraged modern sociologists, political economists, journalists and other social commentators.[32]

Not all of this criticism is modern in origin. Theological precedents for the criticism of 'materialism' can be found in all religions, and church leaders of all persuasions have espoused them since the beginning of Christianity. The philosophy of moral outrage has even more ancient roots: 'everybody knows' about moral decline, greed, self-indulgence, venality, corruption, criminality, materialism, breakdown of community, and so on.

Most criticisms of 'capitalist economics' are well known and obvious enough. Further, in the twentieth century, various communist societies attempted alternative centralised, collectivist practices; none have been able to survive global capitalism. Authoritarian control, five year and ten year plans, austerity, poverty, and periods of mass starvation still occur in a number of state controlled dictatorships, and few would mourn their passing. None of the current alternatives to 'capitalist society' – for example, The Peoples Republic of China, North Korea, Cuba, or Iran – provide any credible alternative to capitalist society and the dominant economic reasoning of neoclassical economic theory.

Ecological imperatives may, however, change the emphasis of cultural and social analysis that has been so damning of capitalist economics and 'economic rationalism'. If the most pragmatic criticisms of 'left' and 'right' (from Churches and conservatism) are combined with an ecological critique, there is definite agreement about major failings of current economic orthodoxy. These can be summarised as: excessive inequalities in the distribution of wealth, over-consumption, waste, pollution, and destruction of natural environments by over-development. This consensus prevails over very different appreciations of 'the system' of capitalism. The big issues over which there is more limited agreement include over-population, climate change and the need for economic growth. As argued in the last chapter, these last concerns will be defining issues for the future of capitalism and the field of economics.

Paradoxically perhaps, there is analytical advantage to be gained from a more restricted, ecologically focused, critique of economic orthodoxy. Among ecologists and economists there is some agreement about the main failures of the neoclassical model with respect to the problems of growth and ecology. These criticisms extend to 'the big three' issues without necessarily demanding over-radical measures in the short term.

The main points of agreement about such limitations of neoclassical orthodoxy are that it requires:

- reduction to a single measure of value;
- restriction of the idea of production to a *capital* and *labour* which excludes the material and biological processes involved;
- an over-restrictive view of 'flows' that can only be described in terms of income, production, consumption, savings, investments;
- exclusion of ecological stocks, flows and reserves (of, for example, minerals, fossil fuels, arable land, fish and forests);
- failure to extend these 'stocks' into public social infrastructure;
- failure to deal with the unequal distribution of income.[33]

Global accounting of ecological stocks, flows, and resources is a hugely complex project, requiring ever-new generations of processing power. However, if we can assume that good estimates are already available, the injection of calculable 'quanta' of matter, energy and life in ecosystems into economic models is not *a priori* impossible; the main obstacle appears to be the intransigence of neoclassical modelling – as indicated in Tim Jackson's work. The transformation of the real value of ecological systems into economic behaviour will require imaginative leaps and political determination to pursue 'hard' options that might include the creation of new markets, such as the carbon trading markets we already see, and new taxes on polluting industries and greater encouragement for renewable industries. Softer options should include more funding for research and development projects that can benefit environments and ecologies – including multi-disciplinary economic research and development – and related educational projects.

The conceptual leaps required go to the very basics of conventional economic understanding. Creating economic ecological values where there are presently none will be challenging for an economic system based on trade and markets. Governments will need to create conditions for the emergence of new markets – such as markets for polluting chemicals other than carbon – and support emerging markets for sustainable goods and services, such as renewable energy systems. Yet, as Australian experience shows, new taxes and higher prices are always resisted by business and consumers – cost minimisation is basic to successful business practice and household budgeting. Governments have to be firm about the necessity for change, and businesses need to understand why; only governments have the legitimate means to maintain the pressure, but ultimately they can always be forced to yield to public pressure – these are subjects in following chapters.

It may be that economic theory is changing as rapidly as is possible. The general acceptance that there are no perfect markets was a breakthrough; the new development of welfare economics gives some hope that 'externalities' can be 'priced in' without abandoning fundamentals.

If economic theory is to change more quickly it will most likely depend on economists becoming more open to insights from outside the discipline. However, the current intellectual isolation of economists, and bankers, was underscored by the recent global financial crisis. According to Bank of England chief economist (and research director), Andy Haldane, '[o]ne of the guilty secrets of the pre-crisis period is that institutions, including banks, didn't form a big part of the models we were using to make sense of the economy. In some cases they played no part at all.'[34]

If we can judge from another of his 'throw way' remarks, it is doubtful that any 'guilt' the Bank of England, or Andy Haldane, may profess will lead to serious engagement with other professions and institutions:

> We're trying to make better sense of social systems like the economy and the financial system. We've already begun to make strides. I have tried to fuse bits of economics with physics, epidemiology, psychology, anthropology and one or two other ologies, to try to make sense of the world [. . .] One of the key elements of our new agenda is a better understanding of how social systems behave under stress. We've started investing in new data sets and databases – social media information and the like [. . .]
>
> Social systems need to go through upswings and downswings – and occasionally need to fail. It's how they fail that matters, ideally in ways that don't tip the economy over a cliff.[35]

BRIDGING THE DISCIPLINARY DIVIDE

Even though many senior economists and bankers appear not to be engaging with the development, global biophysical modelling, pioneered by early generations of systems theorists (including the Club of Rome), has become a major research activity – of interest to many organisations and disciplines. Organisations with global interests, and large regional interests (for example, the United Nations and national research organisations, such as Australia's CSIRO) have a very direct interest in stocks and flows of resources and human populations. This modelling often involves more than geophysical estimates; socio-economic considerations are also important to management and planning in many organisations, agencies and programs. World health, aid, food production, water resources, education, and economic performance all require global modelling. National and regional management and planning involve similar demands. So too do the operations of all businesses. There are many scientists and economists, managers, administrators and consulting organisations whose work involves computer modelling of large systems and efforts to predict their future behaviours.

The connection of biophysical data to economic analysis can be challenging when this involves more than simple calculations with known data. For economists and project managers the security of immediately available resources, known crop yields, established interest rates, and known market conditions enable confidence about short-term outcomes. Longer-term projects involving significant predictions require statistical analysis, mathematical modelling, computer software (and hardware) development, and close familiarity with the history of economic markets, financial products, government regulations, taxation, and the law.

Despite common interests in global modelling, there is a disciplinary divide between scientific ecologists and economists – one can blame economists for being narrow in their calculations of profit and loss, but just as surely ecologists resist the determination of market forces, and the complexities of economic theory that is intrinsically resistant to the intrusions of ecological reasoning.[36]

In general, global modelling by economists and ecologists is difficult to draw together because of different disciplinary assumptions and different practical aims. For instance, the meaning, pursuit, and effects of 'competition' can be different. For ecologists, the survival of a diversity of species is sought after, as is the preservation of quality habitats and species diversity; for market economists the reduction of competition by too many firms is actively sought in order to maximise the extraction of profit as private wealth; this also maximises inequality in the distribution of wealth. Such 'anti-competitive' strategies in supposedly competitive market places are routine strategies that allow economic 'success'. Large scale growth does not require competition or healthy diversity; growth allows economies of scale, the ascendency of large firms, monopolies, cartels and 'globalisation'; growth can discourage competition as small firms are squeezed out of markets by discounting, professional lobbying, and other monopoly practices; and so on. In that context, reference by economists and other corporate professionals to 'ecology' refers to economic practices that are anti-competitive with 'capital' circulating in markets that eliminate diversity[37] might therefore struggle to recognise an economic ecology as a healthy biological analogue; more likely the ecology of economic markets models the degradation of natural ecologies and the biosphere – for most economists that tendency is 'natural'.

Similar paradigmatic differences arise with the use of words like health, vitality and resilience. For instance, economic health and ecological health are as different as positive figures in a balance book are to robust living organisms. The ecologies of natural scientists are about systems with stocks and flows of matter, energy, and life forms. For scientists, these ecologies are 'real' and 'bio-systems', unlike the more abstractly defined 'ecologies' of advertisers, managers and economists.

Words like *ecology, health, vitality, resilience* and *robustness* are rhetorically powerful in any discourse – they imply life and organic intelligence in ways that go well beyond intellectual awareness. The sights, sounds and smells of a nature that is wild and untamed are almost on hand, ready to confer the magical benefits of imaginative association on any customer, client or bystander. However, the power of these words is not only rhetorical – they are useful in describing the behaviour of all systems, and they encourage reference to living systems for examples of 'resilience', 'health' and 'intelligence' – these words are now part of the discourse of systems theorists and many other professionals. It seems that in this new enthusiasm for 'natural' qualities we may have to yield to a new vernacular: a smoothly functioning system is 'healthy' in all accounts; if it can survive stress it is 'resilient'; if it can make decisions it is 'intelligent'.

Nonetheless, paradigmatic disagreements about the meaning of 'competition', 'ecology' and 'health' separate disciplines and professions – and this may not be an ecologically counter-productive situation. As 'deep ecologists' and 'eco-feminists' have argued, the reduction of life to abstract systems by systems theorists and scientists is not necessarily in the interests of life or 'natural rights' – as further discussed in Chapter 8. Such differences are not, however, the only forces that might separate cultural fields, academic disciplines, professions and institutions. Secrecy and competitive advantage are also important considerations. There are many sociological considerations that come to bear in these last respects. For instance, the integration of research efforts across different fields also involves serious competition around the creation of individual careers. Academic success, for example, is dependent on success in publication and participation in the gaining of grants and other support for individual and team based research projects. Further, interdisciplinary work (such as climate change modelling) may not be the best way to gain success in individual disciplines, university departments and schools, or in dedicated research organisations. Organisational contexts are also important in determining the extent to which knowledge is shared through accessible publication. Many scientists and economists are employed in organisations (private and public) where they are subject to agreements that research be 'commercial-in-confidence'. When employment is directly geared to commercial outcomes, peer reviewed publication may not be a desirable outcome for businesses where scientific research (and knowledge) is a condition of market competition, knowledge may not be widely shared at all.

These considerations have great bearing on the ability of economists to 'think outside the square'. However, it would not be sensible to assume that neoclassical economists are less likely than scientists to share their ideas in the interests of global ecology. Nonetheless, economics is a field in need of a cultural revolution – in contrast to new fields like ecology and climate science that are generally more open to changing ideas. These latter fields have not had time to develop a highly codified theoretical core (unlike economics) and their practitioners are more engaged in developing new approaches to problem solving than defending established practices.

Yet when serious problems (such as global warming) threaten global systems, they have the ability to force change and innovation in many disciplines (old and new), and encourage entrepreneurial research to arise widely in response to new demands – theoretical modelling, data analysis and technological innovation all thrive on new problems. Such 'problem oriented' research can also force theoretical development. Climate change, for instance, has forced greater scientific focus on thermodynamic considerations as part of the modelling of global mass and energy flows. These big systems are now dynamic in ways that were once not contemplated at all – heat transfer and storage by the oceans, for example, is now considered critical for the long term modelling of climates. It remains to be seen how the global modelling of climate scientists and ecologists will impact on the global modelling of economists – other than rhetorically.

There are two obvious general conclusions that can be made about the contribution of large scale modelling to practical efforts to reign in global warming: more scientific data is urgently needed *and* more cross-disciplinary analysis involving both ecology and economics are also necessary. Australia's chief scientist, Professor Ian Chubb, has generalised the situation in strong terms:

> Collaboration is essential if we are to see real progress on our goals. We need the new ways of thinking that spark when the disciplines combine. At the same time, we need to keep sight of the unique contribution that every discipline has to make. In a cross-disciplinary world, we are only as strong as our weakest link. We need to be ready to snatch opportunity wherever it lies.[38]

One might wonder how scientific data about 'non-commercial' stocks and flows in global 'commons' – such as the pollution levels of the oceans and atmosphere, or their temperatures – can enter economic equations that might influence the business practices of capitalist firms in competitive markets. It is hard to avoid the conclusion that governments must intervene (in market processes, and the steering of publicly funded research) if businesses are to incur costs for their role in maintaining environmental quality.

Given that governments already do levy fees, charges and taxes for 'externalities' such resource management, risk management, social welfare and carbon trading, one might think ecological sustainability costs should not be too much of an additional stretch. As Jackson's work demonstrates there are ways to price ecological concerns into macro-economic models, but governments, businesses and voting populations need to be persuaded that such moves are economically rational. All recent Australian experience shows that even very modest proposals to levy costs for climate change mitigation (such as new taxes) are always vigorously opposed by those affected. For the economically rational, being competitive is more important than being ecologically sustainable.

Fortunately, economic rationalism is only part of a complex socio-political landscape.

Businesses and voters may not like it, but with political will more can be done without overturning all the laws of capitalist development. The calibration of broader ecological values in new markets will undoubtedly be an excruciatingly difficult project for politicians, forever. But that will be part of the price of survival.

Clearly, neoclassical economic theory raises difficulties for all ecological accounting and planning aimed towards a more sustainable future. 'Economic rationalism' is also at odds with cultural traditions that are broadly compassionate. Part of the difficulty is 'philosophical' – the assumption of selfishness is too limiting to account for all human needs and behaviour; reduction of values to dollar terms is alien in biological sciences, and in the arts, humanities and social sciences; different goals, theories and methods can make cross-disciplinary collaboration difficult. And part of the problem is 'political' and commercial – an economic system that must grow encourages over-population and over-consumption.

In the short term, the commercial interests of large and small firms adversely affected by increased costs due to ecologically related taxes, levies, and other constraints on business practices, will seek to avoid lower rates of profit. In the short term, political parties and governments are necessarily more driven by private sector funding than they are by 'public interests' not accompanied by widespread public outrage.

For this reason government intervention through taxes, regulations, new laws, and enforcement regimes are vitally important for the success of 'sustainable' models of development in capitalist economies. In chapters to follow, it will be argued that green politics and more generally, 'progressive' politics should be key elements in democratic parliamentary processes. The violent extremes of revolution and catastrophe (natural or social) threaten to become global factors in future change, but it is considered that the regulated processes of parliamentary democracies are infinitely preferable. In that context, the possibilities of sustainable development and progressive politics depend upon two main pathways of development –

- new technological developments that can revolutionise economic performance and efficiency, and/or
- new economic models that can factor in ecological constraints.

Typical technological schemes, so far, include the development of innovations that can either integrate with existing industry, agriculture and infrastructure, or more radical 'blue sky' proposals that could change social practices greatly. There are a great many current research and development initiatives producing new technologies for energy production, pollution abatement, communication, transportation, building design, water supply, mineral extraction, food production, and so on. The major hurdle that all new technologies face is the ability to provide a profit on capital investment, whether or not they are socially or ecologically desirable. All new technologies need to generate market demand, and this is premised on the assumption that economies can, and must, continue to grow. The strongest challenges to this logic take the form of arguments about 'sustainability'.

As the following section suggests, some thinking about sustainability is basically science fiction, requiring economic 'decoupling' – an enticing economic term raised by Tim Jackson in *Prosperity Without Growth*. Even if we can exclude those fantasies that seek to avoid basic laws of science, the conjunction of ecological limits and economies that can grow indefinitely requires a level of denial even more insidious than that of climate change denial. The possibility that economies might be able to grow indefinitely, and allow economists to muddle on without changing too many underpinning assumptions, definitely requires consideration – but if this can be demonstrated to be a hollow dream, we need a Plan B. All viable proposals for sustainable pathways necessarily involve both lines of development – new technology plus new economic models. This can be described as a form of 'relative decoupling'.

EXPLORING 'DECOUPLING'

If it is accepted that economies must continue to grow, their current unsustainability is a problem that has to be solved. It is curious that this issue is rarely recognised as the 'show stopper' it really is. Can there be any reasonable basis for the high levels of deferral and denial that hide this issue away from public discourse?

At best, there appears to be one easy theoretical 'solution' to current unsustainability: just 'decouple' economic performance from finite material resources. If economies could be made independent of dwindling material resources and their pollution controlled, they could continue to grow without hitting 'natural' limits – assuming that ever increasing populations could be fed, employed and cared for. This could be the only *rational* basis for the highly relaxed attitudes of governments and businesses. The idea, therefore, warrants closer inspection.

If the production of wealth could be somehow transformed through the use of more efficient, less resource consuming, and less polluting technologies, populations and economies could continue to grow. Eventually population growth would have to plateau, but economies might be able to grow indefinitely. Very efficient recycling, and possibly the importation of new materials from asteroids, might be required. That would be a very high-tech future, enabling much larger human populations to be sustained indefinitely – because new technologies could provide the necessary resources to maintain life supporting environments. Such a transformation of wealth production and ecologies using, ideally, renewable resources and ecologically sustainable processes, enhanced by new technologies, could only succeed if social conditions were also favourable – in the current context this assumes the continuation of liberal parliamentary democracies and market economies well into the future.

Although we are far from achieving this 'decoupling', we can, at least, contemplate the possibility – clearly, the achievement of somehow decoupling economies from existing 'natural' constraints is necessary if economic growth is to continue. That decoupling is not presently possible does not make the prospect any less fascinating for many technologists and economists.

In any scenario, even if humanity lives more simply and peacefully, increasing levels of production, consumption and pollution driven by increasing human populations will require some kind of technological magic to overcome the inevitable exhaustion of non-renewable resources; processes of production will struggle to find replacement strategies. The technological magic most needed now relates to large-scale production of renewable energy by solar energy conversion technologies, controlled fusion, or the capture of cosmic rays in outer space, or some other means that didn't pollute the atmosphere, earth and oceans. Under those conditions global economies could really crack on. Or could they?

In the short term, perhaps they could — but unfortunately, in the longer term, the laws of thermodynamics, and the laws of conservation of mass and energy, remain resolute obstacles. Getting something for nothing is impossible; or, alternatively, getting more of anything (except disorder) is impossible without doing work. In that respect life is subject to universal laws.[39]

In the longer term Earth would most likely continue to heat up because any 'new' energy will increase the average temperature of the atmosphere. From a scientific perspective, global warming, and the destabilisation of climates we currently experience, is very much a thermodynamic process. This amounts to the related fact that thermodynamic considerations provide an ultimate limit to the possibilities of 'decoupling' — even if energy can be produced much more efficiently. Clearly, decoupling remains a science fiction scenario. Earth might be able to somehow export heat to the Moon or Mars; or perhaps artificially generated clouds, or orbiting mirrors, might be able to reflect incoming radiation; however, the capture, production and retention of heat in the atmosphere and oceans necessitate that, into the near future, most ecosystems will just have to adapt to generally warmer conditions.[40]

An 'information society' based on new communication technologies and artificial intelligence is another newly popular idea. The introduction of virtual realities, new virtual economies, and new methods of production (such as laser printing technologies) can all be regarded as information flows that are somewhat decoupled from gross matter and energy. Flows of electrons, quantum encryption, nano-technology and other manipulations of the very small are promising new frontiers indeed, but none so far avoid the 'laws' of thermodynamics and related concepts such as the conservation of mass and energy. Further, ecological impacts will continue to intrude.

'Absolute decoupling' is still very much science fiction. The 'magic bullets' of new technologies all have their limits – there are thermodynamic barriers that define the maximum efficiency of any device, and the ability of life to survive. 'Sustainability' obeys the laws of thermodynamics and all other natural laws; only human made laws are negotiable. Economic processes have limits and possibilities that are defined by *both* the laws of science *and* the imagination of humanity. However, all economics remain fundamentally tied to the material exchanges that define life as we know it.

'Relative decoupling', or doing the same (or better) with less is, on the other hand, an existing technological and cultural phenomenon. Increased efficiencies of production, lower consumption rates, and greater uptake of sustainable technologies are possible right now, and in small measure achieved, because they make good economic sense in any strategy.

New technologies can create greater efficiencies in production, improved planning, more accurate and detailed administration, better communication and many other exciting possibilities, but are not entirely without negative consequences. As discussed earlier in the chapter, the 'creative destruction' of capitalism impacts both human and non-human worlds. New jobs and industries have human costs – typically 'de-skilling', unemployment, ill health and loss of community. The innovation of robots in car manufacturing – or electronic typesetting in newspaper production, or steam engines in factories, for example – all swept aside established occupations, crafts, skills and whole workforces. Environmental and ecological effects are also often profound – industrial plants, housing and infrastructure are made and remade with the progressive loss of natural environments and wildlife.

DECOUPLING GROWTH AND WELLBEING

If we look for changes we can most easily achieve, our personal consumption is an obvious starting point. Consuming less and improving the efficiencies of our energy use are lifestyle initiatives that are in many ways common sense and probably better for personal health. And yet, paradoxically, what might appear to be the easiest pathway to increased efficiencies and decreased ecological impacts – changing lifestyles – is probably the most difficult *collective* long-term step. As we have seen, changing lifestyles is not simply a matter of logic or reason, or just a matter for individual choice.

Social critics have long claimed that consumerism and advertising deliberately distort human ability to distinguish between basic needs and commercially driven desires. Or, as Karl Marx claimed in the mid-nineteenth century, capitalism 'alienates' humanity from nature.[41]

The recent upsurge of interest in happiness and wellbeing as relevant to economic thought can then be seen as a long overdue re-exploration. Left critics have traditionally resisted this line of thought because it has been considered 'counter-revolutionary' to simply lower one's economic and material expectations. Of course that did not deter post-1960s alternative lifestyle pioneers who were quite happy to limit their politics to personal choices, and perhaps even 'drop out', rather than join with angry revolutionaries. Nonetheless, once a certain level of comfortable subsistence has been achieved, in any society, material expectations can be changed without necessarily diminishing happiness or wellbeing. This is what some contemporary economists (and others) are now referring to as 'relative decoupling'.

In any culture, distinctions can be made between 'prosperity', 'human flourishing', and even 'happiness' on the one hand, and economic wealth on the other. Subjective states like 'happiness', or 'fulfilment' are not simply dependent on economic wealth. And conversely, it is widely accepted that a certain level of economic wealth may be necessary for health and happiness, but wealth is not necessarily sufficient to guarantee either state.

Tim Jackson and other economists have provided solid socio-economic evidence showing the extent to which the 'relative decoupling' of wellbeing and economic wealth is a reality in many countries. Life expectancy, infant mortality, and participation in education are similar in a number of countries despite very different levels of wealth. Cubans, for example, fare just as well as Americans or British, or other countries with up to six or seven times as much GDP per capita. Once a certain income threshold is crossed, public health is 'relatively decoupled'.[42]

Current research indicates that once these basic thresholds are reached, wellbeing and happiness can easily follow. For example, Jackson, following the lead of philosopher Martha Nussbaum, suggests that 'human flourishing' is possible without economic growth. Within certain (undefined) limits, life, health, physical security, 'practical reason', affiliation, and play, are already achieved by many people.[43]

Popular usage indicates that ideas of wellbeing are more grounded in physical health and positive life styles that may or may not deliver immediate happiness, but still allow individuals to feel good and productive.

FUTURE DIRECTIONS – GETTING OVER GROWTH

Fundamental changes in economic thought are necessary. Even the most obvious necessary changes – incorporating ecological stocks, flows and resources into economic modelling and recalibrating the values of economic commodities – imply such broad changes to economies and business models that they would certainly impact on public life. Putting a significant dollar value on the health of ecological systems that are not yet economic commodities, or on the health and wellbeing of future generations will require shifts in culture and society – and not least, public opinion. In the short term it is most unlikely that business and governments will stray far from the economic orthodoxies of the 'neo-classical' economic model, which assumes continuing economic growth. There is, however, much that can be achieved using the conventional means of government intervention in markets via new taxes, new laws and regulations, increased government support of sustainable technologies, and public education about sustainability.

Along those lines the Australian research and policy think tank, the Wentworth Group of Concerned Scientists, have recently made a number of highly constructive suggestions. They have recommended five principles that should guide policy formation:

1.   Fix land and water use planning;

2.   Use markets;

3.   Conserve natural capital;

4.   Regionalise management;

5.   Create environmental accounts.

There are at least four concrete steps that should be initiated:

i.   Changing the law to impose a duty of care on all landowners, public or private, to prevent further damage to their land and water resources;

ii.   Reducing carbon emissions by paying farmers, indigenous communities and other landowners to engage in 'carbon farming' – this would be a federal government initiative;

iii. Reforming the tax system to encourage the conservation and repair of the environment;

iv.   iv. Broadening land tax to provide funding for environmental care.[44]

As argued in Chapter 2, all of these desirable changes are part of a bigger knot of problems. Three necessary conditions have been proposed for the avoidance of an ecological crash: climate change needs to be mitigated, population levels need to become at least steady (or even better, reduced), and economic models need to become ecologically sustainable. In short, we have to get over growth – and this means more than economic growth. Economics is only part of the problem.

Each of these conditions is a problem without a simple, or obvious, solution. The ensemble is even more complex and potentially unstable – there are so many ways in which disasters can occur. This unstable big knot is 'the mother of all wicked problems' – there are three elephants in the room.

The first most likely ecological disaster scenario will come from global warming. Whatever happens, if climate change gives us more than about 2^0 or 3^0 C of global warming, the consequences will be very expensive: sea levels will rise by metres; many crops will fail; fresh water will be in short supply; extreme weather will wreak havoc; there will be increased migration of displaced populations; and so on. These are confident predictions made on the basis of contemporary science.

And these possibilities don't necessarily factor in runaway population growth! If that continues, war and social conflict will become endemic, adding to existing poverty, suffering and misery. The best we can hope for is that global population will plateau sometime between 2050 and the end of the century. Most demographers predict this will occur towards the end of the century – at about 9 billion. From the point of view of ecological sustainability, this is a slender thread of hope. These predictions assume dampening effects on human reproduction caused by increasing global wealth, allowing population curves to have the flat 's' shape typical of growing animal populations in normal ecologies. This (perhaps optimistic) scenario builds in the normal effects of crowding, resource decline and disease that we already experience. In a more Malthusian 'sticky end' we can expect a population crash to occur once resources have been exhausted, available space consumed, and ecologically sustainable pollution levels have been exceeded.

The complex, mutually interdependent nature of the three primary problems is easily demonstrated. This depressing fact confronts us all. Simple optimism is not enough, nor will efforts to change the social equitability of global capitalism be enough. Much more needs to happen. Even small improvements that do not contribute to a much bigger ecological vision may prove to be time wasted. Just what needs to happen is still an open problem, but there can be no doubt that the core issue is growth. It is too late for dogmatism; we need pragmatism, and the political will to reach defined sustainability goals.

This is really the only positive conclusion about which we can have confidence. Change will need to be driven by the organised politics of political parties, and the less formal politics of single issue politics and bigger social movements – whatever forms they take. Such a conclusion sounds very like traditional liberal democracy as widely manifest over the last century – and so it is, with one very big caveat. Traditional politics needs an ecological cultural makeover, and more radical Green politicians need to learn from the past mistakes of an over zealous left wing.

Political will is a major consideration in the chapters that follow. The nature of institutional politics in Australia will be explored through the lens of Green Party politics, and some suggestions will be made about the possibilities of 'progressive politics' that is green. More than anything we need a 'pragmatic eco-centric view' to be a vibrant part of popular culture. Evidence suggests that this is unlikely, but we can only make the effort.

It will be argued that we need politics that is 'green', but that this needs to go beyond Green parties. All political parties need to be greened, but we need to understand and appreciate the history and potentials of existing Green parties and the future influence they can have on political culture. An important point to be made in the chapters that follow is that successful Green parties are supported by larger social movements. Some of these movements may be focused on 'single issues' (or are focused on a small range of issues) such as the Australian 'Lock the Gate' movement and the international Sea Shepherd organisation, but there are other political networks (for example, GetUp and the Pirate Party) that are involved in a wide range of community politics. Green politics is not limited to Green parties, nor can it be if mass cultural change is to occur.

Any Green (/green) politics that can be convincingly 'progressive' has to face up squarely to the three big problems of climate change, over-population and economic growth. Any changes to economic thought to come will be to some extent in consequence of these three big problems. There are many ecological and economic battles (and social justice issues) that have to be fought out within the legitimate jurisdiction of local, state and national parliaments, but the global complexion of all these major issues will not go away as a result of small local victories. And most critically, if climate change issues are endlessly deferred in ineffectual international agreements (like the agreements in

Kyoto, Bali and Stockholm) human populations may never have time to recover from the excesses of growth.

The time lines of political careers in international organisations and ecological problems are very different. Further, because the likelihood of successful and popularly acclaimed ecological outcomes is low, the attraction of such issues for most politicians and economists is under-standably limited. Only Green politicians, independents, and other minority groupings, have the political ability to pursue necessarily radical ecological, environmental and economic policies through parliamentary processes.

GREEN POLITICS

INTRODUCTION

Part Two of *Beyond the Limits* begins with a brief historical analysis of green philosophy and politics, and then proceeds with a programmatic critique of Australian Green politics. To some extent this material is a reflection on my experiences as a long time member of the Greens NSW, and my experiences as an academic sociologist in Australia, but the issues discussed are far broader and far more important than that.

The central, optimistic, contention of the second part of this book is that green political analysis and philosophy, Green political parties, and green social movements best illuminate the way forward. There are no easy solutions. Civilisation is only ever one generation away from chaos and barbarism (if television news has taught us anything). Any 'solutions' require some engagement with the inertial sludge of contemporary

political life; in secular liberal democracies social movements and organised political parties require each other.

Green philosophy is difficult to characterise as a single 'position' or
'perspective' since it has developed in conjunction with green politics and a broader green social movement. It has therefore always been
something of a hybrid affair covering a spectrum of beliefs and practices
including 'deep green', 'eco-socialist' and conservative environmentalist
positions. This should be a great political strength – insofar as there is
useful flexibility that comes from ideological pluralism and a commitment to an increasing tolerance of difference. This tolerance is contrary
to an increasingly stereotyped popular media and corporate character-
isation of being Green as being extreme in behaviour and belief. There
may be some truth in the stereotype, but being green (with reference
to life style choices and a broad green social movement – as opposed to
being a member of a Green political party) will be argued to be a survival oriented position increasingly supported by scientific evidence and
'common sense'.

The 'weakness' that comes from pluralism within Green parties is
mainly a result of vulnerability to more focused ideological programs –
such as socialism or 'broad left' positions. Surprisingly perhaps, despite
a post-60s' history including sex, drugs, rock-n-roll, counter-culture
and new age religion, green political cultures are remarkably focused
in their opposition to environmental destruction and over-consumption. A longer history of environmentalism and naturalism is probably
more important in accounting for that very coherent political resolve.
The conflict and political unpopularity that human-centred left politics
can bring to political parties and environmentally focused social movements is discussed at much greater length in concluding chapters, and is
a theme in the political analysis of this book.

These concluding chapters attempt to ameliorate ongoing intellectual
and political conflict within many Green parties by suggesting a new
'view' for green philosophy and politics. There are three broad agendas
in this green way into the future:

1.   A new way forward for green philosophy requires a com-
     mitment to change. A break has to be made with beliefs and

practices that are clearly dysfunctional in the present context. This includes out-dated political ideologies and narratives that promote over-consumption, endless economic growth, and over-population. Scientific knowledge and evidence-based decision making can lead the way, one would hope, towards an environmentally based politics that is pragmatic and 'beyond' left-right politics.

2.   Green philosophy and practice that is fundamentally eco-centric needs to be articulated and promoted. This is a sane and compassionate approach in an over-populated world. The effort required to take an ecological systems view point is suggested as a methodological approach rather than an assertion that human individuals can be other that humans. This needs to become survival-oriented, and quality of life oriented, 'common sense'.

3.   Green politics needs to remain inclusive and continue to be based in a commitment to some version of the 'four pillars' that are written into the constitutions of most contemporary Greens parties: ecological sustainability, grass roots democracy, social justice, peace and non-violence. However eclectic green culture may be, these pillars do provide a necessary focus to sustain Green political programs. What needs to change in Green party practice and policy-making is instinctive, and ideologically driven, prioritisation of human interests over non-human interests. In particular, Green politics and the way forward described in this book should not be overtly (or covertly) committed to the revolutionary class warfare of the doctrinaire left and various forms of 'eco-socialism'. We have to make do with the most successful mode of political organisation so far developed after the French and American revolutions: secular liberal parliamentary democracies.

Together, Parts One and Two of *Beyond the Limits* are a discussion of transitions. How can we manage a transition from the 'apocalypse culture' that has taken over popular culture in such spectacular technicolour style? How can we move beyond growth oriented and consumerist cultures and societies? Knowledge is, as always, the best form of resistance to an overwhelming onslaught of the senses. One suggestion that has been made is that we come to better know our inevitable death, and the kinds of cultural and personal responses that result from the immanence of death. Unlike a dying individual, humanity can move on – but we may have to swap the rose coloured glasses for green ones. Another suggestion has been that we prioritise ecologically sustainable technologies and 'get over' a cultural addiction to growth. To do that we need to know that there are options, and then work to make these options realities. The central suggestion of Part Two, which follows, is that we take green politics and social movements far more seriously – by supporting green social movements and political practices, by voting for green policies, and by thinking and acting 'green'.

This is a 'big' book. Extreme dissatisfaction with the over-contained processes of academic, popular, and political specialisation is behind this attempt to cultivate an interdisciplinary approach to analysis of our ecological crisis. More often in a work of this scope the views of different specialists would be brought together as an edited book, or a set of conference proceedings – there is no shortage of these kinds of works. Such projects can be frustrating for a variety of reasons – most significantly, they can be fragmentary and not demonstrate a sufficiently coherent analysis and commentary. Therefore, although I have attempted to make each chapter coherent in its own right, and focus on issues that arise in particular disciplines, particularly as they are relevant to considerations of our ecological crisis, I have also attempted to sustain a unifying narrative throughout – whilst attempting to avoid overtly ideological analysis. Yet some may find the concluding introduction of 'pragmatic eco-centrism' extremely ideological; that is a risk I am prepared to take.

GREEN CULTURAL DIVERSITY

Come gather round people
Wherever you are . . .
For the times they are a-changin'

Bob Dylan, 1964

Being *Green* was always a politically radical position.
Since the emergence of Green parties in the early
1970s, *Green* has come to signify a 'left of centre' stance that is critical
of consumerism and ecological destruction. *Green* is now a politicised
extension of *green*, a colour that still signifies things natural, but with
increased emphasis on health and 'purity'. Advertisers love *green* because
it helps to commodify 'nature'. This chapter is focused on the politicisation of *being green*, and the diversity of ideas and cultures present in
an international green social movement – out of which Green political
parties emerged.

This sharpening of political focus has involved a diverse field of ideas
– Green political culture has responded to the demands of government
and the steady growth of knowledge in ecologically related fields. At
the same time the 'mainstreaming' of the idea of being Green (that is,

being politically engaged) has enabled the exploitation, by advertisers and political parties, of the attractions of being *green* – as opposed to being *Green*. The colour *green* is such a powerful signifier of nature that it remains somewhat partitioned from *Green* in popular and political discourse – Green is a politicised colour, and a political brand, whereas green is still 'just' about nature, wholesome food, and ecology for the consuming public. This convention survives even with the limited popularity of Green political parties.

Educational curricula are being *greened*. School children cultivate worm farms, grow vegetables, and find their curricula in science, geography, English, and social studies dotted with references to ecology and climate change. Even tertiary academic fields have begun to be more ecologically inclined – the life sciences particularly. By contrast, the humanities and social sciences still struggle to find a way of expressing their green credentials – as can be seen in the curricula of economics, sociology, history, politics, cultural and communication studies courses in Australia and elsewhere. So far, with the exception of economics, accountancy and business studies, the cultural norm in all these disciplines and study areas has been to preserve a broad left hegemony much more aligned with the traditional values of the labour movement than troublesome Green parties.

'Mainstreaming' (or 'popularisation') provides some explanation of how it is that *green* has retained a broad field of reference. In advertising and media discourse, the colour remains bigger than any brand (commercial or political), or any academic discipline, or study area. This is also true in professionalised and specialist discourses. Such broad semantic scope is curiously symbolic of the progress of green philosophy and politics. It is as if the colour is far too basic as a signifier (in all languages) to be pinned down by any particular discipline, paradigm, or ideology. *Green* (*i.e. green*) belongs to everyone; many people will protest that they are *green*, but not *Green*.

Nonetheless, it is intriguing that the establishment of Green parties as part of the scenery of western secular democracies has not seen the emergence of a new Green paradigm, or international political consensus over a green program for tackling the problems of a planet in crisis.

One might have expected, after a flurry of programmatic books and manifestos in the 1970s and 1980s, and the parliamentary successes of Green parties in so many countries, more efforts would have been made to deliver a new Green program that might provide coherent political and philosophical leadership into the twenty first century.

There are many possible reasons why this has not happened. This chapter explores two thematic reasons that have had insufficient airing: the enduring cultural diversity of green politics and philosophy, and the stifling effects of left, and 'broad left' philosophy on the development of a more eco-centric approach in green philosophy and politics. Another reason for the absence of a broadly persuasive new green paradigm is an effective conspiracy by conservative elements of government, business and media to deny climate change and all forms of ecological rational-ism. The deliberate denial of early warning signs over the last fifty years has succeeded in reducing any mass cultural appetite for Green political solutions. This opposition by dominant social institutions is only one side of the problem. The often conflicted 'internal' dynamics of Green party cultures has also worked against the emergence of any thing like a coherent 'paradigm' or political program that might persuade anymore than a few per cent of voting publics.

The net effect of these tensions is the continuing failure of Green parties to be anything more than very occasional coalition partners in government. Generally these parties are oppositional voices and limited in the policy pressures they can bring to bear on governments. Even though electorates everywhere are deeply suspicious of all ideologies, the failure of Green parties to transcend media-driven popular perceptions of them being ideologically extreme – anti-capitalist, anti-development, out of touch with economic reality – has not attracted the support of people who are looking for political forces that might confront ecolog-ical issues first, without abandoning social justice issues, but definitely prioritising sustainability and the ecological health of the planet.

Green parties have serious jurisdictional problems that, from the outset, limit their ability to deal with critical global concerns, such as 'the big three' of climate change, over-population and economic growth. These 'macro' issues require global responses – the co-operation of nation states, and the formation of new bodies with legally enforceable powers. National and regional Green parties can play a proactive leading role, but because (as parliamentary parties) their legitimate policy concerns are restricted, Green parties cannot be the only proactive players. Nor can they be held responsible for the failure of governments to act in ecologically sensible ways. However, Green parties can be held responsible for theoretical and philosophical stasis about the 'big three'. The main ideological roadblock derives from the connection between the growth of populations and the growth of economies. So long as politicians and voting publics believe in the absolute necessity for such growth, there is little chance that any mainstream political party, and certainly no 'left' oriented party, will argue too strongly against growth and the inevitability of global warming and climate change that follows.

However, being a political voice for the environment, endangered species, wilderness, and the natural integrity of ecologies and bio-systems should be the highest priority for Green parties.

As this chapter shows, the roots of all Green parties are so strongly in environmentalist politics and 'naturalism' that prioritising ecological concerns as central should, for historical and philosophical reasons, be an easy transition. The politics may not be so straight forward.

A major problem Green parties face in becoming more eco-centric derives from the entrenched opposition of leftist politics and culture. This is reflected in the diversity of Green party policy concerns and the way social justice issues are widely prioritised at the expense of a coherent ecological critique – or a new Green program – and the confusion and opposition this creates in public perceptions. This diversity can, however, be traced back to the post-1960's emergence of Green parties as part of a great churning of ideas, politics, music, art, lifestyles, sexuality, and everything else. The cultural rigidity of the left has different roots as will be further explored.

Eco-centrism will also find opposition from all supporters of growth economics. That is to be expected, but Green parties do not have to adopt extreme left views to counter that opposition. Environmentally based political parties can become more mainstream in order to gain greater representation in parliaments. As the next chapter argues, 'progressive politics' requires a more central, but still radical, political position. Only in that way can they succeed as change agents in the making of environmental and ecological policy in those parliaments. This chapter explores the cultural roots of 'being green' hoping to show how views that saw the sanity in eco-centrism have survived as the heart of green politics and Green political parties.

THE CHALLENGING DIVERSITY OF GREEN VIEWS

Green politics and philosophy are not an homogenous culture or paradigm. The beliefs of individuals making up an international green social movement are diverse. Even in Green parties, the peak organisational focus of parliamentary engagement, members have diverse backgrounds and beliefs and do not share a common paradigm, or unified set of beliefs. In Green parties the political divide between 'old left' socialists and communists and more eco-centric environmentalists means that today there is only limited consensus about the emphasis and detail of much current social policy, and therefore of future directions also. The cultural differences expressed in these divisions are not sufficiently understood by cultural historians or journalists; even among contemporary Greens (*i.e.* Green party members) the diverse history of green thought is not well appreciated. Among more left leaning Greens there is often a kind of denial that such diversity might be relevant to 'history'. This denial excludes much, including the project of understanding the cultural roots of many older Greens who were alive during the western post-sixties cultural renaissance. That renaissance shaped much of today's popular and academic cultures. Its echoes still reverberate.

The following sections attempt to provide a broader historical review of the formation of a politically inclined green culture. The primary goals and motivations that distinguished an emerging green culture, after the 1960s, involved two signature goals: 'to save the planet', and 'to change the world'. These broad and amorphous goals were shared by many groups and many individuals, and were not simply 'new left' activism. The enormous scope of such a project necessitated holism and inter-disciplinarity – which came easily to many of those who were willing participants in the turmoil and cultural upheavals of the late 1960s and 1970s in Europe, the USA, and Australia. This was not necessarily a deliberate strategy; new ideas were everywhere – in the air, and in the water. The intellectual ferment that characterised the period also happened to draw in much science *and* philosophy as part of the broadly political discourse of pioneering Greens – but the emphasis was on philosophy and science that was 'connected'. Commitment was less about discipline, and more about exploration. Personal development work, including widespread experimentation with cannabis and hallucinogens such as LSD, was also commonplace, and part of 'getting back to nature'. For many these were wild days.

It is a very neglected fact that the early cultural history of Green parties was much more 'countercultural' than it was part of radical left politics. This early history preceded the actual formation of political parties by decades, and merges with a much longer history of environmental activism – and in the West the rediscovery of nature, the land, and 'country' by mostly Europeans, North Americans and new Australians.[1]

Being green has a history that extends back in time before the formation of Green parties. In a longer view, it would appear that post-1960s diversity was only a phase in the inevitable development of more discretely institutionalised fields of ecological thought, the eventual emergence of political parties devoted to Green ideals and, to some extent, the mainstreaming of ecological thinking. For many green activists popularisation of being green was a primary objective – the great hope was that the 'right ideas' would be taken up as widely as possible. Being green was only coincidentally a niche academic or philosophical view, or the captive of any political tendency. For others, the identity politics of being green was more restrictive and tribal.

As participants in a bigger social movement, Green parties and modern green cultures have diverse cultural roots. The contention of the analysis that follows is that environmental politics and 'environmentalism' (broadly conceived as including the defence of ecologies and the biosphere) need to be understood as the most important 'de-centring' forces for future Green political and cultural ideologies. In a long historical view, early conservation movements played a formative role in creating 'environmentalism', environmental politics and eventually Green politics and Green parties as part of an international green social movement. Whilst it is undeniably true that Green parties have come to be increasingly identified, internationally, with left wing politics, this chapter aims to show this to be an unfortunate and dangerous simplification. Human–centred politics will not solve our ecological problems; nor will the ideologically driven identity politics of 'old' and 'new' left warriors, or any similar variety of post-60s radicalism, succeed at the ballot box.

GREEN SHOOTS IN GREEN FIELDS

After the ecological 'big bang' and 'inflationary period' of green philosophy in the 1960s and 1970s, some kind of closure in the discourse of nature-oriented groups, organisations, and political parties was 'inevitable', and sought after. One of the main processes of personal closure involved 'identity formation' around new cultural directions – particularly involving tribal or 'sub-cultural' affiliations. Post-1960's radicals identified diversely – there were hippies, counterculturalists, alternative life-stylers, alternative technologists, new agers, eastern mystics, 'born again' Christians, therapists, Marxists, feminists, anarchists, and myriad others. In many ways an international green social movement started as a 'rainbow alliance' between all these different identities. The formation of Green political parties incorporated many sub-cultural differences, but not all survived the rigours of strong conflict and factionalising that accompany all efforts to become 'politically organised'.

'The sixties' is widely understood to have been a period of protest and rebellion. This was the period in which 'new social movements' emerged to contest established traditions. Traditionally political and social analysis has focused on the way social movements were different from previous revolts, rebellions and revolutions. Typically emphasis has been placed the way that groups organised to react against corporate restrictions and oppression, or the bureaucratic indifference of government and public sector organisations, or patriarchal domination. For sociologists the main post-sixties 'structural determinants' of change in a capitalist social order were class, gender, and ethnicity, but many sociologists also saw problems with a more basic 'instrumentalism', or bureaucracy, that infected all possibilities. The cultural meanings of peace, gender or ecology were (and still are) of far less interest than the abstract social and political structures and processes determining all possibilities. This chapter is intended to show something more about the cultural content of the 'eco' part of what some sociologists still casually label 'eco-pax' new social movements – as if ecological questions were merely peripheral to 'real politics'.[2]

Perhaps the idea of a 'field' of ideas helps express the complexity of the cultural roots of the green movement. Out of a youthful post-1960's 'rainbow alliance' between radical and *avant garde* pioneers, a field of ideas cohered through the concerted efforts of many people who identified with 'being green', and who associated, formed groups, wrote texts, held protests and engaged in various ways with mainstream politics and society. In short, a field of ideas was generated and sustained in social processes that had the common thread of involving people who identified as 'being green' – among other commonalities and differences. This field of ideas and beliefs had many goals spanning local and global issues, but in all this diversity there were, as mentioned, two big ecologically oriented goals: 'saving the planet' and 'changing society'. For early Greens this political project was Earth-centred rather than socially centred. Their 'politics' was not supportive of traditional institutions – radical student politics, for example, was one leading edge, and this was very 'anti-establishment'. In Europe the 'new left' was emerging from the 'old left'.

For those who did 'drop out' and embrace alternative lifestyles – generally involving some kind of communal living arrangements – not many were involved with institutional politics. Voting in elections was rare. The tribalism of alternative life-stylers was always a means to 'getting back to nature'; 'straight' society was alienating. Being social was not an end in itself; being part of something bigger was a journey with no clear end point. In all the different forms these experimental life styles took, the *means* were generally agreed to be important – they should definitely not subvert the *ends*. The idea of a journey made in peace and love may sound terribly clichéd today, yet these sentiments informed early Green political culture, and remain at odds with the procedural ruthlessness of many hard left ideologues in Green parties around the world. Most critically, although the intense melting pot of post-sixties culture was not always political in a conventional sense – artists, musicians, hippies, and many other life style experimentalists often disavowed politics as 'a power trip' – this cultural turmoil was the main breeding ground of modern Green politics. There are other cultural and political sources, but the distinctive spirit of being green (and Green) has its heart in a cultural revolution.[3]

POST-1960S CULTURAL DIVERSITY

The radical nature of Green political philosophy and practice was originally intended as a break with traditional politics. The diversity and eclecticism of the early libraries and conversations of activists and intellectuals today seem curiously 'postmodern' – tradition and contemporary ideas and insights rubbed together in the form of a heady mix of radical politics, indigenous cultures, counter-culture, and new age religion. My own library was probably typical: here Timothy Leary met Karl Marx and Chairman Mao; Abbe Hoffman met Alan Watts, Ram Dass and Krisnamurti; Einstein met the *I Ching*, the Whole Earth Catalogue, and Chief Seattle . . . and so on, in a giddy dance of the worlds greatest works – known and unknown. It was never 'too much' until later, when peace, love and 'changing the world' had been focused in new post-1960s social movements, and the first wave of ecological crisis literature.

Early green culture was consciously 'alternative', countercultural and *avant-garde* in ways that went well beyond books and libraries. No text could fully capture the experience and excitement of a 'new' Earth-centred tribalism that was emerging in Australia, and elsewhere. This was a 'happening thing' – not just a 'head trip' – and was celebrated in Australia through a series of 'alternative' and 'new age' festivals. Most prominent were the Aquarius Festival in 1973, and, from 1976, Down to Earth Festivals, or ConFests, as they are now known. These countercultural festivals celebrated nudity and all forms of radicalism.

The Aquarius Festival was an initiative of the Australian Union of Students and resulted in the transformation of a declining small town in rural NSW, the now internationally famous countercultural landmark, Nimbin. As recalled by Graham Dunstan, one of the Festival's Directors, 'years of protest had made clear what students of that era were against: imperialism, sexism, racism, authoritarianism, industrialism, consumerism and progress at any price.' The Festival was a jubilant celebration of hippy counterculture:

> There were conservationists talking ecology, healers offering wholistic medicine and rediscovering herbs and acupuncture, architecture students and engineers talking about low energy consumption and appropriate technology, post-Illich educational theorists talking de-schooling, foodists offering new diets, bakers offering wholemeal bread, kooris talking land rights, psychotherapists talking about growth and human potential, food co-operatives, videots, alternative media and an array of gurus, guru followers and seekers of spiritual truths. All this and troubadours, shamans, tight rope walkers, dancers, ecstatic singers from the East and soul rhythms from Africa, easy sexuality and drugs to open the 'doors of perception'.[4]

After the Aquarius Festival Nimbin became a kind of rural squat, much to the consternation of the local farming community. Most of the locals eventually accepted the harsh realities of change, and today Nimbin has become the unofficial countercultural/alternative lifestyle community capital of Australia.

The first 'Down to Earth' festival, held at the Cotter Dam (near Canberra) in December 1976, involved political outcasts Jim Cairns (an ex-deputy prime minister), his partner Juni Morosi, and many supporters of the charismatic couple. This next big countercultural festival was another Australian version of Woodstock without the music, and without the need for heavy security arrangements. Thousands participated over several days – anyone could pitch a tent, or tipi, and encounter all manner of organised and spontaneous happenings. The heady mix of Marx, Freud, Reich and feminism espoused by Jim Cairns was far more radical than the very mild anti-corporatism of the Australian Labor Party (*vale* Jim Cairns, who could have easily established the first Green Party in the world), but the emphasis of the festival was alternative lifestyles and counterculture. Organised politics was definitely an unhelpful 'power trip'.[5]

The dynamism of those early post-sixties years has passed, but the impulse for cultural innovation is still present among Greens and fellow travellers. Many of these people want to tackle the new challenges of climate change and an ever more imminent ecological crisis. In Australia, as elsewhere, enthusiasm for change has challenges and obstacles, not least the continuing pressures for conformity to political orthodoxies of left and right. Many supporters of Australian Green parties are not party members and some probably don't vote. Being Earth-centred and ecologically focused can be politically off-centre as part of countercultural tribalism – such as being 'feral' – or just political disaffection. Identifying as Earth-focused, or eco-centric is easily conceivable as an anti-political statement – it is just less common to be so inclined today.

In early green cultural diversity, much published writing addressing ecological concerns and 'ecological crisis' was of historically recent origin, and came after 'consciousness-raising' in the 1960s. Even the traditional ecological wisdom of tribal cultures, such as the North American Indians and indigenous Australians, was received in the context of historical events that were quite recent. That is, invasions and crises – of foreign settlers, industry, disease, industrial scale mono-cultural agriculture, deforestation, and so on – can be traced back through the last few hundred years. This is not a long period of time for the world to have changed so utterly and unambiguously under the pressures of human expansion.

The advent of awareness of global ecological crisis as a galvanising force is probably as recent as Rachel Carson's book *Silent Spring* – the first expose of the global chemical pollution of the mid-twentieth century to achieve a mass audience. The broader perception that humanity dominates nature is earlier – the conflict between Christianity and pagan religions, for example, had been reflected upon by philosophers and historians long before academics and scientists had any professional interest in the decline of nature. Discourse about the ecological collapse of the whole system is actually a 'postmodern' development, requiring science-based evidence to support prior awareness of global pollution, human pathology and general biological decline.[6]

The kind of apocalyptically based ecological thinking that has so inspired modern activists (and many Green politicians) is a late 1960's phenomenon – despite the earlier development of nuclear weapons. Undoubtedly the threat of a nuclear catastrophe during the post-World War 2 'cold war' era stimulated thought about ecological decline but, as registered in early post-apocalyptic literature, the first main worry was the extinction of the human species due to global radiation poisoning caused by war.[7]

Arguably, the disaster nuclear weapons threatened was originally not feared so much as an ecological catastrophe, more as Armageddon – an end to human life on Earth. The fate of other species, ecologies and nature did not become a major cultural issue until less spectacular industrial causes of ecological decline and risks to human health began to be protested 'more professionally' by biologists, medical scientists, the 'Club of Rome', and environmental activists. It took a concerted effort by many activists, who were often scientists, to reveal the bad news and terrible possibilities that await a complacent human society.

The philosophical and academic side of post-1960s ecological writing now has considerable depth and scope, as does writing and broadcasting for mass audiences. There has long been some degree of popular interest in the work of professional naturalists and biological scientists, but the main stimulus for the increasing connection of these different cultural spheres was the movement of tertiary trained naturalists and biologists into the programming of television. The best example is Sir David Attenborough who, as a naturalist, biologist and public intellectual, so effectively legitimated the roles of science and scholarship in early television programing. As discussed in Chapter 3, the transformation of popular perceptions of naturalism as being more than travel and adventure is an important moment in the evolution of public (and academic) awareness of a troubled global ecology.

The increased popularity of books and magazines that gave nature, the environment, and ecology, serious attention (and centre stage) was part of the social and cultural upheavals of the time – and connected to a period of expansion in the tertiary sector of the natural and biological sciences, and technological fields. 'Green politics' and 'green philosophy' developed out of this intellectual ferment. The contributing streams of ideas and perspectives are worth re-examining and categorising (with the benefit of hindsight) because the ecological, social and political issues raised then are of continuing relevance and interest to many Greens and environmental activists – as indicated in the words of Graeme Dunstan, quoted above. The ferment of the decades following the late 1960s clearly demonstrates the cultural diversity of the origins of anything that might be called a Green/green 'paradigm', and shows how (and why) current green philosophy and politics is still at a crossroads between various social and cultural movements. For that reason, the Green/green cultural 'field' is not particularly coherent from a disciplinary point of view.

It also very difficult to draw a line and say, 'this is where green philosophy, or culture, starts', because the study of nature, the land, and country, is a cultural and social perennial. This study, which involves all philosophy, art, and religion, precedes science and everything modern and postmodern. Raymond Williams, one of the founding fathers of the new Western academic specialism of Cultural Studies, has said that the word *nature* is the most complex in the English language. This is because it refers to so much. *Nature* is a very over-loaded signifier.[8]

On the other hand, it is possible to date the formation of social and political organisations – so we do have some benchmarks and points of origin, even if the conversations that preceded and then followed them defy precisely dated beginnings. Therefore we can confidently say, 'this is when a modern political party with a uniquely ecological orientation gains national parliamentary representation in Europe' – the German Greens in 1983, for example. However, as an analysis of culture, this trivialises the question of themes and streams – for which there may be no simple starting points. In particular, once questions of meaning, intention, and political identity are raised it is very hard to be absolutely definitive about historical 'facts'. Such issues require the *interpretation* of evidence, which is a much more open process – and easily subject to deliberate politicisation. These matters are less 'facts' than 'views' or 'perspectives'.

Nonetheless there are some recent historical patterns that might be considered uncontroversial in the current context. Clearly, in the post-World War 2 era, *nature* had become far more than the subject of landscape art and the object of scientific and philosophical study. Nature conservation societies in Europe, the United States, and Australia, had been established and by then had attracted considerable memberships. Nature conservation was becoming part of a broader popular social movement now often labelled 'environmentalism'.[9]

Nature had also become part of popular culture in the form of travel, tourism, and popular mass media presentations of these activities, as well as (more abstractly) in popular science presentations – which were always very impressed with new 'high' technology, such as rocket flight to the moon and beyond.[10]

GREEN MANIFESTOS

The decades following the late 1960's saw a burgeoning of popular literature and visual media that presented naturalism and travel to mass audiences. Popular interest in nature and travel had already been stimulated for over 100 years in the United States and Europe, as the West was won, and new and exotic landscapes and peoples were revealed. Explorers and naturalists, from Charles Darwin to John Muir, published accounts for scientific audiences, and, increasingly in the United States, for diverse popular audiences – e.g. the work of Ralph Emerson, Henry Thoreau, Robinson Jeffers, and much later, Aldo Leopold. In the 1960s and 1970s these latter writers became interesting to new generations of Anglophone travellers, hippies, and other counterculturalists. In that period the broadcasting of naturalism became televised – largely pioneered by David Attenborough.[11]

The new technology of television enabled mass audiences to benefit from scientific fieldwork and laboratory research that would otherwise have remained restricted to small specialist audiences and amateur enthusiasts. After Attenborough had demonstrated there was a ready audience for nature documentaries, others followed, but none could match his enthusiasm and erudition.

His work was highly influential in the building of a greater appreciation of the natural world in Western audiences. Attenborough has always communicated a sense of nature being intrinsically beautiful – even spiritual – but in his later work a hint of unfolding tragedy has begun to emerge. One might hope his nuanced approach has further created public desire to preserve nature as valuable in its own right – as opposed to the creation of an overwhelming and incapacitating sense of loss. Attenborough has become a larger than life presence, but his success has depended upon the availability of large audiences that were part of, or stimulated by a broader green cultural and social movement. Some activists might even claim that his work is far too restrained and that he has been too slow in confronting the dominant institutions that either deny ecological decline or actively contribute to it.

Certainly, all the feelings that Attenborough's work can so artfully manipulate had become part of the written public record by the 1980s. By this time a number of green 'manifestos' had been published – Jonathon Porritt's *Seeing Green* (1984) and Sandy Irvine and Alec Ponton's *A Green Manifesto* (1988) are prominent. The selected bibliographies contained in these books reveal that the most influential works were nearly all published from the early-1970s on. Most of these early texts were informed by science, depending on research that today forms the basis for the new discipline of ecology, and its core interest in questions about the sustainability of natural systems, pollution, public health, climate change, and so on. Many of these issues are today still pursued within the parameters of long established disciplines in the natural and social sciences, but increasingly these disciplines and research organisations are driven in response to problems arising from a broader, newer context of ecological crisis. The impetus for this new phase of problem orientation in scientific research was strongly stimulated by an emerging Green political culture and its determination to 'save the planet'. At the same time, it is important to recognise that the popularity of much early green literature also depended on an increasing public appetite, in reading and watching publics, for more data, evidence, and *science*. The science, and other empirical material, was provided by a limited number of practising scientists who were also activists – such as the Ehrlichs, and later, David Suzuki – and by science trained professionals such as David Attenborough. These pioneers recognised the need to popularise scientific work that was technically 'available', but often sequestered within academic enclaves. The foundation of the early green movement in science based studies, and interpretations, is so important to recognise because the ongoing durability of the green movement critically depends on the ability of journalists, and other popularisers, to stay well in touch with the latest science (and technology). This point has already been made with respect to climate change denial, and will remain a theme in context of the importance of Green party political culture being able to take expert advice, and act upon it with an appropriate sense of urgency.

The natural sciences (the biological sciences in particular) were not the only primary sources of 'real' information (about the environment and natural systems) in the formation of green culture. Political and philosophical ideas were perhaps paramount in the way an emerging social movement was able to persuade hearts and minds that our culture also needed to be changed, as well as 'saved' from real and impending crises in global systems. This uptake of ideas required the reassessment of human values in the context of new information about human systems – the economy, social organisation and the possibility of social justice, most critically.

The most important such programmatic statement to arise out of the green movement is undoubtedly 'the four pillars', originally set out by Die Grunen, the German Green Party, in 1983:

> Our policy is guided by four basic principles: it is ecological, social, grassroots–democratic and non–violent.[12]

The four pillars were eventually adopted by all Green parties – subject to slight re-phrasings in individual party platforms, and the addition of 'peace' to 'non-violence' in Australian constitutions.

These principles are *not* a unique product of Green party think tanks. They are ultimately a distillation from various social movements – which preceded the formation of Green parties, and the emergence of today's international green movement. This needs to be said by way of situating green politics and philosophy historically and culturally. That is, the goals expressed in the 'four pillars' arose from environmental, left-labour, peace, and women's movements – all of which are ongoing international concerns and often broadly allied with green activists. Today's international green movement builds on a history of organised environmental activism that goes back to at least the early nineteenth century; it does not completely overlap with those other social movements (which to varying extents are still ongoing, and different by many criteria). This point will be further examined in later chapters as part of a claim that 'eco-centrism' should become a necessary priority for twenty first century green politics and Green political parties.

Real progress towards the achievement of these four goals is ongoing. Considered in historical terms, there can be little doubt that social justice, for example, has been improved around the globe. Women's rights, indigenous rights, and workers rights are widely (and proudly) enshrined in many laws – even if they are not yet directly incorporated into many national constitutions. The rise of secular liberal democracies has also been a great historical development – as the political historian Joseph Fukuyama has pointed out, the last 100 years has seen an extraordinary acceleration in the development of liberal democracies (most of which are secular).[13]

Ecological sustainability remains the goal that most defines the contemporary green movement. This is true both as a description of popular expectations and the movement's founding philosophical orientations of naturalism and environmentalism. However, despite a much higher level of public awareness of ecological crises, the successes of a large number of activists' campaigns, and an increasing impact of Green parties on established politics, the goal of ecological sustainability is far from achieved and needs to remain an absolute priority for Green parties. However, this goal has (arguably) the lowest level of success of all the four goals. Yet it remains the most important for our continued success as a civilisation. International meetings continue to be held to try and address global ecological issues such as climate change, but the worry is that any agreements made will be too little, too late. As raised earlier, we have probably already reached major tipping points with respect to population growth and the rate of global warming.

EARLY CULTURAL STREAMS IN THE EMERGENCE OF A POST-1960S SOCIAL MOVEMENT

Some readers may find the separation of different cultural streams in green philosophy and political thought to be a case of hair splitting. Indeed, it is likely that many Green supporters are not so analytically concerned to distinguish, as I will, between naturalism and environmentalism, or between social ecology, deep ecology, spiritual ecology and eco-feminism. Certainly, the 'cultural streams' described below are a construct out of a more primal 'soup' of ideas that continue to circulate more in community conversations than in academic seminars. Nonetheless the different perspectives identified are significantly different, and the writers identified as taking these positions tend to endorse different approaches to political life, and strategy. These differences remain critically important in determining why the uptake of green or 'environmental' thought has been so generally limited, and what the best way forward might be. Further, if Green party supporters, and politicians and journalists generally, do not better appreciate the basic philosophical and political differences between these philosophical and political tendencies, the endless loop of left-right politics, and its associated factionalising, will continue to diffuse the truly radical potential of green politics. These issues will be taken up again in the next chapter, which is more focused on future directions. What follows is a brief historical sketch of the philosophical (or 'theoretical') concerns in these different 'cultural streams'. Of course, in the 'reality' of ongoing conversations, these 'streams' overlap and mix in ways that are often very turbulent.[14]

1. Naturalism

'Nature' and 'the natural order' are at the centre of all things human. Deep appreciation and close study of nature are fundamental in all civilizations and cultures – all art, philosophy, religion, and sciences are a conversation about a natural order of which humanity is only a part. As a cultural movement, or style, 'naturalism' is defined by its orientation towards nature as a source of aesthetic and intellectual inspiration. As cultural expression, naturalism seeks to capture the awe felt by being in the natural world. The deepest source of naturalism appears to spring from the perennial human desire to experience wilderness and be alone with 'nature'. Who does not at some time find nature intrinsically beautiful and fascinating?

The strongest contribution to modern ideas about naturalism comes from a very long tradition of nature walking and nature study. These practices evolved into biological and ecological fieldwork, but 'naturalists' were originally 'amateurs' who loved nature and were avid observers of all her inhabitants and cycles – and indeed, all 'her' ways. Appreciation of nature as an aesthetic and intellectual source arises in all specialist and professionalised fields and historically has been defined in many different cultural specialisations: niches, fashions, genres, styles and disciplines. In modern times where human feelings of separation from, and loss of, the natural world appear so profound, naturalism can arise with intensity and angst. This is particularly reflected in the arts – in literature, for example, a 'post-apocalyptic' fictional genre is well established.

Examples of naturalism abound in art and design: nature oriented 'romantics', 'realists' and 'surrealists' occur in western painting, poetry and literature – and, indeed, in all art, design and architecture. Today, arguably, love of nature and 'alienation' from nature, are so intertwined that ecological decline has become even harder to remedy.[15]

As past events in movements, fashions, disciplines and specialisms, naturalism is part of the pre-history of the post-1960's green social movement; as a continuing aesthetic, and scientific and philosophical inspiration, naturalism is the main source of all green culture. In previous sections describing green culture, the natural philosophers John Muir, Aldo Leopold, George Sessions and Arne Naesse have been described as 'pioneering naturalists'; the biologists David Suzuki, David Attenborough, described as pioneering public broadcasters, are also pioneering naturalists; the medical doctors Rachel Carson, Helen Caldicott and Bob Brown were effectively described as 'parents' and elders of the contemporary green movement; they too are naturalists. The list of pioneering naturalists is very long. All these pioneers have advocated the protection of wild places; the increasing alienation of humanity from nature has been a defining problem for them all.

   Naturalism includes the natural and biological sciences – particularly to the extent that they were inspirational to early greens. However, it should be noted that after the 1960s many greens were actually critical of a 'scientific' approach to the wonders of the natural world. There was a view, less pronounced in the twenty first century, that science dissects nature, reducing it to categories and numbers – which is alienating and dominating rather than liberating and spiritual or wonderful – or optimistic. This view extended into a view (and practice) of 'alternative technology' as scientifically minimalist and radically opposed to an industrialised 'high technology'.[16]

2. Environmentalism

Environmentalism is the political expression of naturalism. This is not a uniquely modern expression of political rights and freedoms – although it is only in recent times that an internationally focused (and sourced) environmentally focused social movement has emerged. The term 'green social movement' has arisen as a 'popular' acknowledgment of the broader focus that Green political parties have brought, but without doubt the origins of 'green politics' and a post-1960s green social movement are primarily in a much older environmental movement – that is, in 'environmentalism'.

Concern for nature and the destruction of habitat caused by the increasing encroachment of human populations is ancient. The rise of civilizations and city-states are known to have impacted forests and the availability of natural resources, and resulted in laws regulating the human exploitation of these resources. The development of sewage systems in cities also provides clear evidence that environments and ecologies were managed as early as 4,500 years ago.[17]

However, the pollution and despoliation generated by the industrial revolution was far more intense than ever before. Public concerns began to translate into active and organised efforts to conserve wildlife habitat and protect ecosystems from chemical and industrial toxins, and from the impacts of urbanisation. Groups and organisations that were focused on environmental concerns emerged and actively campaigned for legislative change.

Early environmentalists in Europe and America in the 1800s and 1900s pioneered wilderness protection legislation with the creation of Yellowstone National Park in 1872. The Sierra Club, founded in 1892, is the oldest surviving environmental organisation. As well as protecting wilderness areas in the US, its members today have an international focus – for example, in 1956 concerns about levels of industrial pollutants directly exposed Minamata disease in Japan.[18]

Clean water and clean air legislation were introduced in the US from 1960. *However, the publication in 1962 of Silent Spring* by American biologist Rachel Carson, was particularly influential in drawing public attention to the health hazards of industrial toxins released into the environment, and led to strict regulations in many industrialised countries.

With increasing exploitation of natural capital and large-scale population growth (human populations have doubled in the last 60 years) pressure on ecosystems (such as forests and marine resources) have lead to international groups becoming increasingly proactive. The World Wide Fund for Nature was founded in 1961; Greenpeace was founded in 1971, and Sea Shepherd Conservation Society in 1977. These three activist organisations are at the forefront of non-government organisations seeking to actively enforce international agreements about environmental protection.

In Australia 'environmentalism' is sometimes dismissed as a 'single issue' movement and contrasted with Green politics on that basis. Environmentalism is therefore considered by many Green party members to be more 'conservative' than radical, and insufficiently critical of capitalism. This is different to a North American understanding where 'environmentalists' are often perceived as 'communists' by another name. Neither of these understandings do justice to the true radicalism of an eco-centric view, as will be elaborated in this and following chapters.

3. Left politics

'Left politics' is a highly complex and mobile mix of groups, parties and factions. It is an international social and cultural movement united by critical opposition to capitalism and social inequality. In this view, capitalist social relations are exploitative and dominating – it is capitalist political economy that is the cause of most war and environmental degradation. Within capitalist societies, social class, gender and race all are 'structural determinants' of exploitation and domination. It is difficult to be highly definitive because over time the emphasis of leading theorists has changed to include, only recently, gender and race as key structural determinants of exploitation and inequality. In Australia the intrusions of feminism into a male dominated critical culture has been the most conflictual process – from the 1970s onwards. Ecological concerns were, and still are, minor distractions in what was to become a highly fractious 'broad left' alliance.

After the student riots in Paris in May 1968, a 'new left' emerged from an 'old left' as 'new' interests in gender, race, colonialism and post-colonialism, psychoanalysis and 'domination' were incorporated into a canon that had been itself dominated by Marx, Engels, Lenin, Stalin and Mao. The 'new left' was, in turn, felt to be too highly Euro-centric – and so, in Australia and elsewhere the term 'broad left' is now favoured to indicate a more inclusive and tolerant approach. In the post-1960s historical context the most important philosophical 'factions' were Marxism, Critical Theory, Social Ecology and Eco-feminism.

The rebadged 'broad left' political-cultural movement is still, basically, an ongoing Marxist and post-Marxist project that remains highly influential in Green politics and philosophy. As a cultural force it draws from a wide variety of different factions and tendencies within academic and activist settings, and strongly influences the beliefs and attitudes most left activists and professional politicians apply to social justice issues and campaigns. Its ecological pedigree is not well developed, but most coherently expressed in the writings of 'social ecologists'. A great deal of academic writing about green politics has been strongly influenced by broad left developments in social philosophy and theory, even though the prioritisation of human values and human labour is often at odds with more Earth-centred perspectives. Basic issues in this 'umbrella' of philosophical and political perspectives and issues include:

- the destructive nature of capitalism;
- the domination of nature;
- patriarchal domination and exploitation;
- 'development' and 'underdevelopment';
- colonialism and post-colonialism.

These issues were placed on Green party agenda from the outset of the organisation of the green movement into political parties. There can be no doubting the continuing influence of broad left thought about these issues; they routinely appear in policy and writing that is perceived as Green.[19]

With the exception of 'eco-feminism' and 'social ecology', neither Marxism nor post-Marxism were very ecological at all. The most focused ecological thinkers from the left, at the time of the emergence of Green politics, were the anarchist Murray Bookchin, and the more traditional Marxist, Andre Gorz. Bookchin pioneered the school of 'social ecology', but his work has remained unpopular with the left generally – probably because of his aversion to centralised masculine power structures, and his concern with 'freedom' as something that can be won without surrendering to the politics of class, or the inevitability of male dominated hierarchies. His work remains resonant with the sentiments of many Greens.[20]

Feminism has always been at odds with the male dominance of organised politics. Although there have been many women who accepted the importance of class and class struggle in the development of gender politics and ecological politics, the prioritising of either gender or class as the best strategy for tackling an ecological crisis has not been particularly successful or enduring in either 'broad left' thought, or ecological philosophy. Eco-feminism, like deep ecology, has come to be seen as more an historically important specialisation than the basis of a political paradigm for Green politics. This speaks more to the enduring masculine bias in Marxist thought than the theoretical limitations of eco-feminism.

Feminism remains the most significant development in post-Marxist thought. The male dominance within classical Marxist circles is legendary, as is the masculinity of its thinking. The exclusion of women and women's interests gave powerful momentum to all post-1970s intellectual debates and still remains a necessary ingredient and corrective in contemporary political theorising (and practice).[21]

One point that most academics fail to adequately appreciate is the fundamentally divisive and anti-ecological nature of academic specialisation, particularly in the humanities and social sciences. Specialisation has radical effects on the way that ecological discussions can be conducted. If the founding assumptions and priorities of disciplines and specialisations are human centred, ethical and partitioned from the sciences – as is the case with the humanities and social sciences – then it is unrealistic to expect those who have made careers creating these limited discourses to expend much energy building new paradigms. Indeed, it is more likely that specialists will spend their time defending particular views and exaggerating their importance. This turn of events is all the more likely in highly politicised discourses, or when dominant views have been well established. In Australia (and in Europe and to a lesser extent in the United States) where left dominance over humanities and social sciences is the status quo, resistance to de-centring ideas from new cultural movements has been strong and concerted – even if largely a reflex and reactionary process. This may help explain the particularly chilly reception given by these disciplines to those streams of the newly emerging green culture described below – to 'naturalism', environmentalism, deep ecology, spiritual ecology and 'new science' particularly. The natural bias of specialisation and over-politicisation may also help explain how and why 'new' ideas inevitably come to be re-interpreted and incorporated as part of defensive orthodoxies – thus, gender, race, post-modernity and ecology re-appear as post-Marxist projects in the humanities and social sciences. Who could oppose the moral high ground of social justice and the premise that working class humanity is a cherished part of the whole?

4. Deep Ecology and Spiritual Ecology

As pioneered by Arne Naess (and George Sessions and Bill Devall), 'deep ecology' is a critique of human-centredness that seeks to develop expanded human consciousness as a solution to the 'alienation' of humanity from nature. A main part of this alienation is, in this view, spiritual. The major religions (and particularly Christianity) are, however, regarded by deep ecologists to be a deep source of the separation of humanity from nature. That is why deep ecologists encouraged all nature oriented 'older' religious traditions – including indigenous practices, taoism and Zen Buddhism. So too, like those in the broad left, deep ecologists saw capitalist social relations as alienating and destructive, but capitalism was not considered the single root cause of alienation.

Nonetheless, deep ecologists have been enthusiastic about 'alternative', Earth-centred, political and social structures. As a philosophical position, deep ecology has provided an important critique of human-centredness. Arne Naess, George Sessions and Bill Devall are most responsible for the development of a coherent philosophical perspective.[22]

Deep ecology was attacked by eco-feminists for various shortcomings, including the 'masking' of masculine bias in most spiritual and religious traditions – which is a fair point. On the other hand, perceptions of patriarchal bias in many indigenous, Buddhist and other spiritual traditions, popular amongst the 'counter-culture' and 'new age' pioneers, may never be resolved to the satisfaction of some feminist principles, simply because traditional cultures pre-date the feminist movement and radical critiques of patriarchy. Because the preservation of traditional cultures – particularly their Earth-centred spiritualities – is part of the struggle for indigenous rights, and other post-colonial concerns, masculine bias needs to remain a work in progress for the custodians of these traditions.

In contrast with deep ecology, spiritual ecology is a less well-known project. It is more gender sensitive, but still fundamentally mystical and religious – even if planet oriented. 'Spiritual ecology' differs from deep ecology in being generally theist – sometimes Goddess oriented and sometimes Christian in its basic assumptions. Spiritual ecology and eco-feminism often overlap as a form of goddess worship – the latter being a more concerted critique of religion and being usually a version of feminist critical theory. Both deep ecology and spiritual ecology were however more inclined to go out on a limb for the rights of other species, habitats and wilderness – a tendency that was often opposed by supporters of the rights of 'third world' economies to exploit natural resources. Deep ecology, spiritual ecology and eco-feminism are overlapping categories with respect to their Earth-oriented spirituality, but uneasy companions over issues of religion and politics. Gender equality is probably the main intellectual fault line.[23]

5. New Science

'New Science' is one way of describing those scientifically informed writers who attempt to combine a systems approach with 'out of the box' insights from quantum theory, chaos theory, and other cosmological insights from the frontiers of science. Authors in this category include the scientists Fritjof Capra, Ilya Prigogine, David Bohm, James Lovelock and Edward Lorenz, and many popularisers. The journalist James Gleick is particularly well known for his presentation of Benoit Mandelbrot's 'chaos theory'.[24]

These writers and researchers are also important for the re-vitalisation they have provided systems theory in the social sciences, and for their encouragement to see complex social systems as part of ecologies. The metaphoric possibilities of these new scientific insights are profound

– for instance, ideas such as diversity, complexity, unpredictability and chaos resonate with many lines of enquiry in the arts, humanities and social sciences.[25]

Many of these 'new science' writers could also be considered 'deep ecologists' because they write about Earth as if it were alive, and the source and ground of all human being. James Lovelock, for example – whose work was more closely examined in Chapter 4 – is not overly metaphysical (or mystical) from some philosophical points of view, but his idea that Earth is intelligent and capable of goal directed behaviour (in order to sustain life) is certainly 'out of the box' for most scientists.

It is noteworthy there is a tension between science on the one hand, and deep ecology and eco-feminism on the other. Some post-sixties writers saw science as intrusive and overly instrumental – for instance, the experimental methods employed by some scientists involved cruelty to animals, and scientific medicine had strongly misogynist beginnings. Not only was science capable of directly harming the nature it studied, its theoretical approach could be seen as objectifying and cold in its concern with 'facts' and 'laws'. If nature was alive, science could only register individual organisms and their biological ecologies; the 'bigger picture' was off the scientific radar. Indeed, there is a long-standing tension between science and religion over 'the' meaning, purpose and value of the universe, which goes back, at least, to the rise of science in Western Europe. In general, scientists regard these issues as non-scientific; often they see such 'big questions' as meaningless, pointless and certainly unresolvable – many scientists are either agnostic or atheist. On the other hand, those with strong religious beliefs look to theology for answers to these 'questions', which for them relate to the most fundamental issues of all. Some religious and mystical scientists, and philosophers, have attempted to breach the divide.[26]

Despite all these efforts, the tension between science and religion (and 'metaphysics') is probably unresolvable. Science and religion remain as polarised as ever. Contemporary discourse about climate change, for example, divides between scientists who are most interested in 'the facts' as opposed to religious debate about the morality of human practices that generate climate change. This divide remains, even though scientific cosmology has become so well established that past religious efforts to undermine science – specifically 'creationism' – have fallen into intellectual disrepute.[26]

The very famous (and highly regarded) Stephen Hawking is quite openly 'scientistic' (or 'positivist') as a philosophical scientist. His recent book length assertion that philosophy was dead, and that all remaining big questions were capable of being answered by physics and related sciences is paradigmatic.[27]

His view is shared by most practising scientists and demonstrates why 'positivism' remains an important philosophical position – even though it is opposed to religion and metaphysics generally.[28]

The big questions that appear to interest Hawking most concern the beginning and end of the universe, but he also has a position on 'mind' and 'consciousness' that goes back to the physical brain, neurons, atoms, and the laws of science. While Hawking (arguably the greatest living physicist) may be right about the way scientific cosmology and physics are generally now more interesting and useful than traditional philosophy, the importance of such cosmology in the development of green philosophy and politics in the twenty first century is probably less than it was in the twentieth century. Most politically oriented greens are increasingly engaged in what they see as a struggle for survival, and have less energy for 'new science', or other metaphysical concerns.

In any case, outside professional scientific and philosophical circles, 'facts' and 'values' continue to mix promiscuously. The eco-philosophically inclined writings of scientifically trained writers are not often dismissed as 'positivist' (that is, for reducing questions of *meaning* and *interpretation* to scientific facts), nor are religious efforts to highlight the moral dimensions of climate change rejected. Capra's famous observation in *The Tao of Physics* that modern physicists sound and think like 'eastern' mystics remains intriguing as a suggestion that there are parallels and convergences in all symbolic systems, and that connectivity is basic to all 'being' (and awareness of being).[29]

At the same time it is hardly disputable that professional philosophy is in a phase of decline – the discipline cannot match modern science for new ideas and insights into old problems; further, new areas of 'reality' such as cyberspace and global ecology are the primary domains of new disciplines generated to take up the new spaces and new intellectual opportunities. Perhaps the professionalised discipline of philosophy suffers from a kind of 'mainstreaming' into many other disciplines and interest areas – not unlike the way ecological thought is being (slowly) mainstreamed into popular culture.

THIS IS NOT A PARADIGM

The five broad avenues of thought described above are clearly not coherent in the sense of being a paradigm, or even a perspective. At best they represent a range of ideas that held the attention of many pioneering activists, academics, and philosophically oriented thinkers who were part of a newly emerging post-60s social movement. Many of the authors mentioned above may not be familiar to non-academics, yet the philosophical orientations they represent remain important as a way of describing the fundamental tensions that exist across green philosophies and cultures. The diversity of this modern 'natural philosophy' explains why green politics is conflicted and why anything as coherent as a Green 'paradigm' has yet to emerge. Even if the beliefs of contemporary green activists alone are considered, the fact that some believe in God, gods and goddesses while others are atheists, and some are Marxists whilst others are post-Marxist, and some are science oriented while others are not, should explain why no single paradigm may be possible.

Nonetheless, uncovering streams of thought and old debates at least demonstrates that 'green thought' has an intellectual depth not well appreciated by many journalists and other antagonists of the broad project of 'thinking green'. In fact, there are many other political and philosophical writers who could easily have been included in this very brief survey of early influences. Fortunately, there was a broader context of political and cultural activism that gave context and momentum to these different streams, and provided living impetus to a green social movement. This context included a number of other related social movements: the civil rights movement which galvanised the USA; a

left–labour movement which incorporated Marxist and post–Marxist academics and trade unionists; feminism, which utterly transformed
post–60s political radicalism in the western world; the peace movement;
and more recently post–colonialism, and multiculturalism – including
the increasingly successful struggles of indigenous cultures for cultural
and political recognition, and representation. There have been many cultural forces at work in this post–60s period.

Green politics and early Green parties emerged out of this period of
cultural upheaval and transformation. The genius of the German Greens
was to capture so many of the popular aspirations of that period as 'four
pillars' which might form the foundation framework for a political party
and, as it happens, a whole social movement. This synthesis, driven by
political expediency, remains a brilliant example of the way that theory
and practice can succeed where the individual extremes of either political fundamentalism or academic specialisation fail to ignite popular
imagination, or achieve lasting success.

The four pillars – ecological sustainability, grass roots democracy, peace
and non-violence, and social justice (as they are expressed in Australia)
– are clearly an expression of political and intellectual pluralism. As a
secular over-view of the best political aims of social movements of the
nineteenth and twentieth centuries, it is hard to do better in nine key
words. Yet these goals are still flawed as the key to future success of green
politics. Political progress requires the prioritisation of issues according
to the needs of the day – these issues are increasingly dominated by
the global ecological problems caused by pollution and climate change,
over-population and economic growth.

The separation of five different major cultural influences in the creation
of a social movement is to some extent arbitrary and over-philosophical,
as noted. Any wild and 'happening thing' will resist categorisation on
principle – and so any account will necessarily be incomplete. There
is, indeed, one cultural stream that that might appear missing from at
least two thirds of the account: 'the science'. As noted, biologists and
ecologists were also pioneering activists in the development of ecological insight – without this science, it is hard to imagine what substance
green politics and philosophy could have. Further, the most recent green

cultural heroes are climate scientists and allied specialists who observe, map and describe the fluctuations and problems thrown up by Earth's ecological systems. Any religious debate about the morality of human caused climate change has certainly followed the exposure, by scientists, of 'the facts'.

It seems clear that the 'philosophical' orientation of the majority of these 'streams' is radically incomplete as a representation of 'green thought' because 'the science' on which they all depend for their aware-ness of a motivating crisis is only present implicitly – with the partial exception of 'naturalism' and 'new science'. As philosophical accounts, these streams tend to stand above 'the facts' and compete to define 'the meaning' of ecology, life, society and culture. They do this by situating ecology and nature in an imposed, or assumed, meaningful context – and attempt to define a good way forward, or preferred attitude to the world. None of these streams account fully for the contributions of biological and ecological science (perhaps they often can't because of *a priori* dis-ciplinary distinctions), or the interface between ecological science and politics. The critical importance of not excluding science from political programs is revealed (again and again) by the contemporary problem of climate science denial, and the related problem of adequate funding and recognition for climate related sciences, and for basic ecological scienc-es. Much fuller detail in these stories of neglect and manipulation will hopefully emerge over time.

Just as most Green politicians and activists are not professional phi-losophers or social scientists, nor are they professional research scientists. Some are, but despite this lack, the level of scientifically informed dis-course that occurs in and around Green political parties is much higher than can be found in other political parties. Greens readily accept scien-tific consensus, thus there is little debate about climate change, the loss of species and habitat, and most other associated ecological issues. The same cannot be said about social justice issues, and related philosophical issues. Here differences can be very polarising.

The professional autonomy of scientists has much to do with the fairly ready acceptance by Greens of the importance of distinguishing between scientific research (and scientific knowledge) and the work of political parties and social movements. As discussed, natural scientists are notoriously uneasy with disciplinary transgression and regard politics as a necessary evil, best kept at arms length from the content of research. Of course, most will lobby for funds but not many engage with the broader philosophical and political issues surrounding their work (and arguably running through their work). Scientists with the developed breadth of John Dawkins and Paul Hawking are the exception rather than the rule. For this reason, the work of non-aligned scientific organisations and alliances, such as the newly formed Australian Climate Commission, are so important as a source of reliable scientific information, and as a means of liaising with scientists who value their autonomy.

Science journalism, such as can be found in popular science magazines, also needs to be regarded as worthy of protection. We might otherwise not get to hear about the latest scientific developments and so easily retain an appreciation of science as a cultural foundation of secular liberal democracy.

In summary, the thumbnail sketch that has been presented reveals something of the richness of the cultural origins of the post-60s green social movement and the Green politics that emerged from that social movement. The many issues raised by the movement's cultural pioneers are still relevant and important, and in their diversity demonstrate why it is important for Greens (and greens) to remain pluralist. Complexity is a desirable feature of ecological discourse, and Green political ideology. There are however, further considerations.

STRUGGLING WITH COMPLEXITY

The idea that there should be a unified framework, or 'paradigm', for *green* philosophy and *Green* politics has been dismissed because of the many disciplines and cultural influences already involved, and because of the desirability of 'flexibility' in the face of new and unexpected challenges arising from planetary ecology – and human affairs. Pluralism, or the co-existence of different perspectives is already the status quo in the broader green movement. If there are unifying beliefs and orientations, they are in the form of big goals such as 'saving the planet', the desirability of 'knowing more', and indeed, the 'four pillars'. Philosophers and writers who are nominally 'green' do, however, disagree about the extent to which society and culture should be changed.

The question of whether there *should* be a unified paradigm for *Green* philosophy and politics is quite a different matter. The diversity of ideas (and green philosophies) contributing to the emergence of such an overtly political field as a 'green social movement' has been described above as 'not a paradigm' – partly on the basis that there is at least one profound difference present among Greens that prevents any possibility of agreement about the meaning and purpose of very basic considerations. The coherence of 'left' (or 'broad left') ideas and positions, as opposed to coalitions of more environmental and eco-centric views, is a major fault line in Green politics and to a lesser extent across a broader social movement. There has been more than three decades of ideological struggle in quest of a unified paradigm; there would be many Greens who would agree that any such quest may be a fool's errand.

The appeal for Greens to take a more eco-centric approach might shift existing power relations within some Green parties (that is, diffuse the power of 'the left'), but it would direct more energy and focus towards ecological issues, and it would define ecological sustainability as a priority. This position will be developed in the next two chapters and is presented as part of a discussion of the possibilities of 'progressive politics'. The rationale supporting such a radical view is ultimately survivalist: it is essential that some political parties take up the case on behalf of other species and ecologies. Narrowly defined human interests will lead us all to very undesirable places. No other political parties look like they are remotely in the hunt – under the existing political status quo climate change will proceed largely unchecked, populations will rise without restraint, and economies will continue to grow because of the imperatives of population growth, job creation and reckless consumption. Environments will continue to be degraded, and ecologies will decline and crash. The likelihood of massive human dislocation and suffering looks ominously likely. Climate change alone will do that.

8

GREEN POLITICS AND
GREEN POLITICAL PARTIES

This chapter is an assessment of Green parties and green politics, with an Australian emphasis. The history and politics of Australian Green parties are as unique as those of any country, yet there are many similarities between Australian Green parties and Green parties in other countries – issues, policies, political philosophy and party dynamics – and all Green parties are part of an international green movement. As already discussed, the biggest ecological problems in common are global, even if the beginnings of ecological campaigns and individual politicisation are local – often regional, and issue-by-issue.

Green politics is much broader that the activities of Green parties – Green parties emerged from a diversity of green issues and green philosophical issues. This diversity of interests and approaches is still an important and potentially 'game changing' feature of contemporary green cultures around the world. Party politics is not an option for many activists and individuals who need outcomes in specific campaigns such as those in the anti-coal seam gas movements and wilderness preservation

campaigns. Party politics is a different kind of activity, involving parliamentary processes, bureaucratic regulation, work by committees, and
endless meetings of party members at local through to national levels.
That work is organised, slow, and not for the faint hearted, or for those
of a more anarchist orientation.

Green politics is most fundamentally a social movement – including
individual activism at the level of consumer and domestic behaviour, as
well as more organised campaigns and political parties. Green political
considerations are involved at every level of human existence. Not pur-
chasing processed food, or over-monopolised produce, or composting
and growing one's own vegetables, are all forms of political expression,
no matter how personal and individualised: the consumption of food
and other goods and services is an interconnected process of production,
waste disposal and commerce; personal choices have effects that ripple
through whole chains of connection. In that broad context green politics
is a living network of ecologically oriented behaviour that is continually
emerging. Today, this network is firmly established as an international
phenomenon – ideas circulate, people communicate, organisations form
and grow – and decline and change.

Individuals join green organisations for a variety of reasons – often in
a quest to be more effective achieving their political goals, and involving
desires to care for 'the planet', and anger or frustration with excessive
consumerism and corporate greed. Sometimes galvanising issues can be
as small as an endangered orchid. The conversations and actions that
form the culture of green politics are very diverse but always focused by
concern for environments and ecologies, and the desire to protect them.

These conversations are formal and informal, organised and spontaneous. Symbolic work by artists and philosophers, and many other creative
and thoughtful people, are part of the analysis and rhetoric of 'being
green' and are vital in the communication and interaction that make a
social movement, and inform the practical activities of day-to-day lives.
There is an increasingly extensive green cultural record interspersed at
all levels of expression – for instance, organised politics is such a highly
documented process that successful Green politicians spend far more
time reading, writing, texting, e-mailing, tweeting and phoning than

they do climbing trees, tramping in wilderness, or rallying crowds of protesters.

Green parties are just one focus, albeit a highly important national and 'local' focus in an international movement. Green parties are particularly important as a way of engaging formally with levels of decision making that can compel corporations, government agencies and individuals alike, to change behaviour in favour of environmental considerations.

The persuasive force that organised political parties and social movements can bring to bear in the achievement of collective goals has been demonstrated time and again – in the cases, for example, of religious rights, workers rights, women's rights, indigenous peoples' rights, and gay rights. The rights of other species and ecologies stretch the envelope beyond human rights, but these rights now need consideration. We need other species and ecologies to have a level of legally sanctioned autonomy. Our sense of community now needs to be global.

Social movements and political projects require collective action. Individual self-regulation and personal change are necessary for the success of all campaigns, but individuals also need to work together and communicate in the process. In particular, ecologically enlightened individual action will not be enough to change corporate strategies or government legislation. As the history of political and social change shows, when governments, corporations and media resist change – as they generally will if profits are threatened – it takes the concerted efforts of many people with diverse skills and good networks to bring about lasting change. Enlightened self-interest may be a worthy goal, but time is too short to wait for a total consensus of like minds, all determined to cut consumption, live simply and protect natural habitats. The unavoidable conflict of organised politics will continue to be necessary for the achievement of ecologically rational outcomes.

THE EMERGENCE OF GREEN PARTIES

From the outset, political parties that called themselves Green were trading on a deep cultural association between a colour and a whole non-human sphere – the colour green being universally associated with plant life and nature. Indeed, finding a connection between humanity and all that is non-human requires a philosophical leap that still exercises many minds – and radically challenges nearly every philosophical and religious position. That political parties and a global social movement might symbolically resolve such controversy in a colour is remarkable.

Pioneering modern green philosophers such as Robinson Jeffers, Arne Naess, and George Sessions found their answers to most big questions in nature, as naturalists and philosophers. In their minds, and writings, apparent differences between humanity and the non-human could be partially resolved by the use of inclusive terms such as *nature, Earth, ecology, biosphere* and *Gaia* – but the colour green had not yet been politicised; that was a late twentieth century innovation. For these pioneers love of nature was an occasion for joy, celebration and deep contemplation – much as it can be today, but presumably without the level of angst that attends the contemplation of contemporary environments and ecologies. These early pioneers were what we might describe today as 'deep greens' – being 'in nature' and 'of nature' was, in practice, much more than intellectual reflection. A relationship with nature could also be a transcendent experience, akin to religious ecstasy, but without an external god. *Green grass, blue skies* and *red dust*, for example, signified a natural order that was colourful but uncomplicated by the works of man. For these pioneers the unity of life was, however, not simply a matter for contemplation; 'nature' needed protection, and so they were political – just as many contemporary 'deep greens' are political – but they were political pioneers, as part of their contemplative 'naturalism'.

The contemporary politics of being Green have become quite different from the 'environmental politics' of these philosophical 'founders'. Those people were often advocates for national parks and wilderness, and were networked into various organisations and associations, but did not seek political office. Contemporary Green political thought (and practice) is much more party-centric and pluralist. Philosophically it is divided between a 'deeper' green eco-centric orientation tending toward traditional environmentalism and philosophical views inspired by naturalists, in contrast with a more thoroughly human-centred 'left' position.

Many members find themselves 'in between' and are unclear about the history of these ideological differences.

The emergence of Green parties as political entities is very much a post-1960's phenomenon – as discussed in the last chapter. That time was a period of great cultural transformation. Music, art, politics and 'lifestyles' were the focus of intense scrutiny and change. Political change occurred because of mass phenomena in 'social movements'. Radical processes were most often youthful: *peace* and *love* were slogans that guided many, but not all. Popular culture was catalytic in all cultural spheres – free wheeling university students inspired philosophers, architects, sociologists . . . and aspiring politicians.

Out of this cultural ferment green philosophy and politics emerged as part of a re-vitalised political sphere across Europe, the USA, and Australia. The effects of this period of transformation were, however, global – even if Green political parties did not arise everywhere. By the 1980s green politics had institutionalised in many countries, but Germany became prominent for the scale and success of its greening.

In the context of this post-1960's upsurge of interest in all kinds of radical and revolutionary ideas, the election of 28 Green MPs to the West German Bundestag in 1983 was a *high point* and *defining moment* for environmental activists and an emerging Green political culture. This success built on the work in many different countries over previous decades, and inspired social and cultural movements to carry on with struggles on many fronts, and to more radically think through different streams of thought. The German Greens were not the first Green political party (as discussed below), but the scale of their success seemed to ignite the hopes of green activists and thinkers around the globe. For political ecologists there was dancing in the streets. Finally a radical break through had occurred at the level of parliamentary democracy. Ecologists, feminists, anarchists, socialists, and all in between had reason to hope for continuing change, and perhaps, perhaps . . . a revolution.

Then 'the wall' came down – and for leftists 'revolutionary conditions' in Germany seemed even more promising. . . but, alas, the story of Green politics never did rise to ever more dizzying heights. Green politics remains, for many, a revolution in the making.

Nonetheless, inspired by the success of the German Greens, many other Green parties formed as a loose international alliance. The 'four pillars' that the German Greens established as a party platform were widely adopted as guiding ideals, and as the basis for formal constitutions. In Australia the four pillars were broadened slightly to include 'peace' as a component ideal.

The principles that appear in the constitutions of Australian Federal, State and local groups are shown below, in italics, together with some further explanation:

1. *Ecological sustainability* [not always presented as the first principle];

2. *Grass roots democracy* [as the norm in the decision making of political parties];

3. *Peace and non-violence* [as the default position for all human society]; and

4. *Social justice* [as a legal and moral default position in all human society].

As noted in the last chapter, these 'pillars' are a strategic summary of the goals of many generations of activists, politicians, philosophers and social movements – they are not the unique invention of any Green party. The original 'principles' are defined at considerable length in a Die Grunen pamphlet (cited earlier) and vary only slightly as guiding principles of all Green party constitutions.

Clearly, Green parties are nowhere near achieving any of these goals on a global scale. Radically idealistic as the goals are (and the Australian version is a pragmatic understatement of more extreme positions concerning peace and social justice held by some individual Greens) progress has been made in many countries. Considered historically, widespread public agreement that even some of these goals are desirable, and strategically important, counts as significant ecological progress.

For all contemporary philosophical differences and divisions, the emergence of Green political parties in the late twentieth century is still an inspiring example of contemporary grass roots politics. Green politics shows something very positive about the emergence of new levels of order in complex and conflict ridden social organisations, regions, and countries. It also demonstrates many, if not all, of the perennial characteristics of organised politics – particularly the inevitable conflicts and factionalising that dog all efforts to bring about social and cultural change. While most Green activists have sought to be somehow 'progressive', it is not possible to escape the differences of personalities, goals, motivations and factions that exist in all social groups and organisations. Nonetheless, Green parties have institutionalised 'consensus based decision making' and 'grass roots democracy' as axioms of process and structure. Further, despite the 'natural' hierarchical, elitist, competitive, and often corrupt, downside of 'normal' party politics in all parliamentary systems, Green parties have largely remained grass roots parties with support that extends through wide sections of society.

Green political parties are comparatively small and do not have the levels of financial support enjoyed by their larger competitors. Nonetheless, the prospects for Green parties are generally good. Green parties have not been tainted by the misdeeds and occasional criminality that taint most large parties. Indeed, disillusionment with established major political parties can be found throughout all classes and strata within all societies – despite being often perceived as ideologically extreme, Green parties look relatively clean in comparison. Further, increasing concern about environmental problems in individual societies, and also increasingly at a global level, can help Green parties to move beyond perceptions that are still wedded to a 'left-right' political spectrum that mainly expresses the politics of social class – a shift to a radical 'centre' which would, as presented in the next chapter, be a potentially 'progressive' move.

The long-term prospects for Green parties are also bolstered by the fact that they are part of a broader international social movement that includes many environmentally focused parties, organisations, groups and individuals. The Australian Greens are affiliated to the international organisation, Global Greens. Other green organisations operating within Australia include Green Peace, Sea Shepherd, the World Wildlife Fund, Wilderness Societies, conservation societies (including the Australian Conservation Foundation and the National Parks Association), local environmental groups (including the Landcare network), activist alliances such the anti-coal seam gas movement, 'Lock the Gate' – which registered as a political party in 2013, and also another newly formed ecologically focused political party – the Victorian Save Our Planet Party. There are also two other well-known citizen alliance groups whose broad focus includes environmental campaigning, GetUp, and the Pirate Party. These last two networks have used the Internet to great advantage. Members of Green parties often belong to other environmentally focused groups such as Sea Shepherd and GetUp. Not all those in this network are activists. Many are not – but need no convincing that trouble is brewing.

THE ORGANISATION OF
AUSTRALIAN GREEN PARTIES

Australia is a large and mostly arid island continent, plus a smaller, colder and wetter island to the south, Tasmania. This smaller island is famous in the international Green community for being the home of the first Green political party, the United Tasmania Group, founded by Bob Brown. Christine Milne was also a founding member, and both these pioneering Greens went on to be parliamentary leaders of the national Australian Greens. In 2015 there are 10 federal Senators, one member of the federal House of Representatives, 12 state parliamentarians, more than 100 local councillors, and an Australian membership in excess of 10,000.

The Australian Greens is a co-ordinating political entity that functions primarily at a Federal level of parliament. It is formally a 'confederation' of eight state and territory parties. There is a National Council that is the national decision-making body – it consists of delegates from state and territory organisations. The National Council has no formal executive and decisions are made by consensus.

Each state organisation has its own structure, reflecting the different experiences and possibilities available in the formation of groups, branches and parties around the country:

> The *Tasmanian Greens* has five 'electorate branches' administered by a State Executive;

The Greens NSW has approximately 50 autonomous 'local groups', each with their own constitution;

The *Victorian Greens* is a branch of the Australian Greens with 'regional branches';

The *ACT Greens* is one group;

The *NT* [Northern Territory] *Greens* is a branch of the Australian Greens;

The Greens WA [Western Australia] has semi-autonomous regional groupings based on Federal electorates;

The *Queensland Greens* has branches;

The *Australian Greens SA* [South Australia] is a branch of the Australian Greens with 'local branches'.[1]

This is by far the most diverse (and uncontrollable) party organisational structure in Australian organised politics.

Such a complex organisation has evolved partly in reaction against top down hierarchies as are found in the two major Australian political parties – the Liberal and Labor parties. This organisational diversity is also a direct expression of democratic processes conducted with the autonomy, or semi-autonomy, of states, territories, regions, electorates, and population centres allowed to prevail, as determined by the collective wills of those involved in various Green political entities. All Australian Green parties are in strong agreement that 'grass roots democracy' should be practiced as an ethical value and as an organisational rule. This principle has certainly been an impediment to the emergence of ruling elites, cliques, and factions, but has by no means eliminated them.

Green politics in Australia, like Green politics elsewhere, has been a mix of parliamentary and non-parliamentary activism. It is very clear that Australian Greens have generally regarded themselves as part of a much larger coalition of environmental organisations and single-issue groups dedicated to various ecological and social outcomes. There is an inspiring history of successful campaigns that has laid the foundations for the emergence of new generations of activists – many of whom have become parliamentarians. Some of this history and organisational detail is available on line at the websites of the Green parties listed above, and on various Wikipedia sites. Unfortunately much of the detail of this history including successful (and unsuccessful) campaigns remains oral – and inadequately described in published written form.[2]

Founding Australian Green party parliamentarians began their political careers as environmental activists. Some of those parliamentarians that followed were activists for trade unions and left wing political parties, but the early history of Australian Green groups and parties has a pronounced environmental orientation – most early members saw themselves, fairly exclusively, as environmental activists. However, as the federation of Australian Green party organisations has grown and matured, embracing diversity, a significant number of activists with socialist, communist and ALP backgrounds have joined Australian Green parties. NSW has been the most successful recruiter of left wing activists. Migration from the socialist left of the Labor Party, the Communist Party of Australia (CPA), the Socialist Alliance, and other smaller organisations, began in earnest in the mid 1980's when the Berlin Wall came down, and 'international communism' was largely discredited as a plausible option for activists. In Australia the CPA was disbanded in 1991 – around which time there was a concerted migration of old party members and supporters into Australian Green groups and parties, mainly in Victoria and NSW. The prominence of these 'old left' warriors has fuelled media driven perceptions of Greens as being 'watermelons'. Because it is well known by Australian journalists that not all Greens identify with being 'watermelons' such characterisations function as wedge politics. Understandably, most parliamentarians agree that 'disunity is death'; consequently internal politics can be complex and dysfunctional. In most other states the watermelon syndrome has been less influential and probably contributed positively to the enthusiasm of Greens for social justice issues. In NSW the dominance of old left members (also known as the 'industrial left') has forced conflict over the party's engagement with divisive social and political issues – such as the extent of trade union involvement, the influence of the Socialist Alliance, the anti-Israel BDS campaign (Boycott, Divest, Sanction) and more recently calls for a campaign to 'block supply' – that is, to block the passage of the 2014 Federal Budget through the Upper House of the Federal Parliament; that campaign was unsuccessful. There is a widespread feeling that too much time is spent debating 'old left' ideological issues at the expense of developing an eco-logical program.

Australian Green parties are not generally over-burdened with hard left factions and committed socialists. However, New South Wales remains a place where 'the light on the hill' still shines for many. Sometimes its flickering shadows project images that almost look like history. Some in the Greens NSW, including elected parliamentarians, are highly focused in their efforts to define Green politics as 'left wing'. For them, Green politics and philosophy are an extension of established labour movement and socialist politics and philosophy. Because this requires a selective pri-oritisation of historical events – and particularly the exclusion of much early environmental activism – considerable efforts have been made by them to 'revise' the early history of Green parties, as will be shown below. This 'identity politics' is not restricted to activity within the Greens NSW – broad left and Marxist philosophy occurs very widely as part of Green party discussion and publication, and efforts to create party affili-ations with trade unions occur in many countries.

WHO WAS FIRST?

The question of who was first to form a Green party will probably remain a debating point for a long time. Do we mean which party first called themselves Green, or do we mean which party first prioritised ecological issues, or do we mean which party first had elected parlia-mentary members who called themselves Green . . . or do we mean who started Green politics? Often the German Greens are credited with priority on all counts, but there are good reasons to look more closely at the records relevant to these different ways of being a founding Green party, and to question the question.

Because history is complex the question of where things start or stop is misleading and potentially a strong political construction. Indeed, to claim the point of origin of a social movement, intellectual field, political process, or party (or country), should first raise the question of why one would. Broadly, questions and claims about beginnings need to be placed in the context of who is asking or claiming, who benefits from the answer, and who is disadvantaged. Even more broadly, the basic issue of 'identity politics' arises – whose history and identity is being created, or influenced, and why? In the case of Green political discourse, nobody can claim ownership, or legitimately gain intellectual and political capital by claiming paternity or maternity over a very long and complex green 'conversation' that has occurred across, and within, many cultures. Discourse about the relationship between humanity, nature and other species appears to go back to the beginnings of culture and language. More nuanced questions about the historical emergence of particular ideas, theories, philosophies, cultures and their social relations make sense, but cannot (or should not) be answered as if their fields of relationships relate to space and time in the way that objects do. Conversations are not 'things'; they are processes marked by words and utterances, but not reducible to either.

The importance of these considerations is obvious when one considers political discourse that attempts to define founding moments. In the context of Green philosophy and history, the recent writings of the Australian Federal Greens Senator, Lee Rhiannon, are particularly insightful. In 2013 Senator Rhiannon published a pamphlet in tribute to 'Green Bans' and the role of Jack Mundey in the early history of Australian Green parties. On the first page she makes the following claims:

> 'Our roots go back to the community activism of the 1960s and 1970s.

> Green Bans changed the political weather four decades ago. The decision of the Builders Labourers Federation to down tools when developers threatened urban bushland started a great movement . . .

The German Greens took their name from the Green Bans after the activist Petra Kelly visited Australia in the 1970s.

This was the world's first Green Party and in time the name and principles of social justice, ecological sustainability, grass-roots democracy and nonviolence came back to Australia when the first Greens Party in this country was formed in Sydney in 1984.'[3]

Senator Rhiannon's claims are not new. The narrative about the historical connection between Jack Mundey, the Builders Labourer's Federation, and the German Greens has been made since the mid 1980s. As noted above, from about that time Green politics in NSW became influenced by activists and organisations of 'the left' – guaranteeing much ideological conflict. Subsequently, Green politics in Sydney (NSW) had a particularly conflicted history – and the formation of a national alliance became a very protracted affair – the Australian Greens formed eventually in 1992. Internal disputes among different left factions, including the Democratic Socialist Party, members of 'Labor Greens', and various independents, resulted in a short-lived Sydney Greens party (1984-1991) – which at some point became known as the Green Alliance, with the stated aim of not forming a 'traditional hierarchy party'.[4]

Identity politics were always a major concern, even before the eventual formation of Greens NSW in 1991. As Tony Harris tells the story, naming rights became an issue in the lead-up to the formation of the Sydney Greens because 'it was decided to register the name 'The Greens' with the Australian Electoral Commission [. . . this was] 'to lead to disputes later on.'[5]

What Senator Rhiannon's text attempts to formalise is a narrative of identity, which establishes a trade union (the BLF), and its leader, Jack Mundey, as the founding inspiration for Green politics in NSW (and also in Australia, and the world). In her account, the brief conjunction of 'a group of middle class women who comprised the 'Battlers for Kelly's Bush' . . . set the precedent for cooperation between unionists and community activists.'[6]

Rhiannon's view is that the women were middle class because they lived in Hunter's Hill. It is unlikely that these women were working class in any old fashioned Marxist sense (which is very male centred), but the class position of women continues to be an unresolved argument among women of the left. Do women automatically have the same class position as their husbands? Are we talking about upper-middle class as opposed to lower-, or middle-, middle class here? Are women generally more exploited than men and more likely to be domestic servants of their husbands and partners, if they have them at all? Left feminist class analysis is not a closed book. Nor is the supposed middle class nature of the Green movement a simple matter. As this book attempts to show, ecological concerns cross class boundaries, and will not be solved by a working class revolution – even if it is led by an alliance of trade unions and Green political parties.

Nonetheless, the brief alliance of the 'Battlers for Kelly's Bush' and founding activists of the Sydney Greens with the BLF resulted in the first 'Green Ban' – on an AV Jennings construction project that threatened a small piece of urban bushland. Seeing this as the birthing of Australian Green parties is probably an over-statement. There are other ways of framing that series of events: it might also be said that Green Bans were a short-lived episode ending in a feud between the federal BLF and the NSW branch of the union; that Green Bans were preceded by 'black bans' which also protected environmental values; and that the BLF was de-registered in 1986, and its federal Secretary, Norm Gallagher, gaoled.

Jack Mundey is a favourite father figure on the Green left because he was a prominent trade unionist, and socialist, with ecological concerns. Senator Rhiannon's brief text is intended to demonstrate just how important both urban trade unionism and Jack Mundey have been in the history of the Australian Green movement, in particular – and implicitly how important they should become in this history. Excluded from the frame is a much longer history of local and global activism, including the contributions of Bob Brown, Christine Milne, Milo Dunphy, Peter Garrett, Peter Hamilton, Ian Cohen, Jan Barham, Drew Hutton and many other pioneering Australian activists who fought against the destruction of local habitat. Some chained themselves to trees; many

were assaulted and arrested in a period when there was a great outpour-
ing of outrage and grief over the destruction of forests, ecologies, and
other natural assets.

This was not just an Australian uprising – the ecologically oriented radical tumult of 1960s and 1970s was as much an American and
European process, and was linked to many other causes and processes, as
discussed in the last chapter. But the front line in Australia was definitely
'in the bush' – that is *rural*, despite the millions of disaffected young and
old who were in the cities. The trade unions were then, and now, either
antagonistic or silent about ecologically based campaigns threatening
jobs in the forestry and mining industries. The Green Bans, and later bans
on the transport and export of uranium ore were notable exceptions.

Those who benefit most from Senator Rhiannon's tribute to Jack
Mundey (who, incidentally, deserves rich tribute) are a small number of
dedicated and committed left activists who, to this day, prioritise a particular view of social justice, a top down version of grass roots democracy,
and a centralised, Sydney-centric management structure.

The intended messages in Lee Rhiannon's document go beyond
words. The colour green and the Australian Greens' triangle are prom-
inently displayed on the front and back covers, the dominant interior
headings are in red: this is a watermelon. The impression created is that
the pamphlet is an official message from the Greens NSW (and therefore endorsed by the membership). It is actually a privately produced,
self-published and unendorsed pamphlet. Such apparent looseness of
process is misleading in a party bureaucracy which otherwise attempts
to strongly control the communications of its elected representatives.[7]

For the record, the first Australian political party to have a strong parliamentary voice on ecological issues was the Australian Democrats – the
party was founded in 1977 by Don Chipp, a renegade from the Australian
Liberal Party. However, Bob Brown is widely credited with founding the
first political party with its basis in environmental issues. The United
Tasmania Group were founded in March 1972, and according to Derek
Wall, 'inspired the creation of Green parties all over the world.'[8]

This claim is not uncontested. In a curious twist of trans-Tasman
rivalry between Australia and New Zealand, Dick Richardson (a British

political historian), claims the New Zealand Values Party – also established in 1972 – was the first environmentally based political party.[9]

Unfortunately for Richardson's claim, the Values Party was established in May 1972, three months after the founding of The United Tasmania Group. Controversy rages, nonetheless. The April 2014 Wikipedia entry asserts that the Values Party is 'considered the world's first national-level environmental party that pre-dated any fashionable Green terminology.'[10]

The Values Party contested five elections, but did not gain any seats. 'It did however manage to get some candidates elected to local government . . . In May 1990, however, remnants of the Values Party merged with a number of other environmentalist organisations to form the Green Party of Aotearoa New Zealand, which eventually did gain Parliamentary seats.'[11]

There are many ways to be first.

Europe's first green party, the UK's Ecology Party, was founded in 1973. In June 1970 the Dutch group, the Kabouters won 5 seats in Amsterdam's 45 seat City Council, and a seat in Councils in Arnhem, Altmaar, and Leiden. This group had 'Groenen Planen' (Green Plans) and were probably the first Europeans to use Green as an ecological political adjective.[12]

In an ironic twist, the Dutch Green Plans were inspired by the anarchist group Provos, whereas the Australian Green Bans were inspired by a Communist Party of Australia influenced trade union. And so it seems that even if 'the paradigm shifting Green Ban movement was born in Sydney in the early 1970s'[13], Dutch anarchists had Green Plans before all that. Clearly, Senator Rhiannon's claims can benefit from qualification using very publicly available sources.

THE FIRST AUSTRALIAN
GREEN PARLIAMENTARIANS

In order to further clarify questions about 'who was first' it makes good sense to focus on those individuals who were first elected as 'greens' rather than as members of Green parties – otherwise a very distorted view emerges. Unquestionably Bob Brown has played the most prominent and influential role in the history of Australian green parliamentary representation. Following his leading role in the successful campaign to save the Franklin River in Tasmania from the Gordon-below-Franklin Dam, he was elected to the Tasmanian Parliament in 1983 as an Independent representing the seat of Denison. He was not the first environmentalist to represent the seat of Denison – Norm Sanders, who like Bob Brown had been a director of the Tasmanian Wilderness Society, first won the seat in that same year only to withdraw in order to contest (successfully) for the Senate as an Australian Democrat. By 1989 Bob Brown had been joined by four other environmental activists (Christine Milne, Lance Armstrong, Di Hollister and Gerry Bates), together forming the Tasmanian Green Independents. Bob served in the Tasmanian parliament for ten years. In 1996 he became the first Australian Greens Senator in the Australian Federal Parliament, a seat he held as parliamentary leader of the Australian until his resignation in 2012. Christine Milne was elected as the next parliamentary leader of the Australian Greens.

Jo Vallentine also played a pioneering role as a prominent green activist who became a parliamentarian. She was elected to the federal Senate as a representative of the Nuclear Disarmament Party in 1984, and then in 1990 became the first Greens federal parliamentary Senator in Australia, as a member of the Greens (WA). Jo Vallentine was succeeded by two more female Senators from Western Australia, Christabel Chamarette (1992-1996) and Dee Margetts (1993-1999). In 2002, Michael Organ won the seat of Cunningham in NSW, becoming the first Australian Greens member to be elected to the Federal House of Representatives.[14]

Clearly, as a parliamentarian, there are again many ways to be first. Being first is, of course, not as important as successful environmental campaigns, successful parliamentary policy initiatives, public education about environmental issues, and green networking, but 'identity politics' is in many ways critical to the ongoing formation and resilience of networks and electoral popularity. Being first is not just an outcome of competitive, hierarchical cultures and societies – it is a perennial element in all narratives of identity, myths of origin, and religious cosmologies. It is good to be first.

However, it is also good (and essential) to simply be part of social movements and all progressive social relations. There are hundreds of other individuals not mentioned above who were, and are, Green party representatives in parliaments and councils, who contribute to the organisation and maintenance of local groups, particular campaigns, public education, and so on. Being green has never required social reward as a condition of such self-identification. In some ways, post-sixties legacies of anti-authoritarian and egalitarian human values remain a rather unique and endearing quality of 'being green'.

INSIDE THE GREEN BOX

In the twenty first century green plans are abundant. Every level of government has them, and most citizens have an opinion about climate change and the importance of greening lifestyles. The conversion of societies to sustainability is obviously a huge task. Optimism is helpful; pragmatism is essential. Eco-centric pragmatism, however, is the progressive, maybe essential, direction of future cultural endeavours towards sustainability.

The point has been made that only Green parties are radical enough to drive ecologically focused policies forward in parliaments that are universally limited in their abilities to change economic and social systems quickly, or to pursue policies that are apparently counter to the logic of growth economics. The community needs to be persuaded that eco-centrism is just common sense, even though radical shifts in culture and society are required. However, altruism cannot be assumed. Legislation will be required.

This is one of the main functions of Green parties – to assist in the creation of ecologically focused legislation. The really difficult question for Green parties everywhere concerns their ability to make substantial progress through government processes dominated by large political parties. Yet even as oppositional voices in parliaments, Green parties are a legislative and policy force. As parliamentarians, Greens participate in the normal processes of government and can influence the content of legislation. For small parties, like Green parties, the breadth of expertise required for effective participation in parliaments can be, however, a problem. Policy development over a wide range of issues is challenging even for large parties. In 2014 the Australian Greens had 244 different policy areas drafted as positions and policies. This covered the entire range of Federal parliamentary business arising from proposed legislation, parliamentary debates, and Question Time. Green parliamentarians in Australia are not 'single issue' voices – they are advocates for clean air, animals, indigenous rights, disabled people, impoverished people, refugees, arts and culture, Australian youth, clean and healthy food, home renters, parents, the sick and dying, workers rights and conditions, biological diversity, and so on. The list goes on for 244 items of active policy areas.[15]

The NSW Greens have a smaller list of only 54 active policy areas. This reflects the different focus of State issues (as opposed to Federal issues) – different levels of government legislate for different jurisdictions, and have different powers and responsibilities. The articulation of these policy areas is often based on the research and drafting of working parties, and policy focused meetings at State and branch levels. In 2014 there were only three groups working on policy areas with a strong ecological focus: the Climate Action Working Group, the Futures Conference Working Group and the Sustainability and Population Working Group. There is also an Economies Working Group, and together with the other three Groups, this is the extent of formal group work that might seriously consider matters immediately relevant to the 'big three' problems of climate change, over-population, and economic growth.[16]

This relatively small effort is to be expected because of the dominant concern of State parliaments to focus on promoting economic growth; most politicians so involved actively seek to avoid entanglement with the 'big three' problems.

In federal parliament, the Australian Greens are concerned with the broader issues of clean air, biological diversity, clean energy, environmental principles, extreme weather, global economics, global governance, biodiversity crisis, population, sustainable agriculture, and sustainable planning and transport, but this amounts to just 10 areas out of 244 listed areas – about 4% of the list appear to be directly concerned with the 'big three'. Indirectly, the situation is not quite so dire – many of the 'other' areas listed are ecologically focused, so 4% is a somewhat misleading figure. Approximately 62 areas (or 43%) could be described as 'core' ecological concerns, about which the Australian Greens ought to have policies. These figures are also indicative of the diffusing effect of parliamentary processes on ecological focus – at both levels of parliament. There are other measures that could be introduced to better deal with the ideological drift required by diverse parliamentary agendas – this subject will be resumed in Chapter 9, 'Progressive Green Politics'.

It should be noted that these lists of policy areas do not fully represent the interests and concerns of those two Green parties – there are also campaigns and liaison work with other activist groups that arise from time to time. Nor does such a listing expose the content and particular focus within working groups and campaigns. These can be highly ideological.

If voters are to be persuaded to 'vote Green', and the power of the international green movement is to remain connected to legislative arms in parliaments, eco-politics will need to be mainstream, and much more concerted philosophical effort will need to be made to engage the public imagination about future scenarios. If Green parties attempt to combine broad left philosophy with ecology, as they often appear to do, the outcome will be problematic. Ecological issues will become submerged in a plethora of issues covering the full spectrum of parliamentary business – as raised above, small parties (with small numbers of research staff) cannot hope to do justice to such a huge range of legitimate concerns. It will be suggested that Green parties must focus on the ecological and environmental consequences of policy issues and develop policies accordingly. The general point is that most policy has an ecological dimension and can be situated within an over arching eco–centric perspective.

The 'hard left' and 'the broad left' have a long history of seeking to control the agendas of any political party of which they are part. Committed leftists feel that they have more than 150 years of developed philosophical and political activism to draw from and that they are, therefore, entitled (and needed) to take up leading roles as 'vanguards' of any progressive political movement. The ecological dilemma is that human activity is very much the cause of the decline of planetary ecologies. Totally human–centred politics will not work any longer. In practice this means that socialist agendas and left wing control will lead to limited ecological gains, and guarantee continuing electoral failure. Green parties that are so influenced continue to be of very limited positive interest to voters or ecological activists in different parts of the green movement.

ANYONE FOR A REVOLUTION?

Ecological sustainability is a radical goal in any society. Changing the way power is generated, cleaning up industrial processes, shifting to renewable resources, consuming less, re-valuing economic commodities, and perhaps even lowering standards of living for large numbers of people in wealthy countries would, by any left theoretical criteria, qualify as a 'revolution'.

However, at this late stage of ecological decline it is important to reassess the meaning of the word *revolution* as established by 'broad left' and 'hard left' political ideologies – and co-incidentally, as it occurs within popular understandings.

As has been argued so far, if there is to be any hope of good living standards for following generations, the necessary radical changes would be best achieved through non-violent and democratic means. It has already been suggested that all changes required need to be driven by parliamentary processes, and that economic changes need to involve market processes as well as changed perceptions of very basic commodities – such as the 'real' value of natural resources and the 'true' costs of energy generated by fossil fuels. These changes are already in train, being subjects for debate and discussion in parliaments, 'think tanks' and media.

The next step, to which this book is intended as a contribution, involves more careful examination of economic and philosophical presumptions that are largely still unexamined – and more profound changes in behaviour around consumption and lifestyles. None of this requires violent mass change, nor is it conceivable that these 'conversations' and cultural changes could occur very quickly. In that light, the big question is whether there is any sense in which radical change can 'evolve' and be 'revolutionary' – and also claim a 'radical centre' in politics? This is a question that, appropriately, concludes an assessment, in this chapter, of the dead end of left political appropriation of green politics – and begins a discussion of 'progressive politics' over the following two chapters.

As individuals meet, talk, and form groups, the possibilities and per-mutations grow. An ecologist or mathematician would say that the growth of such relationships generates more complexity in the system. As systems increase in size however, it appears that mismatch between complexity, resource demands, and population numbers, can cause sys-tems to fail. Extreme size does not appear to be sustainable in living systems, prompting systems to reorganise – often violently. In animal and plant systems, populations and ecologies are said to 'crash', but usually there are survivors and new ecologies re-emerge. In human society such radical transformations would be commonly called *revolutions* – and be considered to involve the destruction of 'the old' and birth of 'the new'.

Or at least, that's the view from the left – where it is agreed that total transformations are rare. The 'industrial revolution' of the nineteenth century is probably the best example of a really big change – with major technological change accompanying social transformation, including the re-distribution of wealth. In most accounts by left theorists the 'mode of production' of globally dominant societies changed radically – 'feudal society' is said to have changed (mostly in wealthy European societies) to 'capitalist society'.

The French, American, Russian, Chinese and Cuban 'revolutions' are other well known recent examples of ideologically driven changes of social order. It is arguable that because these revolutions of social orders did not involve the radical changes of 'the means of production' seen in the industrial revolution (for example, the advent of the steam engine) they were not as complete in the extent to which they changed the whole system. Today there are other potentially revolutionary forces in play – pre-eminently the development of new communications technol-ogies and ecological decline. Change in the means of communication is obviously changing much in all contemporary society – just as the invention of the printing press in the fifteenth century and the development of mass production techniques in the eighteenth and nineteenth centuries changed everything in 'pre-capitalist' and 'early capitalist' societies. Could these recent innovations in communication be a revolution in progress?

Because of these well-known historical examples of mass re-organisation, and because of the obvious potential for social change major technological innovations have (for example, the steam engine, nuclear power, the internet, sustainable energy technologies), *and* because of ideologically driven desire for the decline of capitalism, the idea of *revolution* has become a common notion in the vocabularies of activists. It seems easy to argue that big changes in the future will require a *revolution* . . . but there are grave dangers in this line of thought. These dangers derive from the wars, violence and chaos that have accompanied all known major changes in established patterns of national and international capital and power. Another less obvious danger stems from the decades of leftist spin that have already declared the idea of revolution in capitalist society to be understandable only in context of violence and class conflict. Radical political change has been established, by the left (and the right), to be only possible through violent means – popular representations as words, visual images and general propaganda all emphasise such conflict. The possibilities of consensual change to a sustainable society remain to be developed.

In all varieties of left philosophy a proper *revolution* requires (ultimately) changing from private ownership to public ownership – socialism or communism requires the 'overthrow' of capitalism and the era of private ownership, with the creation of a new age of public ownership and public welfare. Just who owns, and controls, the 'productive forces' – including the industries and technologies (or 'the means of production') is a basic concern in this paradigm of revolution. Changing ownership means 'changing society'. This requires a revolutionary working class to wage war on capitalism, however long it takes and by, more or less, any means. In the short term, according to basic Marxism, a revolutionary vanguard of enlightened Green politicians and activists could achieve much in paving the way for revolutionary change. Even if ownership should become temporarily vested in the state including armies, police and associated bureaucracies, no matter because these will all, in theory, become subject to 'the will of the people' and 'the general good'. Through many elegant variations, these are the basic ingredients of leftist revolutionary philosophy. The basic ecological problem is that there is no evidence that public ownership has protected natural assets – other species, or the quality of air, land or water. An industrial mode of production has been dirty and polluting whoever owned its industries; mass agricultural production has been a disaster for forests, endangered species and ecologies, whoever owned the 'broad acres'. New information technologies may facilitate communication and collective endeavours, but these are not intrinsically ecological. State bureaucracies whether capitalist, communist or socialist in name have a long history of being oppressive and violent. Public ownership is no guarantee of public welfare or ecological concern.

Nonetheless, revolutionary narratives persist in Green politics. For example, leftist ideological beliefs have found expression in the way some Greens have seized upon the idea of introducing renewable energy 'to save the planet'. These plans require a rapid, near total transformation of industrial energy generation, and so are predictably unrealistic – they are, in effect, a call for a revolution. This approach will continue to fail, and undermines a more considered and persuasive policy discussion.[17]

So far, the development of mass renewable energy sources in Australia has been mostly limited to the installation of solar devices on rooftops and the generation of wind power in open fields. Some countries have invested in larger scale renewable energy power stations – large, commercially viable arrays of solar thermal and photovoltaic devices can be found in Portugal, Spain and the USA, and large biogas generators are commonplace in Germany and China. Most countries have plans to produce a rising proportion of their national energy budgets from renewable sources, but their targets are all relatively low in proportion to growing total energy requirements.

Important as programs for the development of these and other renewable sources (such as tidal and geothermal power) are, the broader implications of their adoption need consideration. Mass conversion to renewable energy production will require big changes to industrial practices and infrastructure. If policies of total change were pursued, they would entail the closing of all coal mines, oil fields and refineries, gas fields, and the abandonment of most related infrastructure. The flow on effects to the chemical industry and manufacturing industries would be massive. For example, fossil fuels are also a source of organic chemicals used in manufacturing, transport and cleaning, as well as in power generation. Governments would forego tax revenues, jobs would go – and be created in a green energy sector which, as yet, hardly exists. Assuming industry can adapt and change as fossil fuel usage is wound down – and there is no simple consensus about that – the main issue becomes how quickly such changes could be achieved.

In Australia, which is coal-centric, the effects of rapid change would be huge. In the case of closure of mines and refineries – if we can imagine a popular uprising of workers determined to introduce '100% renewables' – the effects on the profitability of industry, and the revenues raised by governments (as taxes) would be enormous. Businesses would fail, and large numbers of working people would become unemployed. This might indeed become a revolutionary situation, but it is unlikely that industry, governments or working people would voluntarily choose such a fate.

Nonetheless, the question of whether Green politics ought to be revolutionary is still effectively posed in campaigns promoting rapid change. Perhaps the question is to what the extent Green culture should aim to be revolutionary. Undoubtedly the phased closure of most coalmines is needed – but taxes must continue to roll in to governments so that infrastructure can be built and maintained, and workforces employed in many industries (public and private). Fossil fuel dependency cannot be curtailed overnight – the social consequences are now far too great.

Many historians and sociologists describe long term changes in society – progressive leftist historians usually find *evolution* and *revolution* of ideas and organisations, and an ongoing *dialectic* between society, culture and *revolutionary* and *radical* individuals and organisations. There is, so far, limited account of ecological and environmental cautionary tales that should illustrate these broad themes.[18]

We might note that in the context of a long and 'hard' left revolutionary tradition, the idea of cultural transition in a relatively unchanged
economic and social system is deeply transgressive – theoretically and
practically impossible, and altogether unthinkable. And indeed, it remains
to be seen whether ecological sustainability can be achieved in capitalist or socialist societies – or authoritarian one party states and military
dictatorships.

We should note that much as the noise, violence, death and suffering
in the chaos of live revolutions may be abhorrent for thinking people,
and despite the fact that we live in global capitalism with diminishing
levels of public ownership, the idea of *revolution* has been a popular part
of the rhetoric of the left – it is deeply encoded in left thought since the
time of Marx. *The revolution* is what will bring about change, and ideally
progressive change – even if it is a continuous revolution. Unfortunately
for the political left, real revolutions have been mostly characterised by
unanticipated consequences, such as authoritarian regimes – police states,
military dictatorships, one party rule, etc. – and anything but progress
in any conventional understanding of human rights; not to mention
the collateral damage to animals, plants and ecologies caused by war
and conflict. All this misery and suffering notwithstanding, these widely
known social and ecological outcomes have only fuelled the determination of some to try harder. This is true even if public conversations about
'the revolution' are no longer quite so loud. History can be repressed, but
it has a habit of turning up in new policies and long strategies – slowly
hatched in silent conspiracies between like minds and kindred spirits.
However the subject is broached, when those on the left talk of *revolutionary politics* the aim remains the revolutionary overthrow of capitalism.

Commitment to such extreme ideas permits a great deal for members
of hard left factions in trade unions and political parties – in party rooms,
branch meetings, street demonstrations, town hall meetings, and on university campuses. After one has seen through capitalism and become
committed to its destruction, the ends justify the means – 'whatever'.
In the vaguely ecstatic state of 'revolutionary consciousness', 'normal'
codes of decency can be abandoned as bourgeois claptrap and the task
of building the revolution given full attention.

In political parties ostensibly committed to 'softer' left, or 'progressive' politics (like Green parties) *revolution* is the stuff of dreams – but this does not prevent agenda coded with these ideas from being extremely destabilising. Ideological sleepwalking by small numbers of 'true believers' can control meeting agendas, the election of office bearers and committee members, and determine the outcomes of discussions.

The goal, and associated political practice, of revolutionary politics is not to be found only in the left of politics. The 'far right' also have these concerns – but, so far, the left in Western politics has been more credible in providing theoretical alternatives to global capitalism, inequality and environmental devastation. However, the experienced realities of socialist and communist states in 'non-western' societies are today rarely considered by western leftists to be good examples of revolutionary politics – a socialist revolution is still a work in progress. According to David Harvey, 'the trick is to keep the political movement moving from one sphere of activity to another in mutually reinforcing ways . . . Previous attempts to create a communist or socialist alternative fatally failed to keep a dialectic between the different activity spheres in motion.'[19]

This (revolutionary) perception veils the more orthodox Marxist strategy of first dealing with the economic base of society. Veiled or not, Marxist 'political economy' is problematic because of its failure to adequately prioritise ecological needs. We do not have time to wait for the 'inevitable' decline of capitalism, or the arrival of suitable revolutionary conditions. Ecological sustainability needs to be prioritised, and we can hope that this will provide the best strategy for changing much else in global economic, social and cultural practice.

There are good reasons for hoping that ecological imperatives might succeed in driving change – unlike the allures of socialism and communism. Any shift towards ecological sustainability will necessarily involve changes at many levels, and whilst such changes may not be revolutionary in the sense of overthrowing capitalism, or totally subverting the free market, they will certainly be radical enough. Some of these changes will be born of necessity – over-consumption, for example, may be dealt with by market forces in the form of price rises as the costs of food and energy rise, and as scarcity of supply becomes more of an issue. Attitudes to nature have already begun to change dramatically – as indicated by the continuing spectacular popularity of Sir David Attenborough's work. Scientists and technologists are increasingly focused on ecological sustainability. Industry is becoming more energy efficient. And so on.

These are all modest beginnings, but are reasons to hope for more. Anybody who remembers back thirty years, or more, would have to concede that public awareness of ecological issues has blossomed in really a few short years. We are in a race against time, and cannot give up.

The efforts of Greens and other environmental activists to counter the excesses of capitalism and industrialism by cultivating ecological 'visions' may seem very idealistic, if not futile. And yet eco–oriented visions are probably our best hope for a future worth living. Most other forms of idealism about global change are just not adequate as prescriptions for the future. The most popular global critiques of the last 150 years – including mainstream and new age religions, and left wing politics, have failed to provide a broadly persuasive ecological critique. Important as their agendas for human rights and liberation may have been (and despite many bad blotches in their copybooks), religion and left wing politics are basically bankrupt as providers of credible morally based ecological philosophy. In the case of the various forms of left wing politics – which for decades have optimistically promised the raising of 'true' and revolutionary consciousness, socialising the means of production, and overthrowing capitalism – the critique has been thoroughly outmoded by changing social and cultural conditions, ecological imperatives, and the authoritarian and violent means used by so many left activists (past and present). It may still be true that we need to change our minds, and change the world, but we also desperately need to think *now* about ecology as if it really mattered, as if it really were the ground of our being.

Two things seem clear: first, no necessary ecological revolution has yet occurred; and second, if, and when, the necessary revolutionary changes are in place, leftists will not consider the process to have been revolutionary.

PRE-REVOLUTIONARY
CONCLUSIONS

The mainstreaming of ecological and environmental concern raises questions about future directions for the Greens. The central philosophical issue is whether Green parties prepare themselves for government by adopting a 'broad left' platform with green trimmings, or whether they can become more effective by maintaining, and further developing, a 'core' ecological perspective – such as the more 'radical' eco-centric perspective suggested in this book. The perception of being radical definitely effects prospects of any political party forming, or becoming part of, government. The more radical perceptions generally are, the more likely a party will remain in opposition. Some might argue that being in opposition at least allows radical voices to be represented – but the issue is how effective such voices can be in changing public attitudes, governing policies and legislation. For that reason, the eco-centrism suggested in the material that follows is qualified as 'pragmatic' and aimed, nominally, at the *centre* of the political spectrum.

If it is to be effective, green politics (like all culture) needs to retain its diversity; this has consequences for political parties. Green parties do not have a consensus view about the meaning and direction of Green. Just what it is 'to be Green' is still a vexed issue when it comes down to parliamentary and party practice, policy making, and philosophical reflection. This vexation has both internal and external dimensions. Within Australian Green parties there are increasing tensions over the prioritisation of issues and the handling of disputes – this tension varies from State to State and territory (and is probably little different in dynamics to that experienced in other federated political parties). Deeper questions about 'identity politics' and the ideological basis of Green politics require a more extended review of cultural influences (partly provided in the last chapter) and organisational history but there can be little doubt that media processes are dominant, along with deeply entrenched 'broad left' political approaches. The role of the media is the least controversial consideration. The battle of ideas, and associated 'internal' struggles over 'identity politics', are least known, and least understood.

However Green parties proceed, public perceptions of them largely depend upon their treatment in mass media. Any good policy or positive achievements can be tarnished or obliterated by a concerted media campaign. Dedicated journalists, media proprietors and manipulation of 'new media' processes on the internet – in fractious collaboration with politicians and their communications departments – amount to a 'fourth estate'. That is, together, they constitute an unelected and hardly controllable level of government. Public policy and our ecological futures depend upon perceptions generated in mass media. This is an often chaotic and superficial process.

Political tensions and conflicts are created and compounded by media desperate for 'breaking stories'. In such a sensational media environment it is easier to report (and market) 'leaders' and personalities than provide detailed analysis or policy debate. Audiences have been conditioned to 'want' a narrative with drama; they definitely do not want to be persuaded or lectured to. For journalists too, personal conflicts rather than ideological conflicts have become more interesting. Perhaps for them this is simply a question of how colour and movement can be injected into the frame, and how limited attention spans can be cultivated.

Like all political parties, Green parties participate in a reactive dance with media. Public 'perceptions' are outcomes of an often highly choreographed exchange process. Predictably, this process creates 'winners' and 'losers' and, in Australia, Green parties have been thoroughly marginalised by mainstream media that are determined to preserve the political duopoly of a Labor-Liberal two party ascendancy. The demonstration of Greens as radical extremists and anti-development 'tree-huggers' has created stereotypes in 'popular' culture that are hard to overcome.

These stereotypes are carefully cultivated in competing parties. Many of the members of these parties are openly scornful and disrespectful of Green parliamentarians and their supporters; their political rhetoric is often (successfully) based on an undying opposition to all things Green (and green). Indeed, for all pro-development lobby groups 'greenies' are a favourite target of abuse. Such is the nature of the 'rough and tumble' of all politics, however, in Australia the sneering is part of a culture of verbal abuse that extends well beyond Green politicians into sport, media commentary, and daily life.

The tough and abusive performances of Australian politicians (across all forums) deserve to be legendary, but this is small consolation to Green politicians who often find themselves the brunt of bipartisan scorn and derision, fuelled by strategically divisive media reportage. Nonetheless, one of the great achievements of the last Federal parliamentary Greens leader, Bob Brown, was to always rise above the boorish behaviour of other politicians and hostile journalists. So achieved was his political professionalism that on resignation he gained a very respectful bipartisan farewell, despite his experience of a long history of antagonistic behaviour from so many 'others'. By contrast the rise and departure of Christine Milne as parliamentary leader was marked by profound lack of media attention – perhaps being a mature female remains a great media liability.[20]

Minority parties like the Greens are treated unkindly in mass media because of a (not unreasonable) perception that they are a threat to economies and the status quo of politics. In Australia, as mentioned, media mostly position Greens as radical extremists. The image may vary – from young, inexperienced, eccentric and unrealistic, to being 'watermelons' (green on the outside, but red on the inside). Either way, the message is still the same: Greens are *extreme* and *unrealistic*. Members and parliamentary representatives are very rarely on the 'A-list' of any mainstream media outlets.

For all these reasons it is hardly surprising that knowledge of the history, philosophy and politics of the Greens is largely limited to in-house enthusiasts. Nor is it surprising that a new green 'paradigm' has not matured after the intense pioneering work of so many activist thinkers. Maybe it is much harder to be optimistic in the twenty first century, but this does not diminish the need for continuing reflection about the way forward. The rich, even if fairly recent, history of green philosophy and politics should be part of this reflection.

PROGRESSIVE GREEN POLITICS

Men and nations will act rationally when all other possibilities have been exhausted.

Katz's Law

The more things change the more they stay the same.

Jean-Baptiste Alphonse Karr
(Les Guepes, January, 1849)

In a future blighted by global ecological decline, governments and public officials will struggle to deal with the consequences of extreme weather and the many issues arising from storms, floods, sea level rise, climate refugees and other displaced persons, whilst attempting to maintain economic stability. The adverse effects will be compounded by over-population. Over-consumption and growth economics will inevitably drive all systems to ecological breaking points. Public health issues will arise from climate change and the toxic overloads of industrial and agricultural pollution. Everyone will be confronted by threats and challenges for which adequate planning will be most likely absent. We face the very real future prospect of lurching from crisis to crisis and can expect that, at the very least, large numbers of people will be angry enough to demand government and corporate responses.

Under these conditions the prospects for break down of civil order seem likely, and unpredictable. These will be circumstances in which new social movements and new political organisations will emerge, forcing existing parties and processes of government to make radical adjustments to deal with inflamed public opinion, and media frenzy.

In the immediate future it is unlikely such apocalyptic conditions will prevail. Most likely we face an era of shortages and extreme weather – storms, floods, fires, and slowly rising sea levels. None of these challenges is likely to cause the decline of western democracy. The question is whether liberal democracies will become more or less authoritarian in response to ecological crises that could effectively put modern states on 'war footing'. Responses to threats of domestic terrorism already show that increased security and surveillance can easily become normalised. Most people accept that difficult times require strong and sometimes undemocratic responses from governments.

If social order does not break down completely in times of prolonged crisis, parliamentary democracies and all political processes will need to adjust to the demands of increased levels of executive decision making, and more limited processes of consultation. What can be less taken for granted are the responses of social movements and popular uprisings. In that context, it will be suggested that Green politics already provides good insights into the future of 'progressive politics' – particularly with respect to internal party processes and the connections of Green parties with environmental social movements, and to a lesser extent, other social movements.

The bigger issue is how liberal democracies can be protected from the authoritarian needs of 'strong' governments that want to lead at times of crisis. If openness, transparency, wide consultation, 'fair play', and related procedural norms can be easily bypassed in the routine functioning of democratic systems today, the prospect of more authoritarian governments should raise concerns. This is the broader context in which any discussion of 'progressive' changes to our existing political systems must be placed.

The idea of any politics being 'progressive' might seem over-stretched. Few politicians shine under the intense scrutiny of hungry news cycles. More than ever, organised politics can seem a cynical exercise in vote capturing and backroom deals. How could this ever be 'progressive'? How can political processes be made more open to publicly driven scrutiny? What if the ground under us should shift and climate change does bring on an era of disaster management? Could politics ever be 'progressive' under such new pressures? Perhaps the first consideration should be the recent political history of 'being progressive'; then the combination of being Green *and* progressive might be better appraised.

A BRIEF HISTORY OF PROGRESSIVE POLITICS

In recent times progressive politics has become something of an apparently 'new' goal for contemporary political ideologies. Whether or not one is green, there is appetite among professionals and mass audiences, for 'progressive politics', however defined. History suggests, however, that 'being progressive' has been 'tried on' by politicians since the turn of the last century – the idea is not new.

The continuing wave of approbation for *progress* certainly says something about the depth of meaning of the word. It also indicates the political importance of rhetoric – all successful political parties pay great attention to public perceptions, re-positioning their policies as necessary, and ensuring that new messages 'get out there'. Most political rhetoric is easily decoded as 'spin' but some words have the magic ability to slip past critical inspection from even the most experienced (and perhaps jaded) voters and journalists – *progress, freedom, growth* and *balance*, in particular. *Progress* is noteworthy because it has such a broad scope, encapsulating optimistic aspirations in any society – including *growth* and *freedom*.

Over the course of the last 100 years, or thereabouts, *progress* has become a much over-used word in the rhetoric of political parties. Indeed, the recent arrival of 'going forward' as a popular phrase in the vocabulary of public relations suggests that the word progress is being given something of a rest. After all, a lot of time and effort has been invested in the idea of progress. It would be a tragedy to see its meaning and promise flattened by over-use.

Nonetheless, despite the popularity of the elegant variation of 'going forward', the cachet of *progress* as a generic political adjective appears undiminished. Fortunately for the word, progress is not capable of being permanently captured as 'the brand' of any one political party, or permanently associated with the rhetoric or policies of any party. One party's progress is another's poison. In the case of values and policies over which it seems hard to dispute an idea of progress – say, with respect to the need for legislation that might better protect children from sexual exploitation – the way forward for conservatives may differ to the way forward for left-liberals. One side will seek to affirm the family and the church as protectors of children's rights; the other will seek stronger legislation and more government attention. In popular usage, however, progress continues to retain the very basic meaning of positive movement towards a goal, any goal. That enables the word to be easily applied to any project, and indeed any set of values. Provided outcomes can be measured as material benefits to wealth, health, or access to services, *progress* is safe from moral judgement, or too much detail.

Such simple semantics do not exhaust the meaning of the word, or account for its continuing attraction to politicians at a time when most political ideologies seem inappropriate to the challenges and conflicts of the twenty first century. More than any other word, progress still represents the 'spirit of the age'.

Progress is deeply part of another idea, that of *modernity*. As discussed in Chapters 3 and 4, ever since the 'scientific revolution' in sixteenth century Western Europe, the idea that knowledge about the world and society might grow, *and* be instrumental in achieving better societies (and military success, and wealth) gained new emphasis. Today those evolving aspirations are sedimented in popular understandings of *progress*, what it is to be *modern*, and what it is reasonable to expect in a *secular liberal democracy*. The word progress is emblematic of all these aspirations – past and present. Progress knows few bounds; however, as a modern idea progress is strongly associated with the possibilities of science, technology and professional expertise. Yet, as we will see, progress is not limited in its usages by continuing association with science and technology – nuanced as that association may have become because of industrial accidents and large-scale pollution. Even religions can call themselves *progressive*.

It would appear that 'progressive politics' is a recurring aspiration for many of those seeking a way forward in troubled political times. Remarkably, this is despite semantic saturation. In, and beyond, the now normal 'institutional' progress of science, technology, medicine, law, education and politics, there is still space for *progressive education, progressive taxation, progressive rock and roll*, even *progressive conservatives* . . . progress clearly has no limits. Even the idea of progress towards ecological goals – towards stabilising our ecological impacts, towards a sustainable future, towards a future worth having – is possible, according to the IPCC and every optimistic commentator . . . and is, therefore, a usefully positive idea. The idea of being *politically progressive* is more troubled, but still useful because of the openness and optimism of progress.

The political usage of the term has been widely canvassed in the UK, USA and to a lesser extent in Australia. Current thinking includes the following propositions:

- that political progress can occur within established parliamentary traditions, that is, within secular liberal democracies;
- that progress should be governed by law and certainly not be the outcome of violent revolution;
- that progressive politics occupies its own political space. It is separable (logically and ideologically) from political conservatism; and it is separable from the radical left and the radical right;
- that progressive politics is not the same as the 'liberal' or 'labour' politics to be found in the major parties in the UK and Australia. The situation in the USA is similar, even though many Democrats consider themselves 'progressive'.

Being progressive has quite a history in North American political culture. Historians and sociologists have described a 'progressive era' of activism and reform around the turn of the twentieth century. Many of these reformers, including pioneering sociologists (noteably William Sumner), were religious and connected to the Protestant social reform and Social Gospel movements:

> The orgies of speculation in the age of robber barons, the mad scramble around the great barbecue, the violent repression of the emergent labour movement, the largely uncontrolled growth of cities, the closing of the frontier, the millions of new immigrants herded into appalling slums and mercilessly exploited in coal mines and sweat shops – these and many more harbingers of crisis and decay brought many formerly complacent clergymen, as well as other concerned citizens, into the Progressive movement. They were all eager to transform America into a country more nearly in tune with the moral message of Christian doctrine.[1]

Commitment to a 'progressive' social movement aimed at egalitarianism and democratic reform carried through to the formation of political parties with progressive goals. In 1912 Theodore Roosevelt ran for president as the candidate for the National Progressive Party, and lost to Woodrow Wilson. In 1924 Robert La Follette was the Progressive Party's unsuccessful candidate, and in 1948 Henry Wallace campaigned unsuccessfully for the presidency as a progressive. Today being progressive has been described as being part of the Democratic wing of the Democratic Party.[2]

North American 'progressivism' has had major successes, being embraced by the administrations of Theodore Roosevelt, Woodrow Wilson, Franklin Delano Roosevelt, Lyndon Johnson, and now, Barak Obama. In the USA, progressivism is today mostly associated with left wing views – which equates, broadly, to interest in social justice issues. It should be noted that being left wing in the USA is a relatively milder ideological position than elsewhere: the rabid anti-communism generated by cold war politics and the Hoover administration appears to have permanently shifted the US spectrum towards the blue end.

Progressivism has been more nuanced in Europe and Canada where even conservatives have called themselves progressive. The conservative Progressive Party of Canada, for instance, was founded in 1920 – but did not win government.

In the UK it seems that all sides of politics are keen to be seen as progressive. The situation was well summed up by Brian Wheeler, a BBC news reporter who described one great convergence in the following way:

> As he faced his final hours in Downing St, it seems Gordon Brown tried to reach out to Liberal Democrat leader Nick Clegg as a fellow 'progressive'. 'I have studied history', the former prime minister is said to have intoned. 'I know that the future of our country is a progressive alliance between two progressive political parties.' Mr Clegg agreed – but unfortunately for Mr Brown it was the conservatives, traditionally seen as anything but progressive, that he formed the 'progressive alliance' with. Explaining his logic, in a speech on Wednesday, he claimed Labour were now 'old progressives', while the Lib Dem / Conservative Coalition were 'new progressives'.[3]

The message for aspiring Green politicians seems clear enough: progress has long lost its innocence, but it's still available. As long as the word retains the simple meaning of going forward in a positive way, without too much other darker baggage, it can remain the aim of Green parties.

PROGRESSIVE GREEN POLITICS

Contemporary views about political progress are generally 'reactionary'; progress would be something 'away' from media driven perceptions of political aggression, mediocrity and dishonesty. Contemporary dissatisfaction with organised politics has also encouraged all large parties in Western democracies to drift 'to the centre'. In political life this is a place of minimal ideological difference – a place where the *status quo* and 'normal' define a political reality that is as non-threatening and non-challenging as possible. Whether voters would currently see progress in movement away from this centre is something of an unknown, but as previously discussed, passion about environmental issues is not universally high. Voters currently 'in the centre' are more concerned about their economies 'flat-lining' than they are with climate change and the state of the environment. Although climate change has the potential to quickly return as 'the defining economic and environmental issue of our generation'[4], Australian voters have a history of prioritising the economy, employment, health and education above the environment and climate change. According to this recent history, the idea that climate change is a major economic issue may take some time to be embraced by voting publics.[5]

Mass disaffection and cynicism about politicians and political systems pose immediate problems for all political parties. Whether or not these perceptions are valid criticisms is hardly worth debating. The major political parties in Australia have been in 'damage control' for some time – as evidenced by their reluctant acceptance of inclusivity as an obvious remedy for alienated supporters, and an enticement for recruiting new members.

Suggestions about 'progressive politics' to be made in this chapter build from this starting point of overcoming alienation by using inclusive measures. Inclusivity must be more than a token gesture – the only way that inclusivity can be 'real' is if party members and voting publics *feel* included. For that to occur, options for individuals to participate in decision-making must be available. In what follows, the best current practice, already instituted in Green politics, will be referred to as 'grass roots' decision-making. This approach to decision-making is arguably the strongest basis for any progressive politics – although the main focus in this chapter is towards Green party politics, many of the arguments made about process are of general relevance to all political parties and their memberships. What this chapter *is not* is a close analysis of the kinds of affiliations Australians have in specific organisations, such as trade unions, political parties, churches and recreational clubs, with projections based on those often declining numbers – in the context of rapidly changing communication technologies it is too early to be definitive about changed social relations or declining levels of 'social capital' (see note below). The assumption made in this chapter is that individual involvement in green politics, formal and informal, is not in major decline and that future involvement will in all likelihood only increase – particularly if the issue of inclusivity is addressed by all 'progressive' social organisations.[6]

The central argument of this chapter is that grass roots decision-making should remain as the basis of green progressive politics because it is the best means of reaching consensus in the blur of issues confronting all green parties. This is not suggested as a form of 'mob rule' – grass roots practices in green politics requires expertise and leadership to be part of decision-making, as has been argued in previous chapters. The focus of any decision-making also qualifies the idea of 'mob rule' – making environmental issues and values 'core concerns' necessarily constrains the scope of policy making, but if it is accepted that all constitutionally bound political processes are constrained from the outset, grass roots decision-making can still be a viable concept, and process, in organised politics.

The strongest way to encourage inclusivity is through egalitarian practices – in contrast, hierarchical and authoritarian systems are 'naturally' alienating. The basic requirements for egalitarian practices are equal political and legal rights – which should not be confused with the idea that equality extends to all aspects of being. Clearly, everyone is different and possessed of different talents and enthusiasms. A progressive political system (and society) can be 'meritocratic' and embracing of specialist expertise, individual excellence, and leadership, without losing the equal rights of all individuals. There must, however, be processes in place to inhibit the development of hierarchies that entrench individual or factional power and control, and that block inclusive processes. Grass roots democratic processes remain so popular among Green party members precisely because these egalitarian principles discourage hierarchies and encourage individual rights and individual expression.

'Grass roots democracy' can embrace change and encourage creativity, innovation, and leadership. This depends on open and transparent

communication in a pluralist cultural context. These are the key requirements for the kind of progressive politics that could both re-engage
dispirited voters, and face up to authoritarian challenges that will arise in
more crisis filled futures. Progressive politics can only rise above rhetoric
if its visions and ideals are persuasive. It will be argued that if Green politics became fundamentally eco-centric it could legitimately claim to be
neither 'left' nor 'right' on the conventional political spectrum; it could
aim for a 'radical centre' in politics. This could be genuinely progressive.

Eco-centrism is central in so many ways: it is Earth centred, it is
survival oriented, it places humanity among other species and environments, it aims to maximise the quality of all life. Further, as a 'pragmatic'
(*i.e.* practical) perspective, eco-centrism can also acknowledge the fact
that the experiences of human beings are unavoidably human-centred.
'Pragmatic eco-centrism', as it will be developed below, is not an absolute stance and metaphysical claim about the possibility of being other
than human – it is a relativising strategy aimed at maximising the 'collective good' for all life on a finite planet that is unavoidably dominated
by human beings. Setting humanity as part of a web of life, or as one
species among many on a planet we share with all other life, need not
automatically prioritise humanity above all other interests. Basically, *ecology* (like *nature* and *life*) is a more embracing concept than *humanity*. It is
quite possible to be both human-centred and eco-centric, but it is not
desirable to be only human-centred – as most political philosophy is.

Currently, the idea that a 'radical centre' could be environmentally
focused is not a topic for discussion in conversations among political
theorists and political parties – particularly in Australia. Conventional
political thought is still wedded to assumptions of economic growth and
increasingly large human interventions in ecologies and environments –
geo-engineering, for instance, is still a popular corporate fantasy for the
solution of climate change that arises in many 'new' proposals. Further,
the traditions of radical thought that most involve Green politics are
from the left – or in many eyes, from the 'far left' – and just reinstate the
old left-right political spectrum.

For those reasons there is very little that could be described as radical
in recent proposals that have attempted to reposition liberalism or social

democracy as 'new' and 'central', as has occurred in the United Kingdom and Australia. For example, the sociologist Anthony Giddens (an adviser to Tony Blair) has described the radical centre as synonomous with 'the third way', a reconstituted form of social democracy. That is hardly radical.[7]

In the USA proponents have been more eclectic, including journalists from *The New York Times*, *Time* magazine, and *The Washington Post*. In an interesting parallel to Australian politics, these publications note a lack of credible voices independent of the two major political parties.[8]

An eco-centric view aimed at the political 'centre' is 'radical' in two ways: it represents a break with the conventional assumption of a political spectrum extending from 'left' to 'right'; and it involves rethinking political priorities around the perspective of environmentalism. Being radical by virtue of being perceived as strongly 'left or 'right' on the political spectrum currently guarantees electoral failure in a country like Australia. Indeed, being perceived as radical by any criteria – by sexuality, by religious belief, or by appearance, for instance, will always make political success more difficult. Therefore, the possibilities of any kind of radical position need to be considered carefully.

At the time of the French Revolution in 1789 when members of the National Assembly divided in their seating to the left and to the right of the 'president', such movement had a clear meaning: supporters of the revolution sat to the left, and supporters of the king sat to the right. By 1791 this had changed to mean 'innovators' sat to the left, 'moderates' gathered in the centre, and defenders of the constitution sat to the right. By the mid-twentieth century this seating arrangement had developed into a political theorem about ideological differences. Political scientists and sociologists had adopted the idea of a linear spectrum to indicate the different class interests of political parties, from those with 'working class' interests being 'on the left' to those with 'ruling class' interests being 'on the right' – or as some saw it from 'lower' class interests on the left to 'higher' class interests on the right. Like any social theory this 'political spectrum' should be understood as a deliberate simplification of a complex world. In recent times theorists have sought to accommodate other social, economic and political ideas along this spectrum – such as authoritarianism, equality /inequality, response to conflict, or ideological spin.[9]

There are obviously many dimensions, or axes, along which beliefs, values, behaviours, and ideologies can be displayed. Nonetheless, more or less belief in individual rights and personal autonomy as opposed to collective interests and the rule of law is still a major ideological difference in Western political systems, and a common sense way that most academics (and students) distinguish between political parties. However, as contemporary politicians rush towards the centre, where perceived differences are most 'balanced', the differences between political ideologies shrink. In the centre, the maximisation of both, say, individual rights, and the right of the state to control individual behaviour for the (perceived) collective good, results in very similar legislation whether one is nominally to the left or to the right.

None of these distinctions refer to the interests of habitat or ecosystems. When Green parties and environmentalists are stereotyped as 'left wing', it is as a result of perceptions that such parties and individuals rely on government intervention to impose restrictive taxes, rules and regulations[10], and because of the prominence of social justice issues in the campaigning and policy development of Green parties. Yet, conservative philosophers and commentators also consider themselves green (but not Green). Viewed from the left, conservatives, conservationists and environmentalists are often lumped together and stereotyped as conservatives, 'neocons' and 'right wingers'. This is an unnecessarily divisive and polarising approach.

Concern for Earth's future is clearly not about 'class consciousness', nor does it derive from any particular social class, occupation, profession, discipline, or age group. Once it is accepted that green politics and green 'awareness' are distributed across society, it is easier to understand that the idea of a left–right political spectrum is a misleading way of characterising Green political parties and more general green orientations and protest. Nor, indeed, is the conventional 'centre' of politics adequately descriptive, given the level of commitment of all 'greens' to low levels of consumption and abandonment of growth economics. By any standards these are 'radical' concerns, and not the 'status quo' concerns of all other political 'centrists'. Being non-human centred is even more radical by today's general standards. Therefore, even the idea that there could be a 'radical centre' in politics is at best a colourful metaphor that serves to emphasise the idea of being Earth-centred (in awareness, behaviour and politics). Having primary concern for the rights and wellbeing of non-human life forms, and ecologies and environments takes one off the scales of conventional political and social analysis. However, in the absence of a better way of describing a 'location' for such concerns, and the politics of Green parties and a broader green social movement, 'the radical centre' seems an appropriate way of describing a point of orientation for 'progressive' environmental and Green politics. As previous chapters have argued, any perceptions that the difference of an Earth-centred frame of reference is socially dysfunctional will certainly soften as the truly radical effects of climate change, over-consumption, over-population and ecological decline become more widely perceived – it's just a matter of time.

CAN AUSTRALIAN GREENS MOVE ON?

The Australian Greens seemed to have achieved something historic when elected Green members became part of government after the Federal election in 2010. The 'two party system' had been challenged, and an environmentally based party had achieved the balance of power in a country dominated by corporate interests and growth economics. Political success also underlined the fact that the Australian Greens were not a 'single issue' party, but rather a multi-issue party genuinely able to share in the running of the country. Indeed to many it seemed that 'the left' in politics had been reshaped for the better. The strangle hold that the trade union movement had exercised over the practices of the left in politics appeared to have been loosened – because it now had to deal with environmentalism as an ally rather than the foe it had often been.

All these appearances were thoroughly tested by three years of government within a still dominant two party system, unsupportive media, and attempts by both politicians and media to woo a public more disturbed than elated by the Greens gaining the balance of power. After the loss of their role in government in 2013 and a return to marginal status, Australian Green parties are back in familiar territory – support in elections at historically average numbers of about 10%.

Support for Green party candidates varies across Australian electorates and election booths, and across different levels of government – most figures fall roughly between 4 to 25 per cent. According to voting analyst Antony Green, '[t]he Greens emerged in the 1990s, reached 5% of the vote for the first time in 2001 and replaced the Democrats as the nation's main third party at the 2004 election. 2010 was the Federal election year in which Green support peaked – 13% in the Senate and 12% in the House of Representatives. This support fell in 2013 to 8% in both houses of parliament. However, support for independents and minority parties (generally) reached historical highs in the 2013 election. Support for non–major party candidates was 21.1% in the House of Representatives and 32.2% in the Senate.[11]

Local council elections (the third tier of government) reveal stronger patterns of support – in one shire (Byron Shire Council) a Green mayor has been elected in the last three elections. There are relatively large numbers of elected Green party councillors across Australian shires.[12]

Some things appear set in the fortunes of Australian Green parties: a national average support of approximately 10%, minority status in most parliaments and councils, relegation by the media, and hostility from major parties and their corporate and trade union allies.

Small parties can, however, play a decisive role in the upper houses of review in the Australian parliamentary system. The national election of 2013 saw the rise (and demise) of PUP (the Palmer United Party) and other micro parties to be able to hold the balance of power in the Federal Senate. As yet, none of the micro parties have taken up environmental concerns. In NSW, after the 2015 election, the Family First Party appears set to hold the balance of power in its upper house, the Legislative Council. Clearly, depending on the continuing fortunes of small and micro parties, Australian Green parties could hold a balance of power in future state and federal parliaments.

There are a number of issues fundamental to the future of all Green parties and politics arising from these recent experiences – whether or not Green parties are cast as 'progressive' and whether or not they hold the balance of power in parliaments. These issues can be condensed into three key questions:

1. To what extent should Green parties retain their affiliation with ideologies of the left?

2. Do the 'four pillars' still form the best framework for future environmentally centred parties?

3. To what extent can Green parties aim for the 'radical centre' of politics?

Failure to seriously address these questions will continue to limit the political appeal of Green philosophy and politics because:

a) Green parties will struggle to retain popular identification as environmental parties;

b) Green parties will not be able to reconcile the demands of prospective government, or coalitions, with the ideological differences currently present in Green parties. Some Green parties will die in an ideological struggle with the hard left and trade union supporters. Many members will eventually despair and leave many Australian parties open to control by an alliance of 'old left', broad left, and trade union activists – resulting in a drop in public support.

c) A two party political system in Australia will be further entrenched as a 'conspiracy' between the Labor Party, the Liberal Party, large corporations, mainstream media, and elites in the trade union movement, the public service, and academe. A strategy of crisis management is the likely dominating outcome.

These issues arise in the Australian political context, but the same, or very similar issues arise in most democratic countries with established Green parties.

MOVING ON

It has become clear to many Greens that the way forward requires the articulation of 'new perspectives' that can 'do things differently'. Arguably, Green parties will need to be seen as expressing 'progressive politics' in order to both retain a support base that includes many of those who define themselves as 'left of centre', and to engage new supporters who may not see themselves as either left, right or centre.

As things stand, the 'four pillars' provide a framework that is fully adequate to embrace the concerns of environmentalists, ecologists, and those of broad left persuasion. The defining issues, previously raised, concern the priorities that a Green political party should have in a 'blur' of potential issues, and the way that consensus is reached about those priorities. The continuation of grass roots democratic processes has been suggested as the best procedural method, and a further shift towards eco-centrism suggested as the best ideological strategy. Together, the principles and perspectives entailed by these two strategies can form the basis for a radically centrist and progressive politics.

That there will always be a 'blur' of issues surrounding politicians encouraged the claim (made in the last chapter) that Greens should forget about 'a new paradigm' – with all the singularity and certainty that implies. A 'perspective' was suggestive as a framework less definitive and prescriptive than a 'paradigm', but still focused and definably different from competing political and philosophical positions. A more deliberate *eco-centric perspective* could justify a different prioritisation of issues for political parties and return Green philosophy to a stronger focus on environmental and ecological concerns.

A 'perspective' can embrace diversity and pluralism and encourage conversations that are not ideologically pre-determined. An eco-centric perspective is intended to extend human interest into the biosphere and allow the 'voices' and interests of other species and ecologies to play a role in human politics. No human expression could fail to be somewhat human-centred, but an eco-centric view would discourage the conditioned reflex of leftists to prioritise short-term social justice issues over longer-term ecological considerations. Such a move might also encourage economists to focus on the costs of delay in setting deep cuts to emissions and transitioning to more ecologically sustainable industries.

Grass roots democracy is centrally important in the political expression of this perspective. Universally, Green party members agree that 'grass roots democracy' is an incontestable principle for decision making on the basis of the broadest consensus possible. In the context of representative democracy and party politics where leadership and 'quick decision-making' are routine expectations, 'grass roots democracy' is a radical ideal, as further discussed below. The most radical proposal for progressive Green politics canvassed in this book, however, involves the need to prioritise the principle of ecological sustainability over the other three 'pillars' of official Green party ideology. All the other suggestions that have been made, so far, about progressive politics are less contentious and could be pursued by any political party. More formally expressed, those general principles of progressive politics include:

Egalitarianism as a core value of any 'progressive' politics – this includes gender equality and equal opportunity;

Openness to change;

General encouragement of creativity, innovation, and expert advice;

Encouragement of leadership models that follow from 'grass roots' principles that are democratic and 'flat' (that is, which are not overly hierarchical), and which allow positions to be filled on the basis of merit;

Prioritisation of open and transparent communication – that extends to multi-lateral negotiation;

Cultural pluralism – that encourages inclusive social practices and tolerance of cultural and ideological differences;

Avoidance of violent conflict at all levels of decision-making, policy formation and implementation of outcomes.

ECO-CENTRISM

The ideological basis of Green parties needs to be grounded in eco-centric principles. As already demonstrated by many generations of ecological activists, this requires the continual elaboration of what it means to think and act 'ecologically' – as basic in identifying as and defining 'Green' (and 'green'). Green parties may have pioneered 'four pillars' as a working position for political parties, but there is a continuing need to refine established policy platforms to more successfully address the current ecological future of Earth. It is critically important that Green parties more closely embrace broader green social movements and a long history of environmental politics rather than being simply aligned with social democratic and traditional left ideological positions – for all the reasons elaborated so far. Such a project requires input from all disciplines and activities with ecological interests. Eco-centrism must be multi-disciplinary and inter-disciplinary; it must be broadly based – and not simply defined by membership of a Green party or occupational group.

Ecology is not, and never has been, a 'single issue'. Our ecology is our habitat, our air and water, our agriculture, our buildings, our transport, our health care, and education – all the systems that support and constitute life. Thinking, and acting, ecologically requires prioritising sustainability, and integrating new methods of design and energy use into our living spaces. Ideally, Green politics should be deliberately prioritising sustainability and an ecological focus. This emphasis could define a key difference between Green politics and other parties and organisations with broad left politics.

The ecological 'litmus test' developed in the first six chapters of this book evolved from the tangle of problems associated with the 'big three': climate change, over-population and economic growth. The challenge for all Green parties is to assess the extent to which they are able to play a role in dealing with the global challenge of these primary causes of ecological decline. Can individual party policies confront the 'big three'? The contention of this book is that unless Green parties become fundamentally eco-centric, particularly parties that are dominated by the political left (such as the Greens NSW), they can do little more than conventional social democratic parties – despite all legitimate concerns for human rights. In an ecological perspective, everything *is* connected. The litmus test is partly ideological, and partly organisation specific: what capacity is there to take on the 'wicked problem' caused by the 'big three'? Is there the 'philosophical' and political will, and is there an available organisational will? The position developed in this book is that only Green parties have made any progress in this direction but have so far failed to put forward any program to address the 'big three', or play any leadership role in developing future pathways.

The philosophical differences known to exist within most Green parties can be profound, and are unlikely to be resolved within any new paradigm. For instance, philosophical positions that have been described as *deep ecology* and *spiritual ecology* are often part of the 'deep green' commitments of many current and past members, but are not views held by all members. Such positions are usually based on a critique of human-centredness, and are fundamentally at odds with Marxist, socialist and *broad left* philosophies. These latter views are much more focused on the priorities of a particular approach to social justice issues; in the end an approach which is rooted in socialist, or any other version of Marxist or 'historically materialist' philosophies, will cause deep divisions in any political party – mainly because of the ideologically based drive for power and control that goes with such views. Pluralism and power sharing do not come naturally, or easily, to those committed (practically *or* theoretically) to the centralisation of political power.

Extreme views of any kind can become particularly problematic when they are highly organised and part of secretive political processes – the communist influence in trade union organisations (and the heavy handed opposition of Liberal governments) is one of the better known Australian examples. Yet, most often the organised processes of political parties simply wear down all but the most determined advocates of destabilising beliefs and values.

This is the difficult reality that confronts many political parties – and a reason why so many individuals prefer to work in the less formal structures available in social movements, or the more focused rules of environmentally activist organisations. But, of course, these 'difficulties' need to be considered in a broad context: relative 'openness', or 'porosity', is also the great strength of secular, liberal democratic parliamentary systems. The protections of the law are often enabling processes: laws against religious and political discrimination, and laws protecting freedom of speech and belief are the cornerstones of all modern democracies. A representative political system should embody such rights and freedoms.

Open political systems also depend on the existence of a number of strong political parties – certainly more than two, in order that issues as contentious as 'the big three' and environmental issues generally can be properly represented in parliaments. Good government depends on strong opposition parties. Therefore it is critically important to maintain a strong Green presence in governments and parliaments. This book has been an effort to strengthen this presence, without being unrealistic about the possibilities of Green parties and Green politics. Optimistically, the ecological future is still open, and still worth fighting for.

Eco-centrism is needed in Green parties as an ideological corrective for the diffusion of over-broad left politics. However, because Green parties are democratic it may always prove to be very difficult to ever overcome the determination of 'old left' warriors (young or old) to preserve Green parties as parliamentary outposts for international socialism and unreconstructed Marxism. It only takes the will of a few to organise blocking and diversionary tactics that can consume much group energy. Nonetheless, whether eco-centrism is pursued within party structures or more dedicated environmental organisations, a pragmatic approach requires clear goals for all practical projects. As a political program, 'pragmatic eco-centrism' would involve the following major strategies:

1. *Assessment of the ecological impacts of all policy proposals, no matter how broad, or purely social, problems and issues appear to be (for instance, transport policy);*

2. *Development of positions rather than policies for all non-core issues (such as work place relations);*

3. *Development of population stabilisation options with reference to carrying capacity scenarios.*

4. *Development of ecologically sustainable economic goals (for example, regarding recycling, job sharing, renewable energy production, natural resource management, and tourism).*

FINDING THE ECOLOGICAL IMPLICATIONS OF ALL ISSUES

For Green politics to be 'progressive' the first major obstacle to be overcome is the ideological rigidity of broad left and old left politics which is unequivocally human-centred, class based, conflict oriented, anti-capitalist, anti-western, and of revolutionary intent – these basic orientations may not be always obvious, but they are very often 'the bottom line' of positions and proposals. Such a focus, when explicit, never has sat well with the strong ecological and wider democratic values of the larger membership of Green parties. An ecologically focused party that even, whenever possible, prioritises social justice issues (however framed) runs the profound risk of alienating its support base, compromising its ecological principles, and allowing itself to become the *de facto* agent of competing parties, trade unions and other, more clandestine, organisations. Social justice issues are intrinsic, possibly determining of outcomes, but not automatically the deciding factor in contests between human interests and the interests of other species, their habitats, and the interests of ecologies and environments.

Pragmatic eco-centrism would be, ironically, 'new' in the context of Green parties in the sense of returning to environmental traditions whilst retaining a much broader social awareness. This 'new' perspective is all about priorities, with the intention of increasing electoral support rather than losing it. Any new environmentally focused parties will definitely need to integrate environmentalism with social reform – without being overwhelmed, or consumed by the complexity of such expanded horizons, or the already established and competing 'interests' in such expanded political fields.

Environmental and ecological considerations generally have major implications for all social policy issues. As soon as the ecological sustainability of any social practice is considered there are many consequences that follow. Sustainable energy policy, for example, entails legislation and cultural change across all levels of government and society. Policy choices, regulation and enforcement with respect to appropriate technology, building standards, workplace practices, health and safety issues and public education, alone, impact most aspects of society and culture. Currently there is a great need for political focus on these very issues – which does not, and probably cannot, occur in political parties that are expected to maximise the competing expectations of economies that grow and industries that pollute. Even if the scope of issues concerned is narrowed to matters concerning 'environmental impact' similar complex and multi-layered policy interactions arise. At least one ecologically focused party should be able to, at least, develop focused policy choices about 'sustainability' – including those areas currently referred to as environmental 'impact' and 'quality', and biodiversity. There is simply not enough time for political and economic change to occur if academic specialisations and professional bureaucracies are left to do most of the policy development work – with those professionals often merely hoping that they will be heard by governments and senior bureaucrats, or that activist organisations will pursue their concerns. Currently we do not even see developed public educational programs that can raise public awareness about major environmental and ecological issues. Part of the blame for that has to be levelled at Green parties that are overwhelmed with the normal run of parliamentary business and 'broad left' concerns.

POSITIONS RATHER THAN POLICIES

As argued, for Green parties there are two main causes of policy dilution and obfuscation: first, the demands of conventional parliamentary practice, and second, the over-broad and over-ideological understandings of social change, and 'ecology', that enmesh 'broad left' philosophy and theory. The 'pragmatic eco-centrism' sketched above, and the critique of broad left social philosophy developed in previous chapters, are intended to counter these concerns. If agreement about 'core' issues requiring detailed policy positions can be reached, as opposed to 'other' areas about which 'positions' rather than policies could be developed, much more time could be spent closely focusing on environmental and ecological issues, and supporting particular campaigns. For those parties with a smaller political representation, the time and energy involved in responding to all the issue platforms raised by major parties is prohibitive.

The development of broad 'positions' about a wide range of social policy issues also facilitates the application of grass roots decision-making. Normally, reaction to parliamentary demands requires elected representatives to respond more quickly than 'grass roots' processes permit. In conjunction with the inevitable factionalising in committees and processes in 'head offices' and state and regional meetings, and parliamentary and media driven demands for 'leadership', grass roots democracy can at best be an ideal that minimises non-consultative processes (but, as argued a fundamentally important ideal).

There is another very good reason to distinguish between core and non-core issues. In Australia, Greens rarely have major disagreement over positions or policy regarding major environmental issues. Grief in party processes, and dysfunctional ideological ferment, generally arises from endless struggle over broad left issues and the desires of some to keep driving Green parties down that ideological road.

Whilst issues concerning international justice, world peace, solidarity with revolutionary activists (armed and unarmed), and public ownership, are divisive issues within Green parties, the environmental and ecological consequences of war, political instability, and military dictatorships are far less divisive. Consensus about these issues is far easier to achieve, and on that basis alone, should remain (or become) core concerns for discussion and policy-making. This will not, however, suit those whose goal is the destabilisation of the 'imperialism' of the United States and its allies, particularly Israel, and the destabilisation of corporate capitalism generally. Green parties cannot afford to be so anti-western and anti-corporatist if their goal is to work within the legitimate structures of liberal democracies. For the sake of all ecologies, there is just not time to waste in pursuit of revolutionary dreams and widely discredited political programs.

Nonetheless, any ecological perspective, by its nature, is holistic encompassing policy areas involving industry, energy, water, agriculture, wilderness, tourism, transport, health and all other areas affected by human impacts on ecosystems. Therefore, Green parties need clearly articulated positions broadly defining desired outcomes – but, as suggested, not always detailed policies for non-core, or non-ecologically contexted matters.

However, the main predicament for Green parties becoming more eco-centric is the likelihood of being labelled as 'single issue' parties (again). A concerted program of public education could easily dispel that idea as a twentieth century misconception of the complexity of any 'ecology'. When it becomes more widely appreciated that the survival of decent human living standards absolutely depends on ecological sustainability, the idea that a more eco-centric worldview is a 'single issue' approach might dissolve as an absurdity.

It also has to be asked whose political interests are most served by Green parties adopting a policy-on-everything approach. As already mentioned, in Australia those interests are the left wings of the Labor Party (which for quite some time have struggled in a highly factionalised party context), left factions of the trade union movement, and various socialist organisations. In strategic terms, the main covert goal is the creation of a perception that 'Greens' form a party of an (imaginary) international working class *and* that Green parties are in solidarity with various radical left wing organisations – in other words, that Greens are keeping faith (and holding firm) with 'the' radical left (hard and soft). This encourages policy development by stealth, and is disastrous for electoral success.

The recent fiasco in NSW in 2012 over the support (briefly) for a BDS (Boycott, Divest, Sanction) campaign against Israel's blockade of Gaza is an example of how this kind of ideological intrusion can go badly wrong. The BDS campaign was largely 'in solidarity' with the international Free Palestine Movement and Hamas in Gaza. It not only had the effect of alienating the Jewish section of the support base of NSW Greens – such a position became very controversial within the membership and was subsequently withdrawn as a position and policy. All this demonstrated a very misplaced radicalism. The issue continues to demonstrate how difficult it will continue to be for parties such as Greens NSW to consensually endorse the radically activist programs of International Socialists, and related political groups.

Public ownership is another highly divisive issue. The belief that all major sectors of the economy should be publicly owned is a fundamental idea of socialism (and communism). If one accepts that private ownership will remain a fundamental of global capitalism, it seems highly fanciful to aim for such a revolutionary economic goal. Even the less ambitious goal that 'core' industries and infrastructure should be publicly owned is so much at odds with current practice as to be counterproductive in the context of creating a sustainable economy. The idea that advanced western societies are going to nationalise banks, manufacturing industries, mining industries, agricultural production, and so on, is absurd. In advanced western economies, 'public ownership' can only occur in the broader context of private ownership: public ownership will never amount to full public control. We need privately owned entrepreneurship to drive creativity and innovation as market based economic phenomena. There is very wide economic and political consensus about these latter ideas – in neoclassical economic orthodoxy, for example, and in emerging work on sustainable economics.

LEARNING TO LIVE WITH LESS

The implications of ecologically sustainable economic goals are radical. Ultimately, under conditions of population growth and decreasing stocks of natural capital, sustainability means learning to live with less – compared with today's standards. This is a scenario that economists and politicians will generally not yet confront. In wealthy countries with growing economies there is not popular acceptance of the fact that the mitigation of climate change will cost money that will affect the public purse, and inevitably slow the rate of growth and profitability of all economies. Indeed, the idea that some measures of austerity should extend to all sectors of all societies will probably never be popular. Such a program will certainly not win elections in the near future.

Nonetheless, these are the realities that Green parties need to embrace. The development of major policies about sustainability – about recycling, job sharing, and renewable energy, for instance – are already serious issues for all Green parties, even if the full implications of ecological sustainability have not been revealed to voting publics still focused on the need for economies to grow.

In Australia, and probably everywhere else, Green parties will most likely become, at most, coalition partners in governments whose major parties will remain wedded to some variant of the economics of growth, for some time yet. It is also the case that Green philosophy and politics is, and needs to be, too radical to be able to quickly reform the existing structures and arrangements of an evolving global capitalism. Certainly, within the next 10 to 15 years, Greens should hope to drive reform toward the low and zero growth economics that are currently unacceptable to most people in rich countries, Green parties have to find a way of keeping radical proposals on the tables of governments without over-alienating their opponents. The costs of 'deep cuts' to carbon emissions, for example, are still unacceptable to Australian governments and most electorates, but the need for deep cuts needs to be pressed unconditionally.

As discussed in Chapter 6, the most important statistic for governments attempting to retain political power is that their economies continue to grow. Two quarters of zero or negative growth officially equals a recession, and that announcement can be trouble for treasurers and governments. Even 'low growth' of around 2% GDP is problematic – all things being equal, growth in GDP has to at least match growth in population numbers, otherwise, unemployment will increase and average living standards will decline.

It may be impossible to provide everyone on the planet with continually increasing living standards. A scenario of continued growth will definitely result in the hollowing out of Earth, depletion of the oceans, increasing temperatures, melting polar icecaps, wilder weather, and conflict over scarce resources. What once sounded like an apocalyptic fantasy now looms on everybody's horizon. Low growth, or even zero growth, may be forced upon us. Global financial crises and increasingly fragile economies may become more the norm than the exception.

Learning to live with less is the most practical approach possible, start-ing now. Living with less does not equate to doing without. Even in wealthy countries recycling, eco-housing design, low wastage, lower pol-luting industries, backyard vegetable gardens, public transport, renewable energy, job sharing, and so on, are active choices already made by many individuals and businesses. Over-consumption needs to be recognised for the waste and greed that it feeds; this is as much a systemic issue as a deeply personal matter. Austerity that was once a condition of religious monasticism and alternative lifestyle achievement more than ever needs to be mainstreamed as an attractive pathway for everyone. Material effi-ciency and frugality have become necessary for mass survival. This need not be a lifestyle disaster.

Individuals may have considerable choice in controlling their con-sumption, but changing whole societies and economies is a different kind of challenge, as discussed in earlier chapters. Yet governments and the providers of goods and services do have options for encouraging lower consumption rates without destroying economies. These are areas of central concern for Green parties.

In Australia the 'aspirational voters' defined by Mark Latham, a past Prime Minister, take far more for granted than the rights of their children to be educated at university, and have access to professional employment, and a commensurate quality of life. They appear to assume that endless consumption and reproduction are the main purposes of life. The 'well off' are not alone with that assumption. Whole populations in both rich and poor countries are aspirational, however such aspirations, and the sense of entitlement that accompanies them, are largely unsustainable. The ability to persuade markets to downsize and make do with less may run contrary to the logic of growth and popular psychology, but unsus-tainability will win out in the end. In that light, learning to make do with less is sensible forward planning.

GOING FORWARD, ECOLOGICALLY

As discussed in early chapters, many commentators, usually impressed by the progressive potentials of new developments in science and technology, seem confident that societies and ecologies can somehow move, or evolve, peacefully to 'another level' – thereby overcoming the dire threats posed by global climate change and ecological decline.

In the 'modern' development of social theory, pioneering sociologists such as Comte, Spencer Marx and Weber were, however, not able to establish laws of social change that might justify such optimism, or that would satisfy any modern scientist; they were all able to find order, structure and patterns of change across societies, but they were not able to establish any lasting 'scientific' basis for the specific prediction of major future developments. From Comte's speculations about 'stages' of social development, to the 'evolution' of social forms in Spencer's work, to Marx's (and Engel's) 'dialectical' historical laws, and Weber's ideas about 'elective affinity' between ideas and social change and the permanency of an 'iron cage' of bureaucracy, all found social limits that resulted in change, but none thought environmental limits could force global imperatives. None were able to predict the destruction of the ecologies that support all societies. None foresaw that there might be an era determined by ecological decline. The assumption that nature was an infinite resource was simply taken for granted – and neoclassical economists to this day have not adequately addressed the problem of environmental limits and ecological decline.

In the broader context of recent Western political and social thought, theory about social change has been polarised since at least the time of Marx between those looking towards forces that would overturn the 'whole system', usually with violence, and those holding faith with progressive developments emerging relatively 'naturally' as 'evolution'. The 'old left' revolutionary option was dismissed in the last chapter (partly as a reminder to all the old left 'comrades' who have been drawn to Green parties as last bastions of hope for revolutionary politics). By contrast the more eco–centric scenarios promoted in this book tend towards evolution with a somewhat quantum twist – allowing for the possibility of radical system reorganisation without the extreme violence of old fashioned revolutions. This is actually a theory of incremental change that can encompass both *revolution* and *evolution*. That would enable progressive politics to be truly radical.

Systems theory in the social sciences, following the work of Talcott Parsons, probably comes closest to the kind of theory that natural scientists would identify as scientific, but the critically neglected aspect in early analysis of human systems is the irrepressibly creative agency of individuals and organisations – that guarantees a level of unpredictability in the behaviour of all social systems. At the very least, unpredictability imposes limits on the utility of scientific analysis in the management of human systems (including economies). Good governance and profitable economic functioning necessarily require a level of creative decision making by expert committees and parliaments. This argument was part of the reasoning of Chapter 6, which raised the limitations of economic rationality – if economists cannot be relied upon to deliver sustainability as a paradigmatic component of economic theory and practice, then governments have to breach the gap; there is not time to wait for critical decisions about the control of climate change to emerge from the well intentioned complexities of economic simultaneous equations.

The need for change driven by recognition of the life threatening nature of 'the big three' ecological problems (climate change, over-population and growth based economics) has been discussed with particular attention to the social institutions of science and technology, economics, politics and governance. However, for any eco-centric view to become influential there has to be broad cultural change – which includes changes in language and the way symbolic relationships with nature are created and used in communication. Discourse that is 'ecologically aware' is already emerging in various institutional settings – and in everyday conversation.

Ecological metaphors and propositions are increasingly common in political discourse. For example, the following lines could arise at any Green party conference (or conference of farmers, agricultural scientists, or biologists):

*Ideological pluralism in democratic settings encourages creativity,
adaptability and resilience;*

*Ideological closure, in any setting, breeds conformity, monocultures and
authoritarian leaders;*

*Biological diversity encourages the health and resilience of species and
their ecologies;*

*Broad acre farming of single crops requires fertilisers and pesticides to
promote growth and eliminate pests, diseases and weeds.*

There are many interesting parallels that can be drawn between political systems and biological ecologies. Such ideas are certainly not limited
to Green party conversations. For further example, we might consider
the possibilities that:

*Creativity in policy formulation requires a level of free interplay and
competition between ideas and options;*

*Complexity of interconnection in any system requires diversity of spe-
cies, or ideas;*

*The health of systems depends on their resilience in the face of threats
such as violence and disease.*

And so on. The behaviour of any system can be considered 'ecological'
insofar as it occurs as a relationship between a system and its environment. Originally the term referred to biological systems in a 'natural'
context, but over the last 25 years, approximately, the term has gained a
much wider field of reference.[13]

In the case of ideas, computer programs and human organisational
structures, the entities in play are not simply biological, and so we can
at best speak metaphorically. This is a useful confusion if one wants to
invade, or ignore, non-human spaces, or if one wants to make a product
appear inviting, enticing and health promoting. Advertisers, for instance,

love the inviting simplicity of all things 'natural'. That is, insightful as ecological metaphors may be, they can also be highly deceptive. In particular, the rhetorical use of 'ecology' as a term for all systems is a pervasive feature of 'greenwash', or the gratuitous referencing of nature and ecology to provide positive support for otherwise questionable practices and proposals.

Yet, no matter how ecologically inspired our thinking may come to be, the momentum of human societies that are out of balance with other natural systems might soon shift the Earth's axis: metaphorically speaking, there is a big wobble in the making. So while we can applaud the optimism of 'greenwash' aiming to propel human societies to higher levels of systems integration – enhancing ecological sensitivities, better exploiting 'free markets of ideas', opening us to the benefits of 'market driven competitiveness' in problem solving and policy making – the wobble remains. The main issues cannot be disguised, denied or ignored. Climate change, over-population and endless growth are the signatures of contemporary human society – they are embossed on every page. No amount of rhetoric can change the fact that the policy possibilities of profit driven, industrially biased, corporate dominated government policy-making machines are necessarily limited.

CONCLUSION:
THE FUTURE

I used to be indecisive but now I'm not so sure.

Attributed to Boscoe Pertwee, 18th century.

If one tells the truth, one is sure, sooner or later, to be found out.

Oscar Wilde

'One last piece of advice,' said Flowers. 'Don't try to understand the whole picture . . .there's nobody in the world who does.'

Robert Wilson, *The Hidden Assassins. A Javier Falcon Thriller*. London: Harper Collins, 2006, p.183.

The future does look bleak.

The 'big three' of climate change, over-population and economic growth seem guaranteed to propel us all into a much less comfortable future. Even though many governments today appear to be tackling climate change by promoting the development of sustainable energy sources, organised politics can only trail behind the overwhelming determination of business and government to sustain high levels of economic growth. Much has been written about these issues; most critical analyses are either technologically focused but politically limited, or when more overtly political, relying on some form of alliance between nation states to provide a level of global governance. Generally, neither of these approaches allows an adequate critique of the political and economic processes that drive global expansion; a positive analysis now has to contemplate human self-interest as an often blindly destructive force. Most popular approaches do not deeply question the sanity of economies that assume endless growth. Radical thoughts about coming to grips with a universal fixation on reproductive fulfilment, or giving rights to non-human entities such as wilderness, animals or trees just cannot enter plans and perspectives that are wedded to the *status quo*. No politics any more radical than those of the US Democrats seem able to emerge in liberal democratic governments for any length of time.

It might be objected that the arguments presented so far amount to a very 'western' account of a problem that afflicts all cultures and societies. If there is truth in the claim by Samuel Huntington, and others, that the power and influence of the west is waning in a clash between seven or eight civilizations that will determine the future of global politics[1], any book written about ecological politics today has to be considered an interim effort: one that will probably be overtaken by global cultural upheavals. The assumption that the west can play a proactive role in dealing with climate change and over–aggressive economic development may be swept aside by cultures and societies more committed to large populations and economic growth. Unfortunately, the contemporary ecological possibilities of all non-western societies are not more inspiring than those we contemplate as a loose western alliance – controlled economic growth in some non-western societies might be more possible, but population control in any society (or civilization) other than China seems a remote possibility. Nonetheless, because climate change mitigation is a global problem now, ecological leadership from the west is vital, whether or not the global influence of the west wanes, or whether or not China, and other societies, also provide ecological leadership.

At the same time, radically based ecological critiques from western commentators have not been particularly inspiring. Here ideological inertia has caused some radical politics to become bogged down in endless debates about the legitimate power of committees and working parties, the need to select the right left candidates, the need to protect the human rights of refugees, war in the middle east, and other very human-centred debates that (appropriately) define the cultures of trade unions and traditional left wing politics. In fact, the long-term aims of the political left have always been to take over 'progressive' initiatives in organised politics, to keep radical philosophy 'on track', and to purge disturbing elements from theory and practice. *And it was ever thus.* Many environmental activists are not closet socialists, but the potentials of Green parties, everywhere, are diluted by their struggles with outmoded political ideologies enshrined in parliamentary processes. The future driving force for ecological change would appear, therefore, to be *green* politics – the politics of a green social movement rather than the politically tamed forces of Green political parties.

The 'pragmatic eco-centric view' promoted in this book is not a 'paradigm' or a 'position'. In the first instance what has been written is intended as a 'wake-up call' to anybody in need of reminding that global human society has the terminal systemic problems of climate change, over-population, and an obsession with economic growth. The diagnosis of this 'wicked problem' is part of a much bigger project, requiring sincere criticism of many aspects of contemporary life and culture that can no longer be taken for granted, or stubbornly retained despite all consequences. Commitment to progressive change is necessary, even if the effort seems futile now.

If Earth's ecology is not to be trashed we need to protect other life forms, habitats, ecologies and environments. This requires sustainable energy pathways, low polluting technologies, less consumption in wealthy countries, and a move away from the assumption that the only healthy economy is a growing economy. Wellbeing, happiness, health and education do not cost the earth. This requires changing economic models, and encouraging more eco-centric attitudes.

There are many concrete things to hope for: in particular, new technologies that might revolutionise manufacturing, provide faster information processing and more efficient energy production – and clean up pollution – are on everybody's wish-list. New technologies might even allow a level of economic de-coupling from material constraints such that some economic growth can stay possible. Higher and higher efficiencies in all processes are conceivable, and entirely new technologies that will radically change material conditions and life-styles are inevitable, based on the historical record, so far. Fearless experimentalism is what we can realistically expect from big industry and big government – unless we can green the agenda.

The devil is certainly in the detail, and the 'view' advocated in this book is not finely detailed – for a very good reason. The way forward does not require too much more ideology (left or right), or highly intrusive governments. The way forward has to be regarded as a 'work in progress' driven by legitimate parliamentary processes and the normal functions of liberal democratic governance, and by the efforts of individuals and groups acting in less formal ways. More science is particularly required – in the sense of more evidence driven decision-making in government (a radical proposal in the context of the current Australian government's approach to climate change and protection of the environment). It would be optimal for these outcomes to be generated in collective, inclusive processes where outcomes and decisions can be negotiated and discussed in publicly accessible forums. We already have the process legislated in many countries – secular liberal democracy in all its national varieties.

END GAME?

The idea that society on Earth conducts itself as a kind of game is attractive for a variety of reasons. Societies and cultures continually negotiate rules and outcomes at all levels of human interaction; most people feel that they are very small players in a large and complex process that has some level of rule governed predictability. Everyone depends on the repeating patterns of language, interaction and the law and the routine outcomes that follow; life is not predictable, but it is negotiable. Daily life is psychologically bearable because it is not altogether chaotic; to some extent most of us approach each new day as if they were in a game regulated with set moves, penalties and rewards. The common assumption that social life is regulated by others enables a level of detachment from parts of 'the game' that are beyond immediate concern. Even if environments and ecologies are considered important, they still can be somebody else's responsibility – being part of other games. Worrying about the environment and other life forms and adjusting individual behaviour accordingly is just not normally in the rules. Why bother, indeed? In such a world a global ecological crisis arises as an increasingly likely 'end game', as chess players might put it.

At present, governments and businesses inch forwards and backwards in rounds of discussions and attempted negotiation – all scripted by other rules and conventions. Everybody knows that power and economic success are institutionalised and highly governed by formal and informal understandings designed to make popular intervention very difficult. Ecologies and environments are, however, oblivious of all the subtleties of human behaviour. Precisely who wins and who loses is far less important than 'the process'. But, if we are in a game it is a very new game. Never before have human beings been able to negotiate the outcomes of global systems. We are at a crossroads.

Of course, most people do not believe that life is a game – and therefore, in the immediacy of daily life, it cannot be. The negotiation and construction of the future is potentially much more exciting, absorbing, dramatic, and 'real' than any game can be. Indeed, most young people are so absorbed with the demands of the present they have little sense of being engaged in an 'end game'. Yet, whatever our age, we are all custodians of the future; the interconnectedness of all life makes us all 'players' and 'punters'.

As a more programmatic agenda, the 'core' recommendations that have been made in this book are strongly cultural. At this stage of the ecological game, any eco-centric view requires:

Acceptance that humanity is only a part of a global ecology;

Acceptance that Earth is finite, and that human exploitation of Earth's resources has encountered natural limits;

Acceptance of the fact that climate change, over-population and economic growth are a recipe for disaster;

Popular pursuit of ecologically sensitive lifestyles – however, whatever;

Recognition of the need for more science and technology relevant to the monitoring of climate change and the creation of ecological sustainability;

Economic modelling that can move towards low, and zero-growth, scenarios;

Educational curricula that include ecological perspectives and thinking as routine in the development of critical imagination and analysis;

Contemplation of the existential dilemma of non-reproductive purpose;

Encouragement and support of Green politics in the media and parliamentary processes;

Encouragement and support of a broader green social movement of ecologically pro-active individuals and organisations;

Encouragement and support of international initiatives – particularly with respect to ecological action, and effective international laws that can regulate individual nation states;

General encouragement of an evidence based approach to decision-making, particularly in the context of secular liberal democracy, the political default position of the eco-centric view developed in this book.

One of the great faults of most books that attempt to give advice is that they subscribe to a 'grand narrative'. Consciously and unconsciously, the commonly known grand narratives of religion and politics assume the existence of God or gods, the absolute moral values of good and evil, and right and wrong. They also assert more negotiable, but still strongly defined, ideas about social justice, and appropriate behaviour. Such overarching principles can bring comfort and security, but they are deceptive. The inevitable intrusion of politics and conflict guarantees turbulence and a good measure of chaos in all human affairs. The success of democratic societies depends on individuals being able to think and act freely in the interests of all. The resistance many people have to ide-ologies, including Green views, comes from a strong dislike of coercion, authoritarianism and moral self-righteousness, as well as the fear of eco-nomic chaos. This is particularly true in Australia. 'Being green' needs to be presented as good sense rather than duty or obligation.

If some measure of ecological sustainability is achieved in the future, it can only be in consequence of definite major shifts in social and cultural patterns:

> *Investment in longer-term futures will outweigh short-term invest-ments and profit taking that is at the expense of the environment and eco-systems;*

> *All organisations and individuals will be more highly regulated by governments in the interests of long-term sustainability;*

> *Professional and academic cultures will likely become highly net-worked and less isolated because of increasing inter-disciplinary collaboration and focus on environmental and ecological problems – such as climate change mitigation, and ecologically sustainable technology;*

None of these shifts could be described as revolutionary, yet they would register as big changes to lifestyles and core beliefs. Institutionalised cultures are, however, by definition, more difficult to change than most individual patterns of behaviour and belief. At present, professions seem unrealistically optimistic and isolated in discrete cultures of expertise. Apart from ecologically attuned scientists – who in Chapter 5 were likened to prophetic canaries – most institutional cultures appear unable to resist the current *status quo*. Most problematically, economists serve growth and profit, and politicians and business people suffer from excesses of institutionalised spin.

Beyond these 'institutional' concerns stand 'the big three' – a truly menacing problem for everyone. Important as the rights and freedoms we currently enjoy in liberal democracies such as Australia are – with all their imperfections – a new turn towards a greener world is imperative. Without eco-centrism exerting a powerful, and popular, political and ideological presence we may need a miracle.

DENIAL

In that context, Australia is a country that can be characterised as being 'in denial'. This denial goes deeper than denial of climate change that, arguably, is abating – even in Australia 'conversations' about climate change are forcing politicians to adjust to changing world opinion. However, it has to be said that the granting of new licenses for coalmines and coal seam gas exploration, clearly indicates that both sides of mainstream politics are wedded to the continued development of the fossil fuel industry, whether or not sustainable energy technologies are slowly introduced into the mix. Australian denial of over-population and the destructive effects of growth economics is far more insidious – and little different to the denial of the developed world generally. Denial is an appropriate description because the science (and mathematics) of a finite world with natural limits has been increasingly convincing since the 1970s. The fact that economies and populations have continued to grow since then, aided by impressive technological innovation is no excuse for refusal of serious conversation about *limits* – about declining resources, about population pressures, about ecological decline, and about the necessary conditions for sustainable development.

In Chapter 1 it was suggested that *denial* has become a highly charged concept; a recent history of denial of genocide in various wars and 'The Holocaust' is memorable, but denial has a longer psychiatric and psychological history going back to Freudian and post-Freudian psychology. All 'modern' western culture has been to some extent psychologised

– indeed, all consumer culture, media cultures and academic cultures incorporate ideas perfected by Freudian and post-Freudian psychology. Because western cultures are highly individualised, the charge of 'denial' strikes a strong chord. Further, post-nineteenth century modernity has become a culture of denial – of the effects of the lifestyles we enjoy, and the ecological genocide attendant on excessive 'human-centredness'.

It is not clear that current psychological theory can, however, grasp the full extent of the level of denial required for 'ecological genocide'. This is apparent in even the briefest of reviews:

The therapeutic method of psychoanalysis postulates that sexual repression, anxiety, neurosis, and perhaps even psychosis, are involved in the ways people deny certain things. The psychological mechanisms of *sublimation, projection* and *transferral* may be routinely at work creating personal realities that are more tolerable than painful 'realities'. A typical psychological definition of denial would be that denial is a 'defence mechanism' that functions to protect 'the ego' or 'self' from things it cannot cope with.[2]

It is, however, only quite recently that theoretical efforts have been made to link the personal 'unconscious' to a sphere of life as broad as ecology[3] – this should at least stimulate inquiry about the extent to which modern psychology can offer any understanding that is not fundamentally isolated from nature. Any 'return to nature' in modern psychology could be described as a post-sixties development, pioneered initially by 'counter-culturalists', and later by a more theoretically focused 'eco-feminism'. The contribution of these latter developments to an emerging Green philosophy and politics was discussed at some length in Chapter 7; the 'return to nature', in the sixties and post-sixties, described there was clearly a rejection of modern psychology. The feelings and explorations of 'deep ecologists' and many other youthful fellow travellers often involved re-visiting the nature philosophies of tribal cultures and 'eastern religions' – typically North American Indian cultures, shamanism, Zen Buddhism and taoism. In many ways this was a return to a pre-Christian pagan history with a 'world spirit' that was part of an ancient natural order. Carl Jung and Joseph Campbell held sway in these explorations

– Freudian psychology, and other post-Freudian psychology, was felt to be without soul.

Theodore Roszak is one writer whose work has incorporated many of these 'counter-cultural' themes. More recently, in writing about 'ecopsychology', he has suggested that the main problem with orthodox psychology and its therapeutic modalities is the ecological vacuum that occupies the theoretical space of the unconscious, or 'deeper' realms of the individual psyche.[4]

This disconnects modern psychology from habitat, and that is a matter of great relevance to any theorising of 'denial'. At best, recent psychological efforts to describe ecologically sourced anxieties experienced by individuals (such 'eco-anxiety'), and any 'eco-therapy' that might be prescribed, can only be part of an account of climate change denial.

It has to be said that any kind of over-personalised psychology is not able to account adequately for the range of social phenomena involved in climate change denial alone. That denial is institutionalised in ways that are at once economic and political, and encouraged through the media and popular culture. Climate change denial is big business. So too is population growth. The assumption that economies must grow is even more sacrosanct.

The socio-cultural breadth of denial, in all its varieties, requires multi-disciplinary analysis. None of the most obviously relevant individual professions diagnose the cultural problem – psychology and medicine are more focused on individual pathology. It takes a more critically distanced discipline, such as sociology, to even begin a diagnosis – one consequence of a sociological understanding of denial (and all psychological conditions) is a ready appreciation that the causes of personal anxiety, dis-ease and dysfunction are not simply the result of individual pathology. The 'causes' of denial need explanation in terms of the institutions, organisations, and cultures that are part of all individuals. It is not enough to simply assert that individuals are 'introverted', 'extroverted', 'narcissistic', 'hedonist' or 'masculine'. They are so only in the context of particular societies and cultures that create, and define, the meaning and possibilities of all personal attributes. Being 'in denial' is no exception.[5]

In the bigger picture (also engaged by sociology) to be effective in creating change, individual awareness needs the complement of some level of organised politics. The desire to change societies and cultures is rarely, if ever, fully satisfied by personal transformation alone. This is one lesson that has emerged from most analysis of post-sixties Western activism, whether the lesson is drawn from the counter-cultures of hippies and rock 'n' rollers, or from the more anarchic tendencies of early Green politics.

Denial also has a considerable ideological history in Marxism and post-Marxism – this pre-dates Freudianism by about fifty years. Marx became famous, then infamous, for the idea that whole classes of people might be deceived about reality – that they might see the world 'upside down'. 'True consciousness', in his view, was revolutionary consciousness that could see through the ideologies of religion and the ruling classes, overcome 'alienation' (from nature and society) and participate in, and know, history as a science of 'dialectical materialism'. The left has been quibbling over the details ever since Marx, but his writings are reasonably clear about the big claims. Indeed, Marx's own theorising about 'false consciousness' and 'ideology' are diagnostics that do appear to have bearing on the question of climate change denial. Marxists would argue that the ultimate causes are actually class conflict, class oppression, and the persuasive ideologies of ruling class capitalists and their lackeys. However, the basic conundrum of why masses of people can remain accepting of conditions which apparently work against their best interests has exercised Marxists (and many others) to this day.

The continuing survival and economic successes of capitalism stimulated much questioning and theory from Marxists that relates to denial. For instance, what causes the deception of the working class masses to continue? What delays the 'inevitable' working class revolution and the overthrow of capitalism? Does mass repression, seduction, or some other kinds of mass psychological mechanisms, explain the failure of such a revolution to occur? Why do voting publics continue to deny the truth of historical materialism and the pressing need for socialism? Although it was well into the twentieth century before 'critical school' Marxists attempted to develop a more thoroughly psychological account of denial – in terms of 'alienation', 'repression' and related terms – the basic idea that populations were being deceived, and therefore might deny the truth, for whatever reasons, appears to have been established by the nineteenth century. Retrospectively, the enlightenment ideal that mere exposure to 'the truth' could bring about change seems naïve; but when we turn to older political narratives – for example, the writings of Macchiavelli, or those of ancient Romans and Greeks – the idea of self-deception is limited. It really did take the twentieth century development of psychology to make *denial* such an interesting, personalised, and 'popular' term.

It appears that although 'climate change denial' sounds like something new (as it is), the denial part of the proposition has quite a history in modern times. 'To say no' is an ancient usage, but to 'be in denial' is much more recent, and signifies some kind of psychological state – a defence mechanism which functions to protect the individual from unacceptable feelings and ideas. Most scholars of climate change denial distinguish between these two usages. How individuals and groups say 'no' leads to one kind of analysis, but why they say no is quite a different concern. The arguments deployed by the deniers can be analysed logically and rhetorically; the individual psychology and collective sociology of denial require different forms of analysis.[6]

In summary, the first kind of analysis goes back at least to the ancient Greeks (reason and rhetoric being established disciplines in ancient times) but the state of 'being in denial' is a typically modern concern with roots in the speculations of first Marx and then Freud. The idea of denial that arises in much of the recent work on climate change generally owes more to Freud than to Marx – insofar as modern psychologists who deal with denial as a personal problem associated with bereavement, and the experience of traumas of all kinds, owe more to Freud than to Marx in their collective thinking.

The invocation of Marx and Freud as relevant to understanding climate change denial may seem rather 'old school' to some, but their comparison raises a very important and somewhat neglected consideration: the difference between individual agency and collective processes are crucial in understanding concepts as broad as denial. If denial were simply a condition that could be corrected with appropriate therapy or counselling, psychological treatment might be fully adequate as a response to climate change denial. Unfortunately climate change denial appears to be a form of mass denial, because even though 'the facts' have been widely disseminated, and 'everybody' should know that we face a disaster, voting publics appear to be fairly relaxed about the matter – the best organised political advocates for strong action, Green parties around the world, still achieve only limited electoral support. We need to wonder why.

As a psychological description of the personal effects of climate change denial it is hard to go beyond the description of dying provided by Elizabeth Kubler Ross. On the basis of her clinical observations of the dying, she developed a model with five stages: denial and isolation, anger, bargaining, depression and acceptance.[7]

The 'five stages of dying' also appear to model the way individuals deal with protracted trauma involving death, and the threat of death. Climate change and the traumas of over-population and economic growth will certainly become increasingly apparent – particularly if individuals are more closely connected to a 'world spirit' than appears to be the case. What the psychological effects of being connected to dying species, dying eco-systems, and possibly even the major decline of the biosphere, will be is still speculation. So far, denial has probably helped 'the big three' to become such a wicked problem, and such an intractably difficult determinant of humanity's future.

If these stages of dying are remotely applicable to mass populations, denial is just the beginning of a roller coaster of emotions, ending in acceptance. No doubt, the intensity of individual responses to the discovery of a dying planet (or at least a mortally afflicted planet) can be sublimated in media and popular culture – but who could say how the emotions of future societies will unfold. And just what it is that we will accept remains negotiable. We are not dead yet.

In the conclusion to *Requiem For a Species*, Clive Hamilton says

> Despair, Accept, Act. These are the three stages we must pass
> through. Despair is a natural human response to the new
> reality we face and to resist it is to deny the truth. Although
> the duration and intensity of despair will vary among us,
> it is unhealthy and unhelpful to stop there. Emerging from
> despair means accepting the situation and resuming our
> equanimity; but if we go no further we risk becoming mixed
> in passivity and fatalism. Only by acting, and acting ethically,
> can we redeem our humanity.[8]

This is an open conclusion. How we act, what is ethical, and what the
meaning of redemption can be, are negotiable – and, therefore, political.
At the very least, an increasing orientation towards the development of
an ecological culture would be a positive response.

SUMMARY OVERVIEW:
PRAGMATIC ECO-CENTRISM

In promoting 'pragmatic eco-centrism' as the ecological perspective
most likely to succeed in the face of impending global disaster, a number
of arguments have been made by way of explanation and definition of
the term:

1.   Humanity is gripped by an **ecological crisis** of our own
     making. The huge forward momentum of climate change,
     over-population and the global imperative of economic growth
     as a cause of continuing human wellbeing, necessarily create a
     'wicked problem' with no easy or obvious solution. The reso-
     lute denial, or rhetorical deflection (by governments, business
     and mass populations), of any latent conclusion that these three
     combined forces constitute an increasingly destructive ecolog-
     ical force, undermines all attempts to be optimistic, progressive
     or creative.

2. **A scientific approach** to the identification, diagnosis and solving of the big three problems (of climate change, over-population and perceived need for economic growth) has been advocated. This is intended as an imperative that is both *anti-metaphysical* and *practical*:

   a) Whilst pessimism is agreed to be unproductive, the non-empirically based optimism of most metaphysical (or faith-based) religions and political philosophies is considered an obstacle; and,

   b) The shift to sustainable, ecologically based models is considered to be, primarily, a practical problem requiring appropriate management, technology and research.

3. The way forward is unavoidably political in the sense of requiring good governance and the exercise of political power. The only formal political practice that begins to embrace ecological philosophy and methodology, so far, is **Green politics**. Green political parties and their ideologies (which may vary) are, however, only part of a broader green social movement which includes a wide range of social organisations and individuals focused by goals that are shared but not restricted by particular organisations. These goals are primarily environmental and ecological in the sense of relativising the place and priority of humanity as only part of a bigger 'web of life'/ global ecology/ eco-system/ 'nature'.

4. **Being green** requires radicalism in at least two fundamental respects:

   a) A break from 'human-centredness' as a taken for granted assumption of philosophy and social practice – that is, a shift in the practices of daily life and the objects of 'common sense' philosophical reflection; and

b)   A break with human-centred politics, particularly the politics of 'left' and 'right'. Because the philosophical narratives of most Green parties have become captured by various leftist agendas, eco-centric party politics has stagnated in Australia, and internationally. The best hope for 'progressive' ecological politics that can honestly confront the 'big three' problems of climate change, over-population and systemic economic growth comes from the political processes of green social movements that occur despite the countervailing forces of organised politics and the coercive constraints of governments, trade unions and businesses. All these dominant social and cultural forces remain wedded to the transcendent interests of human affairs.

5.   **Being pragmatic** means

a)   Being **evidence based** in problem solving; and

b)   Cultivating **'a radical centre'** in politics.

The 'radical centre' envisioned here is a green centre. This requires processes of cultural construction and political reclamation. A central political position that is 'radical' implies a break with the idea that all politics occurs on a spectrum between left and right. This out-dated, human-centered logic effectively excludes non-human interests, and has become an increasingly catastrophic impulse. A space that is Earth-centred is certainly radical in the worlds of organised politics, as demonstrated by the struggles of Green parties everywhere: Green parties struggle 'externally' with other political parties and the forces of 'business-as-usual', and 'internally' with entrenched political differences that need to be better understood.

The 'crisis' that currently exists within Green political parties occurs despite the presence of a 'dialectic' between left politics, Green politics and a broader green social movement. Without doubt, the main break required within Green politics is away from Marxism in its various guises – 'dialectical materialism', 'historical materialism', 'old left', 'new left', 'broad left' and post-Marxist constructions of 'post-modernism'. This is the main ideological challenge facing Green political parties; there is no disagreement about the need to move away from excessive consumerism and 'neo-conservative' agenda that support 'business-as-usual'. However, all left positions are so human-centred that the plight of the non-human world will always be positioned as secondary to human interests. Important as social justice, world peace and non-violence are to human *and* ecological issues, the left (however defined) is insufficiently focused on climate change, over-population and sustainable economics. Its philosophical and political goals and assumptions necessarily promote human interests when broader ecological interests need to be prioritised. The attempt by left politicians to reduce Green politics to socialism, communism, Marxisms (including Marxist-feminism), or any other left construction, can never succeed as an ecological solution because of a fixation on human labour and life as the ultimate source of value, purpose and meaning for all life. Human life is not all life – a basic mistake made by all human-centred thinking whether it comes from the political left or right, from religions, or from the 'common sense' of daily life.

NOTES

PART 1

CHAPTER 1 – WHY BOTHER

1. For example, Naomi Klein has recently coined the term 'disaster capitalism' to describe the way that extreme economic rationalism is imposed in the management of political crises and wars by American political and economic interests – *The Shock Doctrine: The Rise of Disaster Capitalism*. London: Allen Lane (Penguin Books), 2007. We can be sure this is not just the result of American strategies.

2. See L. O. Bygren et. al., 'Change in food availability during pregnancy: Is it related to adult sudden death from cerebro- and cardiovascular disease in offspring?' (*Am J Hum Biol* 2000, *12*: 447-453) and 'Change in paternal grandmothers' early food supply influenced cardiovascular mortality of the female grandchildren' (*BMC Genetics* 2014, *15*: 12). Bygren's studies are a contribution to the newly developing scientific field of 'epigenetics' – the study of the effects of actions and experiences on genes. There is considerable evidence that genes can be 'marked' or 'switched' by responses to chemical agents and experiences such as feasts and famines. See, for example, J. Bernhardt et. al., 'Bacillus subtilis During Feast and famine: Visualisation of the Overall Regulation of Protein Synthesis During Glucose Starvation by Proteome Analysis'. *Genome Res.* Feb 1, 2003; 13(2): 224-237, and www.clinicalepigeneticsjournal.com/.

3. To take one contemporary example from the last war in Iraq: post-war reconstruction alone generated (US)$20 billion in revenues for the energy services company Halliburton. See James Glanz and Floyd Norris, 'Report Says Iraq Contractor is Hiding Data from U.S.' *New York Times*, October 26, 2006.

4. Naomi Klein, op. cit., p. 13.

5. *Science Daily*, March 27, 2014 (accessed online 27/1/2015).

6. Because the Australian CSG industry is relatively new there is little independent quantitative research data about fugitive methane emissions. According to Day *et al.* 'fugitive emissions are estimated to account for 41 Mt CO_2e, Australia, or 7.5% of the nations total green house gas inventory'. See Day, S., Dell 'Amico, M., Fry, R., Tousi, H., 'Preliminary Field Measurements of Fu-

gitive Methane from Coal Seam Gas Production in Australia' (online, posted February 2014, accessed 29/1/2015). Southern Cross University researchers, led by Isaac Sentis and Damian Maher, found that CH_4 and CO_2 levels were elevated at the Tara gas field in Queensland Australia: 'results clearly showed a widespread enrichment of both CH_4 and CO_2 with the production field compared to outside the gas field' (from an email to the Department of Climate Change and Energy Efficiency, 19 October, 2012 – pdf document accessed online 27/1/2015). More is known about emissions in the US - Howarth et al., and others, have reported that up to 8% of gas produced in shale gas operations is released as fugitive emissions. See Howarth, R., Santoro, R., Ingraffa, A., 'Methane and the greenhouse-gas footprint of natural gas from shale formation', *Climate Change 2011*, 106, 679 – 690 (online, accessed 29/1/2015). Fugitive emissions from urban and industrial pipelines may be even more disturbing: 'we mapped CH_4 leaks across all 785 road miles in the city of Boston using a cavity-ring-down mobile CH_4 analyzer. We identified 3354 CH_4 leaks with concentrations exceeding up to 15 times the global background level'. See Phillips, W. G. et al. 'Mapping urban pipeline leaks: methane leaks across Boston', *Environmental Pollution* 173(2013) 1 – 4 (accessed online 27/1/2015).

7. The arguments against any further use of nuclear energy for electricity generation have been established over decades. Greenpeace and Physicians for Social Responsibility are two better-known non-government organisations that continue to argue against the risks of the nuclear industry. From an extensive literature about risks and benefits see, for example, Barry Brook and Ian Lowe, *Why Vs Why: Nuclear Power*. Pantera Press, 2010.

8. According to CSIRO climate scientist, and executive director of the Global Carbon Project, Dr Pep Canadell, new data confirms 'if present emissions trends continue, the world would reach 2 degrees of global warming in about 30 years, a threshold regarded by scientists as triggering the worst effects of climate change.' *The Sydney Morning Herald*, 20/11/2013, p. 14. That's right, page 14.

9. According to one recent survey of political opinion, individual identification of Australians as 'middle class' has been on average higher than identification as 'working class' over many decades. During the period 1967–2013 identification as 'middle class' varied 46%- 57%, compared with 41%-53% for 'working class' identification. Between 1987 and 2001 there was near equality in types of identification (with slightly more people identifying as working class) but this reversal is against the trend. See Ian McAlister and Sarah M.

Cameron, *Trends in Australian Political Opinion: Results from the Australian Election Study, 1987-2013*. Canberra: ANU, College of Arts and Sciences, 2014.

10. Mark Latham, 'Not Dead Yet: Labor's Post-Left Future', *Quarterly Essay.* Issue *49,* 2013, pp. 13, 28.

11. Philip Lowe (Deputy Governor of the RBA), 'Address to the Australian Industry Group 12th Annual Economic Forum'. Sydney - 7 March 2012. - www,aphref.aph.gov.au – house – committee – services – report - chapter 2.pdf (posted 25 August, 2014).

12. This latter finding is common in studies of wellbeing that survey peoples' subjective assessments of their own wellbeing. Clive Hamilton reviewed a number of such surveys (prior to 2003) and reported '[a]t the national level there is a weak positive correlation between a country's income and self-reported life satisfaction. . . it is unlikely that in itself additional income makes much difference to wellbeing in developed countries.' (*Growth Fetish*. Crows Nest: Allen and Unwin, 2003, pp. 24, 26).

13. The Better Life Index used by the OECD reports across eleven categories of life experience. In the 2013 results, out of the 34 participating countries, Australia performed particularly well in the categories *civic engagement* (1), *environment* (2), *health* (2), and *jobs* (7). Despite poor performance on the *work/life* balance (29), Australia scored higher across more categories than any other country – see www.oecd.betterlifeindex/countries/australia.

14. According to the Australian Election Study (cited above), the last four decades are defined by a steadily declining interest in television, radio and newspaper reporting of national election campaigns. Internet usage has increased, as might be expected, but in 2013, only 15% of their sample followed Federal election campaigns.

15. When he was Leader of the Opposition, the current Prime Minister, Tony Abbott, is famous for having described climate science as 'absolute crap'; the current Minister for the Environment, Greg Hunt, argued that a Wikipedia assertion that 'Australia has regular bushfires' entails there is no reason to suppose that climate change might have played a role in the severity of bushfires in 2013. (*Sydney Morning Herald,* October 23, 2013). These two examples are symptomatic of Australia's governmental approach to climate change, ecological decline, and economic policy.

16. For instance in recent years ICAC (Independent Commission Against Corruption) investigations have revealed some Labor and Liberal politicians to be corrupt and potentially criminal, and many others to be highly

compromised. In 2014 the list of recently compromised politicians included parliamentarians (and ex-parliamentarians) Eddie Obeid, Ian McDonald, Joe Tripodi, Tony Kelly, Eric Roozendaal, Arthur Sinodinis, the Liberal state premier Barry O'Farrell, and a growing list of Liberal parliamentarians and staffers challenged by the latest round of ICAC hearings. ICAC's main concern has been that since 2009 it has been illegal for politicians and political parties in NSW to accept donations from developers. Other politicians named as accepting donations from developers include central coast MP's Tim Owen, Andrew Cornwell, Gary Edwards, Darren Webber, Chris Hartcher, Mike Gallacher, the mayor of Newcastle John McCloy, and Sydney MP (and former mayor) Bart Bassett.

17. As reported by the Black Dog Institute, suicide is the leading cause of death among young Australians aged 15-24. Men are at greatest risk of suicide but least likely to seek help. One in seven Australians will experience depression in their lifetime; depression is the number one cause of non-fatal disability in Australia (24%) – www.blackdoginstitute.org.au (28/8/2014).

18. See, for example, Peter Conrad, *The Medicalisation of Society: On the Transformation of Human Conditions into Medical Disorders.* Baltimore: Johns Hopkins University Press, 2007; and Allan Horwitz and Jerome Wakefield, *The Loss of Sadness: How Psychiatry has Transformed Normal Sadness into Depressive Disorder.* New York: Oxford University Press, 2007.

19. Julia Kristeva, *Black Sun: Depression and Melancholia* (Trans. L. S. Roudiez). New York: Columbus University Press, Columbia, 1989, pp. 221 – 222.

20. Theodore Roszack, *The Voice of the Earth: An Exploration of Ecopsychology.* Grand Rapids, MI: Phanes Press, Inc., 1992 and 2001, pp. 320 – 330.

21. Clive Hamilton, *Requiem for a Species: Why we resist the truth about climate change.* London: Earthscan, 2010, pp. 21 – 22.

CHAPTER 2 – THE BIG THREE

1. According to a panel lead by former UN Secretary General Kofi Annan, 'Australia has gone from leadership to free-rider status in climate diplomacy'. The *Africa Progress Panel's 2015 report* groups Australia with Canada, Japan and Russia as appearing 'to have withdrawn from the community of nations seeking to tackle dangerous climate change'. The report noted Australia was on course for emissions to rise 12-18 per cent above 2000 levels after scrapping the carbon price in 2014, compared with a promise of a 5 per cent reduction by 2020 (Peter Hannan, 'Australia singled out as a climate change "free rider"

by international panel', *The Sydney Morning Herald*, June 5, 2015, on-line).

2.   2013 was Australia's hottest year on record. January and September were the hottest months on record. The year also contained the hottest Summer and Spring on record; different States also ran second, and third, for hottest Autumn and Winter temperatures. <2013%20Was%20Off%20The%20 Charts%20%7C%20Climate%20Council.webarchive> 2014 was Australia's third hottest year (See Australia's Bureau of Meteorology website). In his 2015 State of the Union address, United States President Barack Obama said, 'no challenge – no challenge – poses a greater threat to future generations than climate change.' He noted that 2014 was the warmest year on record and that 14 of the 15 years on record had occurred this century (Lisa Cox, 'President targets climate change as greatest threat', *The Sydney Morning Herald*, Thursday January 22, 2015, p. 5). The correlations between global warming, increasing levels of green house gases and extreme climatic events are increasingly obvious, as the IPCC reports discussed in Chapter 5 reveal.

3.   Donella Meadows, Denis Meadows, Jorgen Randers, and William Behrens III, *The Limits to Growth: A Report for the Club of Rome's Project on the Predicament of Mankind*. New York: Signet, 1972.

4.   Ross Gittens, *The Sydney Morning Herald*, 20/11/2013, p. 35.

5.   'A Foreward by Herman E. Daly' in Tim Jackson, *Prosperity Without Growth: Economics for a Finite Planet*. London, Sterling VA: Earthscan, 2009, p. x.

6.   Meadows *et al., op. cit.*, p. 126. This finding was made using a 'World Model' based on data available in 1970. When the model was run with natural resource reserves doubled, population 'overshoot and collapse' still occurred, but this time 'environmental pollution absorption mechanisms became saturated' (p. 127). For all variations, including 'unlimited' resources, pollution controls, increased agricultural productivity, and 'perfect' birth control', 'the basic behaviour mode of the world system is exponential growth of population and capital, followed by collapse' (p. 142). There have many subsequent predictions from global models using better data and better computer models, but those early runs seem prescient, for all their limitations.

7.   Mihajlo Mesarovic and Eduard Pestel, *Mankind at the Turning Point: The Second Report to The Club of Rome*. London: Hutchinson & Co. Ltd, 1975. There have been many subsequent reports written by individual specialists and groups of specialists. None vary significantly from the general message of the first report to The Club of Rome. See for example, Donella Meadows, Jorgen Randers and Denis Meadows, *Limits to Growth: the 30 year update*.

White River Junction: Chelsea Green Publishing, 2004; Ugo Bardi, *The Limits to Growth Revisited*. New York, Dordrecht, Heidelberg, London: Springer, 2011; Jorgen Randers, 2052; *A global Forecast for the next 40 years*. White River Junction: Chelsea Green Publishing, 2012. See also www.clubofrome for more publications.

8. See Lovelock's account in *The Vanishing Face of Gaia*, op. cit., p. p. 110-115.

9. Op. cit., p. 128.

10. Op. cit., p. 128.

11. Eric Night, *Why We Argue about Climate Change*. Collingwood: Redback, 2013, p. p. 4-5. As the environmental scientists P.J. Ballint *et. al.* see it, '"Wicked problems" are large-scale, long-term policy dilemmas in which multiple and compounding risks and uncertainties combine with sharply divergent public values to generate contentious political stalemates' (Balint, P.J., Stewart, R.E., Desai, A., Walters, L.C., *Wicked Environmental Problems: Managing Uncertainty and Conflict*. Island Press, 2011.

12. Knight, op. cit. *p. p.* 141–142. See also Elinor Ostrum, *Governing the Commons: The Evolution of Institutions for Collective Action*. Cambridge University Press, 1990.

13. Knight, op. cit. pp. 85, 87.

14. Knight, op. cit. pp. 11, 4.

15. Paul R. Ehrlich and John P.Holdren, 'Impact of Population Growth.' *Science* 171 (1971): 1212-17.

16. Tim Jackson, op. cit., p. p. 77-82. The first IPCC report also used the IPAT relation to assess the relative impacts of CO_2 emissions. See IPCC. *Special Report on Emissions Scenarios: a special report of Working Group III of the Intergovernmental Panel on Climate Change*. Cambridge, UK: Cambridge University Press, 2001 (accessed at http://www.grida.no/climate/ipcc/emission/050.htm).

17. It has been reported that approaches that give different weightings to each factor have been more successful in accounting for known impacts. See Chertow, M. R. 'The IPAT Equation and Its Variants; Changing Views of Technology and Environmental Impact,' *Journal of Industrial Ecology*, 4.4 (2001): 13-29 (accessed at: http://mitpress.mit.edu/journals/pdf/jiec_4_4_13_0.pdf).

18. Jarred Diamond, *Collapse: How Societies Choose to Fail or Survive*. Camberwell and London: Allen Lane (Penguin Group), 2005, p. 11.

19. Op. cit., p. 6.

20. Thomas Homer-Dixon, *The Upside of Down: The end of the world as we know it and why that may not be such a bad thing*. Melbourne: The Text Publishing Company, 2008 (first published 2006), p. 268.

21. Op. cit., p. 228.

22. Op. cit., p. 295.

23. Op. cit., p. 13.

24. Op. cit., p. 16.

25. See http://www.footprintnetwork.org/.

26. 'In terms of annual averages, the major net receivers of international migrants during 2010-2050 are projected to be the United States of America (1,000,000 annually), Canada (205,000), the United Kingdom (172,500), Australia (150,000), Italy (131,250), the Russian Federation (127,500), France (106,250) and Spain (102,500). The major countries of net emigration are projected to be Bangladesh (-331,000 annually), China (-300,000), India (-284,000), Mexico (-210,000), Pakistan (-170,000), Indonesia (-140,000) and the Philippines (-92,500)'. United Nations, Department of Economic and Social Affairs, Population Division, *World Population Prospects: The 2012 Revision, Key Findings and Advance Tables. Working Paper No. ESA/P/WP.227*. New York: United Nations, 2013, p. 7.

27. On the basis of the UN figures quoted above, relative population growth rates are: Australia 1.77; USA 1.44; UK 1.22; Indonesia 1.26; Sweden 1.51; New Zealand 1.37. Many European countries will experience declining populations by the turn of the century.

28. Ian Lowe, *Bigger or Better: Australia's population debate*. St. Lucia: University of Queensland Press, 2012, p. 190.

29. Amazon.com</Desktop/Peoplequake:%20Mass%20Migration,%20Ageing%20Nations%20and%20the%20Coming%20Population%20Crash:%20Fred%20Pearce:%209781905811.webarchive>

30. According to this UN report (op. cit.): *Small differences in the trajectory of fertility during the next decades will have major consequences for population size, structure, and distribution in the long run. The 'high-variant' projection [. . .], for example, which assumes an extra half of a child per woman (on average) compared to the medium variant, implies a world population of 10.9 billion in 2050 and 16.6 billion in 2100. The 'low-variant' projection, where women have half a child less, on average, than under the medium variant, would produce a population of 8.3 billion*

in 2050. Thus, a constant difference of only half a child above or below the medium variant would result in a global population in 2050 of around 1.3 billion more or less compared to the medium variant of 9.6 billion (p. 4). [. . .] Compared with the results from the previous revision, the projected global population total in this revision is higher, particularly after 2075, for several reasons. First, fertility levels have been adjusted upward in a number of countries on the basis of recently available information. In the new revision, the estimated total fertility rate [. . .] for 2005-2010 has increased in several countries, including by more than 5 per cent in 15 high-fertility countries from sub-Saharan Africa. In some cases, the actual level of fertility appears to have risen in recent years; in other cases, the previous estimate was too low. The cumulative effects of these higher estimates of current fertility levels will play out over several decades and are responsible for significant upward adjustments in the projected population size of certain countries between the two revisions. Second, slight modifications in the projected fertility trajectories of some very populous countries have yielded important differences in long-run forecasts. Third, future levels of life expectancy at birth are slightly higher in several countries within this latest projection; longer survival, like higher fertility, generates larger populations. Lastly, a small portion of the difference between revisions is attributable to changes in the projection methodology used for this revision (p. 2).

31. As Tim Jackson reports the figures, global CO_2 from combustion of fossil fuels doubled in the period 1980-2005. This closely matches the trend for World GDP (Jackson, op. cit. Fig. 5.3, p. 72). Dr Charles Miller (a senior research scientist employed by NASA) reports 'the most recent data suggest that the annual increase is more than 2.75 ppm CO_2 per year . . . when averaged over the last 55 years, the increase has been about 1.55 ppm CO_2 per year' (www. climate.nasa.gov, accessed 20 March, 2015). The 450 ppm CO_2 tipping point (for 2oC global warming) appears inevitable at current rates. And, if Bill Gates achieves his dream of making the whole world middle class within a decade or two, the extra CO_2 emissions from fossil fuel based energy production will be enormous. No number of new nuclear power stations, windmills, or I-phones can save us.

32. Tim Flannery, *Here On Earth: an argument for Hope*. Melbourne: The Text Publishing Company, 2010, p. 268.

33. In Australia Peter Costello, a past Liberal Government Treasurer, asserted that Australian families should aim for three children: 'You should have one for the father, one for the mother and one for the country. If you want to fix the ageing demographic, that's what you should do' (Farah Farouque, 'So will you do it for your country?' www.theage.com.au, 15 May, 2004, accessed 29 December, 2014).

34. Dick Smith, op. cit., p. 6.

35. Dick Smith, op. cit., p. 189.

CHAPTER 3 – GOING FORWARD

1. *Q&A*, ABC, 15/9/2014.

2. Federal government funding of the Commonwealth Scientific and Industrial Research Organisation was reduced by $A114 million in the 2014–15 financial year (approximately 9% of its annual budget); the projected cut over the next five years is $A114 million. The CSIRO's CEO, DR Megan Clark predicted a loss of 500 jobs and eight research site closures (www.news.com. au, accessed 1 June, 2015). The Independent Member for Denison, Andrew Wilkie, has pointed out, 'this latest round of cuts [. . .] was contained in the Appropriation Bills supported by Labor and the Greens in both the House of Representatives and the Senate just three months ago' (www.Andrewwilkie. org, accessed 1 June, 2015).

3. This is true even though all empirical research is subject to statistical variation. Thus although some physics (e.g. quantum mechanics) is essentially statistical, researchers still apply 'laws' and principles that are far more determinative and oriented to prediction than any empirical work in social sciences – particularly economics and politics.

4. For an, at times amusing, account of the political (and occasionally criminal) side of strategically important research in quantum physics see David Kaiser, *How the Hippies Saved Physics: Science, Counterculture, and the Quantum Revival.* New York and London: W. W. Norton and Company, 2011.

5. Al Gore, *The Future.* New York: Random House; UK: WH Allen, 2013, pp. xiv – xv.

6. See, for example, Gregoire Nicolis and Ilya Prigogine, *Exploring Complexity: An Introduction.* New York: W. H. Freeman and Company, 1989.

7. Thomas Homer-Dixon, *The Upside of Down: The end of the world as we know it and why that may not be a bad thing.* Melbourne: The Text Publishing Company, 2008, pp. 6, 246.

8. Jarred Diamond, *Collapse: How Societies Choose to Fail or Survive.* Camberwell and London: Allen Lane (Penguin Group), 2005.

9. Donald Goldsmith, 'The far, far future of stars', *Scientific American: Secrets of the Universe*, Special Collector's Edition, Fall 2014, p. 30.

10. 'In our galaxy, the question is really, "Are there any [other civilizations] now that we could communicate with?" And we could easily be the only one at the moment. Are we the only one ever to have existed? That seems less likely, but it's possible. I wouldn't be surprised if a flying saucer appeared – in that it's possible – but I actually think civilization is probably rare. For biological reasons, primarily.' In an interview with Mathew Stadlen, 'Prof. Brian Cox: "There's a naivety in saying there is no god"', *The Telegraph*, 9/03/2015 – www.telegraph.co.uk, accessed 9/3/2015. Professor Cox's views are more fully expressed in the BBC2 television series, *Human Universe* (2015).

11. These figures are from US government sources quoted by John Dutton (Penn State University, College of Earth and Mineral Sciences) in 'Current and Future Energy Sources of the USA' (www.e-education.psu.edu – 5 October, 2014). In the US, shale gas currently supplies around 15 per cent of gas consumption. In Australia there are rich deposits of shale gas, but they are unexploited, so far. CSG (which is not obtained by 'fracking') accounts for 27 per cent of Australian gas reserves. It is estimated that CSG will supply at least 30 per cent of the whole nation's domestic gas market by 2030, and 50 per cent of gas demand in eastern Australia. Locally available gas supplies are limited in Australia. The Australian Energy Regulator has estimated that conventional gas in the Eastern Gas Market (all CSG supplies are in NSW and Queensland) will last for nine years, while CSG will last for 27 years (www: SBS Factbox: CSG in Australia, 3 September, 2013).

12. Niall Ferguson, *The Great Degeneration: How Institutions Decay and Economies Die.* London: Allen Lane (Penguin Books), 2012, pp. 64, 66-69.

13. In sociology ecological ideas are evident in the early 1920s in the USA. 'Chicago School' pioneers R.E. Park, E.W. Burgess, and R.D. McKenzie introduced the idea of 'human ecology'. McKenzie defined this as 'a study of the spatial and temporal relations of human beings as affected by the selective, distributive, and accommodative forces of the environment' (R.D. McKenzie, *On Human Ecology. Selected Writings.* Chicago and London: The University of Chicago Press, 1968, p.4). Today, geography and demography are the disciplines most likely to pursue such concerns. Sociology has long relinquished territorial claims over the environment in favour of more narrowly defined 'social relations'.

14. The victims of ecological rhetoric are often, unfortunately, the non-human lives that are excluded or exploited as raw materials, or as 'collateral damage' in the very processes that manufacture greenwash.

15. Niall Ferguson, *Civilization*, op. cit.

16. James Gleick describes this effect in the 'chaos' of weather forecasting using computer models: 'For small pieces of weather – and to a global forecaster, small can mean thunderstorms and blizzards – any prediction deteriorates rapidly. Errors and uncertainties multiply, cascading upward through a chain of turbulent features, from dust devils and squalls to continent size eddies that only satellites can see' (*Chaos: Making a New Science*. London: Sphere Books, 1989, p. 20). This might seem to be just like real weather, but we are talking about the behaviour of computer models. The real thing is certainly much more complex.

17. Paul Gilding, *The Great Disruption: How the Climate Crisis Will Transform the Global Economy*. London: Bloomsbury, 2011, pp. 188, 255.

18. For further example see Bob Doppelt, *The Power of Sustainable Thinking: How to create a Positive Future for the Climate, the Planet, Your Organisation and Your Life*. London and Washington, DC: Earthscan, 2010.

19. *Growth Fetish*. Crows Nest NSW: Allen and Unwin, 2003, p. 240.

20. *Earth Masters: Playing God with the climate*. Crows Nest NSW: Allen and Unwin, p. 209.

21. One could level this criticism at Naomi Klein too. After a certain point it is not helpful to focus all the blame for climate change on the ecological irrationality of capitalism and the greed of capitalist entrepreneurs – as if changing those things would fix everything. See, for instance, *This changes Everything: Capitalism vs the Climate* (New York: Simon and Schuster, 2014) and *The Shock Doctrine*, op. cit.

22. The sociologist Anthony Giddens has commented on this in *Modernity and Self-Identity: Self and Society in the Late Modern Age*. Cambridge: Polity Press, 1996, Ch. 4. From Carl Jung to Joseph Campbell, Mircea Eliade (and others), many scholars of myth have described the archetypal qualities of myth. Ancient themes recur across modern religions, in film and literature, and in popular culture (including advertising).

23. Roger Scruton, 'Roger Scruton: Conservatism And The Environment', *ConservativeHome / Thinkers Corner* (www. dated 03/29/2013, posted 28/4/2014).

24. Jonathan Adler, 'Conservative Principles for Environmental Reform', *Case Legal Studies Research Paper No. 2013-9*.

25. See Robert Emmett Hernan, *This Borrowed Earth: Lessons from the fifteen worst environmental disasters around the world*. New York: Palgrave Macmillan,

2010; and Daniel Vallero and Trevor Letcher eds., *Unravelling Environmental Disasters*. Elsevier, 2012.

26. Roger Scruton, *Green Philosophy: How to Think Seriously About the Planet*. London: Atlantic Books, 2012, p. 413.

27. 'Social ecology' is philosophically anomalous among more scientifically based ecologies. As a 'discipline' it is more likely to be found 'off-shore' in independent academies, or relatively marginalised in university structures in the Arts, Humanities and Social Sciences. In universities this is one side of an entrenched divide between scientific and technological disciplines and all 'others'. Natural scientists may justifiably claim to be marginalised by successive governments, but in tertiary structures elite scientists, and the disciplines they safeguard, tend to be more marginalising of others than marginalised themselves.

28. Some scientists regard the impact of human activities on the Earth to have already been so profound as to have initiated a new geological era – the Anthropocene epoch. The term was introduced by Eugene Stoermer, an ecologist, and popularised by the Nobel Prize-winning chemist, Paul Crutzen. Officially we are still in the Holocene epoch, which began 11,700 years ago, after the Pleistocene epoch (and the Quaternary period). See, for example, Crutzen, P. J. and E. F. Stoermer (2000), 'The Anthropocene', *Global Change Newsletter* 41: 17-18.

29. Brad Orgill's *Why the Labor Party Needs its Greens* (2013) – published before the 2013 election – is a recent exception. Unfortunately for Orgill, most Australian Labor Party supporters still regard the previous governing coalition between Labor and the Greens as part of the reason why the Labor Party's support base, and its Federal parliamentary representation, has fallen to historical lows.

30. Clive Hamilton, 'What's Left? The Death of Social Democracy', *Quarterly Essay*. Melbourne: Black Inc., Issue 21, 2006, p. 53.

31. Op. cit. 2010, p. 272.

CHAPTER 4 – PROFESSIONAL OPTIMISM

1. That is, families are a substantively different form of social organisation than the law or other institutions of 'the state', and therefore not directly referred to in the analysis of this chapter. Families form core social relations for individuals in all societies and provide fundamental primary care for individ-

uals – in ways that other occupations and organisations do not. Individuals generally identify with their families whereas they may not identify, at all, with other institutions and professions.

2. The University of Bologna is the oldest university, founded in 1088 as a law school teaching Roman law. Many other 'institutions of learning' that prized 'academic freedom' were subsequently founded in western and central Europe. The modern research based university is widely credited as a nineteenth century German and French institutional innovation. Universities continue to negotiate with guilds, colleges and academies over rights for training and certification. Hilde de Ridder-Symoens ed., *A History of the University in Europe* (3 volumes). Cambridge: Cambridge University Press (1992, 1996, 2004) provides a well – regarded general history.

3. Dictionary definitions of attitude vary slightly; this definition is from the OED, but is consistent with other definitions of common usage such as can be found in Merriam Webster, www.businessdictionary.com, and other online sources. 'Attitude' also refers to physical posture and the orientation of aeroplanes – which are not relevant to this analysis.

4. 'Feeling' is a more general way of referring to the complex flow of sensations and thoughts that comprise our 'inner' worlds. Emotions and thoughts are commonly distinguished, but this may be misleading. It seems to me that 'emotions' are commonly understood to be clear-cut and strong – typically anger, sadness, grief, joy, fear, or hope. Optimism can, however, involve all, and any, of these emotions as part of a 'complex' of feelings and thoughts that may not feel-clear cut, or strong. For that reason, it may be unproductive to try disassembling particular instances of optimism into thoughts, feelings, and emotions – looking forward with hope is the main sense of the word, and the sense that bears most on professional behaviour.

5. There are good historical accounts of many of these events. See, for example, Fernand Braudel, *Civilization and Capitalism: 15th-18th Century*. London: Fontana Press, 1985 (3 volumes); and, Niall Ferguson, *Civilization*. London: Penguin Books, 2012. (First published by Allen Lane in 2011). In the west, the idea of 'enlightenment' has, ironically, also become a reference to 'eastern religions' and mysticism. Enlightenment in these traditions is not a project requiring reason, science, political freedom and associated social institutions. Anyone, anywhere can, in principle, become enlightened. Such enlightenment may be a high achievement, but in contrast with the goals of the European Enlightenment, less definable, more personal, more akin to religious revelation, and does not appear to guarantee social progress. Being 'modern',

on the other hand, is commonly understood to entail some break with the traditional power and authority of religion and monarchy.

6.   In 1931 the British historian Herbert Butterfield had this to say about progress: 'We may believe in some doctrine of evolution or some doctrine of progress and we may use this in our interpretation of the history of the centuries; but what our history contributes is not evolution but rather the realisation of how crooked and perverse the ways of progress are, with what wilfulness and waste it twists and turns, and takes anything but the straight track to its goal, and how often it seems to go astray, and to be deflected by any conjuncture, to return us − if it does return − by a back door' (*The Whig Interpretation of History*. London: G. Bell and Sons, Ltd., 1968, p. 23).

7.   Sociologists refer to a number of defining characteristics − typically, a codified body of knowledge at their core; governing associations and bodies controlling enforceable rules that govern the conduct of their members, and provide for the recruitment, examination and continuing education of students and qualified members; and, clients having the security of 'fee for service' arrangements. See, for example, B. J. Bledstein, *The Culture of Professionalism*. New York: W. W. Norton and Company Inc., 1976; M. S. Larson, *The Rise of Professionalism: A Sociological Analysis*. London: University of California Press, 1977; or any good introductory sociology text.

8.   Historically, the organisation of medicine, the law and the clergy provided strong examples to all those professions that followed their lead in formalising such codes for their members. This was always a necessary step for gaining the support and patronage of monarchs, governments and citizens.

9.   Frederick Jameson's *Postmoderism, or the cultural logic of late capitalism* (London: Verso, 1991) is very articulate with respect to these qualities of capitalism.

10.   This is the basic position set out in by Karl Marx and Friedrich Engels in *The Communist Manifesto* (first published in 1888). On the left there are many versions of what Marx's position was via his subsequent (and earlier) publications, and what the best working model should be. Most express the broad model outlined above (and below).

11.   Mark Latham, *The Political Bubble: Why Australians Don't Trust Politics*. Sydney: Macmillan, 2014, pp. 8-10, 13.

12.   John Hirst, an Australian historian, has observed a narrowness of focus among Australian historians: 'When they write history, they generally study causes with which they sympathise. Some years ago an American colleague of mine expressed his amazement at this narrowness: "There are shelves of

books in the library on the Labor Party, even a small shelf on Communists and the Communist Party, but you are lucky to find two or three volumes on the Liberal Party – but haven't they governed the country for most of its history?" The imbalance is not quite as bad as this. Part of the difference arises because Liberals themselves are not as interested in their history and write fewer memoirs and reminiscences.' *Sense & Nonsense in Australian History.* Melbourne: Black Inc. Agenda, 2009, p. 3.

13. This point is rather neglected by scholars of science – and positively ignored by more 'critical' sociologists, historians and philosophers of science. Just as sociologists tended to avoid speaking too much about 'institutions' other than that they were 'ideological', 'repressive', 'hegemonic', or socially controlling, so too the rise of capitalism was generally celebrated by scholars of science as problematic (rather than enabling). The fact that North American society supports such strong religious communities may help explain the reluctance of 'functionalist' pioneers in the sociology of science to be too enthusiastic about the benefits of secularism.

14. Richard Dawkins had the pleasure of that particular revelation in a recent televised debate with an Australian Catholic Archbishop (ABC, *Q&A*, 10/4/2012). Ignorance of what the average school child knows about palaeontology is not a good look for any public figure.

15. Tim Flannery, 'After the Future: Australia's New Extinction Crisis'. *Quarterly Essay.* Collingwood: Black Inc., *48*, 2012, p.76.

16. Quotes from the television feature 'How many people can live on planet earth?' (BBC, 2009).

17. Even in the extreme case of 'basic research' in science (or 'blue sky research' as it is now often called) – which is often about natural phenomena and principles that operate independent of human interests and values – the governments and organisations that support basic scientists are generally (but arguably not always) committed to the idea of knowledge as a public good. This is true even in the case of weapons research and 'defence' research. There is a very old (and probably unresolvable) debate about the supposed neutrality of 'pure science' and its separation from the processes of application of science for practical purposes.

18. David Attenborough's live appearances in Australia in 2013 were sold out, and large audiences were rapturous. It is doubtful that these audiences were all 'Greenies'. Love for the environment runs deep in the Australian psyche, and spans political divides.

19. Al Gore, *The Future*. New York: Random House; UK: W.H. Allen, 2013, p. 374.

CHAPTER 5 – SCIENCE TO THE RESCUE ?

1. The idea of *modern myth* is similar to the Marxist concept of *ideology* – in the sense of being a source of over-arching meaning. The limited sense of ideology employed in this book is that of a belief system expressing the *interests* of particular groups – professions, industries, political parties, governments, etc. These beliefs may be more or less 'hegemonic', or controlling, depending on particular circumstances.

2. For example, Carl Jung, Joseph Campbell and Mircea Eliade.

3. Arguably, the reliability, and great successes of science derive from its methodology. Indeed, among scientists, and scholars of science, there is a total consensus about basic scientific methodology: science is evidence based – its theoretical structures are open to empirical test, and refutation, on the basis of experimental evidence.

4. In October 2014, the website 'Climate Change Deniers – SourceWatch' listed 81 prominent individuals and 19 climate change denying organisations. Greenpeace (US) has advised that the oil billionaire Koch Bothers have provided $67,042,064 towards climate change denial since 1997 (www. Greenpeace USA – sourced October 11, 2014). In 2013, The Guardian reported: 'Anonymous billionaires donated $120 m to more than 100 anti-climate groups working to discredit climate change science' (www. Guardian – sourced October 11, 2014).

5. These are some of the basic concerns of academic researchers pioneering a new interdisciplinary field dedicated to climate change denial. See, for example, Haydn Washington and John Cook *Climate Change Denial: Heads in the Sand*. London and Washington, DC: Earthscan, 2011; the work of Riley Dunlap and various collaborators – such as Aaron M. McCright and Riley E. Dunlap, 'Climate change denial: sources, actors and strategies' in Constance Lever-Tracy, ed. *Handbook of Climate Change and Society*. Abingdom, Oxford: Routledge, 2011; and Kari Mari Norgaard, *Living in Denial: Climate Change, Emotions and Everyday Life*. London and Cambridge MA: The MIT Press, 2011.

6. See Peter T. Doran and Maggie Kendall Zimmerman, 'Examining the Scientific Consensus on Climate Change', *Eos, Transactions American Geophysical Union*, Volume 90, Issue 3, pages 22-23, January 2009; and, William

R. L. Anderegg *et. al.*, 'Expert credibility in climate change', *Proceedings of the National Academy of Sciences of the United States of America*, vol. 107, no. 27, pp. 1207-1209 (2010).

7. According to Erle Ellis: 'A good [. . .] Anthropocene is within our grasp. Creating the future will mean going beyond fears of transgressing natural limits and nostalgic hopes of returning to some pastoral or pristine era. Most of all, we must not see the Anthropocene as a crisis, but as the beginning of a new geological epoch ripe with human-directed opportunity.' From 'The planet of no return', *Breakthrough Journal*, 2 (Fall 2011); quoted in Clive Hamilton, *Earthmasters: Playing God with the climate*, op. cit., p. 203. Ellis is serious, and not alone.

8. The unguarded informality (and allegedly sloppy methods) of a small number of scientists in the Climate Research Unit at the University of East Anglia were headlined when their computer server of was hacked and confidential e-mails leaked – in 2009. Eventually eight committees investigated allegations of tampering with scientific data and found no evidence of fraud or misconduct. The so-called 'climategate' affair happened to occur several weeks before the Copenhagen Summit on Climate Change and was particularly damaging to perceptions of the integrity of climate science. Climate deniers were able to claim that climate scientists manipulate data to prove false conclusions. *Wikipedia* gives a more detailed description of 'the affair'.

9. There are a number of web sites that list episodes of scientific misconduct – see, for example, the on line magazine *The Scientist* and *Wikipedia*. Scientific misconduct is a broad category that might include bullying, failure to acknowledge student labour, and manipulation of reputational and funding processes. Fraud is an easier offense to prosecute since evidence is often on the public record. The fabrication and falsification of data, and plagiarism are often easy to detect, as any academic in any discipline will know from their teaching and marking experiences. The point that needs to be made is that when there is 'criminal' intent, and when the outcomes cause real and potential harm (as has often happened in medical and drug research), fraud and other forms of misconduct are not always best handled by 'peer review' in the home organisations of perpetrators.

10. The preferred term for those in such research areas is 'inter-disciplinarity', but this implies a level of fusion of disciplines that usually takes much longer than the short time frames required for many current environmental and ecological projects.

11. Lovelock's recent autobiographical account is quite open about his scorn for scientific bureaucracy. See *A Rough Ride to the Future*. Penguin Books (Allen Lane): London, New York, etc., 2014.

12. This was publicly announced in an apocryphal article by Bill McKibbon in *The Washington Post* ('Remember This: 350 Parts Per Million', Friday, December 28, 2007): 'A NASA scientist named James Hansen offered a simple, straightforward and mind-blowing bottom line for the planet . . . It's a number that may make what's happened in Washington and Bali seem quaint and nearly irrelevant. It's a number that may define our future.' See also J. Hansen et. al., 'Target atmosphere CO2: where should humanity aim?' *Open Atmosphere Science Journal*, 2, pp. 217-231, 2008.

13. This is not the case for all scenarios presented in the Fifth Report of the IPCC – see the summarized extracts below. Temperature changes at Earth's surface, for instance, will depend upon how much carbon pollution occurs and the extent to which volcanoes or other natural events contribute to changes. Assuming major carbon abatement, the smallest predicted rise will be 1.7° C by the end of the century, but that will continue to rise after then. The highest predicted change is 4.8° C, and more after the end of the century. The latter scenario would result in a total disaster for humanity.

14. IPCC, op. cit., p. 20.

15. IPCC, op. cit., p. 11.

16. James Hansen, *Storms of my Grandchildren: the truth about climate catastrophe and our last chance to save humanity.* London: Bloomsberry, 2011, p. 14 (first published 2009).

17. Hansen's earliest publications were focused on natural contributions to atmospheric CO_2 – for example, James E. Hansen, Wei-Chyung Yang and Andrew Lacis, 'Mount Agung Eruption Provides Test of a Global Climatic Perturbation', *Science*, Vol. 199 (1978), p. 1065. It was only in the late 1970s that debate about the contribution of humanity to the 'greenhouse effect' gained more concerted scientific and public attention, but most early accounts strongly emphasise the role of natural causes – see, for example, John Gribbin, *Future Weather and the Greenhouse Effect*, New York: Delta/Eleanor Friede, 1982.

18. Ross Gelbspan provides an account of a leaked memo prepared in November 2002 by Frank Luntz, a Republican Party consultant. In a section entitled 'Winning the Global Warming Debate', Luntz says that this debate is where the Republican Party and George Bush were most vulnerable: *'Should*

the public come to believe that the scientific issues are settled, their views about global warming will change accordingly. Therefore you need to continue to make the lack of scientific certainty a primary issue.' Ross Gelbspan, *Boiling Point.* New York: Basic Books, 2004, p. 41 (quoted in Clive Hamilton, *Scorcher: The Dirty Politics of Climate Change.* Melbourne: Black Inc. Agenda, 2007).

19. See, for example, Clive Hamilton, *Scorcher,* op. cit.

20. Op. cit., p. 49.

21. Op. cit., Figure 1, p. 6.

22. Op. cit., p. 69.

23. Op. cit., Figure 2, p. 21.

24. Op. cit., pp. 74-81, 101.

25. Op. cit., pp. 81, 101.

26. Op. cit., p. 120.

27. Op. cit., p. 174.

28. Op. cit., p. 87. Reticence may be a metaphor for active censoring by scientific elites. There are other conflicts 'internal' to science that are note-worthy – at a disciplinary level, climate science is a relatively new specialism and should be assumed to exist in some tension with older neighbouring specialisms, such as meteorology. Similarly, ecology is a new discipline subject to the same internally competitive processes over organisational space, funding, staffing and publication. Social ecology is probably even more conflicted, since it involves both social and natural sciences.

29. Op. cit., p. 171.

30. IPCC, 2013: 'Summary for Policymakers'. In: *Climate Change 2013: The Physical Science Basis. Contribution of Working Group I to the Fifth Assessment Report of the Intergovernmental Panel on Climate Change* [Stocker, T.F., D. Qin, G.-K. Plattner, M. Tignor, S.K. Allen, J. Boschung, A. Nauels, Y. Xia, V. Bex and P.M. Midgley (eds.)]. Cambridge, United Kingdom and New York, NY, USA: Cambridge University Press, pp. 4-20. NB. Internal footnotes, figures and some technical details have been deleted. The interested reader can find all these details in the original report, available online.

31. Lovelock has written many books and articles and collaborated with other scientists – his work with the biologist Lynn Margulis is probably best known. The book that established Lovelock as a cult figure was *Gaia: A New Look at Life on Earth.* New York: Oxford University Press, 1979.

32. James Lovelock, *The Vanishing Face of Gaia: a Final Warning*. London: Penguin Group (Australia), 2009, p.166.

33. 'Let us look ahead to the time when Gaia is a truly sentient planet through the merging with her of our descendants. We will probably both survive and from our descendants could evolve the wiser species that could live even closer in Gaia and perhaps make her the first citizen of our Galaxy.' Op. cit., p.162.

34. In *A Rough Ride to the Future* (op. cit.) this is described as a triumph of home grown simplicity over bureaucracy.

35. See Lawrence E. Joseph, *Gaia: The Growth of an Idea*. London: Arkana, 1991, ch. 8.

36. Toby Tyrell, 'Gaia: the verdict is . . .', *New Scientist*, 26 October 2013, pp. 30-31.

37. See, for example, Stephen Hawking and Leonard Mlodinow, *The Grand Design: New Answers to the Ultimate Questions of Life*. London: Bantam Press, 2010.

38. Lovelock, op. cit., p.162.

39. Donella H. Meadows, Dennis Meadows, Jorgen Randers and William W. Behrens III, *The Limits to Growth: A report for the Club of Rome's project on the predicament of mankind*. London and Sydney: Pan Books Ltd., 1972.

CHAPTER 6 – CHANGING ECONOMICS

1. Nicholas Stern, *The Economics of Climate Change: The Stern Review*. Cambridge, UK: Cambridge University Press, 2007. Sir Nicholas was Head of the UK Government Economic Service and a Professor of Economics at the London School of Economics. He was a former Chief Economist of the World Bank, a highly respected consultant and office holder in many other UK government and non-government organisations.

2. 'An estimate of resource costs suggests that the annual cost of cutting total GHG to about three quarters of current levels by 2050, consistent with a 550 ppm CO_2e stabilisation level, will be in the range -1 to $+3.5\%$ of GDP; with an average estimate of approximately 1%' (Stern 2007, op. cit. pp.239). Under a 'business as usual' scenario, the Stern group estimated the total cost of climate change 'to equate to an average reduction in global per capita consumption of 5%, at a minimum, now and forever.' This figure was reached using an

Integrated Assessment Model, factoring in the risk of a 5-10% loss in GDP with 5-6°C warming (p. 161). Under all scenarios poor countries suffer more.

3. 'The neoclassical synthesis involves introducing the government as the determinant of levels of income and employment, and retaining the traditional analysis of the composition of output, the relative prices of different commodities, the allocation of resources to different uses and the distribution of income.' Paul A. Samuelson, Keith Hancock and Robert Wallace, *Economics: Second Australian Edition*. Sydney: McGraw Hill Book Company, 1975, pp. 676.

4. Economics Nobel Laureate Kevin Arrow has argued that even if the rate of discounting is high (meaning that future benefits will be lower than if the rate of discounting is low), 'the Stern Report's estimates of future benefits and costs imply that current mitigation passes a benefit-cost test'. According to Arrow's calculations, if CO_2 [equivalent] levels are eventually stabilised at 550ppm, 'the benefit from mitigating greenhouse gas emissions can be represented as the increase in growth rate from today to 2200 from 1.2 percent per year to 1.3 percent per year.' Kevin J. Arrow, 'Global Climate Change: A Challenge to Policy'. In Joseph E. Stiglitz, Aaron S. Edlin and J. Bradford DeLong (Eds.), *The Economists' Voice: Top Economists Take On Today's Problems*. New York: Columbia University Press, 2008, pp. 19 – 20.

5. 'So, on the one hand, for purposes of environmental effectiveness and economic efficiency, key developing countries should participate. On the other hand, for purposes of distributional equity (and international political pragmatism), they cannot be expected to incur the consequent costs' (Sheila M. Olmstead and Robert N. Stavins, 'A Meaningful Second Committee Period for the Kyoto Protocol'. In Joseph Stiglitz et. al., op. cit., p.29.

6. *The Garnaut Climate Change Review* (Melbourne: Cambridge University Press, 2008) was commissioned in 2007 by a Labor government led by Kevin Rudd. The final report was released on September 30, 2008. It recommended deep cuts to greenhouse gas emissions, similar to those recommended by Sir Nicholas Stern in 2009. The report was criticised for its economic impacts, naivete about international diplomacy, and technological optimism (assuming clean coal and carbon sequestration technologies would be available within 20 years). In 2015 there is a greater sense of international urgency about climate change mitigation, but the same criticisms continue to arise in most forums.

7. Nicholas Stern, *A Blueprint for a Safer Planet: How to Manage Climate Change and create a New Era of Progress and Prosperity*. London, UK: The Bodley

Head, 2009.

8. Stern, op. cit. 2009, pp. 39, 40-41. Sir Nicholas relates this very clearly to economic growth and population growth; 'If world output were to grow by a little over 2% per annum until 2050, then it [economic growth] would expand by a factor of 2.5 – in other words, it would be two and a half times as big. Halving emissions by 2050 would therefore mean reducing emissions *per unit of output* by a factor of 5 – an 80% cut. If output were to grow by about 3% per annum, then the growth factor would be about 3.3, and halving emissions would involve dividing emissions per unit of output by 6.6 – cutting by 85%. Of course, countries growing more quickly would have to cut emissions per unit of output by more to achieve a given absolute cut in their emissions.' In Stern's view these are all achievable goals, provided governments act decisively, and soon. This relatively simple message provides a much starker view than that provided in the Stern Review – see, for example, the analysis of Stern Chapter 8, 'The Challenge of Stabilisation'. Sometimes more detail is less moving.

9. According to Nobel Prize winning, former World Bank chief economist, Joseph Stiglitz, 'Government can, and has, played an essential role in mitigating . . . market failures [and] also in ensuring social justice. Market processes may, by themselves, leave many people with too few resources to survive' (*Globalization and its Discontents*. London and New York: Norton and Company, 2003, pp.218). Stiglitz does not stray too far into controversy. His analysis of why globalization is 'discontenting' does not extend to discussion of how governments should deal with global pollution, or how economic models might need to change to cope with ecological 'externalities'.

10. There is a well-developed literature critical of models of development that assume western ideals of modernization and that cultivate dependency of 'underdeveloped' economies on 'developed' economies. Andre Gunder Frank's *Capitalism and Underdevelopment in Latin America* (New York: Monthly Review Press, 1967) was a formative text in 'dependency theory'. Much of the literature in this field has limited ecological focus, being more concerned to debunk modernization and capitalist economic theory. The idea that all development should be ecologically sustainable does emerge, more recently, in discourse about 'appropriate development' as well as a growing literature on 'sustainability'. See, for example, Ted Trainer, *The Consumer Society: Alternatives for Sustainability*. London: Zed Books, 1995, and Jonathon Porritt, *The World We Made*, 2013, and *Capitalism as if The World Matters*, Earthscan, 2007.

11. This economic slowdown is partly due the process of debt reduction. By 2012 the combined public and private debt in the USA rose beyond 250 per cent of GDP – for only the second time in US history. This level of debt is common across most Western economies and is linked to the real estate 'bubble' that triggered the last GFC. For a more detailed account of this 'deleveraging' see Niall Ferguson, *The Great Degeneration, op. cit.*, 'Introduction'.

12. When GDP declines for two or more consecutive quarters economists usually describe this as a 'recession'. This way of defining a recession was raised in 1974 by the economic statistician Julius Shishkin ('The Changing Business Cycle', *New York Times*, December 1, 1974, p. 222). Other relevant economic indicators include rising unemployment, and declining real income, industrial production, and retail sales. Economic recessions that extend for three, four or more years are described as 'depressions'.

13. For example, in Australia, when Gough Whitlam's government was voted out in 1975, the 'Khemlani loans affair' had contributed to the perception that the then Labor government was economically naïve and irresponsible. This was despite its visionary optimism and great culturally transformative effects (with the benefit of hindsight). The affair is documented in the Australian Government's National Archives (available online). It was extensively reported by journalists and discussed in a number of books. See, for example, Julianne Schultz, *Reviving the Fourth Estate: Democracy, Accountability and the Media*. Cambridge and New York: Cambridge University Press, 1998.

14. The declining popularity of trade unions and political parties is no doubt linked to changes in working peoples' aspirations. Economic prosperity, and increasing levels of education and self-reliance (all facilitated by new technologies) have changed much, as have the advent of 24 hourly news cycles. Further presentation of this view can be found in Mark Latham's recent book, *The Political Bubble*, op. cit., Chapter 4 particularly.

15. William Baumol, Robert Litan and Carl Schramm, *Good Capitalism, Bad Capitalism, and the Economics of Growth and Prosperity*. New Haven and London: Yale University Press, 2007. Another way of describing this evolution of different types of capitalism is to distinguish between liberal market economies and coordinated market economies. See, for example, Peter Hall and David Soskice (eds.), *Varieties of Capitalism: the institutional foundations of competitive advantage*. Oxford: Oxford University Press, 2001.

16. Tim Jackson, *Prosperity Without Growth: Economics for a Finite Planet*. London: Earthscan, 2009, pp. 90, *et seq*.

17. Anatole Kaletsky, *Capitalism 4.0: The Birth of a New Economy*. London, Berlin, and New York: Bloomsbury Publishing, 2010, p.3.

18. However, as the sociologist Robert Nisbet has pointed out, the idea that societies develop and progress precedes Darwin. 'It is a short step from the eighteenth-century idea of progress and theory of natural history to nineteenth-century perspectives of social evolution. In both centuries the words "progress", "development", "advancement", and "natural history" were very nearly interchangeable.' See Robert Nisbet, *Social Change and History: Aspects of the Western Theory of Development* (London, Oxford, New York: Oxford University Press, 1977 (1966), p. 161). Ideas about growth, development, and stages of growth and development are old, and can be found in the writings of the ancient Greeks and Chinese.

19. Richard Whitley, *The Intellectual and Social Organisation of the Sciences*. Oxford: Clarendon Press, 1984, pp.p. 186, 184. Whitley goes on to observe that '[t]he high degree of analytical coherence, stability and uniformity in the central core of the field is thus accompanied by a diversity of peripheral areas of application which share the same basic training and commitments but otherwise have little connection with one another or the central core' (p.186).

20. It can be argued that the exchanges that occur in caring and nurturing are often altruistic and 'natural' – such as occur in the relationship between mother and child. However, there are always some kinds of 'exchange' involved in nurturance, even if they are not easily calculable in monetized terms. Generally, social life can be easily understood as various kinds of exchange; we exchange gifts, words, feelings and even glances. We expect a level of reciprocity from our friends and associates. We may 'barter' our goods and services without using money. When individuals 'work together' in families and communities, money may not change hands – but even voluntary work is usually performed with the expectation of gaining some kind of return.

21. Riane Eisler, *The Real Wealth of Nations: Creating a Caring Economics*, (San Francisco: Bennett-Koehler Publishers Inc., 2007, pp. 16-17. Eisler lists Barbara Brandt, Nancy Folbre, Janet Gornick, Mona Harrington, Heidi Hartmann, Hazel Henderson, Julie Nelson, Hilkka Pietila and Marilyn Warning along with two men (Edgar Cahn and Duncan Ironmonger) as examples of 'thinkers who have factored in the economic contributions from the household and non-monetized community economy'. She claims these people 'have not been publicised' – but they have started a wave of 'caring economics' (*op. cit.* pp.154).

22. The idea that feminism can be a strategy for disempowering (male) hier-archies of dominance, including Marxism, was established in the 1980s. See, for example, Carole Pateman and Elizabeth Gross (Eds.), *Feminist Challenges: Social and Political Theory*. Sydney, London and Boston: Allen and Unwin, 1986 (Ch. 13, particularly). The preference for a 'strategic' approach, as opposed to the articulation of highly developed philosophical and political positions *and* policies, is similar to the suggestion of a 'pragmatic eco-centrism' advanced in Chapters 8 and 9. Any effective political strategy does, however, require clear-ly articulated goals – but these need not necessarily be developed policies.

23. The possibility that both these views are true has evaded generations of sociologists (and other disciplinary specialists) stuck in dualistic logic traps that force choices between competing views. The most radical philosophical critics of late – typically feminists, 'post-structuralists' and 'postmodernists' – have identified a number of cultural biases at work in all language, conversa-tion and specialist discourses that work against inclusive views. These nor-mally unreflected upon biases include *dualism, hierarchy, logocentrism, patriarchy* and *social class*. None of these biases can excuse deliberately bad behaviour, but they help in understanding how inequalities and injustices have become structured into routine conversations and behaviours. The fact that most of the theorists of these critical views have been unreflective about humanity's intrinsic ecological connections is noteworthy – and referred to in later chap-ters as 'human-centredness', a starting point for the 'pragmatic eco-centric view' introduced in Chapter 9.

24. Emile Durkheim can be credited with contributing most to the institu-tionalisation of the discipline. He pioneered a journal, several books, a depart-ment, and full chair of Sociology – in France, over the period 1887 till his death in 1917. The fact that he was not a Marxist, or a radical social critical still irritates many historians of the discipline – who tend to ignore the social aspect of the discipline's history in favour of 'the ideas', critically important as they are. Sociological ideas can be traced back to the ancient Greeks, on through post-Renaissance European philosophy, and through to Marx, Weber and Durkheim, where they most fully emerge. The idea that there is 'a society' in its own right – something more than the sum total of individuals in it – became most credible in the nineteenth century. Ironically, the importance of the recognition of sociology as an academic 'discipline' is often downplayed by left leaning sociologists (who have traded highly on the status of the academic discipline). For a well-balanced presentation of different sociolog-ical ideas see Lewis A. Coser, *Masters of Sociological Thought: Ideas in Historical*

and Social Context. New York: Harcourt Brace Jovanovich, Inc., 1971 (Second Edition, 1977).

25. Sociology's 'founding fathers' (Karl Marx, Max Weber and Emile Durkheim) emphasised the fact that society and social behaviour cannot be reduced to an explanation in terms of individual atoms. Some other social 'laws', or behaviour determining processes, are always in play. Subsequently the mass popularity of freedoms and choices have made most contemporary sociologists less enthusiastic about articulating social 'laws' (more fundamental than those of legal systems), or 'determinisms' – from sciences such as biology, neuro-science, or from technology or economics. The idea that the natural sciences have fundamentally different rules of procedure than those of interpretive and historical fields (the position adopted in this book) was established in the early twentieth century. Laws of nature based on cause and effect, and high levels of statistical probability, make most sense in natural scientific domains where issues to do with consciousness, meaning, language, culture, and interpretation can be 'bracketed out' in the pursuit of 'objectivity' and repeatable results.

26. See Richard Dawkins, *The God Delusion.* London: Random House, 2006.

27. The tension (/conflict) between individual self-interest and 'the greater good' (including 'society', 'collective interests', 'humanity', 'civilization', etc.) is a basic problem for all modern political philosophies – expressed in the founding works of conservatism, liberalism, and political economy (as can be found in the writings of Edmund Burke, John Stuart Mill and Karl Marx). A professional field like law assumes the distinction, whereas modern sociology (as an academic discipline) can generally 'bracket out' the individual, or argue that it is a social construct – and is, therefore, in a fundamental way, 'imaginary'.

28. See Tim Jackson, op. cit., 'Appendix 2'.

29. Robert Hoffman, *Review of Tim Jackson, Prosperity Without Growth.* CACOR, Feb. 8, 2014 (http://cacor.ca/?page id=1837)

30. Marshall Berman, another 'high left' favourite, famously quoted Marx as providing 'the definitive vision of the modern environment': *[a]ll fixed, fast-frozen relations, with their train of ancient and venerable prejudices and opinions, are swept away, all new-formed ones become antiquated before they can ossify. All that is solid melts into air, all that is holy is profaned, and men at last are forced to face .. . the real conditions of their lives and their relations with their fellow men* (quoted in Marshall Berman, *All that is Solid Melts into Air: The Experience of Modernity.* Harmondsworth: Penguin, 1988 (1982), p. 21).

31. David Harvey, *The Condition of Postmodernity: An Enquiry into the Origins of Cultural Change. Oxford and Massachusetts: Basil Blackwell, 1992 (1989)*, p. 15. Perhaps the best antidote to the compression of space and time in capitalism is actually a return to nature before it is too late (cf. p. 359). What balance of 'being and becoming' is required in that move is certainly well beyond the narrow confines of post-Marxist theory.

32. Sociologists have been highly critical of capitalism. Even early American sociology (before the ascendency of 'functionalism' in the 1940s) had a strong focus on social problems. For example, the early twentieth century work of Thorstein Veblen contains a perspective on consumerism and the 'leisure class', and the idea that industry and business were necessarily conflicted because of the progressive role of technology. 'Veblen was trained as an economist, but much of his life was spent in an endeavour to undermine the assumptions of classical and neoclassical economics which dominated the academic world and which were part of the cultural fabric of American free enterprise' (Lewis Coser, 'American Trends' in Tom Bottomore and Robert Nisbet (Eds.), *A History of Sociological Analysis*. London: Heinnemann, 1979, pp. 304).

33. Cf. Hoffman, op. cit.

34. Andy Haldane, interviewed by Sean O'Neill and Richard Webb in 'Sackcloth and ashes on Threadneedle Street', *New Scientist*, 28 March 2015, p. 28.

35. *Ibid*, p. 29

36. For instance, in a recent report some members of the Canadian Club of Rome complain 'the Association found that institutions both government and academic were not organized in such a way as to support or, in some cases, even to understand a non-partisan, meta-sectoral, meta-national global approach based on bio-physical rather than economic and market relations.' Robert Hoffman, Ed Napke, Bill Pugsley, Gail Stewart, 'The Challenge of Global Systems Modelling: A Report on the CACOR Global Modelling Project', March 18, 2010, p.4. (online, sourced September 9, 2014).

37. See also the discussion in Chapter 3 of Niall Ferguson's ecological insights and 'greenwash'.

38. Quoted in 'Smart Science', *New Scientist* (10 January, 2015, p. 10). In Australia, it is hard to measure the extent that scientific research and policy goals have become more ecologically sensitive or sustainable. Publicly available data such as 'The Australian Government's 2014-15 Science Research and Innovation Budget Tables (Department of Science and Industry, 2014) are

economic audits of limited use in the detailed analysis of research goals. The socio-economic status, or orientation, of Australia's research (or indeed, any national research effort) is notoriously difficult to gauge – as indicated in the introductory remarks by the Minister for Industry, Ian Macfarlane. He thinks that, 'Australia's science and research sector is highly productive, internationally connected and recognised globally for the quality of its research.' However, 'we perform poorly in translating our larger public investments in research into commercial outcomes.'

39. Modern physics (that is, physics after Newton) established a number of basic laws that deal with energy. The conservation of energy is one basic 'thermodynamic' principle – 'energy can be neither created or destroyed'. In other words energy (like mass) comes from somewhere, and goes somewhere. Another basic thermodynamic idea is that energy 'flows' from regions of high temperature to regions of lower temperature, and when it does so it is capable of doing work. However, all devices that use energy to perform work also produce heat – no device is totally efficient. The exploitation of these principles or laws enabled steam engines to power the industrial revolution. Just as surely they define the basic parameters of climate change and the heating and cooling of the Earth.

40. Clive Hamilton points out the big risks involved with geo-engineering schemes in *Earth Masters: Playing God with the climate.* Crows Nest: Allen and Unwin, 2013.

41. See, for instance, Karl Marx and Friedrich Engels, *The Communist Manifesto* (S. Moore, Trans.). Harmondsworth, UK: Penguin (Original work published 1888).

42. Based on UN figures, Jackson's graphs show this to be of approximately $6000 of GDP per capita (in 2005). See Tim Jackson, op. cit., pp. 56-58.

43. Jackson, op. cit., pp. pp. 45-46. These observations do need qualification in the context of global poverty. There are approximately 2 billion people in China, India, Africa and South America who live rurally and are poor. Many of these people have no electricity at all, and have trouble securing drinking water. Their individual carbon footprints are small. There are many other poor people living in urban slums in large (and small) cities and towns. The world's three poorest regions (Africa, India and Latin America) account for 42% of the world's population (2.93 billion in 2012) and generate 19% of the world's GDP. By comparison, the world's two wealthiest regions (USA/Canada and the European Union) have 13% of the world's population but account for

41% of the world's GDP (detailed figures from Thomas Picketty, *op. cit.*, Table 1.1, p. 63).

44. The Wentworth Group of Concerned Scientists, 'Using Markets to Conserve Natural Capital' (wentworthgroup.org, June 2015). See also Ross Gittens, 'Time to right economics of environment', *Sydney Morning Herald*, Businessday Opinion, July 18-19, 2015, p. 6.

PART 2

CHAPTER 7 – GREEN CULTURAL DIVERSITY

1. Most academic histories either prioritise leftists, or completely exclude the role of counterculturalists and alternative lifestyle devotees in creating Green culture – which to this day has strong libertarian, anarchist, and 'old hippy' roots. Undoubtedly, the easy 'laid back' attitudes of some ageing individuals contribute to their neglect in academic accounts. See, for example, Harsha Prabhu and Graeme Batterbury (Eds.), *Rainbow Dreaming: Tales from the Age of Aquarius (Aquarius Festival 40th Anniversary Edition).* Rainbow Collective, 2013.

2. There are many otherwise insightful accounts of 'new social movements'. See, for example Jan Pakulski, *Social Movements: The Politics of Moral Protest.* Melbourne: Longman Cheshire, 1991; Julie Stephens, *Anti-Disciplinary Protest: sixties radicalism and postmodernism.* Cambridge: Cambridge University Press, 1998. Most (if not all) academic accounts are, it has to be said, written with 'specialist' interests uppermost – with the consequence that the cultural heart of post-sixties movements tends to become lost.

3. Arguably many of the ideals of 'hippy' counter culture were a primary source in the development in Green party cultures. 'Consensus decision making', the rule of 'safe meeting practice', and the eventual adoption by the German Greens of peace and non-violence as a primary goal were certainly not invented in left wing politics. Indeed, these ideals could be not be further from the realities of hard left meeting procedure and day-to-day political 'praxis' for those in most communist and socialist parties – particularly those orbiting the Soviet Union and China.

4. Graeme Dunstan in Harsha Prabhu and Graeme Batterbury (Eds.), *Rainbow Dreaming: Tales from the Age of Aquarius,* op. cit. p. 20.

5. This festival is documented in Graham St John, *Alternative Cultural Heterotopia: ConFest as Australia's Marginal Centre.* Melbourne: Faculty of Humanities

and Social Sciences, Latrobe University, PhD thesis, March, 2000. See <www.confest.org/thesis/threephaseone.html>

6. The beginnings of this discourse occurred long after the institutionalisation ecology as an academic specialism, and the arrival of ecologists as new professional scientists employed as ecologists. See, for example, Foster, J. B. and B. Clark (2008), 'The sociology of ecology: ecological organicism versus ecosystem ecology in the social construction of ecological science, 1926-1935'. *Organisation and Environment 21* (3): 311-352. (doi:10.1177/1066026608321632)

7. Neville Shute's *On the Beach* (New York: William Morrow and Company, 1957) – set in Australia in 1963 – was one of the first 'post-apocalyptic' novels in response to the threat of nuclear war. The film adaptation of the book followed along with a number of other films responding to this new threat (such as the US government classic *Duck and Cover*). Although eventually everything will die in *On the Beach* (book and film), the main grief is definitely for humanity. While the threat of global nuclear exchanges may have receded, global terrorism has every potential to become a dirty nuclear event. Presently, radiation poisoning caused by the nuclear industry – nuclear accidents, inadequate nuclear waste and storage regimes, nuclear weapons testing and sub-global war using depleted uranium – is a real and imminent danger to all. For instance, the unknown threat that radioactive aerosols carried in the jet stream pose was chillingly described in David Bradbury's film . . .

8. See Raymond Williams, *Problems in Materialism and Culture*. London: Verso, 1980. A more detailed analysis of Williams' view and the cultural evolution of the word *nature* can be found in Tom Jagtenberg and David McKie, *Eco-Impacts and the Greening of Postmodernity: New Maps for Communication Studies, Cultural Studies, and Sociology*. Thousand Oaks, London and New Delhi: Sage Publications, Inc., 1997, Chapter 1.

9. In Australia, Professor Julius Sumner Miller's television show, 'Why is it so?' (1963-1986), targeted children as an audience, but also managed to fascinate adults with its vaudeville-like take on introductory physics.

10. The optimism of David Attenborough is discussed in Chapter 2.

11. Die Grunen, *Programme of the German Green Party*. London: Heretic Books (Trans. Hans Fernbach), 1983, p. 7.

12. This is a developing theme in Francis Fukuyama books starting with *The End of History*, (*op.cit.*) and more qualified in *The Origins of Political Order* (London: Profile Books, 2012). His work has been controversial, but his sup-

port for liberal democratic governance is still influential (and reasonable). As he concludes in *The Origins of Political Order*, '[t]here is, however, an important reason to think that societies with political accountability will prevail over one's without it. Political accountability provides a peaceful path toward institutional adaptation (p. 483).

13. Carolyn Merchant's introductory discussion of social ecology and critical theory (in Caroline Merchant (Ed.), *Ecology: Key Concepts in Critical Theory*. New Jersey: Humanities Press, 1994, pp. 1-25) was an important stimulus in the teasing out of these different cultural streams. My last four categories (left political theory (and practice), deep ecology, spiritual ecology and 'new science' are similar to the categorisation used in Professor Merchant's introductory discussion of social ecology and critical theory, but the addition of 'naturalism' and 'environmentalism' are a response to the strategic narrowing of thought about things green that typifies left academic thought, no matter how 'broad'. Most of the content presented below is, however, different as perspectives on left political thought.

14. 'Alienation' was a term developed by the 'young' Karl Marx to express the separation of humanity from not only 'nature' but society and 'reality'. Capitalist social relations were understood to be the cause of a state of profound human isolation and misunderstanding of political, economic and social life. See, for example, Karl Marx, *Economic and Philosophic Manuscripts of 1844* (Edited With an Introduction by Dirk J. Struik). New York: International Publishers, 1964. The sense of alienation intended in my text is restricted to *feelings* of loss and separation and is not intended in the broad Marxist sense.

15. For an account that is critical of the 'romantic' tendencies of 'drop-outs' see, for example, David Dickson, *Alternative Technology and the Politics of Technological Change*. London: Fontana, 1974. By the mid-1970s a well-developed 'critical' (and 'socialist') view of science and technology had emerged in Britain and Europe – to which David Dickson was an important contributor. The academic specialism of 'science studies' emerged in this intellectual environment – see, for example, the *Radical Science Journal* (first published in 1974).

16. See, for example, http://en.wikipedia.org/wiki/Timeline_of_history_of_environmentalism

17. (http://www.britannica.com/EBchecked/topic/543339/Sierra-Club)

18. This broadening of left culture in Australia was also a reaction against the domination of British and English language traditions. In Australia,

post-Marxist thought first developed under the influence of European feminism, the Frankfurt School, and the translated works of Jurgen Habermas. This began in the decade of the 1970s, approximately. Around the period of the 1980's in Australia, even broader left influences arrived in the form of 'post-structuralism'. The high-powered intellectual influences of the French theorists Deleuze, Guattari, Foucault, Derrida and Lacan were not well appreciated by old school Marxists and Marxist-feminists. For some this continental migration was a welcome relief from the tedium of Marxist orthodoxy; for many it was just too difficult and not worth the intellectual effort. Post-structuralism is still a niche product on the left, and very much 'high theory'.

19. Murray Bookchin's masterpiece is *The Ecology of Freedom*. Palo Alto, California: Cheshire Books, 1982.

20. Much more could be said about the role of the Frankfurt School (and subsequent 'critical theory') and post-structuralists in 'broad left' discourse. The work of Adorno, Horkheimer and Marcuse introduced psychology and culture to many Marxists – work that was in turn refined by Jurgen Habermas. His complex writing remains a challenge for many on the left. Post–structuralism is an even more demanding linguistic turn in 'broad left' thought. The 'deconstructionism' of Derrida, for example, is legendary. In general, Marxists and post-Marxists have declared themselves to be 'anti-naturalists' in the sense of denying 'essentialism' or the idea that there are values that somehow pre-exist the work of humanity. This makes the relationship between ecologies, gender, and class relations in all societies a difficult project for all left theorists.

21. See, for example, Bill Devall and George Sessions, *Deep Ecology: Living as if nature mattered.* Layton, UT: Gibbs M. Smith, 1985; Michael Tobias ed., *Deep Ecology.* San Diego, California: Avant Books, 1985; Warwick Fox, *Toward A Transpersonal Ecology: Developing New Foundations For Environmentalism.* Boston and London: Shambhala, 1990; John Seed, Joanna Macy, Pat Flemming, Arne Naess, *Thinking Like a Mountain: Towards a Council of all Beings.* Philadelphia: New Society Publishers, 1988. Macy and Seed promote a Buddhist approach to deep ecology. If the rejection of orthodox religion and theism is considered a defining characteristic of deep ecology, the introduction of Buddhism begins to blur the boundaries. Buddhism (generally considered) is much more religious and codified in its relationships with deities compared with shamanism and other tribally based indigenous traditions. Developing a relationship with Earth may be more of a philosophical work in progress for Buddhists

than for shamanic traditions (which historically preceded Buddhism and remain more 'animist' and less centred on contemplative meditation).

22. See for example, Charlene Spretnak, *The Spiritual Dimension of Green Politics*. Santa Fe, N. M.: Bear and Co., 1986; Charlene Spretnak, *States of Grace*. San Francisco: Harper and Row, 1991; Carol Christ and Judith Plaskow, *Women Rising: A Feminist Reader in Religion*. San Francisco: Harper and Row, 1979; Paula Gunn Allen, 'The Woman I Love Is a Planet' in Irene Diamond and Gloria Orenstein, Eds., *Reweaving the World: The Emergence of Ecofeminism*. San Francisco: Sierra Club Books, 1990, pp. 52-57; John Cobb, Jr. 'Process Theology and an Ecological Model', *Pacific Theological Review* 15, no. 2 (Winter 1982), 24-27, 28.

23. See, for example Fritjof Capra, *The Tao of Physics*. London: Wildwood House, 1975; David Bohm, *Wholeness and the Implicate Order*. Boston: Routledge and Kegan Paul, 1980; Ilya Prigogine and Isobelle Stengers, *Order Out of Chaos: Man's New Dialogue with Nature*. New York: Bantam, 1984; Gregoire Nicolis and Ilya Prigogine, *Exploring Complexity: An Introduction*. New York: W. H. Freeman and Company, 1989; James Lovelock, Gaia: A New Look at Life on Earth. New York: Oxford University Press, 1979; James Lovelock, *A Rough Ride to the Future*. London, New York, Melbourne: Allen Lane, 2014; Edward N. Lorenz, 'Predictability: Does the Flap of a Butterfly's Wings in Brazil Set off a Tornado in Texas?' Address at the annual meeting of the American Association for the Advancement of Science Washington, 29 December, 1979 (cited in Gleick, *op. cit.*); James Gleick, *Chaos: Making a New Science*. New York: Viking, 1987.

24. As a consequence, these ideas became influential in the 'post-modern' and 'post-structural' thinking of philosophical sociologists such as Jean Baudrillard, Gilles Deleuze and Felix Guattari.

25. See, for example, Stephen Toulmin, *The Return to Cosmology: Postmodern Science and the Theology of Nature*. Berkeley: University of California Press, 1982; Charles Birch, *On Purpose*. Kensington: New South Wales University Press, 1990; Paul Davies, *The Mind of God: Science and the Search for Ultimate Meaning*. Harmondsworth: Penguin, 1992.

26. Stephen Hawking and Leonard Mlodinow, *The Grand Design: New Answers to the Ultimate Questions of Life*. London, Toronto, Sydney: Bantam Press, 2010.

27. This view was formally established by the 'Vienna Circle' in the 1930s, and has been carried forward as a default philosophical position by subse-

quent generations of scientists. See Leszek Kolakowski, *Positivist Philosophy: From Hume to the Vienna Circle*. Harmondsworth: Penguin, 1972.

28. Capra, op.cit., supports the claim of philosophical parallelism in his first chapter ('Modern Physics – A Path with a Heart?) with quotes from Robert Oppenheimer, Niels Bohr and Werner Heisenberg. Capra's mysticism, and that of a number of other countercultural physicists, is placed in the context of US government interest in new technologies of communication in David Kaiser's amusing account of *How the Hippies Saved Physics* (op. cit., Chapter 3).

CHAPTER 8 – GREEN POLITICS AND GREEN POLITICAL PARTIES

1. Based on information compiled from the websites of the various state, territory and national websites.

2. Available 'hard copy' sources include Ian Cohen, *Green Fire*. Sydney: Angus and Robertson, 1997; Bob Brown, *Memo for a saner world*. Ringwood, Victoria: Penguin, 2004; William Lines, *Patriots: Defending Australia's Natural Heritage 1946-2004*. Brisbane: University of Queensland Press, 2006; Geoff Law, *The River Runs Free*. Ringwood, Victoria: Penguin, 2008; Alice Hungerford, *Up-River: Untold stories of the Franklin River activists*. UpRiver Mob, 2013; Harsha Prabhu and Graeme Batterbury (Eds.), *Rainbow Dreaming: Tales from the Age of Aquarius (Aquarius Festival 40th Anniversary Edition)*. Rainbow Collective, 2013. Films and music have also been produced – see Hungerford, op.cit., for further references. Campaigns in Tasmania are the most fully and publicly documented; archive material still tends to be restricted to private collections, but some is finding its way to public libraries – e.g. the Rainbow Archives in the State Library of NSW.

3. Lee Rhiannon, *Green Bans: Inspirational Activism. A tribute from Lee Rhiannon and the Greens NSW*. Surry Hills, June 2013, p.1 (of 9 pages).

4. 'Australian Greens' (https://en.wikipedia.org/wiki/Australian_Greens) pp.5. Accessed 28/06/15. According to the NSW party co-ordinator Hall Greenland, 'when amalgamation with Bob Brown's Tasmanian movement was first mooted, Brown was hesitant owing to what he perceived as the "anarchic leftism" of the Sydney movement.' (first quoted in 'The Australian Greens Party', *The Monthly*, cited above).

5. Tony Harris, *Basket Weavers and True Believers: making and unmaking the Labor Left in Leichhardt Municipality, c. 1970-1991*. Newtown, NSW: 2007, p. 204. Hall Greenland (the convenor of the Greens NSW, 2014 –) led the charge to

outmanoeuvre all those who might otherwise have formed the first Australian party called 'The Greens'.

6. Op. cit., p.6.

7. In 2012-13 some members sought to expel elected representatives who allegedly deviated from a briefly held party line condemning Israel, supporting Palestine, and invoking a ban on Australian trade with Israel. The majority of the party membership was found to be unhappy with this extreme view and the accused were not expelled – despite a very protracted and strenuous campaign.

8. N. Derek Wall, *The No-Nonsense Guide to Green Politics*. Oxford: New International Publications, 2010; quoted in Wikipedia – http://en.wikipedia. org/wiki/Green_politics – 23/03/13, 6.21 pm.

9. Dick Richardson, 'The Green Challenge: Philosophical, programmatic and electoral considerations', in Dick Richardson and Chris Rootes (Eds.), *The Green Challenge in the development of Green Parties in Europe*. London and New York: Routledge, 1995, p. 4.

10. Wikipedia <http://en.wikipedia.org/wiki/Values_Party> (5 April, 2014) attributes this quote to Christine Dann, 1999 ("From Earth's last islands: The development of the first two Green parties in Tasmania and New Zealand". *Global Greens*. Lincoln University. Retrieved 2014-02-23.)

11. Wikipedia, op. cit.

12. Wikipedia, op. cit.

13. Op. cit., p. 4.

14. Based on information from the websites of the Tasmanian Greens and The Greens WA.

15. As listed on the website of the Australian Greens.

16. These priorities are relatively unchanged in 2015 – see the website of the NSW Greens.

17. For example, Greens NSW parliamentarian Dr John Kaye's '100% renewables NOW' campaign.

18. But see Kerryn Higgs, *Collision Course; Endless Growth on a Finite Planet*. Cambridge (Mass) and London: The MIT Press, 2014.

19. David Harvey, *The Enigma of Capital*. London: Profile Books Ltd, 2010, p. 228.

20. Moments of respect for Green politicians are rarely reported in media. On the retirement of Christine Milne, Liberal Defence Minister Kevin An-

drews tweeted about the newly elected leader Dr Richard Di Natale: 'Does it really matter who will lead the freedom hating Greens? Their anti-family & community destroying policies remain' (Michael Gordon, 'New Greens leader plays down talk of internal rift', *Sydney Morning Herald*, Thursday, May 7, 2015, p. 7).

CHAPTER 9 – PROGRESSIVE GREEN POLITICS

1. Lewis Coser, 'American Trends' in Tom Bottomore and Robert Nisbet (Eds.), *op. cit.* (Ch. 5), p. 288.

2. 'What is a Political Progressive?' www.goldparty.org/ poliprogressive.html (11/06/13, p1).

3. www.bbc.co.uk/news/uk-politics-11785483

4. Asserted by Australia's Labor Party leader, Bill Shorten, in response to the announcement of an agreement between the US and Chinese governments to curtail greenhouse emissions at meeting in Beijing, prior to the G20 Summit hosted in Brisbane in November, 2014 (Tom Allard, 'Shorten backs action on climate', *Sydney Morning Herald*, November 15-16, 2014, p. 31).

5. A few weeks after Bill Shorten reaffirmed his commitment to the fight against climate change, as noted above, a Fairfax/Ipsos poll revealed the order of issues of most concern to NSW voters to be (in order of priority) health, education, employment, state finances, CSG and mining, law and order, and then the environment (Sean Nicholls, 'Health tops issues influencing votes', *Sydney Morning Herald*, November 25, 2014, p. 9).

6. The declining memberships of trade union organisations, political parties and churches was noted in Chapter 3, and has been of continuing interest to social scientists. Despite these declining numbers, if the broader idea of 'social capital' is used, Australia is still appears to be a relatively prosperous country: 'There has been growing involvement in community festivals, environment-repair events, and other intercommunal activities. This indicates strong residues of goodwill, and the possibility of inclusiveness such as has operated to make gradual improvements in the quality of life for most Australians since the end of the Second World War.' Eva Cox, 'Australia: Making the Lucky Country' in Robert D. Putnam, *Democracies in Flux: The Evolution of Social Capital in Contemporary Society*. Oxford and New York: Oxford University Press, 2002, p. 357.

7. Anthony Giddens, *The Third Way and its Critics*. Polity Press, Chapter 2.

8. For a longer review that demonstrates the very mixed quality of these conversations see the Wikipedia entry 'radical center'.

9. As discussed in the work of Bob Altemeyer, Norberto Babbio, Charles Blattberg, and David Boaz, respectively – see Charles Blattberg, 'Political Philosophies and Political Ideologies', *Public Affairs Quarterly* 15, No.3 (July 2001) 193-217.

10. See, for example, Naomi Oreskes, 'Merchants of Doubt', *Cosmos* 38, April/May 2011, p. 41.

11. See 'Antony Green's election blog: Record Vote for Minorities at 2013 Federal election' (sourced 16 November, 2014).

12. See the various State Greens party websites for more details.

13. Ernst Haeckel is often credited with inventing the field he defined (in German) as 'oekologie': '[b]y ecology we mean the whole science of the relations of the organism to the environment including, in the broad sense, all "the conditions of existence . . ."' (in *Generelle Morphologie der Organismen,* 1866). This has been disputed – see R. Clarke, *Ellen Swallow: The Woman who Founded Ecology*. Chicago, Follett, 1973. Ellen Swallow introduced the term 'oekology' in 1892; other contenders for being first include Eugenius Warnung (*Oecology of Plants: An Introduction to the Study of Plants* (1895) and Carl Linnaeus (who was an early eighteenth century influence on Charles Darwin). By the late twentieth century academics in cultural studies took the idea of nature to another level asserting the existence of different kinds of 'nature' – effectively trying to 'naturalise' machines and artificial intelligence as part of all ecologies. See, for example, Mackenzie Wark, 'Third Nature', *Cultural Studies,* 8(1), 115-132, 1994. The recently institutionalised academic field of 'social ecology' installs humanity as a dominating part of the natural order.

CHAPTER 10 – CONCLUSION

1. Samuel Huntington, *The Clash of Civilizations and the Remaking of World Order*. New York, London, Toronto and Sydney: Simon and Schuster, 2003 (1996).

2. For example, see Kendra Cherry <psychology.about.com/od/theories of personality/ss/defense mech-5.htm>.

3. For example, Glenn Albrecht has identified chronic stress as measurable on an 'Environmental Distress Scale'. See G. Albrecht, G.M. Sartore, L. Connor,

N. Higginbotham, S. Freeman, B. Kelly, 'Solastalgia: The distress caused by environmental change', *Australasian Psychiatry 15* (S1), S95-S98 (2007), and N. Higginbotham, L. Connor, G. Albrecht, S. Freeman, K. Agho, 'Validation of an environmental distress scale', *EcoHealth* 3 (4), 245-254 (2006). Daniel Smith asks whether there is 'an ecological unconscious'. See Daniel B. Smith, 'Is there an Ecological Unconscious', *NY Times*, Feb 2010.

4. See Theodore Roszak, *The Voice of the Earth: An Exploration of Ecopsychology.* Grand Rapids MI: Phanes Press, 2001(1992), pp. 68–73.

5. There is much more that can be said about 'the social construction of reality'. In particular, the idea that there are 'paradigms' and 'world views' are sufficiently well known to justify some further remarks. More specifically, the idea that there are 'paradigms' that determine scientific research and scientific 'world views' has been well canvassed in a large specialist literature (See, for example, Steve Fuller, *Thomas Kuhn: A Philosophical History for Our Times.* Chicago and London: The University of Chicago Press, 2000). There is little dispute among sociologists (and philosophers, historians and cultural theorists) that everyday 'reality' and 'perception' is to some extent determined by 'socialisation' and 'enculturation' – which is to say, we are all 'programmed' by parents, schools, peers, media, and so on. The extent to which 'paradigms', 'world views', ideologies, or 'cultural programming' are impervious, or conversely, capable of change, remain at issue. An eco-centric 'perspective' is intended as a contribution (by rational means) to any cultural programming – which, in all cases, is assumed to be relatively changeable.

6. Haydn Washington and John Cook run through both these lines of analysis in their excellent overview *Climate Change Denial: Heads in the Sand* (op. cit., Chapter 3). Kari Mari Norgaard's book *Living in Denial: Climate Change, Emotions and Everyday Life* (op. cit., Chapter 3), shows the value of a typically ethnographic style of sociological analysis. Her study of a rural community in Norway details avoidance patterns provoked by an unusually warm winter in 2000 – 2001. Riley Dunlop and his collaborators are perhaps the most established group of sociological researchers – see for example, Dunlop and McCright, 'Climate change denial: sources, actors and strategies' in Routledge's *Handbook of Climate Change and Society* (Ed. Constance Lever-Tracy), op. cit., Chapter 3.

7. Elizabeth Kubler Ross, *On Death and Dying.* Simon and Schuster, 1969.

8. Op. cit., p. 226.

INDEX

C

H

M

N

O

Objectivity, 120, 138, 149-150, 363

Oceans, 38, 42, 94, 146, 155, 204, 208, 314

Ocean temperatures, 38

Oil, 42, 50, 58, 61, 90, 281, 353

Old left, 126-127, 227, 230, 244, 266-267, 303, 308-309, 316, 336

Over-population, iii, 3, 5, 36, 61-63, 65-68, 70, 72, 88, 117, 127, 129, 138, 165,
      198, 205, 214, 221, 225, 252, 275, 289, 301, 306, 317, 319, 321, 323, 326,
      328, 333-337

P

Paradigm, v, 41, 91, 135, 186, 188, 190, 224-225, 227, 235, 246, 251, 254-255,
      272, 279, 287, 304, 307, 323

Peace movement, 48, 251

Pluralism, 220, 252, 254, 304-305, 307, 318

Political cultures, 10, 220

Political economy, 43-44, 48, 179, 181, 191, 244, 283, 363

Political practice, 283, 335

Pollution, 3, 6-7, 21, 23-25, 29, 39, 42, 44-45, 54-55, 62-63, 65, 85, 90, 92, 95,
      103, 107, 129, 154-155, 174-175, 178, 181-183, 190-191, 195, 198, 204,
      206-208, 213, 233-234, 237, 243, 252, 289, 293, 324, 339, 342, 355, 359
      see also global warming, toxic spills, ecological decline, fossil fuels,
      fracking, the big three

Popular culture, 10, 18-19, 144-145, 214, 221, 236, 250, 261, 330, 333, 348
      see also Apocalypse culture

Population pressure, 49, 60

Positivism, 250

Post-apocalyptic worlds, 4

Post-marxism, 245, 331

Postmodernism, 136, 366

Profession, 40, 122, 131, 135, 146, 151, 300

Professional cultures, 4, 10, 13, 123, 131

Professionalisation, 116

Professionalism, 5, 99, 120, 151, 161, 287, 351

Professions, iv, 19, 79, 89, 103, 115, 117-120, 122-124, 128-131, 135-136, 138-
      139, 161, 171, 200, 202, 327, 330, 349, 351, 353

Psychological, iii, 8, 16, 31-32, 69, 73-74, 328-333

T

U

AUTHOR BIOGRAPHY

Tom Jagtenberg is a published author of books and articles about science and various cultural fields. Tom was a senior lecturer in the Department of Sociology, University of Wollongong, and an adjunct senior lecturer in the School of Natural and Complementary Medicine, Southern Cross University. He has qualifications in science, engineering and sociology – a BE (Chemical and Fuel Engineering, Hons 1, UNSW), an MSc (Liberal Studies in Science, Manchester University) and a PhD (Sociology, University of Wollongong). His books include *Eco-Impacts: New Maps for Communication Studies, Cultural Studies, and Sociology* (with David McKie), *Four Dimensional Social Space* (with Phillip D'Alton) and *The Social Construction of Science*.

Tom's interests, whilst being inter-disciplinary, have always had a focus on nature and the environment. Since his student days he has been concerned with the representation of nature in disciplinary fields as diverse as science, sociology, cultural studies and communication studies, and in political life. He has been a strong critic of the exclusion of non-human interests from academic fields and political parties. As his latest book suggests even Green political parties are limited in the extent to which they can be advocates for other species, their habitats, and even human environments.

After 30 years of research, teaching, administration and research supervision Tom retired from academic life to live in Northern New South Wales with his partner.

ACKNOWLEDGEMENTS

My partner Becky has been my strongest critic and chief editor. Norman Thompson and Sandra Heilpern have been particularly supportive and helpful in the production of the book. Many other friends and colleagues also supported and encouraged the production of the text: Barbara Stander encouraged me to work through the economics section; Lach inspired me with his tireless journalistic endeavours; my friends and colleagues in Green politics helped with vigorous discourse over many years. My publisher Evan Shapiro and his partner Jacqui Owen at Cilento Publishing and Green Avenue Design deserve particular thanks for their design and production skills.

My mother listened patiently to a text she thought was pretty much common sense. But I do take final responsibility for the views and criticisms expressed in *Beyond the Limits*.